21 Ways to

Success in Therapy

A Complete Consumers Guide to Counselling and Psychotherapy

A Therapist's Guide to Empowering the Client Role

Complete, practical and accessible

"Therapy is a powerful instrument of change which does not come with a user manual"

EmpoweringYourTherapy.com

Twitter: @ahmad_mamood

YouTube: Dear Therapist

Edition 1.02

Mamood Ahmad

21 Ways to Success in Therapy

Published by PT Publishing (Bracknell, UK)

PathTherapy, St. Marks Road, Bracknell, RG42 4AN, UK

Empoweringyourtherapy.com

First Edition

ISBN: 9781701757370

The information in this book is not intended or implied to be a substitute for professional medical or healthcare advice. The author disclaims any liability directly or indirectly from the use of the material in this book by any person.

Dedicated to all worldwide consumers of therapy and particularly those clients who have been failed by bad therapy. This book was written because of you. Your voice and struggle have not been forgotten.

Therapy is truth, in heart, mind and body

Summary of Contents

Introduction

If you are considering the possibility of counselling or psychotherapy, or if you have already begun the process, and would like to ensure you get through therapy successfully* and make the most of the experience, then this is the book for you.

You can be successful in therapy because of one fact: although the foundation of therapy is built from the competence of your therapist, no matter how good that foundation is, it is you who ultimately makes therapy work (Lambert, P., 2007; Bohart, A.C., 2000). This book teaches you how to be successful* in therapy.

This book is for both clients and therapists. For clients, this book can be used as a general learning resource to help you get the most from your experience, or as a reference to access when you need help, such as when you're feeling confused, unsafe, overwhelmed or stuck. For therapists, trainee therapists and tutors, this book illuminates the heart of the client struggle to achieve their goals through the instrument of therapy. It can be used as a source of reflection both in the classroom and in practice.

You will find in this book all the ways in which to make therapy work. If you prefer, you can think of them as teaching foundations to take charge of your role and to make judgements on what you can do to help yourself and be successful, whether it's finding the right therapist, becoming more feelings-focused, building awareness or recognising when the time is right to bring therapy to an end. The road to healing and growth can be a daunting prospect, but by selecting and applying the knowledge gained here, you will be in charge of your own growth and development.

This book came about because many clients have asked me what they need to do in therapy to achieve their goals, and although this concern can come up any time, it often happens at the first session, as it did for Joe.

Joe entered therapy really enthusiastic and hopeful. He told me about his struggles at work, such as in keeping deadlines. People expected so much of him, he found it difficult to say no or to take time out. He felt run down and tired, and he had been signed off work. He felt he had let people down. After about 15 minutes, he looked towards me expectantly and said, "Well, that's all really. I don't have anything else to say." There was a pause. He asked, "What do we do now?"

"What do we do now?" or rather, "What can I do to be successful?" is the frequently asked question that led me to reflect upon how it could be answered, not only practically and completely, but also in a way that would maximise chances of success (of course as long as the problem was suitable for therapy and clients had means of access). This book is the outcome of that challenge.

I approach the question from a coaching perspective, because I believe mastering therapy, in other words getting good at making use of therapy, is something that can be taught alongside the organic therapeutic process. The rationale behind using a coaching approach is this: if you master tennis, you win matches; if you master business, you grow it; if you master therapy, you overcome your problems. By taking this perspective, I can teach you, based on my experience as both a therapist and a *therapy coach*, to master the tool of therapy so you can improve your chances of being successful in achieving your goals.

What does mastering therapy mean? It means combining knowledge about how change works in therapy and what clients do to be successful (backed by experience, evidence and theory), and it is using that knowledge to teach you to gradually become proficient at using therapy.

Although therapy taps into your innate skills of sociality and awareness, it isn't always intuitive; it has its own method, which is used to help you (see Way 1). After all, what other relationship exists where people get undivided attention for an hour, and where there is an implicit assumption that you'll be gradually peeling back the layers?

This book answers the question of how to use therapy well by looking at therapy through the lens of learning theory, and by teaching you what works so you can appropriately apply it. This approach is neutral to any particular therapeutic approach or problem(s); I call it *therapy coaching*.

By teaching you to use therapy as a tool, you are not only taught how to use the instrument of therapy, and of your therapist, but more importantly, you are taught how to use yourself within it. The therapy coaching approach described in the 21 ways:

- Teaches you how to use therapy effectively, efficiently and safely. Whether it's how to become more insight focused or to use your innate skills of awareness, the ways will teach you how and why these things can be important.

- Validates and normalises your experiences of therapy. You'll find that any difficult experiences you have during therapy are not uncommon, whether it's sharing difficult experiences, trying to please the therapist or finding it hard to be vulnerable. These ways will help you feel that any concerns or worries you have are acceptable.

- Provides support and strategies for dealing with obstacles along your therapeutic journey (an equivalent of outside support/supervision for clients). Whether you feel therapy is stalled, your therapist says something you don't like or you're thinking about ending, these ways will give you perspectives and strategies for working through obstacles you run into along the way.

- Helps you identify areas you can explore and reflect upon therapeutically based on what you learn about yourself when reflecting on or applying these ways. How you are in therapy and how you use therapy is a potent source of therapeutic material you can use in your journey. If you thought ending was just about ending, or being a good client was just about being a good person, these ways will help you reflect more deeply about these themes and whether they relate to your problem(s).

- Makes you feel more confident about the path you're on in therapy. With a good-enough therapist and good support, these ways can help you feel more confident that you're on the right path for you and in making important decisions, whether it's selecting the right therapist, when to initiate the ending or getting further professional support.

- Provides a single comprehensive, accessible and practical reference for clients and therapists, which describes client difficulties, issues and concerns in making their therapy work.

Here is a condensed example of how Mary was taught to master the instrument of therapy and so help herself on her journey towards recovery:

Mary emailed me because she was not able to find a therapist to help her. Her problem was that she had found it very difficult to be on her own, especially when she did not have much to do. Silence could be a scary place. She entered therapy 12 months ago but did not think she was closer to feeling better. She went through four therapists in the year. She said, "None of them really helped; they seemed okay and nice, but every time either she left or she got referred on to someone else. I don't know what's going on with me?"

As I was not her therapist but her *therapy coach*, my role was to teach her to use the tool of therapy well. I asked her to fill in a questionnaire that included 50 questions about her experiences, including what her ideal therapist would be like, what types of feelings she shared, did she understand awareness, what she tended to talk about, did she trust the therapist, or even whether moving therapists could be related to her problems. Eventually, after 30 minutes or so, we were able to pinpoint some of the difficulties she could work on. We prioritised finding ways to teach her to:

- *First, express her feelings of frustration at the process and at the therapist for not being able to get very far (basis of Way 4).*

- *Second, she should not make the decision to stop working with a therapist until she has expressed all her feelings and her rationale (basis of Way 20).*

- *Third, understand why she found it difficult to express what was going on in her mind and to take the therapist on a journey inside her experiences (basis of Way 5). We agreed she would reflect and write down in a diary her experience, and if possible, share it with the therapist.*

- *Fourth, tell the therapist that silence is uncomfortable (basis of Way 4).*

- *We also worked on a personal hierarchy of difficulty in sharing (see "How to use the ways") to look at how she could gradually build up towards sharing safely.*

I reminded her that these were teaching points and that she should go at her own pace. After all, no one expects to be good at something straight away, particularly if they're not used to sharing feelings. Of course, as an expert about herself she is free to choose not to use any of the advice given, but she had now been informed so the choice was hers to make.

After a month, she sent me the following email: "As soon as I took the step of reading my diary to my therapist, explaining how it's really difficult to share, things slowly started to move. I still find it really hard but I understand it more. This therapist really understands me and knows I don't want to be pushed along quickly or feel pressured. The others just had not got me."

This example demonstrates how easy it is to assume that clients know how to use therapy well. Of course, her therapeutic journey may have only begun, but I couldn't help wonder if she had known about these foundations earlier, including asking the therapist for help, she would have been able to help herself and thus overcome her problem sooner. With the right foundations (based on Ways 4, 5 and 20 to be exact!) in place supporting her therapy, Mary was in a strong position to overcome her problem. Without good foundations, the building is unstable and this applies to therapy too. There are foundations that fuel your therapeutic journey, which allow your story to unfold.

There is a lot of information both online and in books, however its weaknesses are that it is fragmented, it may not be of a professional standard, and, importantly, it requires you to know what you need to know (not always easy unless you're an expert within the profession). Given the aforementioned importance of your role, I developed this "one-stop" reference resource to support your therapeutic journey.

The 21 ways are aligned to what makes therapy work. By learning and judging when to apply these ways, you can be more confident that you're using therapy effectively, efficiently and safely. It does not matter what type of therapy you decide to use, your problem, life experiences, symptoms, what you talk about or even the therapist. If you learn and earnestly apply these ways, you are likely to be successful. You will heal, recover and grow.

Welcome to yourself.

TIP: If you're in a hurry and want to decide what to focus on or find specific information look at the table of contents (Appendix H) or the Quick Start section below and in Chapter 2 – The 21 Ways. I also recommend you read the "Important Bits" section below before reading any other parts of this book.

* Success in therapy is very much dependent on what you consider to be a successful outcome (as long as it's achievable through therapy of course!). See Chapter 2 – What does success in therapy mean?

If you have any feedback or questions related to this book, please contact me at ma@paththerapy.co.uk or empoweringyourtherapy.com

Youtube: Dear Therapist

Quick start

This book is centred on the 21 Ways in Chapter 2 and the rest of the book supports developing further understanding about those ways, the process of therapy and frequently asked questions about therapy. The table below shows the purpose of each chapter so you can get started in the area that most interests you.

Chapter	Title	When to read?
1	Getting started in therapy	To understand what therapy is, why and how it works and what it can be used for. To understand therapeutic options. Topics include: what to expect in the first session, contracting, ethics, confidentiality and your rights in therapy.
2	**The 21 Ways (The main body of this book)**	**You want to learn, assess and apply the 21 Ways for success in therapy.**
3	Essential tools that make therapy work	While the 21 ways embody the tenets of success in therapy, these essential tools apply aspects of these ways in practice. To learn, assess and apply specific therapy tools which make therapy work both inside and outside the therapy room.
4	Oliver's journey	To learn about a therapeutic process through Oliver's journey (A humanistic exploration of a client's journey)
5	Process themes in therapy	To understand common process themes that are relevant to the ways in this book. Themes include idealisation, inner critic, the fixer, and love in the room. This chapter provides perspectives and strategies for exploring these themes. *This chapter may be of more interest to therapists.*
6	Understanding	You want to understand a bit more about the

Chapter	Title	When to read?
	the therapeutic process	theory of change in therapy, what changes and a model of how the process unfolds.
7	Client topics, questions, and concerns	You have a specific questions or concerns you want to learn more about. From boundaries to false memories, over 70 topics, questions and concerns about therapy are covered.
A	Survey of consumer concerns	Clients have many concerns about starting therapy which are separate to overcoming their problems. Based on research, I describe them here.
B	International mental health support numbers	Links to mental health support numbers and professional membership bodies
C	Further Support	How you can get further professional support about therapy (Also see way 21)
D	Client Concerns	A checklist and suggested way of approaching the therapist about your concerns about therapy
E	Further Reading	Further reading resources such as example case studies and books that support these ways
F	References	To identify references used in this book
G	Worksheet exercises	Exercises to support your therapy
H	Full table of contents	Complete table of contents

Who is this book for?

This book is written for anyone who is curious, considering, beginning or in therapy, as well as wellbeing and mental health professionals.

This book is also written for trainers and trainees of counselling and psychotherapy. By including topics and scenarios within the curriculum, students can explore the client's role and what they can do to support them. This book can be used as a bridge between training and practice to help trainees understand challenges clients can face in using therapy and their therapist.

For therapist, although much of this information will be familiar, a number of therapists have commented that this book enabled them to step back from their individual work and amplify their pre-existing awareness of the collective voice of the client and the universal patterns within it.

Because many of the ways and material apply are about learning about yourself, you may be interested in this book from a self-help perspective too.

Important points

If you have specific concerns you wish to understand, I suggest reading the table of contents or the "Quick start" section in this introduction and Chapter 2 – The 21 Ways, to quickly find the appropriate information. When reading and understanding the ways and material in this book please bear the following in mind:

- This book is not a replacement for therapy, the therapist or the organic therapeutic process. The intention is to empower your therapy process and strengthen the work you are doing, not interfere with it. If you feel safe, consult the therapist about strategies and decisions you make as a result of reading this book.

- There is no expectation that you will be able to use all these ways straight away. In fact it's more than likely you will not until you feel safe and ready. You should go at your own pace.

- Not all ways need to be present for your therapy to be successful. These ways are for reflecting upon what is needed in your therapy, so you'll need to use your judgement to determine their applicability. As with all important matters in life, you are a free to choose what is useful and what isn't.

- This book is geared towards change. Not everyone wants some specific thing or to overcome a problem or to achieve a goal. If you feel you are getting what you need in therapy through the therapist, perhaps a space to talk and be heard, then you can consider which parts of this book are relevant to you.

- This book is based on generic therapy processes and is neutral to any type (or modality) of therapy. It has been reviewed by a number of UK qualified therapists across the spectrum: psychodynamic, person-centred, existential, integrative and CBT. This does not mean that all therapists will agree completely with all the material presented. Therefore, it is highly recommended you talk about things that come from this book with your therapist.

- The book assumes you are working with a "good-enough" therapist (See Way 2 for why I use the term "good enough") —one who can accept all your feelings and work with them, with empathy and acceptance. They can make occasional mistakes but overall, you feel safe with them. Therapists may give their perspective, even counter to yours, but they do so with your interests in mind. However, just like all professions, there is no guarantee how well informed or sensitive your therapist is (See Way 19: Watch out for signs of inefficient, poor or harmful therapy).

- The examples provided are condensed and imaginary to demonstrate particular learning points in action. They are not intended to show, in true time, how things can unfold in therapy. The examples are largely insight-oriented to be able to demonstrate ideas briefly, rather than the nuances of the process. Any examples, suggestions and interpretation of factors related to difficulties are just that, ideas for you to reflect upon, they are not meant to be taken as literal reasons for your problems. That is for you to work through in therapy.

- This book is written for international consumers of therapy. However, since each country may have its own variations e.g. competence standards, I have written for a UK audience and indicated where international variations may exist depending on your country or region.

- While these ways apply to all counselling and psychotherapy approaches, at the beginning of each way, I have suggested "approach variations" to describe how strongly a particular school of therapy may emphasise or deemphasise a particular way.

- There is a lot of information in this book to allow for a complete range of client experiences to be explored. If you feel overwhelmed, you can either focus in on what you're looking for (see Table of Contents or the Quick Start in Chapter 2 – The 21 Ways) or stop reading. You can dip in and out of the material when you need help.

- I emphasise your role in this book because it's the only role you can control and use to influence your therapy. It is not my intention to make you feel like it has been your fault or is your fault that your therapy did not work. After all, you need a competent therapist to work with. However, in writing this book, I wanted to ensure you have a comprehensive and professional source of support at your disposal.

- I recommend you consult your doctor/physician to way out any undetected underlying medical conditions which may be affecting the way you're feeling. For example, an overactive thyroid may produce symptoms of nervousness, anxiety, and irritability (source: NHS England).

- This book's focus is on therapy. It does not mean other forms of support such as psychiatry, medication, support groups, psychiatric hospital, specialised treatment and rehabilitation centres, are not needed or viable alongside therapy.

Note for therapists

Because these ways focus on mastering therapy as a tool, they do not intrinsically interfere with your own way of working because they are focused outside of any particular approach, problem, content or even the client's process (although client's reflection based on these ways may contain vital sources of process information). These ways are intended to reinforce the work you are doing, rather than interfere with it. The ways do not invalidate your personal "art of therapy".

An educative component, alongside client process can be an important part of fuelling the client's recovery and growth. Teaching relevant parts of these ways to clients, in your own empathic style, either as a brief intervention in live therapy, homework or bracketed-off coaching, can be used as another way of empowering the client role. Needless to say I am not suggesting the ways are used to rail-road the client's process and tear down protective layers.

You may also find these ways useful as a rational way of assessing and understanding where the client is in their process, and thus determine what interventions to apply. You may also use these ways as another way of justifying your approach, including working towards endings.

The scope of therapy education

This book a complete resource for educating and coaching clients about therapy, and about what they can do to make it work. Thera-education's core focus is on using the tool of therapy outside of any particular approach, problem, content, or even the client's process. Thera-education is intended to reinforce the client's work by being as transparent as possible in what we know could help them, whether informed by practice or evidence. Although the range of educational interventions is diverse, contextual and broad, they fall into six possible areas, which I cover in this book.

The first area, unsurprisingly, is the education of consumers who are contemplating or beginning therapy. Examples include how and why therapy works, what it can be used for, finding a therapist, and access options, as well as confidentiality and guidance on what to do if you're struggling to find the right therapist. It can also include elements of psychoeducation, such as self-care, and an aetiology of mental health problems. Traditionally this is the area where the most information is available to consumers online.

The second area of education is in relation to the therapeutic relationship and the ways in which clients can use the therapist for help. This could include why the therapeutic relationship can be important, the relevance of feelings about the therapist, and giving permission to provide feedback. Other important topics could be relational ruptures, endings, erotic transference, and dependence. Clients may not be aware of these, or may not have even consciously thought about asking the therapist for help, thereby informing them that the relationship is safe, even if they may not feel it.

The third area is what clients can do for themselves to help their process: the client role. This may amount to helping clients understand that therapy is a collaboration: staying committed and turning up. However, the range of potential useful interventions can go far beyond that, especially if we look to the heart of therapy. For example, common factors posit what is present and helpful in all approaches of therapy, and interventions can be designed around them, so we may provide education and/or experiential practice for awareness and reflection, expressing here-and-now feelings, recognising process rather than content, and joining the dots by looking at the way past experiences contribute to current difficulties. This is the area where the least amount of practical advice is available in consumable form.

The fourth area is about the therapeutic process or roadmap. Clients often want to know how the process works, how long therapy could take, what to expect, and what others have done to overcome similar difficulties. Behind these questions often lie a client's understandable need to feel hopeful. Therapists may provide evidence of their approach being suitable, examples of what helped others, case studies, and even details of the process delivered in a way in which clients can easily absorb. Familiar examples include "people can feel worse before they feel better," "therapy is a process," or "sometimes people can get in touch with feelings that are dormant but it isn't always the case." Roadmap education could be problem specific. For example, a client who has been diagnosed with PTSD could be educated with, "by experiencing those memories from a distance, reappraising or changing their meaning can, over time, help restore a sense of safety. You won't forget the memories but they will become less distressing". By providing a roadmap, albeit a fluid one, clients can feel they are on a hopeful path.

The fifth area of education is where consumers, either in or out of the therapy room, may ask questions about therapy, safety, extra therapeutic matters, the relationship, and their role. For example, clients may be worried about what they'll discover, whether they are about to be brainwashed, boundaries, false memories, or other forms of support including medication. Questions can be split between those that can be answered in a way that is generally true e.g., does therapy blame parents, and those that are enmeshed in the client's context, for example a question presented as a worry such as feeling the therapist isn't on their side. There is significant but fragmented information available to consumers in this space, however, clients can always surprise you with questions you've never encountered.

The sixth area of education is where clients want further contextual support because they are confused, stuck, or feel harmed by therapy, and for whatever reason cannot talk to the therapist, or they have already done so but things remain unresolved, and they want a second opinion. For example, they may be unsure whether something happening in therapy is "right," whether they should continue their therapy. The may feel nothing is working or even that therapy has left them with long lasting wounds. In these cases non-directive and contextual support will most likely be needed because clients could need emotional support and need to question their own decisions (sounds like therapy!).

Beyond these core six areas (and more experimental) is to educate clients through reflective exercises on relevant process themes which arise because they find themselves in therapy. A client's instinctive beliefs about how they should use therapy, and how they should conduct themselves could reveal much about his/her inner world. Familiar examples could include "the good client," "am I normal?" or "I shouldn't be here because others have it worse." These themes could help to understand the influences which may contribute to their problems. I introduce these themes in Chapter 4, but for a more thorough treatment see my other book "Client perceptions in therapy".

Further support for clients

If you need further professional help with your therapy process see Way 21: Get help from outside therapy if needed. You can also contact your country's regulatory, governing body or voluntary membership body to determine whether they provide any further support (See Appendix B for main UK bodies). See Appendix C for details of additional *therapy coaching* for your process.

Chapter 1 – Getting started in therapy

This chapter aims to give you a good understanding of what therapy is, what therapy can help with, and how and why it works. It will help you understand therapy options, the therapeutic contract, your rights, the process of finding a therapist, and what to expect in your first session.

What is therapy?

Therapy, also called psychotherapy or counselling, is an activity by which you meet with a therapist to work on problems in your life. These problems can be wide ranging from relationships, behaviours, life decisions, traumatic experiences, bereavement as well as bodily symptoms such as panic. Therapy may also be used by people seeking self-improvement and growth unaccompanied by any specific problem, because you just want to be the best version of yourself, whether it's seeking life purpose or seeking to understand yourself better. Ultimately, beginning therapy can be a big step toward being the healthiest version of yourself and living the best life possible.

This activity of therapy is primarily based on talking to explore thoughts and feelings in relationship with the therapist who is skilled, through training and experience, in helping people resolve these types of problems. The activity of therapy is held within a relational space, where you, your problems and any content that comes up is accepted with empathy. Therapy does not offer medication or diagnose mental health issues, unless the therapist is appropriately trained to provide diagnosis, although those may be sought alongside therapy through a psychiatrist and/or a psychologist. The therapist may use a variety of tools or techniques based on their own training and skills to help you during the process. There are a number of types of therapies (often called modalities) which therapist have trained in. Popular therapies include Cognitive Behavioural Therapy (CBT), Person Centred, Psychodynamic, or Integrative therapy. Although these modalities differ in theoretical approach, or what they believe helps clients change, they all universally agree that the relationship between the client and therapist is the foundation for good therapy regardless of the modality they practice. Therapy may be provided either individually, between you and a therapist, or as a couple, group or family, called individual, couples, group and family therapy respectively.

International Variation: In some countries the term counselling can refer to support, coaching, listening and advice giving, rather than therapy. If you're unsure whether you're receiving therapy you should talk to the provider. A suggestion could be to ask whether they are using a particular modality as the basis for counselling. Samaritans UK is one example of a listening service rather than a counselling one.

If you're deciding whether therapy is going to be a good choice for you, you can also take a look at the things therapy is not.

Therapy is not about judging you

Therapy is not about telling you you're bad in some way or forcing you to do or talk about things you don't want to or telling you that you need to do better in therapy. Therapy is an open invitation for you to be yourself as you are, not as you may believe the therapist expects you to be. Therapy is about providing an accepting, empathic and safe environment for you to work on what you want to. If you feel nervous about sharing something that you are embarrassed about, those feelings are accepted too and it is quite normal; you can go at your own pace, when and if you're ready. Similarly, if you feel you're not "performing well" in therapy (See Way 10: Watch for the good client mask), therapists welcome that and are really accepting of it, even with big silences or with your anxiety in the room. They want you to feel you can be yourself.

Therapy is not just turning up

Therapy will only work if you actively do the work. If you're reluctant to be in therapy or you have expectations that turning up will be enough then its unlikely therapy will be successful. You will have to take part actively to stretch those mind and thought muscles. While physical exercise requires dedication, so too does therapy. Therapy is emotional training for wellbeing.

Therapy is not a magic pill to life's problems

Although a single session can be enough to help you, therapy is an opportunity to explore, gain better understanding and insights. You don't usually get fixed by just talking to someone and they come up with a fix for you, it's more reasonable to say the skilled therapist creates an environment by which you find your own answers and heal yourself. You will have to put in the work, so be prepared to put in the required time and effort to achieve your aims.

Therapy is not advice giving

Therapists don't give advice about decisions in life. For example, don't expect the therapist to advise you on whether you're better off leaving a relationship, or whether to confront your parents about an issue, what they will do, through their expertise, is to help you to work out answers to your own questions. Only you can possibly make these decisions, you know you better, what you need and what works.

Having said that therapists, may give possible interpretations on what and why some of the things you're working are occurring, such as the impact of your childhood on the way you think and feel now. They may also advise on other services that may be able to support you outside of the service they provide, such as addiction support groups, mental health crisis lines or other supporting treatment options.

Therapy is not providing a friend who will listen
Therapy is based on a relationship called the therapist and client relationship, it is its own type of boundaried relationship alongside others we have in life such as friend, father or mother. While friends can offer support, therapy is based on solid theory and the experience of the therapist to help you overcome psychological difficulties. It is not a friendship because to be friends it would need to be reciprocal. Instead it provides a space where you don't have to worry about a friend's opinion and are free to set the agenda. It is its own relationship and it can even be deep and caring but it exists within boundaries to help you get the most from the experience.

Therapy is not an emergency line
If you're in sudden crisis or emergency involving mental health, therapy is not generally for emergency access to help. As part of the therapy contract your therapist will make clear the service they provide and the boundaries of it. The therapist may signpost to out of hours support and emergency services. If you are concerned about getting help outside therapy it is recommended you raise this with your therapist.

Therapy is not at core about diagnosis and treatment
Some people may have or want a mental health diagnosis. Examples include autism, bipolar disorder, borderline personality disorder or post-traumatic stress disorder. In therapy, the diagnosis can help the therapist gain an initial understanding and even inform the way they provide therapy, but therapy sees that very much as a starting point and seeks to look behind the label to the whole person. Therapy is more about understanding the whole of you – the inner you, your story, feelings, what has shaped you and how that relates to any problems you share. In therapy, the therapist will be recognising you as more than any diagnosis or symptom; they will see you as a whole, unique and complex being. This does not mean therapists are against treating mental health issues with medication or don't believe in diagnoses; it just means they are trained to help with these issues by working within the context of your whole being, informed but not blinded by any diagnosis you may have.

Comparison with other psychological professionals
International Variation: Different countries or regions may use different professional names to those described below or use the same names but mean something different.

Therapists, in terms of counselling and psychotherapy, can often be confused with other types of wellbeing and mental health professionals and there are definitely overlaps, because ultimately they deal with mental improvement. Here are other types of professionals and the main differences in comparison to therapists.

- A Coach looks to identify and make changes a person needs and wants and what is holding them back from achieving it. Coaching looks at the issue, in the "here and now" and changes needed both internally and in the world to obtain confidence needed to achieve these goals. It's not typically associated with creating deep awareness of the past and how it impacts the present.
- Clinical Psychologist. Psychology is the scientific study of the mind in the way people behave, interact or think, both consciously and unconsciously. Psychologist may be skilled in diagnosis, for example a personality disorder.
- Psychiatrist. A psychiatrist is someone who has had medical training and has decided to specialise in the study of mental disorders. This includes their diagnosis, medication, management and prevention. Psychiatrists often work on a broad range of cases alongside an area of expertise and research.
- Mediation. Mediators often work in workplaces, human resources and independently. They work to resolve differences between people. For example, difficulties with an ex-partner, or a work colleague.

Keyword: Here and now refers to what challenges and issues you are experiencing currently in your day to day existence rather than focusing on the past. The past may come up but the focus is on the now.

What problems can therapy be used for?

Therapy can be useful for many psychological problems. It can be used for complex and severely distressing problems, such as suffering from a psychosis where you hallucinate or hear voices, to life stresses such as feeling low due to work stress. In most cases, problems will be comorbid, where a number of problems coexist. Here are brief descriptions of the major categories of problems that people come to therapy for. This list is not exhaustive but indicative.

Life stresses

Although a degree of stress is a healthy part of life, stress can build up incrementally and cause a variety of issues and symptoms, such as difficulty sleeping or a general sense of feeling tired and run-down. Specific stresses in life may include bereavement, relationship breakup, life-changing illness, work difficulties, financial difficulties, family troubles, or children not leaving home. Stress does not have to be related to negative experience; positive events can be stressful too, such as moving houses or getting married.

Anxiety

People with anxiety respond to certain objects or situations with fear and dread, as well as with physical signs of anxiety or panic, such as a rapid heartbeat and sweating. Fears could range from health anxiety, phobias (e.g., fear of spiders), and social anxiety to a general feeling of anxiety that may be continuously experienced.

A particular anxiety called OCD (obsessive compulsive disorder) is where people have constant thoughts or fears that cause them to perform certain rituals or routines. The disturbing thoughts are called obsessions, and the rituals are called compulsions that try to cancel out those obsessions. An example is a person with an unreasonable fear of germs who constantly washes his or her hands.

Mood Issues
With mood related issues you may have persistent feelings of sadness, or fluctuations from extreme happiness to extreme sadness. Your moods may combine with other emotions such as anger, emptiness, numbness or tearfulness. The most common mood issues are depression and bipolar disorder.

Trauma
You have been through a traumatic event like a car accident, victim of crime, war, rape, serious life changing medical procedure or even a near death experience. Even though the event is past you don't feel you've processed it yet. For example, you have flashbacks as if you are reliving the event, get emotionally triggered, feel your nerves are fraught or you just don't feel yourself anymore.

Relationships
Relationship issues include difficulty forming relationships, affairs, betrayal, abuse, sexual intimacy issues, communication and trust issues, separation and divorce, family issues and parenting conflicts. Relationship issues can be worked on in therapy either individually, in couples or within families.

Psychosexual Issues
Sexual issues which have a psychological basis to them such as loss of libido, fear of sex, painful sex, premature ejaculation, erectile dysfunction and performance anxiety.

Psychotic disorders
Psychotic or psychosis disorders involve distorted awareness and thinking. Two of the most common symptoms of psychotic disorders are hallucinations - the experience of images or sounds that are not real, such as hearing voices -and delusions, which are false fixed beliefs that the sufferer accepts as true, despite evidence to the contrary. Schizophrenia is an example of a psychotic disorder. It is common for these types of issues to be treated with medication alongside therapy.

Addictions and Habits
Addictions can develop from many activities, including drinking alcohol, taking drugs, eating, stealing, gambling, gaming, social media, work, having sex and using the Internet. Often addictions begin as a result of how these activities make people feel emotionally and physically. These feelings can be pleasurable - triggering a powerful urge to carry out the activity again to recreate the 'high'. This can develop into a

repetitive cycle that becomes very hard to break, affecting how you feel about yourself, personal responsibilities and relationships. Equally there are other habits with negative impacts, which can include self-harm, hair picking, excessive scratching or biting nails.

Eating Disorders

Eating disorders involve extreme emotions, attitudes, and behaviours involving weight and food. External signs include being seriously underweight, bingeing and purging or bingeing by itself. Anorexia nervosa, bulimia nervosa, and binge eating disorder are the most common eating disorders which can involve underlying feelings of and cycles of stress, worry and shame.

Self-Worth, Identity and Attachment

Usually not separated out as an issue but manifested as part of other problems when you present in therapy. For example you may have low self-worth, which is an opinion you have about yourself and your acceptability and goodness. You may be struggling with identity issues associated with your sexuality, spirituality or cultural heritage and feel something is missing. Sometimes, with *attachment* issues, you can also struggle with fearful feelings of abandonment, separation anxiety and rejection as a pattern in life, which can then impact your current relationships. For example, needing to control the other persons activity in case of rejection or loss.

Keyword: Attachment. In a psychological sense attachment issues occur as a result of specific patterns of ingrained behaviours in relation to carers. For example, a child who is not allowed to explore and feel a sense of safety may become insecure. Attachment theory believes some issues with relationships can carry forward into adult relationships, such as excessive distrust of a partner.

Personal Development & Growth

You can be on a journey exploring life, its meaning and your relationship with the world as well as your own beliefs. It's not uncommon for people to explore their own purpose, spirituality, life project(s), ageing, life stages as well as death anxiety. People often want to be the best person they can be whether it's in relationships, the community, or being more self-aware of your own conflicts and issues.

Personality disorders

Sometimes people can be diagnosed with a Personality Disorder where people have extreme and inflexible personality traits that are distressing to the person and/or cause problems in work, school, or social relationships. This can interfere with a person's ability to cope in life. Examples include antisocial personality disorder, borderline personality disorder, obsessive-compulsive personality disorder, and paranoid personality disorder.

Psychosomatic Illnesses

You've heard it said that the mind and body are connected and your wellbeing is influenced by both. Although medical issues can't be cured by therapy, the relationship you have with your illness and how it makes you feel, such as your stress about the issue, can be worked on in therapy. People come to therapy to manage medical issues such as cancer, pain, IBS and fertility. Many medical issues can have an associated stress element and thus therapy can help you manage this.

How to spot the psychological signs early

The truth is, most people entering therapy do so when there is a significant or critical issue that cannot wait. Wouldn't it be nice if you had spotted a potential issue earlier and saved yourself a lot of time, money, and pain and improved your quality of daily life? For example, people may enter therapy for hearing voices, compulsive thoughts, panic and anxiety or depression. However, when things are slightly off, or when it feels you trudge on regardless, these could be some signs where therapy could help you pre-emptively. Here are some ways to spot whether pre-emptive access to therapy could be beneficial.

Remember to check with your physician/doctor in case there are other medical issues involved.

Generally not yourself

What's your norm? You may find yourself feeling angrier and your moods change more than you expect, or it may be that you feel more sadness. Maybe you may feel more lonely and shutdown. This may combine with feeling fatigued and having difficulty sleeping or concentrating. You're just feeling more "off" than normal, and what you feel may be uncontrollable or even unexpected. If you feel out of sync with your norm, then it could be a sign to take action.

Engaging steadily in more unhealthy behaviours or substances

You are moving more habitually towards using substances or harmful behaviours as a way of coping and feeling better. This maybe in the form of alcohol, aggression, drugs, food, sex, and self-harming. You may feel you're moving into a cycle where it feels it would be difficult to let go of the need.

Self-care doesn't work

You're feeling run-down and tired, and your natural rhythm of life and flow is out of synchronisation. So, you go the self-care route to help; after all, you've done it before – you take breaks, rest and go on holiday, or you get support from family and friends. However, you still feel fatigued and run-down, and you are have difficulty concentrating and sleeping, and something does not feel right.

Stressful events
There are so many generic life events that sometimes come up, from bereavement, loss of job, financial worries, divorce, or even moving houses. If you feel weighed down by life events such as guilt, shame, and fatigue coupled with no space or time to care for yourself, therapy could be a good option.

You lose interest
Have you stopped doing the activities you ordinarily enjoy? This may be social life, work or a hobby. If so, ask why. Many people find that emotional experiences, low mood and difficult events keep them from participating in life activities.

Traumatic event
You have been through a traumatic event like a car accident, or you have been the victim of crime, complex bereavement, war, rape, serious life-changing medical procedure or even a near-death experience. Even though the event has passed, you don't feel you've processed it yet or you may feel your nerves are fraught or you just don't feel yourself anymore.

Impartial outside support
Sometimes, we can feel confused, and we don't know what direction to take and need to make an important decision. However, it's hard to think straight if you have no one to talk to or when people are giving you mixed messages and have their own agenda. For example, you are trying to make a decision to move abroad, but your family wants you to stay and you can't think straight and feel guilty. Therapy can provide a safe space for you to explore your feelings, understand where they come from, resolve conflicts, alleviate confusion and make decisions.

Understand yourself better
For some people, therapy is an opportunity to grow by becoming more aware of themselves. There may be things about your history, spirituality or identity that you want to explore, or you just want to know why you are the way you are and what stops you from achieving your life goals. Understanding why we think, act, and feel the way we do can be extremely empowering. That understanding can lead to insight, which once revealed, can help channel how you want to direct your life now and in the future.

Faltering relationships
You may be feeling more and more disconnected with your partner and seem to have lost feelings of trust or are developing anger, jealousy, possessiveness and resentment. You may also find it hard to resolve conflicts or make plans for the future. Rather than wait for things to get worse, relationship counselling could be used to restore and understand what is causing the feeling of distance between you. Remember, this can equally apply to families, between siblings, parent-to-child or

even with a friend. You can invest time into the relationship to get your needs met and the relationship back on track.

Why does therapy work?

So, you're in the therapy room. You sit, you talk and you're listened to attentively with empathy and acceptance. Depending on the type of therapy, the therapist may offer their thoughts and feelings as well as employing a number of different techniques. You would be forgiven for asking, "How can this possibly work?" and "Surely if it were that easy, anyone could do it." Part of the confusion could be because you perceive the therapist to do actually very little; there may be less structure or no fixed roadmap to get you there. Well, I hope in this section to demystify why therapy works.

In his book *Why Therapy Works* (2016), psychologist Louis Cozolino provides a detailed explanation of how and why therapy works from a neuroscientific perspective. I have summarised these as five fundamental ways the therapy process works: by understanding yourself better, by establishing a better relationship with yourself, by experiencing and connecting with your thoughts and feelings, by social bonding, and by moderating fear. Not that all are mandatory for the therapeutic process to be beneficial, but they do reveal what goes on within to effect change. Underpinning that change is our innate mental capability to find imaginative ways to express thoughts and feelings (the unfettered mind) and the innate ability for our brains to develop new mental paths (neuroplasticity).

Understanding yourself better

When you attend therapy, there may be any number of problem areas you're working on, such as an inability to make relationships or to manage difficult feelings, or a general sense of something wrong. Particularly where these issues become a pattern or are repeated as a general way of being, the reasons for them prevailing may remain out of awareness to our conscious minds. Through the safe process of therapy, where you mind is allowed to explore you inner world freely, these more unconscious experiences can be brought out into the therapy room to see how they play a part in your current problems.

*Keyword: The **unconscious,** also called the subconscious, is the set of mental activities within an individual that occur without awareness. Therefore, the unconscious can affect the patterns of a person's behaviour, thoughts, and feelings. Therapy can reveal the unconscious through talking and expression. Some believe that the unconscious can also be revealed in dreams, body language or even slips of the tongue.*

For example, although not always necessary, therapy enables revisiting of your childhood experiences to form new narratives and understandings towards your past.

Through this process, you can understand the long-lasting effects childhood has had upon you, including your beliefs and behaviours. By allowing for new perspectives to be formed, new possibilities may awaken inside. These insights can begin to shift unhelpful unconscious patterns you may have learned from the past. Therapy allows exploration, self-understanding, and self-reflection to facilitate change within.

Improving your self-relationship

Self-worth is how you judge yourself. While there are external things like work satisfaction that can build your self-worth, the type of self-worth that people often have difficulty with is self-judgement, which is not tied entirely with external achievements such as personal success, wealth or being appreciated. Self-worth is a deeper sense of judgement and feelings about yourself, such as feeling damaged, unworthy of love, abandoned, or self-loathing. These themes can remain static, having been "created" in our history of childhood, social, cultural, family relationships, school and society. For example, feeling secure with parents and being able to explore and make mistakes is going to be positive for your self-worth, but being persistently scolded, abused, bullied and feeling a lack of belonging in the world is not a recipe for creation of good self-worth. Therapy gives you the skills to reality test maladaptive beliefs, behaviours, and emotions in order to reappraise your worth now. Through the care of the therapist, you can reinstate your sense of self-worth by accepting yourself more and changing the judgements you have towards yourself, thereby restoring a sense of "okayness."

Keyword: Reality test *is the objective evaluation of a belief, thought or feeling. For example, you may assume a colleague at work is ignoring you, but there may be many other explanations, such as them having a lot on their mind.*

Experiencing yourself

Ever heard the phrase "What does your heart tell you?" "What are your feelings?" or even "Don't just think - feel!" Contrary to popular belief, this is not about making you cry, although that is one possible effect. It simply means not only thinking, analysing and interpreting, but also being in emotional contact with what is and has happened by using the language of emotions. That process can bring out emotions, even anger and sadness, where the thoughts and emotions come together in an experienced reality. Therapists often talk about felt response or visceral reaction; it's as if the body has connected both head and heart. It's not just a rational response, such as, "I know it was difficult." It's an experience: the body shakes, the emotions come forward into the room perhaps with anger and you feel the emotions through your nervous system. You're connecting your thoughts, emotions and body sensations together to heal.

Sociality and bonding

We are naturally social creatures, and our minds have evolved to connect with others in very useful ways for purposes of survival. We always existed in groups, and forming secure attachments with others is a natural way of destressing, and gaining support, protection and love. The benefits of good relationships to our wellbeing is an unarguable truth. Therapy taps into this innate need as a healing agent, by providing a secure attachment with a therapist. How does the secure attachment form with the therapist? By them offering an accepting, empathic and sometimes deeply relational connection. Through the connection, therapists become attuned to your needs, to what is said and also unsaid, and to establish a tentative theory about what is going on for you. From this place, the therapist gets to feel what it's like for you and uses those feelings therapeutically.

Soothing fear

The amygdala is the part of the brain that detects dangers for the purpose of survival, and can trigger fight or flight mechanisms that are very useful to our survival and to deal with a threat. However, the brain can become sensitised to threats based on past experiences and believe a current situation is something to be alarmed about, when it is not. This may be emotional triggers, spiders, relational patterns, needles or active trauma with flashbacks. Through the secure but challenging environment of therapy, people can work on their thoughts and emotions by gradually confronting these perceived dangers and thus desensitising or inhibiting the fear reflex to a realistic baseline.

Unfettered mind

Allowing your mind to freely express itself is a critical part of healing because it allows you to find out who you are and what's wrong. It enables you to think abstractly and imaginatively to express ideas in novel ways through a combination of language, stories, memories, dreams, metaphors, associations, feelings, body senses and intuition. These inbuilt capabilities can help open up your internal world to discover who you are and what is wrong, which in turn can allow you to drop what is no longer needed and to understand what you now need. Therapy, through the safety of the relationship, allows your mind to freely wander, explore and discover.

Through the safe container of the relationship with the therapist, this inner world can be opened up to explore and imagine the kind of future you would like now. For example, by thinking about what it would be like to wake up tomorrow and have what you need and to visually see what that would look like. Stories create identity and spark the imagination, setting the direction of a new future.

Here is a condensed example of a client allowing her mind to free associate in a creative way.

[Agnes feels alone and is losing hope in her life]

Client: I really feel hopeless; it's like I can't see out of the rubble.
Therapist: What do you see in that rubble?
Client: I see lots of big boulders all around; it's dark and no one is there.
Therapist: Can you describe what you see?
Client: It's dark, and cruel. I don't have the energy to get up, it seems. It's not nice at all.
Therapist: So little energy.
Client: I just need a hand up. If only I could get a hand up.
Therapist: Do you imagine anything, anyone who could give that to you?
Client: Well, my son. I feel so warm and light with him.
Therapist: Is that something you could imagine?
Client: Yes, I can. He is there for me and cares. {Client shows emotion.} I feel a bit lighter.

Neuroscience

From a neuroscience perspective, the mind is plastic or neuroplastic; like dough, it can be shaped through learning. Neuroplasticity is the brain's ability to reorganise itself by forming new neural connections throughout life. Therapy experientially changes the brain and literally creates new pathways of thinking and feeling.

There are many examples in this book that show how the process of therapy works where the mind shifts through new insights and felt experiences. These shifts literally create new pathways and reinforce hope and belief to catalyse your process in therapy.

Here are some examples of clients achieving a shift in therapy:

"I don't know exactly what happened. I felt upset a lot of the time during the past few weeks. It was painful but I just feel a bit better. I could not tell you exactly why and how this helped me but it has."

"[Karl was feeling low moods.] Understanding how I was shutting off my feelings about my partner and how that felt for her really helped. I was in a loop with her, which continued to make me feel isolated and uncared for. But taking the risk and saying what I felt just made things so much better between us. I still get low moods but they don't last as long now."

"[Amarpreet's bereavement.] I had put so much focus on feeling guilty for not being there for my mum at the moment she died because I had to go to the bathroom. But I almost forgot that maybe she would have wanted it that way, and it really was not my fault it happened that way. I know we loved each other."

"[Kate was traumatised.] Reprocessing the memory and events and the physical shock of seeing my mum having an affair seems less distressing now. I used to relive the moment so much, but now it's not as stressful. It really feels I can let go now."

Assessing Therapy Options

In this section I'll give you an overview of considerations to determine the therapeutic options (for the right therapeutic approach and therapist, see Way 2). In this section you will:

- Determine your options for access to therapy.
- Consider whether you wish short or long-term therapy.
- Consider the use of tools therapists may use.
- Consider any preference you have for the therapeutic setting.

Accessing Therapy

Access to therapy will depend on where you live and any cost constraints. You may live somewhere where there are no or few options for therapy, or where there is a wide variety of options across public, charitable, private, insurance, and workplace sectors. Access points may include:

- Public services. You may be in a country where free, albeit limited, types of therapy are available with an upper limit to the number of sessions. For example, in the UK CBT is commonly available for a short duration, although other types of therapies such as DBT and EMDR are available depending on the type of problem being experienced. Access may be through a referral (in the UK via a doctor) and may involve being on a waiting list, sometimes for many months.
- Workplace schemes. You may be part of an organisation that offers health insurance that includes therapy. Typically, therapy through workplace schemes are short term in nature.
- Charities. You may have local access to therapy services who operate as a charity. The service may be free at point of access, operated on a sliding scale based on personal circumstances, or as a lower cost option than private therapy.
- Privately. Private typically means you would be paying for therapy, either out of your own pocket or by an insurer. Private therapy, depending on your location, tends to offer the most options, shorter waiting time, and flexibility to work longer term. Therapists may operate individually or as part of an agency.

Where you have no suitable local access to therapy, you could consider online or phone therapy as an alternative. Where you have a therapist who works or is a citizen of another country, they may not be able to offer you therapy due to your country's legal regulations. For example, it is not legal for a UK therapist to offer therapy to US citizens, unless they are licensed to practice in the US.

International Variation: Different countries will have different access options to therapy.

Short-term vs. Long-term Therapy

Therapy can last anywhere from a single session to 5 years or even more. There is no way of determining exactly how much time your healing and recovery will take place. The most you could say is that the type of problem, the number of coexisting problems, how entrenched and severe the difficulty, are associated factors to duration of therapy, but there is no formula.

Therapy differentiates between short-term, or sometimes called brief or time limited, therapy, normally between 6-12 sessions, and long-term therapy. Short-term therapy is generally directed to a single specific goal, which focuses the work. Examples of goals could include managing work stress better, overcome driving anxiety, or improving communication in relationships. Short-term therapy is also an option if you are time or cost constrained or as a way of determining whether therapy is right for you. Where access to therapy is provided by public or insurance providers, they will typically offer you short-term therapy, although there may be exceptions.

Short-term therapy may open up other problems and emotions that you were unaware of prior to undertaking short-term therapy. If you're worried about this, then speak to the therapist. Therapists should be able to offer referrals, options, or suggestions for further help if that is the case.

Long-term therapy is open-ended, where the scope and goals of therapy have no fixed constraints. You may share with the therapist what you would like to work on, but the agenda is fluid and open-ended. There are some issues that might benefit more from a longer-term commitment, such as abuse or addictions.

If you feel you may wish to switch to longer-term therapy from short term, then you can ask what options are available early in the process, and whether the therapist would be able to switch to a longer-term model.

Therapeutic tools

As well as talking therapy, therapists may introduce a number of tools into therapy to help with your healing process. The purpose of these tools is invariably to help you explore your thoughts and feelings, learn new ways of being, and deepen your understanding of yourself. If the therapist introduces these tools, you are totally in control if you wish to engage with them or not. You may worry about your competence to use the tools, but it isn't about being "good" at using the tool, it's about using the process of expressing yourself through the tool to heal and grow.

- Drama using theatre techniques for healing. Drama therapy (Psychodrama) is its own modality.
- Role play. Where you and the therapist act out parts to learn about new ways of being, such as development of empathy, conflict resolution, or assertiveness.

- Dance uses mind and body techniques for healing. Dance therapy is its own modality.
- Sand tray work. Use of sand to create concrete manifestation of a client's inner world using sand, water, and miniature objects.
- Pebble work. Use of stones to represent ideas and feelings such as with relationships.
- Cards. For example, emotion cards enable people to understand and express feelings.
- Art is a creative way of expression. Art therapy is its own modality.
- Mindfulness. Mindfulness is the psychological process of bringing one's attention to experiences occurring in the present moment, observing and flowing with it.
- Hypnosis. Hypnosis is a state of human consciousness involving focused attention and reduced peripheral awareness, which it is believed enhances your capacity to respond to suggestions made.
- Animals. Animals such as horses and pets are used in the healing process. Equine or "horse therapy" is its own modality.
- Virtual Reality and computer-assisted interventions; for example, in the desensitization of phobias and fears.
- Music therapy. Music therapy is its own modality.

Therapeutic Settings

Therapy is typically offered at the therapist's organisation or their home office. However, therapy may also be available in a number of different environments such as your home, in outside spaces, in your work office, or even in noisier environments. In the digital age, therapy can also be available through a number of mediums as well as classical face to face. This includes traditional phone, web cam, email, instant messaging, and internet phone/audio systems.

Sometimes people prefer the convenience of home, phone, or online access to therapy, or it may be because it is not easy to visit the therapist's office due to lack of transport, disability, or an accessibility need. Another reason is safety, as people who have suffered a trauma such as a crime could be reluctant to meet someone face to face in private and may be more comfortable working online or in an open public space. In other cases, people may have difficulties that prevent them from meeting face to face, which is why they are accessing therapy in the first place, such as fear of leaving home, having a phobia of open spaces, or a general social anxiety of meeting someone new. For some, therapy can be anxiety-provoking, so having another medium for accessing therapy can provide a transitory or longer-term way of accessing therapy.

Whatever method(s) you choose or negotiate with the therapist, it's important that you feel comfortable doing so and feel safe from being overheard, so, for example, having no one in the house when you are online with your therapist. For online systems, the tools used by the therapist must use secure encryption to protect against interception, which is analogous of minimising the possibility of someone listening in to a room. The other type of threat to online security is through anyone who can potentially access your computer device, whether desktop, laptop, tablet, or smartphone. If someone is able to access your device, there is a possibility they could access your files, emails, and recordings on your computer or, even worse, install software called "keylogging" which could record all your messages and sessions in stealth for viewing later on. Whatever method you choose, if safety is a worry, talk to the therapist about risks and what protections are in place.

Self-Reflection
1. What options do you have for access to therapy, including funding?
2. Do you prefer shorter and goal-directed therapy? Why?
3. Do you prefer open-ended therapy? Why?
4. Is the option of switching with the therapist you first meet from short- to long-term therapy important to you? If so, ask your therapist whether that is a possibility.
5. Are you able to gain access to therapists from your preferred approach?
6. Do you have a preference for types of tools used during therapy? For example, mindfulness.
7. Do you have any preference for the environment you're going to be in? For example, home or internet.
8. Are there any risks to being overheard in the environment? For example, access to your computer.

Your rights in therapy
All competent therapists must adhere to ethical as well as competence standards when working with you. You have a lot of power and rights in therapy, and here are the most significant rights, although there are many others too:

- Fair treatment, with dignity and respect.
- The therapist puts you as their primary concern.
- You can ask questions about anything related to your therapy.
- Expect the therapist to be professional and competent. They only work with you if they're able to within their limits and competence.
- Right to privacy and confidentiality unless harm to yourself or others is a concern.
- Freedom to say "yes" or "no" to methods employed in therapy and ultimately therapy itself.
- Freedom to talk or not talk about anything.

- To know what information is kept about you, with consent, and copies provided on request.
- To have access to a complaints process.

Typically your responsibilities are no more than turning up, paying for sessions, providing any essential information required, and not harming the therapist. There may be other responsibilities depending on the therapist or the organization, for example, not coming to sessions intoxicated. Essential personal information you provide may vary, but it could be as little as your name, doctors, and contact details.

Having a lot of rights does not mean the therapist does not have a right to refuse something you suggest; it is collaborative, after all. For example, referring you on is based on putting you first as their primary concern.

International Variation: Each country may have its own regulatory or generally accepted ethical standards

Disclosure

Before you meet the therapist, be mindful that, although therapy is confidential, there are limits to what the therapist can keep to themselves without talking to someone else. In most cases, the therapist will tell you if they are thinking of or will need to disclose material. Disclosure may be to a doctor or another support service, law courts, social services, or even the police.

Therapists tend to use a catch-all statement: "I have to disclose if I feel you or another person maybe at serious risk of harm," which can specifically include though is not limited to:

- Harm to a child or vulnerable adult through abuse, including neglect, sexual, financial, or physical abuse. This is not limited to children in your family but can be any child that you discuss.
- Serious criminality including terrorism and money laundering.
- Legal trial. If the therapist is asked to take the stand as a witness, they will be subpoenaed and therefore cannot hold matters in confidence.

Therefore, there are limits and, contrary to popular myth, therapists are compelled just like anyone else to testify in a law court if mandated. If you are worried about disclosure, you can ask the therapist at the initial session (or any subsequent session) what their stance to disclosure would be.

International Variation: Each country may have its own regulatory or generally accepted disclosure standards

Process of finding a therapist

Obviously you can use your gut instinct to choose a therapist, but I feel you can really help yourself more, especially if you are embarking on longer-term therapy or have not had the best experience, if you can meet a number of therapists, ask some questions, get to know who they are and their philosophy, and get a feel below the surface. The process of finding a therapist usually involves shortlisting potential therapists, talking with them, asking questions, assessing them, and, if necessary, repeating the process.

Shortlisting possible therapists

Shortlist a few therapists if you can rather than picking the first that comes up so you can compare and contrast. Maybe you'll find a list of potential therapists through the internet, which can give you a profile and experience to help, but I would also say not to reserve too much judgement on the profile itself because of your initial perceptions. Some therapists may not be good at the written word, so visit or talk to them if possible. Sometimes you can also get a referral or recommendation, e.g., from a doctor or a friend of a friend, but don't assume they are the right therapist just on that basis.

If you use a therapist that someone you know is using or has used in the past, consider how you feel about it. For example, what if the therapist already knows about you through them, or you need to talk about the person who recommended the therapist? Therapists may also believe it is in your interest if they know about this, especially if they are a current client. I suggest talking about that in the first session so boundaries are understood and concerns clarified.

Many find a therapist through insurance schemes, workplace, or public health agencies and are offered a therapist based on availability and/or location. However, even then you could ask whether there is a possibility of consulting with a few therapists, even by phone or email if possible. If you have no options but to work with an assigned therapist, but you feel you cannot work with them, an alternative may still be possible.

Talk to potential therapists

When you have a potential shortlist of therapists, it is a good idea to talk face to face, although telephone or, in some cases, online are also good options. Therapists often use voicemail to avoid interruptions during their client sessions, so don't be surprised if you don't reach your chosen therapist immediately. Leave a message and they will return your call. In some cases, the initial session may be provided to you for free or it may be chargeable. The therapist should be clear about any charges for the first session. In the UK, you'll find most private therapists are happy to chat on the phone for free for a short period.

You can find out whether the therapist feels able to help you with your problem and discuss practical matters such as whether they have appointments at a time and place that suits you and how much they charge. To make a decision, I suggest you think about it before making a final decision. Other therapists may ask you directly, but you should not feel pressured to make up your mind immediately. You can simply ask for time to make a decision; you are free to choose.

Ask questions

If you need to ask questions, you should not be afraid to ask them during the process of making up your mind. Therapists should welcome questions. This conversation will also give you a sense of what the therapist is like and whether you would feel comfortable working with them. See the section Way 2 under "Questions for the therapist" for ideas and choose the questions you feel are important to you. I know clients can find asking questions difficult, especially if encountering therapy for the first time. This may be due to ideas of politeness or feelings of anxiety, or lack of confidence, some of which you may be coming to therapy for in the first place, but it could be beneficial to ask questions. This feeling of reluctance to ask could also be due to a power imbalance or a preconceived idea of authority, like that of a doctor-patient relationship, or you may feel that you should not ask questions for fear of causing offence or presuming that they would be seen as challenging or rude to the therapist's authority, but in order to get the therapist you want, I really feel you need to go in and ask questions that are important to you. One way to mitigate this feeling of discomfort over asking questions prior to visiting your therapist is to ask them whether it would be okay to ask them questions including about their experiences. If you wish, you can forewarn them; you're not looking for them to fail.

In my experience, most clients don't ask any or many questions; ultimately it is all "proof is in the pudding" and that is okay too. If you feel uncomfortable asking questions, it's an opportunity to respect your own feelings. You are free to choose.

Assess them

After your first meeting, take a bit of time to reflect upon what you experienced. Way 2 "Find the right therapist and approach", provides guidance on assessment. You can also complete the "Self-Reflection" exercise in that way.

If you're embarking on long-term therapy or are unsure of the fit, you could just take a leap of faith and try out the therapist for three to six sessions before deciding, or even ask for short-term therapy. If you can, I would recommend this if you aren't quite sure and have no better options, as the initial session may not be representative of what therapy would be like with the therapist, and the therapist may be still getting attuned to your needs. Just like in real life, a partnership can eventually be successful even if you're unsure at first.

Many people don't find the right therapist the first time and in fact it may take a while to find a good match for you. If this happens to you, it is not your fault. You have already decided you would benefit from therapy, so it is worth trying again. Also, it's easy to assume that you would be using one therapist or approach to recover, but that is not necessarily the case. As with any journey, you can meet a number of people along your way.

The first session

Congratulations! You're ready to meet your therapist. The first session, sometimes called the initial session, consultation, or initial assessment, is there for both you and the therapist to determine if you are a good fit for each other. You'll figure out if the therapist is right for you and the therapist will figure out if they believe they can help you.

Here are some things you can do to make the most of your first session.

- Read through Way 2 Find the right therapist and approach, and this section to identify anything that may be relevant to discuss at the first session.
- Be ready to state what is "wrong," your thoughts, and your feelings. If you feel you will struggle, you can always write it down and take it with you.
- Inform the therapist if you have any significant needs. See the section below.
- Inform the therapist of the ways you like to learn. For example, if you're neurodiverse, you may prefer visuals rather than working with feelings.
- Ask questions if you wish. You can ask about the therapist and their philosophy to determine if they are right for you. See the section "Questions for the therapist" in Way 2 for ideas.
- Be open and honest about your feelings. Remember, the "good enough" therapist will offer a safe and non-judgmental environment and work with you "as you are."
- Remember that therapy is a process and is not generally considered a fast fix.

Informing of significant needs

Prior to meeting your therapist, you may hold concerns even before you meet them, for which you can make preparations or ask questions beforehand.

Some immediately practical concerns reported by clients include:

- Does the room have access to nearby toilets?
- Do the facilities have disabled accessibility?
- Whether access is discreet or via a waiting room. In some cases, you may be asked to wait in a waiting room with others, while in other settings you're hardly ever going to meet anyone prior.

- Is the place safe? For example, will there be other people in the building? Sometimes clients can feel safer during the day with people around, while others prefer that no one else is around.
- Having an emotion or fear triggered. For example, fear of being alone with the therapist and trigger words or situations that cause flashbacks or phobic reactions.
- Don't feel you'll be able to talk at all to the therapist. The therapist may be able to assure you or find a tool to help with your expression, such as art or emotion cards, which provides a different activity to talking that does not need you to be intensely focused on the face-to-face encounter.

If your anxiety or fear is of concern, you may wish to take a trusted person with you; they can wait outside or, by agreement with the therapist, be allowed into the initial session so that you can get more comfortable.

While the therapist will not be able to control everything, at least you will be forewarned in what to expect and the therapist can learn about any significant things you're worried about prior.

What to expect at your first session

Therapists tend to have different approaches to assessment for the first session. The session may be totally open-ended, with no or only a few questions being asked, and you talk as you wish about what is going on. Alternatively, the assessment may be more prescriptive, where you're asked a list of questions which they complete in front of you, or they may even ask you to complete a questionnaire before or during the session.

Unless you are there with a therapist who is skilled in diagnosis, and that is what you want, therapists won't diagnose you. Mental health diagnosis can only be carried out if they are qualified to do so, typically the field of psychiatry and clinical psychologists, and would likely to be over an extended time or a number of hours or sessions. Either way, as a minimum they will want to understand why you are seeking therapy, any symptoms you are experiencing, and some background. If you feel you will find it hard to express these, you may wish to take some notes with you to provide, read, or explore with the therapist.

Here are some questions that you are likely to need to explain or respond to at the initial session:

- Why are you seeking therapy? What issues and symptoms are you experiencing? For example, because of bereavement, feeling low, or work stress.
- What impact does the issue cause you? For example, your problem might be causing difficulty at work, sleep issues, or panicky feelings.

- What are your expectations of therapy and the therapist? For example, you may only have time for a set number of sessions or want more direction from the therapist.
- What have you already tried to help yourself? This may include past therapy.
- Some information about your background. For example, when your problems started, previous history of problems, or even a description of your family constellation (which is to understand where you fit in your family relationships).
- Some therapists may ask about whether you're on medication or have a mental health diagnosis.

Of course, the initial session is an opportunity to assess the therapist and ask questions. See Way 2 "Questions for the therapist" to assess what is important to you.

Also, let them know if you have any concerns about the counseling contract, such as disclosure and record keeping, that need to be explored at the first session (See the section below titled "Understand and negotiate the contract").

During or towards the end of the session, the therapist is likely to indicate whether or not they could work with you. If not, a number of reasons may be given (See the next section, "Why a therapist may not be able to work with you"). The therapist may then ask you to think about it and let them know if you wish to continue, while other therapists may ask you directly whether you wish to continue. You should not feel pressured to make up your mind immediately; you can simply ask for time to make a decision because you are free to choose.

If you decide to begin therapy, you may also be asked for personal information, such as:

- Personal contact details
- Doctor's name
- Next of kin
- Previous history of emotional or mental health problems
- Current medication
- Any previous suicidal attempts

If you are worried about the collection of this information and its purpose, you should talk to the therapist. Generally, therapists do not share information without your consent or only if mandated (See Disclosure). For example, you may be concerned that by providing doctor information, confidential information could end up on your record and be shared with an employer.

In this section, I bring together the considerations from a therapist's perspective of why they may not feel they are right for you. Where the therapist might not be able to work with you, some may find that in itself stressful and that it triggers feelings of failure or rejection; however, you should bear in mind that the therapist is working in your best interests so there will be reasons for their decision. It may feel like a rejection and that can be discussed with the therapist or your next one, but to look at it another way it shows that the therapist is being ethical and kinder to you by being realistic and knowing their limits. Therapists come from a range of backgrounds, experience, and personal perspectives, so all therapists will naturally have different perspectives and opinions on whether they can help you. It's no one's fault; this is a stepping stone in your journey, and you can learn from it. In most cases, therapists may be able to offer a referral and signpost alternative services that may cater to your needs.

Expertise and level of experience

A therapist may simply be unable to work with you due to lack of expertise, inner resources, and experience. Sometimes the more severe and distressed a client, the more a therapist will consider whether they have the internal resources to work with you. For example, therapists without sufficient experience in working with psychosis or schizophrenia may feel that you will not be served best by them. It could equally be that the therapist has chosen not work in certain areas due to their own self-understanding and limits. For example, a therapist may have decided not to work with addictions because of similar issues they experienced with a caregiver growing up, or they don't have enough knowledge in that area.

Meeting expectations

A therapist may not wish to take you on because they cannot meet your expectations. This could include basic needs around timing, duration, and frequency of sessions, or it could be based on whether they can meet your expectations of the outcome. For example, you may have a limited number of sessions you can attend to achieve your goals and they don't feel it's realistic. Some therapists may believe that they can't help you because of these constraints, while others would be freer to work with you within those constraints, leaving you to decide what is best. Either way, the therapist should be open about whether they feel they can meet your expectations.

Relational issues

The therapist is trained to provide you with a safe and impartial zone where you and the therapist can work untainted by outside interference. If they know of you previously or know someone else who knows you, that is likely to be a reason for not working with you. Another reason could be they have worked with or are working with someone you know. Other times it may be that you are in close proximity, such as neighbourhood, inside a community or club setting. You and the therapist will need to consider whether this will interfere or make things awkward. Feeling awkward in therapy is not what anyone would want, as it can interfere with talking about feelings and disclosure openly.

Therapists that work with groups or couples also may consider the dynamic of working with people for the same reasons. In addition, they will carefully consider whether they can work with you in multiple settings, such as individually and then within a couple. The reason for these boundaries is in order to create an impartial and safe place where you're both able to work unfettered from unnecessary interference.

Agency policies
Some public services, workplaces, and insurance providers assess you prior to agreeing to take you on as a client and thus actually seeing your allocated therapist. The provider may have their own set criteria prior to taking you on. For example, an agency may not take you on if you're under 18, or if the problem is related to substance or domestic abuse. This can sound unfair, but it will have to do with risk or scope by which the organisation operates.

International Variation: Each country or region may have its own regulatory or generally accepted ethical standards that therapists must adhere to in taking clients on.

Understand and negotiate the contract
So, once you start therapy, you'll agree to what is usually termed a therapeutic contract. It provides an agreement of how you will work together. Usually clients will accept the agreement, but if you need more flexibility in the agreement, it may be worth understanding it further and talking this through with the therapist, particularly at the initial session. Most therapists are likely to have a written or electronic contract for you to read and perhaps sign, while others state their contract verbally. The scope and content of the contract can vary from therapist to therapist, but here are some considerations.

Remember, if anything is unclear to you, there is no reason why you can't ask for clarification.

International Variation: Each country or region may have its own regulatory or generally accepted contracting standards, e.g., for Pre-Trial Therapy (PTT).

Timing
As well as looking at your time and day availability, you could consider your best mental timing. What you want is to be engaged and to be mentally alert as much as possible; certainly you don't want to be really tired. For example, if you are going to

therapy at 8 a.m., it can be beneficial because you have more energy. On the flip side, you may be tired after therapy and going to work may be difficult.

Frequency
Typically, therapy is conducted face to face once a week for 50 or 60 minutes. However, if you or the therapist feel more or fewer sessions are needed, that can be discussed. Sometimes clients may be under severe distress, for example, from trauma or grief, so you may wish to have more therapy. Sometimes therapists may be able to offer a tentative backup slot so that it can be used if really needed. Further, it may be that you feel a long session would be beneficial, so 60 minutes or even 90 may be possible as long as both you and the therapist are able to agree and work effectively for that duration. For example, it is common for EMDR therapy sessions to last 90 minutes.

Fees and cancellations policy
The contract should clearly state the fees and the cancellations policy. Some therapists may offer free, low-cost, or reduced rates based on a sliding scale and you can confirm these with the therapist.

Method and scope of delivery of therapy
Most therapy is conducted face to face at the therapist's office. As discussed, other settings for therapy, including online, phone, or even outdoors, may be possible.

While most therapists only work at allotted times with you, they may allow you to express feelings in between sessions, such as via secure email. This may be something that can be negotiated by exception, but with clear boundaries such as the frequency and time to respond.

Regardless of the method, the contract should state the boundaries of the service provided. For example, DBT therapy may involve individual sessions, as well as phone coaching for help in between sessions.

Session recordings
No recordings are allowed to be made in therapy unless you give prior permission or it's part of the contract you agree to. Therapists may request recordings be made for various reasons, including to gain help in supervision, reflect on the case, research, or to record a case study for training and development. Remember that in all cases you have a choice whether you wish to do so. If you do provide permission, you should understand the purpose, who it will be shared with, and how and when the recording is to be destroyed.

Keyword: A supervisor is a therapist who is trained in providing support to therapists. Therapists work with supervisors to enable them to do the best work they can with you. Therapists don't use identifying information when reflecting in supervision.

Be clear on what therapy you're receiving

You may be wanting a particular therapeutic approach or to use a particular tool, so the contract should make it clear on the type of therapy you will be receiving. For example, if you were expecting EMDR, make sure that is clear in the contract. Some therapists, particularly integrative therapists, may use a range of orientations, but if you wanted to focus, say, more on CBT, clarifying that with your therapist will help you get off to the right start. Of course, the therapist may have an alternative view, but that is something you can discuss.

Confidentiality

To work on the issues you want to work on and to disclose information you need to, it could be worth considering the limits of confidentiality and disclosure. Therapists usually have a clause about keeping things confidential, unless they are legally bound or there is a risk of harm to yourself or others. What this typically means is that therapists are duty bound to report children's safeguarding issues, terrorism, and money laundering. It is also a myth to think that a therapist is in a privileged position and even if they were subpoenaed to court they would plead, "Sorry, sir, that falls under client and therapist confidentiality." The reality is that therapists can be asked to give evidence or support a case just like any member of the public, so there is a limit to confidentiality.

Pre-Trial Therapy (PTT)

If you are called as a witness in an upcoming trial, you need to inform your therapist at the initial session. Before undertaking therapy, you should discuss this with your legal team and the prosecution prior to starting therapy to ensure it does not impact on the case. In many cases, you may need to seek permission. The reason is that as a witness your evidence may be vital to a case, and if you are undertaking therapy, or where the therapist does not work with you within PTT guidelines, it could jeopardise the case. In addition, the therapist may need to prepare specific PTT notes about your therapy, and there is always a possibility they could be called as a witness to a trial. Although therapists may not have a statement in their contract regarding PTT, it needs to be brought up by you for this reason.

Prosecution services generally prefer you to undertake non-directive approaches to therapy such as person-centred therapy, rather than more directed approaches like psychodynamic therapy.

Similarly, if you are being prosecuted where a case is being brought against you, the same principles of telling the therapist apply so that nothing is detrimental to you.

You can ask the therapist what guidelines they follow in working with you if you are going to trial. For example, the therapist is not to ask leading questions about the crime or ask you to reprocess it.

Record keeping

Therapists vary in their approach to confidential record keeping from just keeping appointment dates/times to more detailed factual information. In-country ways and legal requirements will need to be followed by the therapist for the handling, processing, sharing, and destruction of personal information. If you are concerned about recording keeping, discuss that with the therapist. In most countries, you will have a right to get access to any information stored about you, what it shall be used for, how it is handled, modified, and destroyed. For example, in the European Union, GDPR consent has to be provided by clients to store personal information.

Custom records and reports

If you need the therapist to keep records in a particular format, produce assessment reports, or letters produced, you should convey this up front, so the therapist can determine whether they can meet your needs. This applies equally if you are looking for letters and records to be produced for use by other organizations, such as doctors, work, courts, probation services, and social services. There is always also a possibility that the therapist may not be able to meet your needs, so it's always best to check.

Contact boundaries

This makes clear what is allowable contact between you and the therapist. Most therapists only work at the allocated timing and are not operating a crisis line. However, some may work with you within limits such as allowing messages between sessions. It is important to note that the therapist relationship is different to a friendship and certainly would not extend outside of therapy. Therapists won't connect with clients online or on social media.

About the therapist

You should receive a statement of the therapist's background, qualifications, membership to any standards body or licensure, insurance, complaints process, and approach to therapy. This will provide confidence that the therapist meets requisite standards of practice.

21 Ways to Successful Therapy

Way 18: Use essential tools that makes therapy work

Way 19: Watch out for signs of inefficient, poor or harmful therapy

Way 20: Don't walk away from therapy without talking to the therapist

Way 21: Get help from outside therapy if needed

Chapter 2 – The 21 Ways

"You can clean a room, change its décor. Or you can knock a few walls down for a larger room or an extension. Or you can decide to bring the whole structure down to the ground and rebuild"

This chapter covers all 21 Ways—the teaching foundations of what you may need in order to learn to be successful in therapy.

Introducing the ways

Why 21 Ways? Well let's face it, not everyone has time to digest a lot of material, particularly if you want to focus in on something specific. For each way you can read its condensed idea, to see if it resonates, followed by an explanation, supporting examples and scenarios, as well as practical strategies to apply in or out of the room. The learning is further reinforced through an exercise section for self-reflection, activity, further resources and a quiz to check your understanding.

If something resonates with you, I suggest spending time on it and, if appropriate, follow it through into therapy (see "How to learn the ways" later in this section). Of course, you can speak to your therapist about its relevance, or if you prefer, seek outside professional support (Way 21).

Broadly speaking, ways 1-14 relate more to the "doing" of therapy as a general sequence by which the process tends to unfold (see Chapter 6 – Understanding the therapy process), while ways 15-21 focus more on the assessment, recovery and efficiency of your therapeutic process.

Since the therapist provides the groundwork for your therapy, you will not be surprised to see that five out of the 21 ways (Ways 2, 4, 16, 19, 20) relate to your therapist. You will also find a further seven ways (Ways 5, 6, 7, 8, 9, 10, 11) relate to how you can use the other instrument of therapy—you—in generating the change you require. Whether it's using feelings, awareness, insight or perspective, you'll learn how to effect change. This, together with the relationship with the therapist, makes therapy therapeutic, and more than "just talking".

Having ways to learn and follow does not negate the fact that learning takes time and practice. You'll get the benefits from following the ways through self-reflection, or in the room over time. Therapy can be seen as a continuum, an organic process that unfolds, but by mastering the tool of therapy you can add fertiliser, especially if your process is withering.

In this introduction to the ways you will learn:

- What I mean by success in therapy.

- A quick start guide to help you find the way(s) you want to focus on.

- Guidance on how to learn the ways and develop a personal hierarchy of difficulty if you're struggling with it.

- How ways may vary slightly depending on the therapy approach and duration.

When working on these ways you should apply the principles outlined in the "Important bits" section in the main introduction to this book.

What does success in therapy mean?

Success in therapy is very much dependent on what you consider to be a successful outcome (as long as it's achievable through therapy of course!). For the purpose of this book success means some form of lasting change, rather than using therapy as a safe place in which to be heard or vent (although that could lead to change too!). Therefore, what I mean by success in therapy is to change something within you and/or your life which, through the process of therapy, you have decided is right for you. However, success can't just be measured by resolving problems, healing or achieving goals, it could also be about acceptance of your position, becoming more empowered, or making difficult decisions (including ending therapy if it's not working).

Therapy can be useful for many psychological problems. Presenting problems can include stressful life events, relationship issues, addiction, fear, trauma, anxiety, depression and a whole range of psychological wellbeing and mental health difficulties (See Chapter 1: What problems can therapy be used for). In most cases success will have something to do with alleviating confusion, distress, unwelcome symptoms and harmful behaviours. For those using therapy for self-development success may be deemed to be based on becoming more self-aware and being the best version of yourself. Success does not necessarily mean extinguishing the difficulty completely, it could be what you consider enough change to function better, or be able to live within your situation.

Quick Start – Which way should I focus on first?

If you want to dive straight in and work out the way(s) you want to focus on, then use the table below for a summary of each way and when it may be important to learn.

Way	Title	When to read?
1	Learn all about it	You want to know about therapy, how and why it works and what to expect You want to understand why learning in therapy can be uniquely challenging

Way	Title	When to read?
		You want to learn how to approach learning about yourself in therapy (learning to learn)
		You want to know about your rights in therapy, ethics, contracting and confidentiality
		You're unsure if therapy will work for you
2	Find the right therapist and approach	You are trying to find the right therapist and approach for you.
		How to work out if a therapist is competent
		You're having difficulty finding the right therapist for you
3	Work on feelings related to hope and motivation	You are looking to build hope and commitment towards life and therapy
		You have lost hope and/or motivation
		You are thinking about suicide
4	Use the therapist as a resource	You want to know about multiple ways you can use the therapist to help you
		You're looking for new ideas to help reinvigorate your process
5	Express yourself from your point of view	To learn about the importance of self-expression
		You're struggling to open up
		You want the therapist to take the lead
		You're unsure whether to disclose something difficult
		You're concerned about changing your story because you did not tell the truth before

Way	Title	When to read?
		You're unsure what to focus on
6	Allow feelings and watch what hinders them	To learn about the benefits of being feelings focused
		You want to learn how to express feelings more
		You are struggling with expressing or getting to feelings
		You are struggling with finding the source(s) of your feelings
7	Understand yourself through awareness	To learn about the importance of awareness and why it's the heart of change
		You're struggling to change
		To learn strategies for using and building awareness
8	Consider what makes change undesirable	Understand struggles within you that could block your therapeutic change process
		You feel stuck in the process
9	Put it all together by understanding your story	To understand the benefits of being insight focused
		You're looking for ideas on how to become more insightful
		The importance of building a story of "you" in being insightful
		How to recognise possible patterns and unifying theme(s) which hold you back in life
10	Peel back the layers	To understand the benefits of vulnerability, and working with all parts of you
		You don't understand the potential benefits of sharing many parts of you

Way	Title	When to read?
		You want to share broader and deeper aspects of your personality and history
		You want to understand who you are; your authentic self
		You're struggling with going deeper and showing all parts of yourself in therapy
11	Seek the truth and then "the" truth	To understand the importance of checking out your truth in reality
		To understand why we can all make false assumptions
		To assess potential bias in thinking patterns
12	Weave in ideas of acceptance and responsibility	To understand the importance of acceptance and self-responsibility in being able to change
		Strategies for using acceptance during therapy
		How self-responsibility and acceptance can link to catalyse change.
		How change can manifest in therapy
13	Put what you learn into action	To understand the benefits of taking action outside of therapy
		You're struggling to take action outside of therapy
14	Use your feelings about endings in therapy	Learn how endings can be an important part of therapy
		How historical endings can hold source(s) of difficulty
		You're confused about when to end

Way	Title	When to read?
		You're struggling to end
		To learn what you can reflect upon during the ending phase
		Why therapists may initiate the ending
		Perspectives on dependency on the therapist and/or therapy
15	Don't let things stay stuck without taking action	What you can do if you're stuck in therapy and making little or no progress
		Why stagnation is a feeling that contains therapeutic potential
16	Do your fair share in building a good relationship	What you can do to help build your relationship with the therapist
		Strategies for working with issues that interfere with the relationship
17	Reflect on whether you're being distant or caught up in feelings	Understand how distancing yourself from feelings could impact your process
		Understand how not taking a step back from feelings could impede your progress
		Your process is stuck or faltering
		You tend to be more analytical or tend to be too feelings focused
18	Use tools that make therapy work	Learn, assess and apply tools that apply aspects of the 21 ways in therapy (Chapter 3: Essential tools that make therapy work).
		Your process is stuck or faltering
19	Watch out for signs of inefficient, poor or	If you are unsure whether the therapist is working competently

Way	Title	When to read?
	harmful therapy	Understand why assessing competence is not always easy
		How to work with therapist "grey areas" of competence
		Understand the signs of overt unethical and harmful practices
		Strategies to keep yourself safe if you feel a strong emotional pull towards the therapist
		You have a complaint
20	Don't walk away from therapy without talking to the therapist	If you are considering leaving or ending therapy without telling the therapist
		Understand the potential value of talking to the therapist before you initiate an ending
21	Get help from outside therapy if needed	If you need further professional help outside your therapy
		Why outside help if you're confused, emotionally overwhelmed or you feel lost can be beneficial
		You would like to understand more about these ways
		You want to reflect deeper on a particular problem with another professional

Way structure

Each way consists of the following structure:

- **Way title.** The name of the way.

- **A quote.** I use quotes to deepen your understanding of the way. If you don't understand the quote immediately then you can reflect on it at a later date.

- **Condensed idea.** A summary of the key message(s) and ideas contained within the way so you can quickly determine whether it's something relevant to you.

- **Description:** The core of each way may contain a number of sub topics. Each description is typically supported by summary case example(s) to support understanding.

- **Scenario:** A number of scenarios that frequently occur in therapy, with practical suggestions for you to reflect upon.

- **Exercises:** Self-reflection exercises, activities, and a quiz to strengthen your understanding of the way. These exercises can also be used as a source of self-reflection by trainee therapists during their training.

How the ways make therapy work

The 21 ways in this book centre on what makes therapy work. The knowledge in this book has been developed from five sources: my own experience of a decade in practice as an integrative informed therapist, peer review across the four schools of therapy, client experiences, theory and evidence.

Drawing out themes from clients' perspectives, e.g. from books, social media and experience, this book has been designed as a response to those perspectives, including concerns about misinformation or harm caused by therapy. Examples include: does therapy brainwash people, love in the room, how to determine if the therapist is working competently, and what to do if you don't feel therapy is working for you.

Evidence also provides a useful source of practices that deliver better outcomes. For example, clients giving the therapist feedback (Richards C, 2019) and repair of ruptures in therapy are often beneficial to outcomes (Lambert, M, 2017).

The common factors theory of therapy posits that all types of "good" therapy have things in common that make therapy work. This book is also informed by those factors. Here is a summary of how the ways align to theory and best practice:

- To stay hopeful and dedicated in seeking your truth regardless of obstacles that may make the journey bumpy (Way 1, 3, 21).

- To create an evolving foundation of safety in relationship to yourself, the therapist and the therapy process, in order to do the work needed (Ways 2, 16, 19).

- To allow your thoughts, feelings and presence, including silence, to be expressed so they can be heard within you and by the therapist (Ways 5, 6, 7, 10).

- To reveal multiple facets of yourself, your personality and deeper core feelings—the things that you normally keep away from, or are even out of reach (Way 7, 8, 10).

- To be vulnerable by allowing yourself to be visible in all your judgements about yourself or others, whether they are harsh, joyful, vain, proud or ashamed (Way 10).

- To gain awareness and insight into your being. You may discovery why, how and for what purpose you are the way you are (Way 7, 8, 9).

- To break through any protective layers, whether they are within you, between you and the therapist or between you and the process, and which prevent you from making contact with places that—out of awareness—you didn't know existed but are needed (Way 9, 15, 16, 17, 20)

- To understand the differences between your truth, reality, your authentic parts, those parts that are no longer needed and those that still serve you (Way 9, 10, 11).

- To work on wholeness, self-responsibility, and acceptance (Way 9, 10, 12).

- Work collaboratively with the therapist (Way 4)

- Look at emotions, thoughts, memories, situations and problems from multiple points of view (Way 7)

- Develop empathy and compassion towards the self (Way 12)

- Continuous process of attempting to face things you may avoid (emotions, memories or situations) which are needed to alleviate difficulties (Way 3)

How to learn the ways

Everyone learns in a unique way and at their own pace, some people like to think and analyse, some like to be visually taught, some like the idea of group thinking and others want to learn by trying things out in practice. Similarly for these ways, you can reflect on how you like to learn and utilise them.

Here is some guidance on learning and applying the ways in this book:

1. Understand the way. Here are some ideas to develop your understanding:

    a. Set some time to aside to think about the ways.

    b. Write down what you understand about a particular way (or even what you don't understand).

    c.   Complete the exercises at the end of each way.

    d.   Discuss and share what you understand. For example, with a trusted friend or if you're in training with your peers or lecturer.

    e.   Go online to my YouTube channel "Dear Therapist" where I discuss these ways with professionals and those who want to share their story.

2.   Assess whether the way is relevant to your therapy.

    a.   Why do you think it is or is not?

    b.   Do you have any worries about using it?

    c.   What do you hope to get out of applying it more?

3.   Talk about the way with your therapist if you feel it's important and if you feel safe to do so.

4.   Try a way (or an idea/tool) out in therapy. Remember, it's a learning process so many of the ways you won't be able to contemplate using until you get to a certain stage in the process, while others may not be relevant or needed. Apply the way to a point that is challenging but also safe (see below "Developing a personalised hierarchy of difficulty").

5.   Once you have tried out an aspect of the way, reflect on it. Did you feel it went well? Do you think that the therapist helped and handled it well? Is it something you want to continue using in therapy or in life?

6.   If you need further help, seek therapy coaching about your process from a qualified therapist (See Way 21).

Developing a personal hierarchy of difficulty
Each of the 21 Ways in this book represents something to learn in order to become proficient at using the instrument of therapy. Some of these ways you may be able to follow through in therapy easily, while others may be more difficult, not least because of the encounter with the therapist. However, if you feel that a particular way resonates with you, you should explore it deeper and become better at applying it in therapy.

Here I suggest a way of gradually becoming more proficient and confident at using the ways. For each way, or an aspect you decide to use, you can rank the tasks based on a personal difficulty rating. You can assign a score to the difficulty of the task from 1 (easiest) to 10 (hardest). Here is a template when approaching something difficult with the therapist, beginning from the easiest to the hardest task, you can adapt it to develop your own personal hierarchy of difficulty.

1. Understand the way. Identify why it feels important to you by reflecting on it. Some may prefer to write it down, think it out or even expressing an art form to describe it. If you need further support in understanding, seek further help (Way 21).

2. Understand the barriers that stop you using the way in practice. Does it relate to the problem you are working on? Is it because you need to understand it more? Or is it hard to say it out aloud to the therapist? Write it out and read it back to yourself.

3. Talk to your therapist about the way you're trying to work on and see if they can help you with it. For example, "I find it difficult to show my feelings sometimes".

4. If you find it difficult to talk to the therapist face to face consider sending your thoughts and feelings via secure email, or take your notes in to therapy to read out.

5. If you find it difficult to share something, start by talking to them about the difficulty without talking about the specific problem. For example, if you want to share a historical abuse you can say "there are things I want to share but I am worried about saying it out loud". By doing so you may eventually become more ready, or you may decide not to share.

6. Ask a few lead-in questions to the therapist to introduce an idea or concern you want to bring into session. By leading in you may be able to broach the subject more confidently. For example, if you have strong feelings about the therapist, such as anger, indifference or attraction, you could depersonalise it by:

    a. *Using an external source of knowledge: "I was reading this book that talks about feelings created in the past that can follow you into new relationships. What do you think about it? Is it real?" and then "Do you think it applies to me?"*

    b. *Your difficulty expressed through another person: "I talked to someone who said they had a hard time leaving their therapist. Does it happen?"*

    c. *Your difficulty expressed towards others (not the therapist): "I think sometimes that happens to me. I get strong feelings when I like someone and then I get so upset and end up think about them so much, and when they leave, it really hurts."*

7. Once you feel ready, talk to the therapist directly about an idea or concern you want to bring into session.

If you cannot apply the way, decide whether implementing it can wait, or whether it is something you need to work on to take your healing to the next step in your journey. Alternatively, if you need to break through a barrier and you find it too difficult to talk to the therapist then seek further support (Way 21).

This book's central philosophy is based on *therapy coaching*, just as a swimmer who is coached improves in their sporting ability, and achieves their goals, similarly coaching you on therapy means you will be able to achieve your therapeutic goals.

The ways are applicable to all types of therapeutic approaches, whether it's individual, couples, family or group therapy; whether it's one session or long-term therapy over years. The ways are, by design, about mastering the instrument of therapy, and about using the feelings they invoke, rather than working on the specifics of your problems, symptoms or your individual story.

For example, regardless of the type of therapy or its duration, you can go from being closed off to saying what's on your mind. You can become more vulnerable, checking out whether your feelings are true, and talking about your feelings about the therapist or others. Similarly, if you find it difficult to open up, or you have difficulty with endings, that could be a valuable source of material for exploration in therapy.

I believe that all good enough therapists will receive you using these foundational ways in therapy. However, given the diversity of therapists, their experience, theoretical orientation and backgrounds and their own unique style of working it is hard to generalise how much emphasis a therapist would hold towards a particular mode of working described in these ways. For example, would a cognitive behavioural therapist (CBT) be better equipped to work with you expressing your feelings about them, or would you be best served with a psychodynamic therapist? In theory the psychodynamic therapist would be more appropriate, because it's an intrinsic part of their theoretical approach, but that does not mean you won't get a lot out of sharing your feelings with a CBT therapist.

Ultimately, good therapists will be able to work in an empathic and accepting manner regardless of whether they are familiar with working in any of the ways described in these ways. Therefore, there are no obstacles to what you can talk about with your therapist if you believe it's relevant. Good therapists will welcome it and can give their perspectives too, even if it's simply to mirror back your feelings.

Having said that, I will give some brief guidance on how strongly a particular school of therapy, *in theory*, emphasises or de-emphasises the ways of working described in this book. If a particular way has not highlighted a variation it simply means the school of therapy is neutral to it. Remember not to take this as definitive for all therapists and therapy approaches.

For a description of each school of therapy see Way 2: Find the right therapist and approach.

Insight oriented therapies

These therapies are very much geared to working with your feelings towards the therapist (Way 4). It may de-emphasise the relationship somewhat (Way 2, 16) in favour of bringing out deeper feelings you may be unaware of, but it does not disregard the importance of a good relationship. Unsurprisingly, this school emphasises an insight-based orientation (Way 9).

Humanistic therapies

Humanistic therapies are intrinsically geared towards working in the client's own way. These therapies tend to work with whatever you bring, including "here and now" feelings towards the therapist. In that sense it is theoretically neutral with regard to all these ways. There is usually more of an emphasis on developing the relationship (Way 2, 16) in comparison to other therapies. Humanistic therapies don't emphasise interpretation or analysis (Way 9).

Cognitive behavioural and solution-focused therapies

Cognitive and behavioural branches of therapy (including solution-focused therapies) de-emphasise working on deeper feelings, particularly around childhood and the past (Way 10), while emphasising rational thinking (Way 11). They do emphasise an action-orientation approach to achieving your goals (Way 13). There is also less of a focus on understanding your feelings towards the therapist (Way 4). There are forms of therapy in this branch such as cognitive analytical therapy (CAT) and schema therapy which do focus in on childhood experiences.

Integrative/Eclectic

These therapies mix various approaches so how therapists emphasise these ways will largely depend on their background, training and experience.

Variations for couples, group and family therapy
Couples, group and family therapies can also be based on a particular school of therapy – humanistic, insight oriented, integrative/eclectic or cognitive behavioural. The exception is for family therapy, where you may find therapists trained specifically in *systemic therapy* which tries to help the family understand each other by looking at the whole family system in order to improve the quality of relationships and function, such as by changing behaviours and resolving conflicts.

A significant difference with couples, group and family work, compared to individual therapy, is that the work you do will be in relation to others.

While none of these therapies lose individual focus, they are more geared towards relational feelings and difficulties within the family, couple or group in order for you and other(s) to function better together, for example, exploring difficult communication, understanding patterns of behaviours, being able to listen to others' perspectives and giving or receiving personal feedback. Because of these differences, you'll be listening to and understand others much more rather than expressing your feelings from your point of view (Way 5: Express yourself from your point of view), and you'll be using others as a resource, as well as the therapist (Way 4: Use the therapist as a resource). You'll also use awareness and listening skills to help you understand feelings—both yours and others' (Way 7: Understand yourself through awareness). Because time will be focused on everyone in a couple, family or group, you'll not have the time for focused, deeper inner work as you would individually (Way 10: Peel back the layers).

In summary, working in couple, group or family therapy is about everyone working on change collectively as well as individually, while in individual therapy the change is more focused on your own change.

Now the ways.

Way 1: Learn what it's all about

"Learning is a process not a goal. The process is the goal"

Condensed idea:

Condensed idea: Therapy can be considered to be a talking cure, however, the essential purpose of therapy is to help you move towards experiencing your truth in heart, mind and body; live within it and direct it. Truth comes from learning about yourself in relation to others and the world. An open and curious attitude towards therapy and what you know about yourself allows you to learn more. Start by learning about therapy and how it works (See Chapter 1), and if you have any particular problems, such as anxiety or depression, you can learn about them too in Chapter 3: Tool #14: Psychoeducation.

Approach Variations: Applies to all approaches of therapy. The subject of learning is primarily yourself, but in couples, group, and family therapies you will be learning about others as well.

Congratulations; just picking up this book and being curious is a great way to take charge of your process of healing and growth. As you learn about therapy and what you can do to help yourself, you will begin to feel you're on the right path, instilling confidence and hope in the benefits of therapy.

This first way teaches you that therapy itself is learning about yourself in relation to others, and to the world.

In this way, you will gain a good understanding of:

- What therapy is and how it works (supported by Chapter 1).
- How learning about yourself can be uniquely challenging.
- How best to learn in therapy (or learn to learn).
- Strategies for working with doubts about therapy.

Defining therapy

"The essence of a cup is to hold water"

What is the fundamental purpose or essence of therapy? Isn't it to meet your goals, recover, heal, and grow? Well, yes, but not directly, because that is your desired outcome rather than its essence or purpose. Well then, isn't it about talking in a safe, confidential place with a trained therapist, about yourself, your feelings, and concerns, such as stressful life events, relationships, negative thoughts, and behaviours? That certainly is closer, and is usually the sort of answer that is provided to the public. But no, that is the activity of therapy, rather than its essential purpose.

When talking about essence we are referring more to the purpose or indispensable quality of something. For example, the essence of a cup isn't filling it up, holding it and moving it to your mouth. The essence of a cup is to hold liquid, and that is what makes the cup a cup. It is a universal feature across all cups. This essential feature enables you to be able to drink from it.

So what are the essential features of therapy? The essence of therapy is to help you to *move towards experiencing your truth in mind, heart and body, to live within your truth and direct it.* Breaking this down, the essence of therapy can be stated as:

A process of experiencing
Just as you cannot swim by dipping your toes in at the edge of the pool, therapy is an experience within a therapeutic relationship (or with others in case of group and couples therapy). The relational connection and its safety is the learning arena for therapy, much like the swimming pool is the learning arena for swimmers.

A process to uncover your truth
Imagine yourself as an iceberg, with the tip being what you know about yourself and all the rest hidden under the water. This is a common image given in psychology to help you understand that you don't know as much about yourself as you may believe. So in practical terms it's really important to be open to the idea that you don't know everything yet, and therefore there is hope. You don't want to be in a position where there is no new learning because that's a dead end.

In therapy you'll likely discover new things about yourself, sometimes a relief, sometimes difficult or even painful, but this gives you more to explore which could be vital for your healing journey. This does not mean you need to discover everything, learning, after all, never truly ends, but it needs to be enough to allow you to achieve your goals.

A process of learning to live within your truth
Your life may be extremely challenging, whether it's because of stressful life events, trauma, or anxiety. However, you can only live within your own reality, your mind, body and capability, so implicitly therapy works to help you find a way of living within your own truth, regardless of the situation, and the difficulties it presents. That does not mean giving up on change; it means being in contact with your reality, including parts of you which represent your core feelings and needs. From realisation of your truth, change is possible.

A process of directing your internal and external life from the ground of your truth
As you learn more about yourself and experience your reality, quite often you can encounter change. Once you are living more in your truth and revealing your core feelings, beliefs and needs, you can direct yourself in the world through that understanding. Change many be directed internally, within your body and mind, or

externally through actions you take in life. For example, internally you may truly learn to let go more of things you cannot control and liking yourself more, or externally you may decide to focus on establishing better boundaries in your relationships.

The therapeutic method

"As I sit here feeling and experiencing your world, I'm going to watch you heal."

Now that you understand the essence of therapy, the method by which therapists work can be understood in the context of "how do you help someone experience and discover their truth?"

The therapeutic method can be quite confusing and counter-intuitive for many, especially at the beginning, because it's probably very different to the way you're used to learning and talking about yourself to others, especially to a stranger. Unlike a traditional teacher in school or the workplace where there is a mix of instructor-led and experience-based teaching, therapists don't teach you about yourself directly (although they can offer possibilities—particularly insight-oriented therapists), rather they apply a method which helps you teach yourself about you, within the safety of the therapeutic relationship.

Therapy's method is akin to you taking the therapist on a journey inside your experiences, such as your concerns, events, and feelings. Within your world the therapist can experience first-hand the terrain of your world, as if they were in it. So the way the therapist helps to solve your problem is through you solving your own problem ultimately. It has to be like this, it's your mind, your life and only you ultimately know what's going on and where you need to get to. This is why *you* are the secret to your success in therapy. This is the method of learning which all therapies employ regardless of approach, theory or technique.

Of course, on any significant journey, there may be twists, turns, pauses and obstacles, and no two journeys are the same. The therapist knows this, but they also know the best way is to "trust the process" because it works best when you allow them to stay as a welcome and active guest on your journey, rather than taking over. By trusting the process, therapists know that regardless of the problems, your mind will find its way home.

Therapists are very aware of the dynamic between giving you things to "do" or telling you lots, versus allowing you to "be". It's a fine art, because it's very tempting—even for therapists—sometimes to feel the need to apply a formula, or a technique in order to help, when in reality mostly you need space to travel along the journey.

This does not mean that therapists never make suggestions, use techniques or ask direct questions, but even with those interventions it's still more about you taking them on the journey inside your heart and mind. When therapists provide interventions such as interpretations, feelings, metaphors or stories, they are very aware that your interaction is what matters the most.

So this all means in practice that any concerns you may have about therapy not being useful because the therapist does not *appear* to be doing much in terms of giving advice, opinion or guidance could be because they are trying to help by applying the therapeutic method of being with you, and in time you'll allow them on-board your journey. This is why the relationship is fundamental to the process; without someone you trust, how do you allow someone in to your experience?

Given that this is the way therapy teaches, you too can "learn to trust" the process to get you where you need to be (unless there is some other issue present such as stagnation or poor practice).

This is the proven method which can eventually lead to you experiencing your truth, living within it and directing it. From there change is possible.

Difficulty of learning about the self

Learning about yourself has challenges that are not comparable to other types of learning. Firstly, as described previously, the therapeutic teaching method can seem counter-intuitive in comparison to other types of learning, such as in the classroom. The other key difference is that the subject of learning is "you", where you learn about yourself. On the face of things this is not intrinsically an issue, because as humans we have the ability to mentally make space in order to observe and study ourselves. However, there are five problems when it comes to learning about ourselves that can make the therapeutic learning experience uniquely challenging.

Looking in the mirror

Becoming aware of why you are the way you are or feel the way you do requires you to look inside yourself. This may not be something you have been taught, but it is usually intrinsic to therapeutic change (See Way 7: Understand yourself through awareness).

The Iceberg

If what you know about yourself is the tip of iceberg then it follows there may be a lot to uncover and work through before you achieve your version of success. Therefore, it's difficult to fix the learning process to a time frame.

Gaining mental space

Therapy geared towards change requires you to become more aware of yourself and to "look in the mirror", and it isn't always easy, particularly if you're in a state of lost hope, severe distress, or confusion. You may find you're not able—particularly at the beginning—to do much self-reflection because your mind is running away with the difficulties you're experiencing, rather than being able to take a step back and reflect.

So it can be challenging to focus on self-awareness immediately—it's a process after all. Gaining mental space between current events and the process of developing self-awareness can be a goal in itself.

Conditioning

The way we see ourselves, others, and the world itself is programmed in through our life experiences, relationships, environment, culture, family and identity right from the earliest moments of our life. We see ourselves and the world through our own glasses. This is not a problem in itself, after all we have to learn from somewhere and be someone. However, learning can be unhelpful if it goes against what you need now, or if it underpins the problem you are trying to overcome, such as addiction or abusive relationship patterns. Therefore, the therapeutic challenge is likely to involve you deconditioning yourself against anything that no longer serves you.

Protective layers

Life can be a struggle, it can hurt, be traumatic or chaotic, but ultimately we are primed for survival. In order to survive we can develop protective layers within, which help us to function in the world, and to fit in. However, these protective layers can also cause internal disturbance and harm, such as an unresolved trauma, or experiences of not being heard and validated. For example, you may develop a protective layer (or guard) which keeps people from knowing you because of your past experiences of being harshly criticised.

These protective layers can very much link to the problems you are trying to overcome. Whatever the reason for protecting yourself, the layers can be difficult to reach, explore and experience because they can "hide" parts of you even from yourself. Making contact with these protective layers, understanding their purpose, and even understanding what lies under them is all a part of seeking your truth.

Of course you're not to blame if you find it hard to get to the "core" part(s) of you, your feelings or problems. The mind is very good at keeping things away from awareness because of its need to help you survive and function. The mind, once it learns a particular way, finds it difficult to let go or undo its learning. It can take time, but it can be worth it.

In a practical sense, if you become frustrated with the time that therapy takes, or because the therapist cannot fix you directly, I hope, with this knowledge, you will understand why therapy can take longer than perhaps you had hoped.

Learn how to learn

"Learn to learn again. How learning is supposed to be done!"

When you think about learning what comes to mind? Perhaps being taught in a classroom or learning a difficult life lesson? Maybe you had a good experience and enjoyed learning? On the other hand you may have difficult memories of learning, possibly due to a heavy cocktail of criticism, bullying, shame and guilt which made you feel not good enough.

Similarly, as therapy is a form of learning, it too can bring out feelings about being "good" or "bad" at learning. If you identify strongly with being competent, or if you are used to becoming proficient at something given time, it can stir unfamiliar feelings when you're used to overcoming challenges. If you have had bad experiences of learning then those familiar feelings may also come out in therapy.

Of course you may be able to pick up the instrument of therapy really well, have a predisposition towards it, and you might not even need to know anything in this book! After all, much of therapy is based on using or tapping into innate abilities like feelings and awareness.

To clarify, learning in therapy is not like classroom learning or being taught by a critical parent, it's about learning in a safe place, where no one is there to judge, criticise or blame you, and no one expects you to be "good" at therapy. Instead, therapy is a safe container where you're learning about yourself and ultimately what you need, in your own time and space. Not everyone is good at everything and you, too, may be better at certain subjects and activities more than others—whether it's competence in relationships, in groups or in a job. Therapy is a learning process, and the therapist won't value you less if you're finding it confusing or difficult.

In this section, I'll go over the most important learning-centred attitudes you can develop for a positive and effective learning experience both in life and in therapy. *Learning to learn* positively will take time to achieve for most, particularly if you've not had a good relationship with learning in the past. So in this sense therapy can also be a way of restoring your hope in the learning process, and could open new opportunities in life too. Because learning is such a useful life skill, it too can be explored in therapy.

Maintain an "I don't know" attitude

An attitude of curiosity and "I don't know" can be the most powerful way to learn because it allows the possibility of learning something new. Without this belief you may inadvertently slow or even hold back your process because there is little or nothing to learn. This isn't about being modest about your capability, it's about recognising that learning never ends no matter how good you are at something, including learning about yourself.

If you're a swimmer trying to improve your breast stroke you'll really need to learn to assess yourself in order to help yourself (as well as take the advice of an instructor). You may realise your arms and legs are not coordinated and will need to focus in on that part of your learning. At other times it may be learning to breathe and relax. You can't do it all in one go, it's a process. On the other hand, if you believe there is nothing more to improve your progress will be slower. Being open and honest about what's going on leads to better learning, whether in swimming or in therapy.

Although you are an expert in matters of yourself, it can be really important to be open to the idea that the therapy process may eventually be really helpful, even if it is difficult or you feel indifferent about it at the moment. For example, give the therapist a chance because sometimes it takes time for you both to get on the same wavelength, and not everyone clicks or sees progress immediately. Give therapy time to brew, and by doing so you're practising being open to the learning experience. This does not mean ignoring feelings, or dismissing moving on when you have tried, it means allowing for the possibility that therapy will be of benefit.

This kind of openness to learning allows you to be more honest or objective about your experiences: to see things as they are and bring them into awareness. Rather than being self-attacking or self-protecting you can work towards being compassionately objective. For example, if you find yourself wanting to be self-sufficient, yet you notice that you are pretending it's not the case in the room, you can acknowledge it as your truth rather than ignore it. Recognising this type of mismatch can make you feel vulnerable because being found out, being wrong or discovering that you are not all-knowing can bring up difficult feelings and penetrate protective layers inside. If that is you, then it's another opportunity to explore in therapy.

Learning works best when you're open about what's going on for you, including not wanting to share with the therapist or even not wanting to acknowledge what's going on. This is because you're working from a point of honest objectivity, rather than being removed from reality. When you bring these honest reflections into therapy, the process can often be catalysed. Of course if you become aware of ignoring something you can acknowledge that too, and in doing so you *are* practising being open and honest.

Learn through experience
It is not enough to read and understand something without trying it out and applying it. It is the same with this book, with therapy or with swimming: learning is an experience. This is often the reason why self-help books are not always enough for self-development, there has to be an experience alongside what you learn. Through experience you gain the confidence in what you've understood.

Learning is a personal journey, only you can do it
Learning is a personal journey. There is hope that you will be aided and well supported to carry out your learning; everyone needs a good parent or teacher, but you already know that is not always the reality of life. Support or no support, only

you can do the learning, whether it is class maths, self-development or learning about yourself in therapy. Of course it is wonderful to have a good enough therapist, and if you bring yourself into therapy you can be taught in the unique way therapy teaches. If not you will need to be prepared to make a decision to find another therapist because it's your personal journey not the therapist's.

Learning goes at your pace

Learning happens at your own pace. We are not all built the same, we have individual personalities, biologies and life experiences. Therefore, you cannot compare the recovery times of two people with similar problems, because underlying the problems will be their own unique and nuanced circumstances.

Similarly you may find it easier to apply some ways more than others. As with all learning you can't run before walking, so focusing more on the process rather than the goals, although not easy, can be empowering.

Not everything works for everyone

Ideas from your therapist or even this book are not one size fits all, you decide whether something works or is appropriate for you. Equally, don't ignore ideas without being open to them, assessing or even trying them out first. The ways in this book have passed the test of time; they align to what makes therapy work, so there are a number of things you can learn and apply in therapy that you will find useful. An important point to remember is that just because something does not work or make sense at a point in time, does not mean it may not in the future, it may still be an important part of your therapy.

Learn safely

Using these ways and dedicating yourself does not mean you should harm yourself in the process. It certainly would not be good for learning if you decided to bench press twice as much weight as you did last week. You could put your back out or injure yourself in some other way.

This applies to all the ways expressed in this book too. In therapy, advance at your own pace; if you don't feel that you can apply a way then you can challenge yourself to accept how you feel (Way 12: Weave in ideas of acceptance and responsibility). For example, you may not be ready to disclose something that's happened to you, tell your therapist how you feel about them, or ask for help. Equally it does not mean taking a back seat and not challenging yourself. Just advance as far as you can, which may involve some discomfort, but not harm.

Learn by taking acceptable risks

To learn you have to try new things out - going out of your comfort zone. Doing the same thing again and again may reinforce what you've learnt, but if you want to learn more you have to apply new ideas, theories and try things out.

Learning is catalysed by trying, taking a chance and making safe mistakes, all of which can be seen as much-needed steps towards your goals. If they lead nowhere you can tick the process off as complete and have no regrets because you tried. By learning through experience and assimilating the knowledge gained, you're one step closer to success.

Taking risks in therapy is whatever you find difficult. Taking a risk could include sharing something difficult, being more vulnerable, acknowledging a truth, sharing feelings about the therapist, or even acknowledging you've said something unfair. In most cases the risk is an internal sense of risk, because good therapists accept you as you are. However, the risk could include worries about consequences, such as the therapist ending therapy, or whether you or someone you know will get into trouble.

Here are some examples of risks and their potential learning:

- You feel dependent on the therapist and therapy so much so it is blocking your therapy process. You feel bad for having these feelings and for letting the therapist down. You take a risk and tell the therapist.

- You get angry at the therapist and regret it later. You are curious about the anger and its nature and use it in therapy to have a dialogue with them, which in turn moves you towards trusting the therapist more.

- You raise a concern to the therapist and they dismiss or criticise you rather than work with your feelings. You learn that you had an inkling that the therapist was not the one for you. You regret not changing therapist before, but now you know to trust your feelings more as a result.

- You want to disclose something important in therapy. You're worried about confidentiality so you take steps to find out their policy. Once you're content with the policy you bring up something difficult but important, and as a result you feel relief and an increased sense of safety in doing so.

Here, all these risks are not mistakes, they are lessons learned heading you towards the outcome. Taking a chance could be the most important part of your therapy.

Unlearning can be just as important as learning
Learning is not always about new skills, it can be just as much about unlearning or taking away something you typically do. For example, you may want to working on unlearning your tendency to dampen down feelings by exploring your inclination to think it's always your fault or your opinions don't count. If you are learning to change, then taking away what you learnt is often a big part of learning.

Learning as the goal
We've all done it—spent time wondering or thinking about what it would be like to

achieve a desired goal, whether it's getting a dream job, building that house extension or swimming better. However, the feeling of achieving goals can be short-lived and fade away; we all know that, eventually, goals are going to be replaced by new ones, which is part of life. Not that we should not celebrate an achievement!

Understanding this can be liberating for some, as you can imagine experiencing a process more easily than simply being goal-directed. Just like the spaces between the notes make the music, so it's the same in life, a process of learning and experiencing. The goal is not the goal, the process is the goal.

Now I have laid down the principles of adopting a good learning attitude you should remember that this way of learning can take time, often in parallel to your recovery process. Go at your own pace.

Scenario: I don't know if this will work

Cheryl sat down and explained her problem. She was struggling to control her drinking. She used it as a way of managing her anxiety, but now it was no longer working. She felt she had tried everything, from support groups to self-help techniques and even therapy. She said she came to me because I had helped someone else she knew with a drinking issue. I asked Cheryl if there was anything helpful or missing in what she had done so far. She replied, "I've already let out my feelings before and don't want to do that again here, what I want from you are some techniques so I can feel less anxious when I'm stressed". I had heard her frustrations and replied, "You've been discouraged with all the work you've done and it has not worked." She answered, "Yeah, do you know what will work?" I replied "I don't know exactly, but I will try my best". She looked back and I was unsure whether that was the answer she really wanted.

In this example something was clearly amiss with Cheryl's experiences of therapy. If you are having trouble understanding whether therapy could help, even if you've tried before, here are some practical suggestions:

- Remember how the process works. It has to work with you taking the therapist on your journey rather than the other way around. So even though a therapist does not give you a "fix", the fix is usually within you, and taking them on that journey with you. This doesn't mean techniques are not important, but they are part of the learning process.

- Embrace the principles of learning to learn. You may have tried therapy before and it may not have helped; embrace the motto "This is someone new so I won't know unless I try". So although it is frustrating to be stuck and not to get anything out of therapy you can try and see whether a new therapist is best placed to help you (See Way 2: Find the right therapist and approach).

- Try before you buy. Make a short term commitment, say three or six sessions before making up your mind about therapy or the therapist.

- Rationalise. Make a list after the session of anything you found useful. This enables you to take in an evidence-based view of whether you're getting anything out of therapy.

- Work with your motivations (see Way 3) to examine your underlying feelings about entering therapy and whether you're ready.

- Therapeutic approach. Maybe the type of therapy is not suitable for what you need at the moment. For example, Cheryl may be more suited to a cognitive behavioural and solution-focused therapy because the past therapist was focusing in on her childhood.

- Seek help. If you get stuck and don't know the direction therapy should take, seek further support (Way 21).

Exercises

Self-Reflection

1. What have been your experiences of learning?

2. What was good or missing in your experiences? What do you believe would have been more helpful to your learning?

3. What underlying beliefs about learning do you have? For example, do you talk yourself out of learning something new? Or is learning something new anxiety inducing?

4. How do you like to learn? What do you need in order to learn best? What puts you off learning?

5. Who have been the most influential teachers in your life? Why?

6. Who has let you down or had a negative impact on your learning experience? Why?

7. Does it feel okay to make mistakes? Or does it bring out negative feelings?

8. Is there anything you would like to change about your approach to learning?

9. Which of the attitudes in "learning to learn" would you like to be able to adopt?

10. Compare and contrast your therapeutic learning experience with your general learning experiences.

11. Are you concerned about therapy being able to help you? What are the reasons why it won't work? And compare them to the reasons why it could work.

12. Read Chapter 1 – Getting started in therapy, and then answer:

    o   Can you describe your problems?

    o   What experiences may have led to the problems you're working on?

    o   Do you have any particular concerns or questions about therapy?

Resources

Here are resources that support this way to set the groundwork for your therapy:

1. A good understanding of therapy, what it can help with, and how and why it works (Read Chapter 1: Getting started in therapy)

2. Understand options for access to therapy, short and long term therapy and preference for therapeutic setting (Read Chapter 1: Accessing Therapy Options).

3. Understand how particular psychological issues occur and their possible impacts. If you have been diagnosed with a particular mental health problem you can learn all about it too (Chapter 3: Skill #14: Psychoeducation).

4. Learn about therapy by reflecting on the example case of Oliver (Chapter 4). Remember, this is not an example to imitate or expect, it is to help you understand the inner workings of a process.

5. Read about any topics, questions or concerns you have about therapy, such as stigma, anxiety about therapy, medication and therapy, boundaries or any concerns you have about starting therapy (See Chapter 7: Client topics, questions and concerns).

6. Read the section "I know" (Chapter 5: Process themes in therapy) to learn about reflecting on openness in therapy.

Quiz

1. What is the essential purpose of therapy?

2. How is therapy different or similar to other types of learning? What are some challenges of learning in therapy?

3. Is the use of therapy for venting or talking, without a specific goal or problem in mind, a good use of therapeutic time?

    a.   What are some of the difficulties in answering this question?

4. Why is it important that clients try to take the therapist on a journey inside their experiences?

5. What practical advice would you give to Cheryl (see scenario: I don't know if this will work) to give her hope in her new therapist, if anything?

Way 2: Find the right therapist and approach

"Swimmers learn within the safe container of a pool; clients learn within the safe container of a good therapeutic relationship."

Condensed Idea: *Work with a trusted therapist whom you feel safe with, who has experience with working on problems your experiencing and who believes the approach you are taking with them has potential to help you achieve your goals. However, therapist competence isn't just about qualifications and experience; it's as much about how they are within themselves and with you. Therefore, use gut instinct, feelings and logical reasoning when assessing your therapist. Therapy is a personal journey, so be prepared from the outset to change therapist and approach if needed (see Way 18).*

Approach Variations: *Applies to all approaches of therapy, although relational styles may differ based on approach.*

International Variations: *Each country or even region will have its own standards for competence.*

In this way, you will understand and learn how to assess your therapist, based not only on standards and experience, but relationally too. In order to assess the therapist you will understand differences in therapeutic approach, questions you can ask the therapist as well as reflecting upon the kind of therapist you're looking for.

Overall, there are four considerations when selecting a therapist:

- Adheres to professional standards

- Has experience working with problems your facing

- Is the right relational fit for you

- Uses a therapeutic approach that is right for you and the problem(s) you are experiencing

In this way, you will be provided with lots of information on considerations, questions and guidance for selecting a therapist and therapeutic approach. If you're unsure or in a hurry, then you can keep it simple by following the guidance within the condensed idea part of this way.

Therapist standards

Prior to shortlisting therapists, some basic criteria need to be considered, such as qualifications, insurance, experience, specialism and licensure. Therapists may require a formal regulatory license to practice in some countries while in others there are voluntary membership bodies that assure standards. Regulation by law provides a level of protection to clients because they verify reasonable standards of practice, such as qualification, ethical practice, continuous development, supervision, insurance, as well as offering a complaints procedure. The same can be said of voluntary bodies, however there is no legal basis or centrally governed standard for practice, even though membership bodies may enforce the same criteria for membership as in regulated countries.

One advantage of using someone who is licensed or part of a voluntary membership body is that you already know they meet a professionally recognised standard and there is usually a complaints process. Although being licensed or registered with a reputable body provides a level of assurance that therapists meets accepted standards it does not necessarily mean they are the best therapist for you.

TIP: Voluntary membership body's standards may vary quiet a lot. It is recommended you use a therapist for an established and reputable body. This will vary depending on the country you are in. For example, in the UK UKCP, BACP, BPS are recognized and reputable member organisations although there are many others.

International Variation: Each country or region may have its own regulatory or generally accepted voluntary standards

Therapist experience

Therapist experience with the problems you are working on is highly desirable but is not always a show stopper and grey areas do exist. On the basis that therapy is generally more about the whole person and the healing process of therapy is mostly a creative process, I would not completely way out someone who is not experienced with your problems. What is important is that they have awareness of the types of problems you are experiencing, contraindications i.e. know of any practices that could be harmful, and some theory – additional specialist skills and experience can certainly be helpful but the foundation of the relationship needs to be in place first without which expertise on its own is unlikely to compensate. Therapists are already ethically obliged not to take clients on who they don't feel they have the background to work with.

The problems and approaches below, although not exhaustive would usually require additional training, qualifications or experience to work with beyond the standard qualification unless of course the training specialised in one of these areas in the first place. For example, a therapist base qualification may already include or be focused on children's therapy.

- Dissociation and Post traumatic stress disorder (PTSD)
- Eating Disorders
- Personality Disorders

- Attention Deficit Hyperactivity Disorder (ADHD)/Attention Deficit Disorder (ADD)
- Autism/Aspergers
- Developmental disabilities
- Young Children (usually under 13)
- Couples, Group or Family Therapy

If you are unsure about standards of experience and qualification for your particular problem you can seek third party advice from various governing and membership bodies that assure standards for therapy (See Way 21).

International Variation: Different countries and regions may use different regulatory or de-facto professional standards of practice.

Therapist relational fit

Finding a therapist who meets professional standards of practice and is experienced with working on problems your facing, depending on where you are in the world, can be the easier part of finding the right therapist, and in many cases that can be all that is needed. You do a search, find someone who meets the standard and has experience of working with the types of problems you are experiencing, you meet them and the rest is history as they say.

However, like a good foundation for a building, the whole therapy process is built upon establishing a safe relationship with your therapist. What happens if you aren't so lucky, don't find the right therapist or even keep seeing a number of therapists and just cannot find "the one". You may be working long term with a therapist on very complex and deep wounds where the quality of the relationship comes very much to the fore. The mantra many therapists would adhere to is "it's the relationship that heals". After all, regardless of the experience and qualifications of a therapist, someone who you don't gel with or does not appear to fully understand your perspectives, can put you on shaky ground for recovery.

Therefore, you should spend time learning about how to find a good relational fit. You can also combine this activity with learning how to spot signs of poor practice (Way 19: Watch out for signs of inefficient, poor or harmful therapy).

In this section, you will learn to:

- Understand why a "good-enough" therapist rather than an ideal or perfect therapist can be beneficial and more realistic

- Understand the difference between *relational quality* and *relational connectedness*

- Understand how relational styles can differ depending on the therapeutic approach practiced

- Assess the relational fit

Good enough therapist

The therapist does not have to be perfect or indeed tick all your boxes, but "good enough". I use the term "good enough" therapist throughout this book but what does "good enough" really mean? The phrase "good enough mother" was termed by a british psychoanalyst, D.W. Winnicott. He coined the term to express the idea that while a mother starts by sacrificing her needs to fulfill her child's, such as sleep, later in development the mother allows for small frustrations, for example a delay in responding as the child starts to cry. She is not "perfect" but she is "good enough" in that the child only feels a slight amount of frustration which gives the child space to learn about her place in the world and develop. I refer to the term "good enough" therapist throughout this book to allow for that development, the therapist may not always be attuned to your needs in the room, a good therapist is never able to be "perfect" at all times and know what is going on or what you need, but they can be "good enough" and that is not only realistic but equally may even be an important part of your healing. Good enough therapists may frustrate you a little but that also allows for new learning.

Please note that although originally the description was focused on female mother, in the modern setting it is any primary caregiver or caregivers, regardless of gender.

Relational quality and connectedness

The quality of the relationship can be seen in two interrelated ways. The first is relational quality (or relational competence), and the second is relational connectedness (or relational feelings).

Relational quality is about how the therapist is with you in the room. The practice of therapy is based on the therapist providing a secure relational space, consisting of empathy, acceptance and their presence. These core skills are central to why therapy works, so when it comes to evaluating the therapist, relational quality is something you can assess. For example, if the therapist is consistently distracted from what you're saying, then that isn't showing relational quality and is very likely to interfere with your therapy.

Therapist's relational quality can also be understood by comparing and contrasting it with other types of relationships because it can help you think about what type of person who makes you feel safe to be around or share feelings with. Think about your experiences of people who don't make you feel safe to share and your reasons why. For example, perhaps they are abrupt, judge you, try and fix things without listening, or even talk at you rather than with you. Bottom line is, you don't feel seen by them as a person. This does not mean they don't have qualities you like, but they aren't the person you would choose to open up with. Whatever your needs are to feel safe, if they are not met, you are hardly going to feel secure in sharing your feelings and vulnerabilities.

Similarly with a therapist, there are a set of core relational skills that therapists learn that have been shown to be fundamental to helping your process. The good news is that therapeutic relational quality is something, with a bit of education, you can learn to assess (See: Assessing the relational fit).

On the other hand, *relational connectedness* is a more subjective experience. Relational connectedness can be more readily compared to how you experience or feel in a relationship, whether with friends, family or work colleagues. You will already be aware of how you connect or "spark" with some more than others, where there is something intangible about why you connect with them, sometimes deeply, more than others. You may experience this type of connectedness with someone you barely know, don't see very often, or don't know anything about. On the other hand, you may feel connectedness gradually over time. Similarly, in the therapeutic relationship, relational connectedness is something you can consider when coming to assess the therapist.

Relational Styles – Insight oriented vs Cognitive vs Humanistic
Before making a judgement of what you felt about the therapist, understand that because of the therapists own modality they may seem appear a bit more "aloof", or even distant. For example, a person centered therapist can be perceived as being warmer or relational than a psychodynamic therapist. Although it's very difficult to generalise, psychodynamic or psychoanalytic therapists may appear to give you less in terms of a warmer fuzzy feeling, don't appear to engage in small talk, or disclose much about themselves, even at a superficial level. This perceived "aloofness" may exist to allow your feelings that are unconsciously held to naturally appear in therapy. While a person centred therapist can appear more personal, familiar and allow you to focus on wherever your mind takes you, a psychodynamic therapist may gently challenge you, for example by bringing you back to focus on things you may be unconsciously avoiding. This is not to say psychodynamic therapists are any more or less empathic and accepting or that person centred therapists don't challenge, but they are informed by their own theoretical modality which influences their relational style. Regardless of the relational style, they are ultimately there to work for you in overcoming any problems you present with regardless of modality.

For therapies that are more treatment based, short term or structured like CBT, the feeling you have towards the therapist may be somewhere in between the Psychodynamic and Person centred therapist. Again this is just a generalisation as individuals ultimately work in their own way regardless of modality, and many aim to work with a person centred relational base regardless of the approach they utilise.

Assessing the therapist

So, how do you assess the therapist? Well, for most, it's going to be about how safe you felt overall.

You can reflect upon:

- Did you feel comfortable with them?

- Can you imagine being able to talk freely about the things you want?

- Are they accepting and non-judgemental of you and your issues? Did they make you feel guilty or ashamed?

- Did you like their character? For example, were they open and honest when asking questions?

You could leave it at that and that may be enough, but I often find clients are very curious about perspectives, particularly when they have difficulty finding the right therapist or encounter a relational concern (See scenario below: Help! I can't seem to find the one!)

How you assess the therapist, just like people you meet, is always going to be subjective because you're going to see the therapist through your own "glasses" or perspective. You may already have an implicit approach to judgement, such as using your gut feeling or intuition over how connected you feel. Further, everyone comes into therapy with a different set of relational needs, such as warmth, respect, directness or assuredness. Your approach to judgement may also be based on a belief, for example, a sixth sense, a higher wisdom, a guide that moves through you to help make decisions. Even if you do not feel you have a style of judging, you *will* have one, because your mind will be doing it for you out of awareness. This is something you can be curious about if you wish.

At the outset, remember assessment should not about the therapist getting everything right; it's about being good-enough, taking into account inevitable differences in relational style. For example, you can't say a therapist is definitely not good on the basis of a single occurrence of being interrupted or you did not feel an instant connection. No matter how much you assess the therapist, there are no guarantees they will be "good enough" for you; it's about maximising your chances to find someone suitable for you. What is right for you may not be right for someone else. Quite often, finding a therapist is as much about getting to know your feelings and what you need to feel safe in the therapeutic relationship, which in and of itself can be useful in all types of relationships.

Regardless of your approach, explicit or implicit, usually there are three dimensions: gut instinct, connectedness and logic usually associated with judgement. If there are any conflicts between these three, then you can use that as input into the therapeutic process.

Your gut instinct
There is a lot to be said about using your gut instincts or intuition, rather than using heart feelings or rational thoughts. There are a few practical reasons for doing this. First, because relationship can take time to build, you won't have all the sense information to fully assess them, so using your gut instinct is an option. The other reason is your natural instincts are primed towards safety and survival, built into your DNA and developed throughout life. So, by trusting your instincts, you may already have the inbuilt wisdom to gauge whether you're going to feel safe with them.

However, gut feelings don't necessarily mean they are 100% reliable either. You will likely have had an experience where you made a judgement that turned out to be very different later. This judgement can work both ways, for example, someone you instinctively thought was considerate turned out not to be the case or vice versa. Of course, if you find your instincts not to be the most reliable source of judgement, then you can assess them based on relational connectedness and the qualities of competence below. Of course, if you believe your instincts are usually off the mark, it could be a subject of exploration in therapy.

So, use your instincts; after all, they have got you so far, but also use them wisely by considering feelings and logic too.

Relational connectedness
How did the therapist make you feel? This can be a continuum between three points: negative feelings, no feeling whatsoever to feelings of deep connectedness. At the very least, you should experience a "neutral feel" towards the therapist, particularly if they display good relational quality (See below).

Relational quality
Rational thinking can provide an opportunity to check whether your gut and feelings accord with your rational thoughts. If there is a conflict, then you can reflect on it some more before making a decision.

To help you rationally assess the therapist and to continually monitor the therapist's relational quality, I have provided a 6-point rational assessment tool called EPAIY-S you can use to determine how the therapist is with you.

- Empathy and acceptance. You feel they listen with empathy and acceptance to what you are saying without judging you. Therapists may challenge or suggest what may be going on for you, but they do so without it being forced upon you.

- **P**resence. On the whole, they are very present, understand what you say, and it feels they are fully with you in the room.

- **A**ssuredness. They don't appear to be out of their comfort zone or to be overwhelmed by what happens in the room. This does not mean they are stoic and emotionless, but they exhibit an overall air of confidence. A therapist must only work within what they have training or experience working with.

- **I**nner balance. They work in an emotionally consistent and balanced way with you, even when things are difficult, not progressing, or you're frustrated with them. This does not mean they approve or agree always; they can bring in their perspective, but they work openly with your feelings, rather than shutting them down. Any responses are given in an adult manner that allow therapy to continue, rather than being critical or blaming.

- **Y**ou focused. They keep their focus on you, what you need, and your process. They work in your interest, not their own. Examples include, not using you to share personal life frustrations, helping you to eventually live independently of therapy or referring you on if they do not have the right experience to work with you. They may share personal details but it is still focused on helping you. They also work within agreed boundaries of the service, such as session times.

- **S**upporting factors. They support their practice with self-care, supervision and ongoing self-development as well as having insurance. These factors are external to sessions but reinforce their competence to practice.

Further considerations
If you don't feel relational connectedness, but they exhibit good relational qualities, it does not mean you won't be able to get what you need out of therapy. This is because the therapist provides what is considered good practice for the process to be able to work.

However, sometimes you may encounter strong connectedness or feelings towards the therapist even when they don't exhibit good relational quality too. In this case see Way 19: Watch out for signs of inefficient, poor or harmful therapy.

I hope you find the right therapist for you, and many do without much effort or hardship. However, people don't always find the right therapist the first time, and in fact, you may take a while to find a good match for you. If you're unsure, you can consider contacting another therapist or trying a number of sessions. It's not a precise art and ultimately, you will have to decide.

Questions for the therapist

Generally, you'll be doing most of the talking during the first session, so as well as getting a feel for how they are with you – empathic & accepting, present, assured, inner balance, and you focused (EPAIY-S), I recommend asking questions to corroborate how they made you feel.

The table below shows possible questions and rationale for why it may be an important question to ask. Choose the ones that are most important to you although I feel Questions 1, 2, 3 are the ones you will always want to ask. As well as these questions you should also remember basic contracting questions like time, frequency and duration (See Chapter 1 – Getting started in therapy: "Understanding and negotiate the contract").

Some therapists may be reluctant to answer certain question where they feel it would mean disclosing personal information such as "religious affiliation" or "what led them to do therapy", because they don't feel comfortable with the disclosure, or because of their therapeutic approach. Hopefully, they will explain why they don't wish to disclose. From experience, this has the possibility to bring out feelings of awkwardness, embarrassment or even rejection in clients but hopefully the therapist will handle this well by still being empathic and understanding. If they become defensive and don't handle a well-meaning question you can use that as input into your decision. As a general principle, therapists should always answer questions that are directly relevant to you and the work you are doing, and are more cautious when at the edge between work and personal disclosure. That is not to say therapists will never disclose personal information but they do so in your interests.

Ref	Question	Why it may be important?
1	Do you think you can help me?	Wanting to know whether therapist believes as far as they are aware that they can help
2	Have they worked with these types of issues?	Wanting confidence that therapist has worked with similar issues successfully
3	Are you licensed or part of a membership body that adheres to best practice, ethics and complaints process? And have insurance? And are supervised?	Therapist meets acceptable standards of qualification and ethical practice

Ref	Question	Why it may be important?
4	How do you intend to work with me and my issues?	To understand therapist's philosophy and the way they will work with you. The approach and tools they will use.
5	How do you handle difficult feeling with clients?	If you believe you can exhibit strong emotions in general or towards the therapists such as anger and fear.
6	Do you think you'll be able to work with me long term? If so how long?	You want to feel secure that therapist will be able to work with you long term or you will be very hurt if abandoned by the therapist.
7	How do you understand my problems? And goals?	That the therapist has heard you, paid attention and understands you.
8	What do you think about diagnosis and medication	That the therapist is working with all of you not just labels.
9	How will you keep me safe in therapy?	Worried about confidentiality or you can get relationally hurt if you get too close to someone.
10	What is your confidentiality and disclosure policy? How will I know what I can safely share?	You are worried that something you wish to talk about may need to be disclosed outside of therapy
11	How will I know when it's time to leave? How long will therapy last? How will we review progress? How do you work with endings?	Wanting to understand review, feedback and ending process
12	Do you follow Pre-Trial therapy guidelines?	To ensure that the therapist works within guidelines so not to jeopardise a pending case you are involved in.

Ref	Question	Why it may be important?
13	What do you do if you can't work with someone or need to refer someone on? What areas of mental health would you not work with?	To ensure they will only work with you because they are able to. So you can their limits.
14	Will you have time and energy for me?	They are able to have time and energy for you in the room. For example, they may mention self-care or ensuring less than 20 client hours per week. **Note that some therapist may be reluctant to answer this question due to personal disclosure.**
15	What led you to do therapy?	Can get a feel for therapist's journey and life experience. **Note that some therapists may be reluctant to answer this question due to personal disclosure.**
16	What do you do to develop yourself and your learning?	Therapist continuously learning is important to you. For example, signs a therapist is working on new things may mean they avoid stagnation, keep up to date with mental health problems and are aware of themselves. **Note that some therapists may be reluctant to answer this question due to personal disclosure.**
17	How much time have you spent in therapy?	They understand themselves so understand and creates confidence on their maturity. **Note that some therapists may be reluctant to answer this question due to personal disclosure.**

I often receive this type of comment or question from people struggling to find a therapist to help them.

> *I have seen various therapists over the year but none have helped me much so far. I am not very hopeful of finding someone who can help. What do you recommend?*

What happens if you keep going from therapist to therapist and can't find the right one for you? If you can, you should explore these feeling with your therapist before leaving or beginning with a new one (Way 20: Don't walk away without talking to the therapist first).

Although it's difficult to be concrete and say what could be happening, here are a number of possibilities you can reflect upon.

- You've just been unlucky. Just keep looking and if you run out of options, extend the geographical reach of your search. Other options include online or phone therapy.

- There is something amiss in the way you're using therapy or choosing the therapist, which isn't helping you get the most out of your experience (read the Quick Start guide at the beginning of this chapter and self-assess anything which resonates).

- You need to give it more time before you leave. Sometimes, therapy can work fast; sometimes, it needs more time and priority. For example, you could try six sessions and then review them.

- You need a different modality or approach. For example, couples counselling to work with relational issues, or cognitive-based therapies that are more forward-looking rather the based on the past.

- You are not choosing appropriately qualified professional therapists who have experience working with your problems

- Anything in this book which could springboard your process. This book is by design geared towards the difficulties that can block your process (So see Ways 1 to 21).

Here are more relational reasons why someone may find it hard to find the right therapist.

- Some characteristic of the therapist puts you off therapy (see Appendix D: Inventory of client concerns for a range of possibilities). Perhaps it's their gender, age, feelings of authoritarianism, or they feels distant and could be judging you. It may even be the stigma of being in therapy or a belief that you should be able to help yourself.

- You tend to dampen down your feelings, don't trust them, and tend to go along with what the therapist is saying; therefore, you are not making choices that are based on what you really need.

- You have an ideal of what the therapist should be like, which disappoints you when they don't meet it. You can reflect on your ideal therapist and ask whether it is realistic or you can ask the therapist what you need. For example, more input, less input, warmer, or slower.

- You want to change but there are unexplored parts of you that make you tentative about change (see Way 8: Consider what makes change undesirable).

- The encounter with the therapist is problematic and relates to your difficulties. For example, someone who is fearful of social situations may find the therapist encounter difficult too.

I would recommend writing your own journal with your feelings, needs, and fears and make it part of the therapeutic journey. Through self-reflection and having an inner dialogue with yourself you may come to see what is creating the confusion or repeated pattern of going from therapist to therapist. This can help you release and get in touch with your feelings rather than dampen them down.

You can use these reflection questions as a starting point:

- What did you feel about each of the therapists? Was there some background need that was missing?

- Did you feel safe with the therapist enough to allow them into your inner experiences, or did it feel difficult?

- How does being in therapy make you feel about yourself?

- How do you normally experience relationships in life? Are there any parallels with the therapists you have seen so far?

If you're not able to get anywhere after talking to your therapist, I would recommend seeking professional advice to talk through your feelings. For further support, see Way 21: Get help from outside therapy if needed.

Therapy approaches
As well as finding a therapist, there are a number of therapy approaches, sometimes called modalities, to choose from. Although, in general, it is thought that the overall

relational fit, relational quality and experience of the therapist is more determinate of better outcomes, the modality may also be important too.

There are over a hundred different types of therapeutic approaches available and unless you already know the type of therapy you're looking for it can feel like a minefield. Generally Cognitive Behavioural Therapy (CBT), Person Centred, Psychodynamic or Integrative therapies are the most practiced and evidenced therapies available. However, that does not mean they are necessarily the only ones that you should choose, there are many approaches to therapy that may be beneficial.

Your choice of therapy may be limited depending on where and how you access it. If you have a strong preference, you may have to use a private therapist. However, remember that your relationship with your therapist is the foundation of therapy regardless of whether or not a particular approach is important for you. Therefore, if you feel the type of therapy is going to be important you may wish to shortlist prospective therapists from a particular orientation or pick a mixture from different orientations first.

Although there are many therapy approaches, they can be generalised as belonging to one of the six schools or groups of therapy:

Analytical insight-oriented therapies – Therapies such as psychoanalysis, Jungian and psychodynamic theories are geared towards gaining insight into yourself, how you think and act by exploring your experiences as well as making the unconscious conscious. There is usually a focus on childhood experiences and the nature of feelings between the client and therapist.

Humanistic therapies – Therapies such as person-centred, Gestalt and existential therapies emphasise the individual's own natural potential to heal and grow. These therapies deemphasise therapeutic interpretation but rather work with the whole person in an atmosphere of empathy. Humanistic therapists believe people are inherently motivated to fulfil their internal needs and their individual potential.

Cognitive and solution-focused therapies – Therapies such as cognitive behavioural therapy (CBT), solution-focused therapy and EMDR emphasise how thoughts, feelings and behaviours work together to impact your life. They focus more on how you want to be, in the context of the past and your memories, rather than looking deeply into childhood development.

A next wave of cognitive behavioural therapies such as acceptance and commitment therapy (ACT) and mindfulness-based CBT (MBCT) combine principles of acceptance (including mindfulness) into their approach.

Integrative or eclectic therapies – These therapies tend to use different elements of different schools of therapy and apply them in a way that is suitable to the client (sometimes called client centred therapy). With schema therapy, although it theoretically stems from CBT, could be classed as an integrative therapy because it combines CBT, insight-oriented (psychoanalytic) and humanistic (Gestalt) ideas within it.

Expressive therapies – They use creative arts including the body as the central tool for your work, such as art, dance/movement, drama, music or drama. The emphasis is on expression using these art forms, not being good at the art.

Couples, group and family therapies – These therapies are geared towards individual and collective goals. For example, improving relationships, developing interpersonal skills or helping each other's change. While none of these therapies lose individual focus they are more geared towards helping you and others overcome difficulties and function better together. They can also be based on a particular school of therapy above – humanistic, insight oriented, integrative/eclectic or cognitive behavioural. The exception is for family therapy, where you may find therapists trained specifically in *systemic therapy* which looks to help the family understand each other by looking at the whole family system in order to change behaviours and resolve conflicts.

Is the approach important?

The short answer is that it matters when it matters. It may matter because it's more suited to your personality or preferences, or because of the types of problems you're experiencing. You're likely to be met with alternative views depending on who you talk to and your context, so it is difficult to say definitively which therapy type will be best for you and your particular problem(s).

Here are some guidelines for the selection of a particular school of therapy. Remember, this list is not exhaustive and should be seen as suggestions for selection, not a recommendation.

- If you believe that early childhood development and the unconscious, that is the things that you're unaware of, is a driver for your issues, then an insight-oriented therapist, e.g., a psychodynamic therapist, may be appropriate. This therapy may offer more suggestive interpretations of how your problems may have developed and how it relates to your difficulties.

- If you believe by focusing on the present within the context of your history, you can change your thoughts, feeling and behaviours, then cognitive behavioural and solution-focused therapies may be appropriate. You want to focus less on the unconscious or the past, but rather on solutions based on here-and-now problems.

- If you believe that you can, through an empathic therapeutic relationship, work through your problems because you believe in the innate ability of your mind to find its way, then humanistic therapy, such as person-centred therapy, may be appropriate.

- If you believe no one orientation is best, then an integrative therapist who uses a mixture of approaches may be appropriate.

The following types of therapies have been created around specific problems, although not necessarily limited to just dealing with those difficulties:

- If you believe you are suffering because of Trauma or Post Traumatic Stress Syndrome (PTSD) then Eye Movement Desensitization & Reprocessing therapy (EMDR) or Somatic Experiencing may be appropriate.

- If you have been diagnosed with Borderline Personality Disorder (BPD) or Bipolar Disorder then Dialectical Behavioural Therapy (DBT) maybe appropriate. DBT typically involves homework, individual and group therapy.

- If you have been diagnosed with a Personality Disorder then Schema therapy may be appropriate

- If you are having a relationship issue with your partner then Couples Therapy maybe best. If the relationship is an issue either with a partner, sibling, parent or friend, couples therapy can offer a space for you to both work through your relationship difficulties. Relationship therapy may involve individual therapy alongside couple therapy.

- If you wish to have a young child access therapy then a qualified Child Therapist may be appropriate, particularly for children under 11.

- If the whole family is encountering issues as a whole, such as due to individual mental illness, substance abuse, eating disorder, or communication issues, then Family therapy may be appropriate. In family therapy the whole family attends together to work on identified problems. Family therapy sees family as a system that has its own dynamics rather than just individuals.

- If you wish to explore your problems in a supportive group with people who maybe struggling with similar issues then Group Therapy, sometimes alongside individual therapy may be appropriate. Common issues may be explored such as difficulties in forming relationships, patterns of painful relational experiences or addictions. Group therapy offers the opportunity to form relationships, learn about yourself through feedback, and to give feedback as part of the healing process.

- If you are having sexual difficulties that are of a psychological nature then Psycho-sexual therapy may be an option.

Exercises

Self-Reflection

Before embarking on finding the right therapist, consider your needs:

1. Do you understand what to do to check if a therapist meets the minimum standards for practice in your country?

2. What important qualities do you want from your therapist? For example, warmth, age, gender, reputation, status, authoritative, and direction giving.

3. What do you need in order to trust the therapist?

4. Do you have any views on the type of therapy you're looking for?

5. Do you have any concerns about beginning therapy (see Appendix D for possibilities)

6. Consider questions you want to ask a prospective therapist (see: Questions for the therapist within this way)

Reflect, compare and contrast your therapeutic relationship with your own perceptions about relationships:

1. Are relationships important to you in life? What type?

2. What is your ideal type of friend? Or partner?

3. Do you make connections with people easily?

4. Do you often feel disappointed with relationships? If so, why?

5. Do you find that after meeting a number of therapists, you cannot feel a relational connection with the therapist?

   o Why do you believe that is?

   o Are there any parallels between how you feel with therapists and other relationships?

6. Do the answers to these questions change what qualities what you are looking for in a therapist?

Resources

1. Consult the following resources if you want to understand more about therapeutic approaches

    o   Good Therapy (https://www.goodtherapy.org/learn-about-therapy/types)

    o   BACP (https://www.bacp.co.uk/about-therapy/types-of-therapy/) or

    o   UKCP (https://www.psychotherapy.org.uk/about-psychotherapy/types/)

2. Chapter 1 - Getting started in therapy. Learn about therapy options, rights in therapy, the contract, confidentiality and disclosure

3. Review Way 19: Watch out for inefficient, poor or harmful therapy

Activity

1. Close your eyes and allow an image of the type of therapist you would like. Write down what would they look like and be like, what would they say and how would they be with you.

2. Write down a list of qualities you would like from the therapist.

Quiz

1. For the scenario below, how would you answer it?

    I have seen various therapists over the year, and none have helped. I know I am the sort of person who needs direction and doesn't like talking about the past much. Isn't there a way of getting better that doesn't involve that?

2. What's more important the relationship with a therapist or the approach? Or both? How do they interrelate?

3. Do you understand the therapeutic contract and its purpose? (See Chapter 1)

4. Why may it be important to assess a therapist's competence on how they are with you as well as qualifications and experience?

5. How do you rationally assess the therapist's relational qualities? What are some of the difficulties in assessing relational competence?

6. Why is it useful to assess feelings as well as rational thoughts when finding a therapist (Hint: Way 11: Seek the truth and then seek "the truth")

Way 3: Work on feelings related to hope and motivation

Condensed idea: Hope and motivation account for a large part of the reason why clients achieve their desired outcomes in therapy (up to 50% Bohart, C. 2000). Therefore, exploring your feelings connected with hope and motivation, both towards life and therapy can be an important part of your process.

Approach Variations: Applies to all approaches of therapy.

Hope is a held belief and attitude that things will be okay, even in difficult circumstances. It is an optimistic state of mind in which you believe and expect a positive outcome. Hope doesn't mean being unrealistic, it is believing that there are always new avenues to go through even if you don't fully realise it on a particular path.

Motivation is having reason(s) to act or behave in a way which satisfies a goal, desire or purpose. Hope has strong links to motivation. Hope and motivation work reciprocally because hope gives you the will to act, which in turn reinforces hope. Similarly, helping yourself can increase hope. For example, if you enter therapy and your engagement with the therapist gives you hope it can motivate you to commit to therapy and your healing process.

In this way, you will learn to work with feelings related to hope and motivation. If you've lost hope or the will to act, your therapist will work with you on it, either directly or implicitly as part of the problem(s) you are experiencing. Remember, therapists don't shy away from dark or difficult feelings, because they are your reality, and often within them lie the way forward.

Working with lost hope

Trigger warning: Please do not read this section if you may be emotionally triggered.

Tony sat down and explained that he had been having a very hard time during the year. He was losing his relationship of ten years. He was becoming more and more isolated; not talking to friends or family and staying indoors. He had an online life in which he could not only work and shop online, but also numb out his feelings by browsing the Internet. His distress and anxiety could get so high that the only comfort he had was the bag of drugs he had locked away in a cupboard. He knew he had a way out if it got too bad.

If you feel hopeless, numb, in distress, or you are in a dark place please read this. I don't wish to talk you out of your place of hopelessness or tell you what to feel, what to do or how you should be. However, I would like to share a few practical things for you to consider in relation to the feelings of hopelessness and the way therapy can ease it.

You are not to blame for feeling hopeless
Feeling hopeless equates to the accumulative weight you're carrying from events now, and from the immediate or distant past. You're not weak, a bad person, worthless or defective. You did not do this to yourself. If people in the past or now have told you to "pull your socks up" and get on with it, that can also apply if you're physically injured. Sure, everyone is different with a different biological imprint and life experience, but that doesn't mean they would not be affected, because problems manifest themselves differently. You are not alone in your experience.

Hopelessness is proportional to the pain you are carrying
Hopelessness just means you are in pain somewhere; you have lost your direction and sense of worth in the world. This pain may not always be visible; it does not necessarily come out with emotions, anxiety or distress, it can equally come out as numbness, emptiness or being zoned out without feeling or thought.

Hopelessness is not right or wrong, neither is it immoral or a character defect. Of course, you may feel that you are to blame and defective, and even if you have regrets about actions you have taken, deep down there will be a reason. The therapeutic process teaches us that there is always a reason for your feelings, thoughts and actions, it's just that you are not aware of them yet. Give therapy a chance and you will gain insights about yourself, which can instil hope.

Would you tell a loved one or friend in your place to just get on with it?
People may react badly to your hopelessness, usually not because they don't care, but because of their own fears. Their frustration can come to the fore because they don't know what to do to soothe, comfort and help you, because they have never been taught themselves. Instead, they try to get you to push through the pain. Remember: that's their struggle not yours. Therapists do not argue you out of your feelings, judge you, or tell you to "pull yourself together", instead they accept you as you are, even in the darkest place, and from that point change is possible.

If you're suicidal
If you are suicidal and feel you will experience relief as a result of death, this is not true because you can only feel relief if you are here to feel it. Feeling relief is for the living. Even in the darkest of times, when you feel life is pointless you may be able to find a hook, a reason to live. Consider whether there is someone or something that needs you, or that you'll miss:

- A partner, child, family, friends or a pet, perhaps.
- A just cause or purpose.
- A creative passion that you wish to pursue.
- A future version of you who wants to live, who feels better and has a purpose.
- Appreciation for the wonder of nature and the planet.

If you can, message, text or call someone you trust, even if you can't talk specifically about what's happening in this moment.

Take a leap of faith

Remember to take it step by step. People do overcome being in a very dark place. As badly as you feel now, there are many others in your shoes right now and many more who have been through what you're experiencing who empathise with you. You may not know them, but I am sure many would want to be with you. You can overcome this, because those that took a "leap of faith" in the moment to take it step by step, minute by minute, day by day, week by week say how much they were glad they did.

Channel your feelings

You can consider other purposeful options even if you can't overcome your hopelessness immediately. If you're ready, you can channel your feelings to help others—and in turn yourself too. Many find ways to make use of their feelings. Some write blogs, campaign for better mental health services, find a creative hobby or use humour, while others create support groups online or volunteer to help those in a similar position. You can give and receive by doing so. Can you convert this energy into something which you may find meaningful?

Take the first step to get help

You can call people who are trained and who care.

Therapists, on the whole, are passionate about their job, they care even if they charge money, because you can't buy someone's care. Call one now. If you feel you can't speak on the phone or talk face to face there are services that work with text messaging, instant messaging, phone and even email. Just by doing that you could relieve some pressure.

I can't be with you but wish I could. If you are feeling hopeless please give yourself a chance and call someone. You can:

- Make an appointment with your physician or doctor.

    o Call your local emergency service or go the accident and emergency department if you have seriously harmed yourself

- Pick up the phone and talk to someone you trust.

- Call a support number (see Appendix B).

- Seek a therapist (see Way 2). If you are worried about confidentiality there is usually no need because thinking about suicide is not the same as telling someone you have a plan in place for it. Therapists know that clients can be in very dark places and are trained to work with you. Everyone at some point has suicidal thoughts. (Seek advice about the confidentiality policy if you're concerned about disclosure).

Work with your motivations

Of course, if you're feeling hopeless it's understandable that even taking the small step of asking for help can be daunting. When you don't have hope, you may have little energy or motivation for therapy, or for any effort to change your situation. However, it can be a useful exercise to pinpoint the factors preventing you from taking action, in other words the underlying reason for your feeling of hopelessness or feeling that you cannot take action. For example, you may have no hope in therapy because you won't be good at it, or because you think the therapist will blame you. See the self-reflection questions at the end of this way and ask whether this is really true, or whether it is based on bad experiences.

In this section, I describe some of the ways in which you can explore hopelessness and your motivation—specifically, how life experiences can lead to hopelessness, disappointment in learning that the therapist can't fix you, your readiness for therapy and self-help strategies to increase hope and motivation.

What leads to hopelessness?

This is something to explore in therapy. However, if you've experienced continuous exposure to oppressive situations in which you've had no free agency to apply your own *will,* you can learn hopelessness regardless of your current situation. For example, you may have felt too overpowered to make decisions, to have your own feelings, or perhaps you were neglected. In short, your life experiences themselves could, amongst others, be what is keeping you in a hopeless state and manifesting itself in low moods of hopelessness. Linking these feelings to life with your therapist can open new avenues of exploration.

Hope in the therapist's ability

For many there is deep disappointment in the therapy process when they hear or realise that the therapist cannot lead them directly out of a problem, rather it's the other way around. Ultimately, it's your responsibility, albeit with a guide, to heal yourself. This mirrors life, because no one can take responsibility for your life regardless of how much you may wish it were the case. Therefore exploring these feelings of disappointment with the therapist could be a useful activity.

You may not be ready

On the other hand if you're not in a position to prioritise your time you can consider whether it's the right time for you. In the fast paced lives we live in, with the desire for continuous production, productivity and progress it is all too easy to add one more item called "therapy" into your busy lifestyle. If you already have a workload full to the brim or overflowing, therapy itself, because there is a time commitment, ends up taking a backseat or becomes another tick in the box activity of life. Ultimately, it may be that you don't have time yet. So really consider whether you have the energy, time and priority to give to therapy.

However, if therapy cannot take a back seat, then look to see if other things can wait, and be honest about your reasons for not being able to prioritise therapy. That does not mean the other extreme of forgetting other things in your life, it just means that you give priority to care of yourself and your healing.

If you're ready to begin therapy

If you've taken the step to begin therapy, you do not have to go all out with full dedication on day one, you can build your dedication gradually. You can start simply by turning up, giving it a chance and building on that. Not all problems require long term commitment, you may get a lot out of a single session or short-term therapy.

To maximise your success in therapy, try to see therapy as a continuous learning activity rather than a fix, and as far as possible, commit, prioritise and regularly engage in it. There is no doubt the more committed you are to your healing process the more likely you are to see results. Just like any learning objective, dedication can pay off. Because therapy can be a nuanced process it's important to give it a trial run and stick with it, even if you feel a bit uncomfortable, because you don't know until you have fully tried it.

Therapy is not always a straight line, it may involve difficulties and obstacles, but remaining committed to the learning process usually leads to results. Therapy builds mental muscle by allowing for healing time in and between sessions.

Ways to increase hope and motivation
Take action

- Take a leap of faith and try therapy or seek support. Take it step by step and see where it leads. If you're not ready for therapy you may need more time to move from contemplation to commitment so delaying it is all part of the process.

- There are countless ways to begin helping yourself in small ways, many of which can be done from home. For example, connecting with others, acts of kindness, helping others or seeking a purpose.

- Apply self-care (Chapter 3: Tool #13: Self-care)

Explore feelings

- Tell your therapist. There is no need to hide feelings or thoughts about not being hopeful, or to hide your tentative feelings about therapy. Working through these feelings can, in itself, help to ease concerns.

- Explore underlying feelings about motivation. For example, is there a fear of failure, or a wish that someone had helped you in the past but didn't? (See Chapter 3: Tool #9 Expose underlying feelings).

- Use Way 6: Allow feelings and watch what hinders them in order to fully explore hopeless feelings in therapy.

- Understand whether the problem you experience may relate to how you feel about therapy. For example, you may have difficulty trusting, therefore you don't trust the therapist implicitly. Explore the possibilities with the therapist.

- Even if you're over the feelings of hopelessness, keep monitoring it and talking about it so that you minimise the chance of a relapse.

Scenario: The tentative client

If you're unsure or tentative about entering therapy then it can be a worthwhile exercise to try to understand whether there are deeper feelings behind your reluctance.

Adele reached out to me for therapy because of problems with anger. She would feel anger particularly when her girlfriend socialised without her. She would often ask for proof of her whereabouts, a Facetime call, a picture or a message. At the first session she did not show and then disappeared, ghosting me. A few weeks passed, she reappeared apologised profusely for not cancelling the first session, but really needed my help. I agreed.

At the first session, she described her feelings which were linked to being abandoned, first by her mum, then her dad. She said she really needed help and wanted to resolve this. To me she appeared committed to working on herself. However, before the next scheduled session she cancelled and never returned. I wondered what was going on for her, and whether she really knew. Was it to do with sharing difficult feelings? Was it because she was not ready? Was it something I said she did not like? Or was there something else going on? I would likely never know.

Adele is an example of someone being tentative about therapy. Her motivations and concerns were difficult to ascertain. If you find yourself being tentative about therapy, particularly at the beginning when you don't feel fully committed or engaged, you can explore those feelings with the therapist too. Here are a few reasons that clients have for not starting or faltering at the beginning (see Appendix

D for a list of possible concerns you, too, may have about therapy, the process and the therapist):

- Time, effort or money.
- Not feeling hopeful.
- Not convinced therapy or the therapist can help.
- You feel uncomfortable sharing your feelings.
- You have not found the right therapist yet.
- You're not ready for change. See Way 8: Consider what makes change undesirable.
- There are matters in life and the past you are concerned about revealing to your therapist (or even to yourself).
- Stigma and impact of going into therapy.

If you have particular concerns about therapy you can find more information about these subjects throughout this book as well as in Chapter 7: Client topics, questions and concerns. It can be important to share your concerns, or lack of hope with your therapist.

Exercises
Self-Reflection

1. At what times in your life have you felt hopeless? How have you been able to become more hopeful?

2. Do you feel hopeless now in your life, or at the thought of meeting a therapist, or do you even doubt the therapy's ability to help?

    a. What, in life, contributes to making you feel hopeless? For example, work, body, finance, family?

    b. Describe the underlying beliefs and feelings you have. For example, anger, disappointment, no one cares, or I don't belong (See Chapter 3: Tool #9 Expose underlying feelings).

    c. How did these feelings come about? How do you think you learnt them?

3. What resources or support do you have if you feel hopeless? Think about people, things you like, or even a future version of yourself.

4. What would make you feel more hopeful now? Or take the pressure off to feel even 5% more hopeful? For example, a call to a friend, an act of kindness or a walk.

5. What are your feelings about entering therapy? Do you feel hopeful? (See Appendix D for possibilities).

6. Are you ready to change? Are there any obstacles or things that you will miss, or possibilities you are fearful of if you were to work on change?

7. Do you have time and mental space to undertake therapy?

   a. If not, do you want to prioritise therapy? If so, what can take a back seat to give you mental space and time?

   b. If you can't dedicate yourself immediately, do you prefer to gradually ramp up therapy or would you prefer to wait?

Quiz

1. Name four practical ways you can help someone if they feel hopeless. Do any of those ways help you?

2. How would you help Tony in his feelings of hopelessness (see the beginning of this way)?

3. What advice would you give Adele (see Scenario: The tentative client)?

4. What advice would you give Adele if her reason for leaving therapy were to do with feeling defective for disclosing her behaviours?

Way 4: Use the therapist as a resource

Condensed idea: The therapist themselves could hold the key to your recovery.

Approach Variations: Applies to all therapeutic approaches. In couples, group and family therapy you will be using others as a resource too. For example, to ask for help, feedback or to clarify feelings.

If there is one way above anything else, I would say it is to learn to use the therapist. As a natural part of the process, you will be expressing your thoughts and feelings to your therapist, thus using them.

However, the therapist can also be used in a number of additional ways that may not be so obvious at first. In this way you will understand the potential benefits of using the therapist in these additional ways. Whether it's a general question about therapy or psychological problems, feeling stuck, examining your relationship with them or for feedback, the key may be sitting right opposite you.

As a relational reference

Approach Variations: Psychodynamic, Psychoanalytic, Interpersonal Therapy (IPT), and Schema therapy are specifically geared towards using what is going on between client and therapist in the room as a constructive part of the process. That does not mean you cannot us the same approach with other types of therapies, because most therapists will be aware of the therapeutic potential of your feelings towards them.

Are you coming into therapy where relationships are in the foreground of the work? Then it can be useful for you to reflect upon and talk to your therapist about what you feel about your relationship with them, and compare and contrast that with any other relational difficulties you experience.

Here are some ways people may experience their therapeutic relationship:

- You idealise the therapist. There are two particular patterns that frequently occur when clients think about the therapist being ideal. The first is that the therapist needs to *be* the ideal meeting a near perfect expectation; the second is the therapist *is* the ideal! In the former clients are dissatisfied because the therapist doesn't meet ideal expectation and the later they are idolised as being near perfect.
- You keep the therapist away. You inadvertently keep the therapist away from helping you fully usually out of your own awareness. For example, by not acknowledging their care or contribution.
- You want to be "the good client." You not only want to perform or do well in therapy but a lot of that is related to pleasing the therapist.
- You feel a deep feeling of dependence on the therapist, which may include emotional, romantic or erotic dependence. They occupy a large part of your

mental space, thus interfering with your therapeutic goals (See Chapter 5 – Love in the room).

- Your feel indifferent or nothing about the therapeutic relationship. They occupy none or little of your mental space.
- You don't particularly like the therapist and have negative feelings towards them (See Way 19 to determine whether they are not working competently with you).
- You see them as better than you in some way e.g. more attractive, competent, academic which interferes with your process.
- You feel the therapist is judging you even though rationally there is no reason to feel that way (See Way 2 for how to rationally assess the therapist).

Here are some ways you can open up exploring this topic with the therapist:

- "I heard there are patterns in how we relate to people based on past experiences"
- "I wonder whether there are similarities I can explore here with you?"
- "I wish to compare relationships in general to our relationships. Is that okay?"

How you feel about the therapist, whether positive, neutral or negative could be influenced by your learnt experiences. For example, if you have had bad experiences with men all your life, it may interfere with you feeling safe. There is nothing wrong with feeling that way, but it's better to be aware of it and explore it with them. You can also use this knowledge when finding a therapist.

To review progress

Use the therapist to review your therapeutic process, goals, learnings, and your relationship with the therapist.

Some therapists review progress regularly with you; others may leave it up to you. Sometimes, the therapists may not even mention the possibility of a review, and if that's the case, there is no reason why you cannot take the lead on it.

Regardless of the logistics of the review, the review can be useful for any number of reasons, maybe even for things lurking that you don't even know of yet! You can review progress and focus your therapy as well as consolidating what you've learnt so far.

As part of that review, you can also reflect on your relationship with the therapist too. How do you see the therapist? What more do you need from them? Do you feel safe and able to talk about what you want? This can be useful input not only for building a better relationship but also can open up further insights in your process.

Sometimes even the therapist may ask about your relationship with them:

Therapist: "How do you think we're doing? Is there anything you need from me that could help? I know sometimes you said it's hard to say what you need in relationships. Is this an opportunity? For example, is there at any point something I did or said anything that you minded?"

Client: "Well, there was one thing [smiles]. When you end therapy, it can be abrupt, which can feel uncaring to me."

Therapist: "Well, that's great. I really want you to be able to say what you feel in sessions, etc."

You could also ask the therapist for feedback too, but be aware: generally, therapists act as a mirror to help you arrive at what you believe you need, so don't be surprised if they return what feels like a question with a question or reflect back what you say. In short, a review can bring into focus why you're there and what you want out of therapy.

Possible subjects for review include:

- Review or focus in on your goals
- Identify areas you want to work on
- Review progress and what you have learnt so far
- Review the relationship with the therapist
- Concerns about endings
- Concerns about stagnation or blocks
- Give feedback on what is working what else you need from the therapist
- Ask questions including asking for feedback from therapist
- Concerns about the process
- Celebrate where you are now
- You're confused about where things are going

As a sounding board for the process

Approach variation: Depending on the question asked you may or may not get a direct answer to questions when you ask the therapist, particularly when it comes to the therapists personal disclosure. Usually integrative, cognitive behavioural and solution focused therapies will provide more suggestions in answering questions.

Lost for ideas on what to work on? Maybe there is a missing piece to the puzzle you're trying to discover or you cannot find a way to express an idea. You don't have to wait, you can use the therapist to help you along. In many cases, the therapist may reflect back to you what you want help on and what you feel about it, but they may do it in a way that gives you more space or another strand to focus in on, to deepen your understanding of your questions.

Here are some things you could ask:

- I need help opening up
- Is there anything you feel I could explore more?
- I'm stumped and don't know what to say
- Is there something you think I have missed or I am not aware of?
- Do you have an idea of how these things happen?
- Questions about how the process works
- Questions about the rationale for the therapist working with you in a particular way
- Explanation of something the therapist said
- Ask about activities you could do between session to help your process
- Questions about mental health problems such as depression, anxiety, fear. This sort of question is called psychoeducation (see Chapter 3 - Tool #14), and it can help you understand your problems better.
- Anything you're curious about. For example, what you have seen or read (perhaps even matters in this book!)
- What they feel about what you have suggested or said?

For role play

Approach variation: Usually more relevant to integrative, cognitive behavioural and solution focused therapies

Is there something you find difficult to express in life? You can ask the therapist whether they can roleplay communication skills you are working on. The most popular role play that comes up in therapy is that of being able to communicate effectively, resolve conflicts, and to share difficult feelings with family, friends or work colleagues.

I recommend everyone to practice communication skills (Tool #10: Empathic interpersonal skills) either in life or with the therapist, particularly if you're having relationship difficulties. This teaches you how to use appropriate language, be empathic, express your feeling and still retain boundary's in relationships.

When feeling blocked

A sign that things are stagnating is when you feel like nothing is progressing, even after months of therapy, and you appear to be looping around content without insight or shift. You have stopped learning and therapy feels "flat" in the room. You may be "doing" a lot in therapy but nothing moves you any further and no new insights form. It may be that you don't feel much during therapy, and nothing appears to be whirring inside you. It can feel like you're in a forest that has no path or purpose. Examining the feeling of being stuck is really important because it can either make or hinder your therapy. Given its importance to the process, I dedicate Way 15: Don't let things stay stuck without taking action, to this important subject.

To keep the relationship on track

There is a general consensus in the therapy world that having a good-enough relationship is a key to a strong foundation for change; otherwise, you could be on shaky ground. Given the relationship is so important to the outcome, you can do your fair share to keep your relationship on track and to deal with any obstacles along the way. Your fair share involves communicating your needs and telling the therapist what is bothering you.

In my experience of therapy coaching, relational issues with the therapist are the most discussed concern. These issues can come up from time to time, and of course, the therapist does not have to be perfect but good enough. If you are able to, you can take charge yourself to raise any issues in the relationship.

Because of the importance of the relationship and potential difficulties I devote a whole way "Way 16: Do your fair share in building a good enough relationship" on this matter.

When ending

It's perfectly acceptable for you to end at any time. However if you feel safe it can be beneficial to talk through your reasons first (See Way 20: Don't walk away from therapy without talking to the therapist).

Exercises

Self-Reflection

1. Do you like your therapist? What qualities do you like about them, feel indifferent about or maybe even dislike?

2. Are there any new ways you would like to use the therapist?

3. Do you believe what you feel or think about the therapist could relate to your problems / goals?

Quiz

1. Under what circumstances could it be important to reflect upon or even share your feelings about the therapist?

2. Why would rehearsal for a difficult conversation be useful?

3. Why can reviewing progress be important?

Way 5: Express yourself from your point of view

Condensed Idea: Therapy is a process of learning about yourself by taking the therapist on a journey inside your experiences. Therefore, learning to openly express yourself from your point of view is central to achieving your goals.

Approach Variations: Applies to all therapeutic approaches. In couples, group, and family therapy, you will be listening to others express themselves from their point of view.

In this way, you will learn the importance of expressing yourself from your point of view, and strategies on how to overcome difficulties opening up.

You will learn to recognise and utilise strategies where the difficulties relate to:

- General problems such as anxiety
- Disclosing important material to the therapist such as being abused
- A pattern of wanting the therapist to guide and reassure you
- Not knowing what to talk about

Expressing what's going on in your heart, mind, and body is really important in therapy. Only through your expression can both you and your therapist experience and understand your world. Although therapists may talk more at the beginning to help you open up, eventually you'll need to learn to do most of the talking yourself. Therapy is a collaboration, but in the long run it's you taking the therapist on a journey inside your experiences, not the other way around.

Of course, therapists do express themselves from their perspective too; they can express feelings, ask questions, structure sessions, set the agenda, offer feedback, or suggest what may be going on for you. Expressing yourself does not mean you do not use the therapist (see Way 4: Use the therapist as a resource). If you are stuck, need feedback, or have questions, you should feel free to ask. By sharing what you need you *are* expressing yourself from your point of view.

Note: Expression in therapy is primarily about talking but also includes body movement, silence, and non-verbal communication.

Scenario: What if opening up is too difficult?
Therapists recognise that opening up for some can be the hardest part of therapy and they have no preconceived expectations of how you "should" be in therapy, whether you find expressing yourself difficult or are not ready to. They will work with you "as you are" with empathy and without judgement. They take time and will not criticise or blame you for whatever you experience. They are there to help you.

Clients who are initially anxious about opening up quite often find their worries or anxieties diminish considerably once their feelings and experiences are validated and normalised. Sharing difficulties opening up can take the sting out of the encounter.

Difficulties with opening up can of course be very much related to the problem you're trying to overcome, as it was for Fran.

> **Fran** *always kept herself to herself. In school, girls would often shame her in front of the whole class, laughing and pointing at her: "Err, look at her, she's weird, what's wrong with her, why doesn't she say anything!" Fran would put her head down, looking towards the floor so she could escape. She didn't want anyone to see her upset. Instead, her anger would come out towards herself while alone, going from anger to tears. Years later, the tears dried out and she spoke little about herself. Fran entered therapy as an adult wanting help to stop fearing social situations.*

> *Fran felt really awkward in therapy. Her mind was rushing, trying to find things to say. Often she would get upset or angry with herself in front of the therapist because she could not open up. She found therapy so hard because of her difficulties in expressing herself in front of a stranger; it felt like so much pressure she would often go home with a migraine.*

For Fran, the therapy encounter was emotionally triggering, at least in part due to her social anxiety. Often, difficulties opening up relate to your experiences and the problems you're trying to overcome. If you recognise that your difficulties with opening up are related to your problems, it can be a useful way of reinterpreting your therapy, because instead of seeing opening up as an obstacle to begin therapy, it can be seen as being a central theme to your therapy. Developing awareness of your underlying feelings about opening up can provide you and your therapist important areas to explore. For example, feeling that you're going to be judged, or you won't be able to manage emotions, or feeling embarrassed are all worth exploring.

Of course this is not the only reason why opening up could be difficult. In Appendix D – Inventory of client concerns, you'll find the most common concerns that clients have reported, for example, worries about personal ability, consequences of change, or whether the therapist will understand you.

Regardless of why you are having difficulties, here are some self-help strategies for you. As everyone is unique, you will need to assess for yourself which of these strategies would help.

Be safe
If the encounter is too distressing, then tell the therapist or even stop the session.

You don't want to hurt yourself emotionally by pushing through when you are clearly distressed. Consult your therapist and doctor.

Use the therapist

Remember, therapists are very familiar with difficulties in opening up and are experts in guiding you through the process. If you are already in therapy, you can explore the difficulty of opening up with the therapist. Although the therapist is likely to guide you, here are three strategies you can ask for:

- You can reflect on what you need from the therapist to help you open up; for example, maybe all you need is space and time, rather than being under pressure to talk.
- Ask the therapist to see if they can ask you questions that you can answer, rather than having to come up with things to say.
- You can also ask the therapist if they can do something with you that isn't directly face to face. For example, use emotion cards or an expressive art (remember, art is not about being a good artist!). Another example, is to use a notepad and pen to communicate.

By taking the step to express your difficulties and needs, you're already on your way to opening up.

Evaluate expectations

Clients can often put so much pressure on themselves to "perform" or be a "good client" that it can get in the way of opening up. If you recognise this in you, then that is likely to have therapeutic value, so it's worth telling your therapist about. Remember, therapy is about focusing in on you and your goals rather than coming up with things to say to fill silence or please the therapist. So even if you're silent, which I know can be awkward at first, you can learn to become more comfortable with it.

Dear Diary (Chapter 3: Skill #11)

You can consider using a diary to write about the topics you want to express, including difficulties you are having expressing yourself. Write a few points down and bring it into a session as a point of reference, or even send it in securely prior to your session. Expressing yourself in writing can be a good way to learn to develop confidence in opening up.

Consider other sources of expression

Consider whether there are other sources you can draw upon to gradually open up. In Skill 10: Ideas for expressive material, for example, you'll find an idea about expressing how you would like to be in the future. If you find it easier to talk about certain subjects, then that is the important first step.

Many clients forget that what they experience in the here and now (Chapter 3: Skill #4) can be a useful source of expression. This is where you take a step back to notice your feelings, body sensations, and thoughts and verbalise them with the therapist. For example: My heart is running fast, I feel awkward, or I feel like escaping.

Consider online therapy
Consider whether another medium, such as phone calls, outdoor therapy, or instant messaging approaches, would make opening up easier. Many online therapists are able to move from instant messaging, to phone, to face to face therapy as and when you are ready.

Let things brew
If you're not ready to open up because you don't feel quite safe yet, then you can wait until you're ready. Like in most relationships, building trust can take time and although it's difficult now, that does not mean it won't change over time. You don't need to feel you owe the therapist trust, it's a process like in every relationship.

Consider ending therapy
Alternatively, if you believe it's not working because of the particular therapist you're seeing, you can consider ending the relationship with that therapist. See Way 14: Use your feelings about endings for guidance on when to end.

Remember, however you express yourself, the therapist will work you as you are, with empathy and without judgement.

Scenario: What if disclosure is too difficult?
And then there was the subject of what Fran really wanted help with. Being raped by her mother's boyfriend. She was frozen then and she is frozen now.

For Fran, disclosure of her rape in therapy is a scary experience and the range of underlying feelings that make it scary is something that will most certainly need exploring in therapy. However, her reasons for holding back are likely to fall into one of more of the following areas:

- You're just not ready to talk about a particular problem or experience.
- The disclosure is loaded with feelings about being judged and you feel it's something shameful or embarrassing.
- You're worried that you or someone you know will get into trouble because of the disclosure. For example, in the case of a criminal act that someone you know has committed.
- You think what you share would be used against you, whether by an insurer, employer, court, or government.
- You don't want personal information to be stored or shared. For example, in therapists' records or to friends and family.

- Some other unique reason. For example, you don't want to disclose because the person won't be in your life when therapy ends.

As it happens, Fran was not so concerned about telling the therapist. What she was more worried about was her mother abandoning her because the therapist reported it. For Fran, disclosure did not feel like an option.

For further discussion on the limits of confidentiality in therapy, see Chapter 1: Disclosure.

Given the dilemmas clients face and the possible repercussions, it's not surprising if you feel some reluctance to disclose. Most often in my experience, a client's worries about repercussions are usually unfounded, but it depends on the context. If it's a worry, then you can use the following self-help strategies to help you towards feeling safer about disclosure.

Find out the facts
Many clients can be worried about what the therapist will do with information they disclose and whether it will harm them in some way. If you are worried about the confidentiality of what you disclose, you could open up a dialogue by asking what the limits of confidentiality are. Often therapists and organisations have a written disclosure policy.

Use the therapist
If you're finding it difficult to disclose something important for your therapy, you can start by exploring your worries about disclosure rather than disclosing. Through that process, you'll be exploring your feelings of reluctance and in doing so may feel more comfortable to disclose.

Use a content free approach
Many therapists work with you in a "content free" way, so you don't have to disclose. Using a content free approach, the therapist directs you into your experience and you talk about feelings and sensations rather than disclosing what happened. Some therapies, such as EMDR, EFT, Focusing Therapy or NLP, contain *"content free"* protocols within them. Other approaches may include the use of metaphor, art, and sand trays to help you through your feelings.

Talk to your therapist to see whether they can work this way and whether it could be beneficial given the context of your goals.

Other strategies described in the previous scenario apply here too:

- Online therapy, particularly where the service is provided anonymously. Anonymous services can still have limits of confidentiality.
- Consider writing a letter to read out loud or securely send to the therapist

- Consider whether you can allow yourself more time before disclosure. Maybe you aren't quite ready to disclose but you're working towards it.
- Consider whether you feel safe enough with the therapist and whether you need to end therapy.

Ultimately, you are free to choose whether you disclose or not; you can wait or decide at a later date. If the disclosure is important to your process, then you will have to look at whether it's something you can realistically work on without exploring.

Scenario: Wanting the therapist to guide you

When Fran began to express herself, I noticed she would say a few words and then pause, look at me and wait. I wondered what Fran was expressing to me when she did that.

If you catch yourself wanting to use the therapist's perspective a lot or wanting to stay away from your own, then you can be curious about the nature of your experience. You can use it as a source for exploration.

Here are common reasons:

- You need guidance on what to do.
- You believe that's the way therapy should be done.
- You want the therapist to focus the agenda or structure.
- You don't feel safe yet. For example, you feel judged or don't trust your therapist.
- You don't want to say the wrong things and so need for them to reassure you.
- It's too difficult for you to stay within your own experience and just express whatever is going on (see Way 16: Reflect on whether you're distant from feelings).
- It's a way of life. For example, you're not used to taking "air space" or having people listen to you.

Whatever your need for staying outside of your own point of view, it is an opportunity to explore it in therapy. It may even relate very much to the problem you are working on.

Scenario: Untold truths and lies

In my experience of therapy coaching, clients can often be worried about changing their story, or revealing something important later on during the course of therapy. You may feel that doing so would be like being caught telling a lie, or you may have concerns about being criticised or blamed for doing so.

You may have worries that the therapist will think badly of you (say, because of having an affair). Or you may hide things because you fear you will not be believed, and sometimes you may hide things to avoid confronting your feelings and the truth.

Another reason for being selective is that you may hope that you can get what you need from therapy without going into the underlying issue. For example, anger management may be more about changing thoughts and behaviours around the anger rather than looking inside the anger, although a content-free therapy approach described prior may be a way around this reluctance.

Of course, with a good therapist this is not the case at all, as it just represents who you are at a point in time. They are not lies or secrets. Your therapist knows that therapy is a process and your story can unfold in various directions, they are there to accept you as you are, not how you should be.

To help you understand how valid and normal it is to withhold or distort your truth here is a list of the most common distortions or concealments in therapy (Farber, A., 2019):

- Minimisation of impact including severity of symptoms
- Exaggeration of progress
- Suicidal thoughts, self-harm, and emotional distress
- All things sexual including history, fantasies and sex life
- Substance use and abuse
- Trauma
- Clinical progress and feelings about the therapist
- Insecurity about yourself
- Pretending to like therapists comments or suggestions
- Reasons for missed appointments or lateness
- Pretending therapy is more effective than it is
- Life regrets
- Pretending to do the homework
- Not saying you want to end therapy
- Something illegal
- Opinion of the therapist
- Feelings about your body
- Family secrets
- Things parents did that affected you

If any of these are relevant to your therapy and you are ready feel free to change the narrative.

Sometimes particularly if your analytical minded you may wonder what it is that you need to focus on to get the most out of therapy. This can itself cause confusion and frustration regardless of whether you are working towards specific goals or are working in an open ended manner. This is not something that can be answered in absolute terms because it depends on your circumstances. But it is an understandable particularly if your mind is overloaded with possibilities or you have a set number of sessions to work with.

However, experience and theory indicates that the mind finds its own way once it begin expressing yourself. So what may seem irrelevant or way off mark can branch off into very important therapeutic material over time. In practice this means "trusting" your mind to eventually know what's important to bring up.

Here are some more ideas to reflect on in therapy:

- You can accept that you don't know (See Way 12: Weave in acceptance into therapy)
- What pops up in the here and now is usually a good start to expression
- What you push away as difficult when determining what you need to talk can often be something to talk about
- Ask whether what you are talking about relates to your goals
- Tell the therapist and let them guide you in their own way

This type of worry can occur when you're in a hurry or may be related to your problem too. This is something of course to talk to your therapist about.

Exercises
Self-Reflection

1. How comfortable are you with talking about your thoughts, feelings and perspectives?

2. How much do you usually share about yourself with friends, family, colleagues, and strangers? Do you listen more or talk more?

3. How do you feel about the prospect of sharing with a therapist, even things you have never shared with anyone before?

4. What, if anything, in this way applies to you?

5. If you have trouble expressing parts of yourself, reflect on why that is.

6. What do you need from the therapist to be able to freely share what you need to?

Activities

1. Develop a hierarchy of difficulty related to opening up, and then apply that in practice. A generalised hierarchy was given in the section "Applying Ways Using a Hierarchy of Difficulty" earlier in this chapter.

2. Try opening up more with people you feel safe with.

3. Start a journal (Skill #6) to write down your thoughts, feelings, and experiences regularly as a means to open up.

Resources

1. YouTube channel "Dear therapist" (Launched 2020)

Quiz

1. Why do you think inside-out expression is important in therapy?

2. What advice would you give Fran to help her in expressing herself?

3. What advice would you give Fran about her difficulty in disclosing the abuse she suffered?

4. If Fran left therapy without disclosing would that be the right thing for her to do? What advice would you give her?

5. Name two reasons why people may keep things short and look for reassurance from a therapist?

6. What advice would you give someone who posts this question on the empowering your therapy message board?

   Does anyone else struggle with an overwhelming fear of what your therapist thinks of you? Will she believe your story? Will she think you're making a big deal out of nothing? I replay everything I say in session over and over again and I think it's keeping me stuck. I don't know how to trust others at all but need help.

Way 6: Allow feelings and watch what hinders them

"You say your feelings are wrong, first look for reasons why they may be right"

Condensed Idea: If you have feelings, allow them to rise from inside you, to be talked about or displayed, regardless of how irrational, illogical, confusing or embarrassed you feel. Explore these feelings and understand why they make sense as you work towards rationalising them.

Approach variation: You are unlikely to be able work through all of your deeper feelings if you are in couples, family, or group therapy. In shorter term therapy you may not have time to work through all of your feelings, so setting a focus can be important. Cognitive behavioural and solution-focused therapies tend to emphasise rational thought rather than deep exploration of feelings (See Way 11: Seek your truth then seek "the truth").

In this way, which reveals the importance of working with feelings in therapy, you will learn:

- The significance of feelings in therapy.
- How difficulties in expressing feelings can manifest themselves in therapy.
- How feelings can be dampened down or lay dormant.
- Strategies for finding the source(s) of feelings.
- Strategies for becoming more feelings focused.

Your feelings are never wrong from a therapeutic perspective, just like the readings on a car dashboard are never wrong (well, rarely!). If the engine is overheating, it tells you to do something about it, otherwise the car may break down. Similarly, feelings are indicators that something needs attention before change can happen, whether it's a tweak, a significant overhaul or something you need. Acknowledging feelings doesn't mean you don't want to change; it points you to the change needed for your wellbeing. Feelings are to be respected for what they are and explored as windows into what is going on, and when you have worked them out or *processed* them, change is possible.

Ignoring feelings can be like changing the lightbulbs when the engine needs fixing. Similarly, if there is a mismatch between the sources of feeling(s) and solution(s) to your problem(s), you could end up working on something that is less relevant in the hope you'll strike gold.

Remember, like all the other ways, respecting feelings or allowing feelings is a process. It does not mean you will be able to do that immediately. For example, if your feelings have been dampened down, getting in touch with them can take time. Similarly, feelings don't always have to be explored, you're free to choose.

What do we mean by processing feelings? Processing feelings means to become aware of them, understand them, to gain perspective(s) of them or even experience them bodily so they can be healed. A metaphor of healing taking the plaster off a wound, caring for it, letting it air, bandaging it up, and allowing it time to heal.

Scenario: Bypassing feelings

A common pattern in therapy is to dismiss feelings as wrong, unacceptable or scary, which results in leaving the feelings unprocessed and unresolved. However, instead of rejecting or criticising your feelings, therapy allows you to process them and— when appropriate, to use and convert these feelings over time. As an example, therapy does not generally look at feelings such as anger and try to manage them away, although that may help. For deeper issues, their root(s) would need to be understood to heal its source. Feelings can be embraced and understood in therapy.

A narrative of ignoring or pushing past strong deep-rooted feelings may sound something like this:

> Paul: "You know, I really felt hurt by my friends [eyes tearing up] over the weekend. I don't know what it is about me, that I feel people ignore me and my feelings. This happens a lot; it hurts, but I have to get over it, think more positively and not depend on people to meet my needs or get so attached to them."

> Therapist: "I can see you are hurting underneath [long pause]. You're really trying to push through and think positively. You can do that but I'd really like to understand the part of you that felt angry and sad for being left out."

It's tempting, especially when you feel strong feelings, to rationalise them or "fix" them away, but if you feel something, you feel it! Ignoring those feelings would be equivalent to ignoring a child's feeling and saying, "Don't be silly, just grow up!" That is not to say that rationality is not important (See Way 11) or challenging—whether there is evidence for feeling the way you do or not; it may be a very important part of this solution but give feelings enough airtime first. Allow understanding, nurturing, self-care and even love to be provided to the feeling parts of you.

Respecting your feelings is a core part of caring for your wounds.

Scenario: Bringing in Dampened Feelings

"Gurnal was very agreeable, he liked to be liked, hated being judged and never got into conflicts. Only the fantasy bubble of being "good" had just been broken as he sat opposite me full of anxiety and hurt. He had come to realise his wife had controlled every aspect of his life: from what he should wear and eat, to who he should meet. He had become isolated from friends and family because his partner did not like them. He

now asked "Where was I all this time? It's like I lost myself but I don't know who 'myself' is!"

For some, feelings may be so dampened down, that you don't trust your feelings, or that you emphasise others' feelings more—including the therapist's—more than your own. This may be because you believe others know best, so you don't listen to your own feelings. You may "give in" to others because you feel you are wrong, or because you don't see the point since others don't listen. If you realise that you tend to quieten or damp down your own feelings then I recommend exploring this further and bringing it up with your therapist.

Sometimes your feelings may be hidden so far deep inside you they that it will take much work before they come to the fore. Feelings may arise which were previously unsighted, sometimes at the peak point of your change process. Although this may not happen for you, the distancing and dampening down of feelings can occur over a long period of time, as a way of coping or even surviving in life. The feelings become like a dormant volcano. Examples of dormant feelings may include a bereavement, a trauma, or even a painful memory; all forgotten but sat within the body and mind, like an old unattended wound.

Dampening down your feelings can have consequences in the therapeutic process too, such as stagnation in therapy, not being able to share difficult feelings or remaining with a therapist who is not right you.

Having feelings may be overwhelming in therapy so it is important to feel safe. For highly distressing or very low feelings this could mean staying somewhere in the middle between having feelings and being present with the therapist in order to process them. Speak to your therapist if you have concerns about triggering strong feelings, remembering that strongly felt feelings could be a much-needed part of your process.

You can find an an example of how dormant feelings come to the fore in Chapter 4: Oliver's journey.

Scenario: Finding the source(s) of your feelings

It may also be difficult to allow or explore feelings because there does not appear to be a reason for them. This can confuse both you and those around you.

As your feelings are triggered, you could get caught up in them and instead of owning them, you end up protecting yourself from them by blaming yourself or others as a way of coping with the confusion. Creating mental space to look below the surface and gain an understanding of these emotions, particularly when things have cooled down, is often needed.

Stephen had a huge release of anger a few weeks back. He had been tidying up some of his wife's bathroom items; they had both been meaning to get around it. However, when his wife returned, she told him that he should not have moved her things and she "would have eventually cleaned up." At that point Stephen, very unusually for him, went into a rage. He was very surprised, and so was his partner.

After much exploration of his feelings, he uncovered many factors that led up to that point. He came to realise how he tried to contain his feelings, rather than take steps to work through them. In particular, he felt his partner had not listened to him for a number of years, and he could not understand why she could not think like him too. Then there was his own history of not sharing feelings, being dissatisfied at work and feeling anxious about the future. He found some of these feelings related to unresolved feelings from his past, in particular how his family never kept a financial safety net, which made him worry they would be kicked out of their home.

The anger expressed towards his wife gave him a window to explore what lay beneath the emotions, rather than go straight to a logical solution which assumed feeling had to be fixed rather than being heard. This example also shows how feelings and reactions can have many strands that can appear to be unrelated to symptoms but are more about discovering and processing frustrations that have not yet been aired.

You may not know why you are feeling a certain way, but by giving your feelings time and space, you'll pick up some possibilities as your process unfolds. It is pretty rare to not find some possible reasons for feeling a certain way.

How do you get to your feelings?

Deeper feelings aren't something you can directly pull out of the bag. In fact, if you make it an objective to get to your feelings it often becomes more elusive. Rather, getting to your feelings—especially if you're unaware of them or they lie dormant— can come about spontaneously or gradually during the process. Mostly, all you can do is to freely explore your experiences and let the relational container of therapy do its job.

You can start using the language of feelings when expressing your experiences. Here are some ways to describe feelings:

- Label your feelings. For example, jealousy, anger, emptiness, excitement and rage.
- Describe the feeling as a picture or image. For example, confusion may be expressed as mist and hopelessness could be described as being in a dark well.

113

- Describe where a feeling is in the body: its colour, texture, shape, temperature and intensity.
- Associate feelings with memories and events in which you had similar feelings.
- Using metaphors, stories or myths which represent your feelings (see Chapter 3: Tool #7: Stories and metaphors).

You can also observe any language you use which minimises feelings. Of course many of these are feeling-based and can be explored too:

- I'm not normal or I'm crazy
- Others have it worse
- It's not their fault
- I'm to blame for how I feel
- Self-criticism. For example, I never get it right or I shouldn't feel this way.

You can also familiarise yourself with the various forms in which feelings can be expressed:

- By using "I feel…" or "I felt.." statements.
- As live bodily felt sensations.
- As a lack of feeling sometimes called emptiness or numbness.
- As feelings which you quickly close off as being difficult, shameful or wrong.
- A mismatch between what you say and how your body expresses itself. For example, talking about difficult experiences and smiling or laughing over them (minimised feelings).
- Silence.

You can also observe and reflect on whether you are keeping a distance from your feelings through your awareness of them (see Way 17: Reflect on whether you're being distant or caught up in feelings).

Learning to acknowledge more of your feelings can be a difficult path, especially if have come from an environment or family where feelings were not shown or allowed. You may also feel guilt or shame for talking about feelings out of a sense of disloyalty, or even fear of consequences. In other cases it may be that you have an inbuilt way of shutting down feelings through self-criticism, believing no one is interested, which causes you to believe that feelings are "abnormal". So allow your feelings to surface in stages and work on what interferes with their expression. Of course, this does not mean you should share feelings if you are not ready, but if you are and you feel it's important, then take steps.

If you have difficulty talking about feelings you can use similar strategies to those presented in Way 5: Express yourself from your point of view. However, here are a few additional strategies specific to feelings and emotions:

- Tell the therapist that you have difficulties talking about your feelings. Therapists usually have many methods to help you.
- Talk about any obstacles that stop you talking about feelings. For example, feeling that you would be betraying someone if you shared what you really felt.
- Talk about your historical experiences of showing feelings when growing up.
- Use awareness to determine whether you are minimising or criticising your feelings inadvertently.

Where possible don't shut feelings out of therapy—even if you don't like them, are confused by them, feel ashamed, self-critical or feel they are irrational—until they are understood. Your own subjective feelings are going to be an important source of the work you do in therapy.

Allowing feelings does not mean that you don't stand back and check out their truth (See Way 11: Seek your truth and then the truth), you will in time, and that can be important too. But unless there is a safety concern, allow your feelings to breathe, because allowing them to be expressed, processed or felt in the room is a big part of what makes therapy work.

Exercises
Self-Reflection

1. What are your beliefs about feelings? Do you, your family and friends show feelings?
2. What is your approach to expressing feelings?
3. What is your family's approach to expressing feelings?
4. Do you generally try and figure out why you may be feeling a certain way? For example, happy, energised, excited, sad, emotional, angry, low, numb?
5. Do you believe your feelings are balanced and in accord with the trigger that made you feel something?
6. Have you ever felt emotions without understanding why it was happening or what was causing it? For example, anxious, feeling low, emotional, and angry.
   a. Does your lack of emotion or high intensity of emotion sometimes surprise you?
   b. Do you have some examples where you felt unexpected emotions? Trace back from that time and write about what was happening five days before the situation and whether there were any stresses or triggers. Remember, stresses may be a lack of a need, e.g., feeling lonely.
   c. How long has this been happening? If this has been happening for a long time what factors do you believe contributed to your current feelings? Consider writing your life story to see if it reveals any new ideas.

    d.   If you can't figure it out by yourself, try and ask others whom you trust and know.
7. Do you share feelings in therapy? Are there feelings you want to share but are not ready to do so?
8. Are there any feelings or beliefs which inhibit you from sharing more of your feelings?
9. Do you want to share more feelings? If so, develop your own personalised hierarchy of difficulty for sharing feelings.

Resources

1. Chapter 5 – Calm the inner critic. Learn how self-criticism can interfere with sharing feelings.
2. Chapter 5 – But I had a good childhood. Describes the difficulties of sharing feelings about caregivers and families.
3. Way 17: Reflect on whether you're being distant or caught up in feelings.

Quiz

1. Why can it be important to talk about feelings in therapy?
2. Give three reasons why someone may find talking about feelings difficult.
3. Why do dormant feelings occur?
4. How can the expression of feelings differ based on personality and neurodiversity e.g. Aspergers.
5. What life impacts could be a consequence of dampening down or minimising feelings? Why can it be difficult to "get to" feelings?

Way 7: Understand yourself through awareness

"Awareness, awareness, awareness...the gateway to another world."

"The unexamined life is not worth living" (Socrates)

Condensed idea: Use awareness to become conscious of what's happening or has happened so you can explore its meaning. Awareness is the heart of change because it is the gateway to understanding and experiencing what's going on and therefore what may need to change.

Approach Variations: Applies to all approaches of therapy. In couples, group, and family therapy, awareness will extend to others too.

Awareness is the bringing in of new information that was previously unknown into your consciousness. This could be from the present, the past or from an imagined future; it could be located inside you or outside in the world. It answers the question of "what's happening, happened or could happen?" and once you've brought something to your attention it can be used to gain situational understanding and to piece together a story of you or others (see Way 9: Put it all together by understanding your story).

In this way you will learn the importance of awareness in enabling change. You will understand:

- What awareness is and why it's so important.

- Strategies for building awareness.

- How awareness of "process" helps identify the feelings that underlie your words as well as the way you express yourself in the room.

Look around you right now. What do you see, what do you hear, or smell? By bringing your focus to your surroundings you become aware. You experience your environment moving from the background to the foreground. This is what awareness is—focusing in on yourself in relation to events, memories, people and the world with an attitude of curiosity. Awareness allows things that you did not notice before to come into your consciousness, in other words to look at yourself in a mirror. This is much like the way a scientist works: by observation they collect information that can be used to increase their understanding.

Through awareness you learn to make yourself the subject of examination and curiosity. Without awareness you can focus on difficulties and vent frustrations, but change can be difficult because you may not be aware of what's going on inside you that is really causing difficulties, and therefore may need to be worked on, healed or changed.

Awareness is perhaps the most important thing you can learn to be successful in therapy. The more aware you are the more you discover, and the more you discover, the greater the possibility of self-understanding. Through awareness over time, you begin to remove your filters or glasses, which keeps your truth out of sight or distorts it. Awareness is the gateway to your process of change because you can't change things outside of your control, so the hope lies within, to make the inner change.

Here are some examples of awareness (noting that the precondition for these statements is that you were unaware of them previously):

- I am aware that when I am around my boss my body tenses up and I get nervous.
- I am aware that when I talk to my therapist I end up talking about my day-to-day activities rather than the problem.
- I am aware that whenever I have an argument with my partner I start drinking more.
- I am aware that part of me is scared to leave my partner but the other part wants to stay because it will be easier.
- I am aware that whenever I look in the mirror I see someone I don't recognise.
- I am aware that I use sessions to vent about others rather than focusing on my hurt feelings.
- I am aware of a memory of being abused by my father.
- I am aware that my therapist irritates me when they change the subject.
- I am aware that my mother was not emotionally there for me during my childhood.
- I am aware how my father abandoning me has contributed to the anxiety I feel when my partner leaves me alone.
- I am aware of new memories coming up of being traumatised.
- I am aware that I don't tend to use self-awareness a lot.
- I am aware that I use therapy to try to fix or control my external situation.
- I am aware my partner looks sad (externally located awareness).

How to build awareness

Awareness can happen spontaneously while you're talking, and your mind automatically brings in new information to the foreground. Awareness can also come about through curious observation of yourself as you reflect on experiences, past, present or imagined. If you want change in therapy and it's not something you're used to doing, then I recommend you develop and practice awareness.

Here is an example of using the "catch yourself" approach to awareness in which you reflect on unexpected reactions, including feelings or behaviours.

> Nadia was standing in the first class queue waiting to board her plane home. From behind a lady walked up to her and asked, "Are you waiting in this

queue?" Nadia responded quickly with indignation, quipping in a sarcastic tone, "Yes I am! Are you?" Nadia didn't think too much about the incident until she started to look back at it. She started to wonder why she reacted so aggressively at a lady asking her a simple question. This was the beginning of her awareness, looking inwards at herself rather than at others; there was something going on inside her that did not make sense. She took her awareness of the reaction to therapy sessions to explore it.

She spent time being curious of her reaction and realised this was more about her deeper feelings of being treated less fairly than others. She had reacted to feelings of being questioned when she was in the queue because she had felt like a second class citizen most of her life. Of course, her sense may have been right, the lady may have judged her, but it may also have been to see if she could go past her. For Nadia, the truth in the moment wasn't important, she knew she could not change others, she could only change herself, according to what her experience had revealed. Her wounds were still raw inside. In her mind she thanked the lady for showing her that these angry feelings needed her attention in therapy.

If you're not having moments of awareness, either spontaneously or by curious observation you can reflect on the reason why. You can self-assess (thus practising awareness) or speak to your therapist if you want to work on increasing your awareness.

Here are some signs you may not be using much awareness in the room:

- You tend to focus more on venting (important in therapy too!) about situations and people rather than talking about yourself.

- You talk more about difficulties and symptoms rather than actual life experiences.

- You don't bring in too much personal material.

- You don't allow yourself to recognise feelings within you. For example, the therapist annoying you, or being distant from your feelings (Way 6: Allow feelings and watch what hinders them).

- You spend little time bringing into the room what you felt, thought or did in relation to experiences.

- You focus all or most of your attention on fixing things outside of your control, or things that you can only influence (can be very important too!).

Possible signs you may need to bring in more awareness into your process:

- You cannot explain why you feel the way you do.

- You feel stuck or haven't met your goals. By nature, therapy is about your truth so if your goals have not been met or you feel stuck, that could be a sign that there is more awareness to come.

- You cannot explain your behaviour—for example, controlling, avoiding or aggressive.

- You cannot describe the way you express yourself in therapy—for example, analytical, feelings-focused, venting, reflective, careful or insightful.

Strategies for building awareness:

- Practise being present and expressing what's happening in the here and now (see Chapter 3: Tool #5: Here and now).

- Practise using focusing and mindfulness techniques (see Resources section of this way).

- Practice "catching yourself" as Nadia had.

- Write a reflections diary at the end of each day or as things catch your attention.

- Notice any mismatch between what you say and what you feel or really want to say. If you find a mismatch—that is being aware. For example, I am aware that I am listening to someone but don't want to.

- Notice your body and mind as you talk about certain subjects. For example, do you get tense talking about yourself, or does your heart start to race being more vulnerable?

- Notice feelings you have towards various people. For example, you feel guarded, excited, annoyed or angry.

- Make a note of situations where you show emotion. For example, unexpectedly when reading or watching a film, or when talking to a friend who has had similar experiences to you.

- Notice if there is anything you push away from being brought up in session. For example, filling in silences or not wanting to be in therapy.

- If there is a lot of talking and little silence in the room, slow things down to allow awareness to surface.

- Be curious about your process (see 'Awareness of process' below).

Awareness of process

A significant part of the work you do with your therapist is to understand what lies beneath your words and actions. This can occur naturally where you speak and the therapist hears and experiences what you say. You build awareness of your world and so does the therapist.

Awareness can also be used to notice any inconsistencies between what you say and what may be going on deeper inside, or in what you really think and feel. Knowing how you really feel is not always easy as it may be hidden from you and/or the therapist. Understanding what is below the surface of feelings and behaviours is sometimes called "awareness of process".

Here is an example of awareness of process outside of the therapy room:

> Imagine you challenge your partner because he's been grumpy and short-tempered with you over the past week or so. You ask them continually what is wrong and they continue to answer, "Fine. Just fine".

> However, because you know them, their tone and body language, you believe there is more to it. Although you are asking what is wrong, your process may actually be, "What's the point in this relationship if he won't trust me with his feelings?" Therefore, the content is the question and the answer, but the real issue is NOT the content; it's the process that "he does not trust you." Awareness of what you really feel, that is "What's the point" comes through self-awareness.

> Of course, he will have his own process going on too, such as "She doesn't really care" or even "I don't have an answer to give, so I'll say I'm fine." But the point is he may not be even aware of his process enough to say "I don't feel you care about me".

> In this case, it is very easy to see that the consequences of leaving out "process" information could deny a meaningful relationship or even result in separation. What is really going on is left unsaid, that is, you feel your partner does not trust you and your partner feels you don't care. Without this vital "process" information, neither of you know what's going on. It leaves out the possibility of understanding, empathy, care and resolution of the conflict; instead it blocks and stagnates the relationship.

This is very similar to the therapeutic process, by not being aware of significant "process" information about what's happening beneath your words and actions. In relation to therapy, the therapist and yourself, it can have unintended consequences to slow, or even halt the process of recovery. However, once discovered, it has potential to open a "royal road" for your work in therapy.

Awareness of process also applies to your relationship with the therapist and the way you express yourself. A lot of this book is about you becoming aware and catching your process. For example, you can observe after a session whether your expression tends to be analytical, feelings-focused, venting-focused, inner change-focused, external change-focused, careful, reflective or insightful.

So, let's look at a couple of examples of how awareness of process can come about in the room:

> In the process of "Am I crazy?" Louis expresses himself over the course of 10 minutes about his feelings towards his work colleagues. The therapist notices a pause where Louis changes the subject and starts talking about decorations on the wall. Something similar happened in the previous session. The therapist asks "I noticed there was a pause and a shift between your feelings. I wondered what happened for you?" Louis explains that he felt uneasy when talking for that long, and that the therapist must have been thinking he was crazy. Here the client was aware of his process so he stopped talking, but through the therapist's curiosity his process was made available to explore in the room.

> In the pattern of "I'm a good client", you may be unaware that you are wanting to perform and to please the therapist, but as you work more in therapy, you come to recognise the "mask" of being a good client has more to do with feeling scared of "getting things wrong". So becoming aware of the process of being a "good client" can get you more in touch with what's going on and so work with these feelings in the room.

> In another pattern, "relational cracks", you are consciously aware of feeling irritated with the therapist. You put it in the back of your mind, but it inadvertently infects the process and blocks you from feeling comfortable around the relationship and from being more vulnerable. You are not fully aware that this is hurting your process. The therapist is also unaware of your irritation at his suggestions. Eventually, therapy ends because it's not going anywhere. The chance to repair the foundation of therapy is lost.

> In the process "careful" you become aware that when you express your thoughts—particularly about your personal life—you rehearse what you say to the therapist in your mind first. You catch this process and tell the therapist.

In therapy, I recommend always asking, especially when your process is stagnating, "Am I aware of my process?" as this, in my experience, is a valuable tool of therapy, and unlocking its potential is a key to successful therapy. Being able to say "I don't know" is okay too because that is your process, your truth.

Strategies for becoming aware of your process are very similar to those in building awareness. Here are a few more:

- Check in with yourself and ask, "Why did I say that?" and "Is it my truth?"

- Check that you are actually saying what you intended or meant to say.

- Be aware of anything you push away, censor or exclude from saying to the therapist.

- If there was no one in the room would you say something different?

- If you get a sense of being protective or even outwardly angry or defensive ask yourself why.

- Become aware and notice any time you push away thoughts and feelings, including those directed towards the therapist.

In Chapter 5 I provided some further examples of process themes relevant to ways in this book. I hope this gives you a start in understanding the idea of "process" and the types of process, leading you to look at becoming more aware of your own process.

If you want change I recommend you develop awareness. So just be curious, notice what you say, what you don't say, what you know or what you don't know. Grow your awareness about your nature and how it reacts. If you have awareness then change is possible.

Exercises
Self-Reflection

1. Are you using awareness in therapy and life? Do you have any examples?

2. Reflect on the last time you had a conflict, either spoken or unspoken, with someone.

    a. What do you notice about it?

    b. What was your experience like?

    c. What were your thoughts, feelings and actions?

    d. Is there something you are aware of now that you did not realise at the time?

3. Provide some example of process that you have noticed within yourself or others.

4. Is awareness something you want to learn to apply more in therapy and your life?

Resources

1. Chapter 3 – Tool #2: Reflection.

2. Chapter 5 – Process themes in therapy. Provides "process" themes that are relevant to the 21 ways.

3. Mindfulness. There are many good teaching resources on YouTube for mindfulness. I suggest a search for "Jon Kabat-Zinn". Mindfulness can help you build awareness because it asks you to take notice.

Quiz

1. What is awareness?

2. Why is it so important to therapy? And even life?

3. What do we mean by awareness of process?

4. What is the relationship between reflection, insight and awareness and how do they interrelate? (See Way 9 to understand insight)

5. Can you identify any statements in this extract that bring in self-awareness? Or lack of awareness?

Over the weekend my sons came to see my husband. You know what, they ignored me and spoke to their father. I could not believe how rude they were to me. They don't know how hard it has been. Not a word. Don't they know how hard it is to look after their alcoholic father? Where were they? They are just relieving their guilty consciousness. I'm the villain. I've told them time and time again to share feelings. I'm not having it.

Way 8: Consider what makes change undesirable

Condensed idea: Explore what would be lost if you change and the difficulties you will face doing so.

Approach Variations: Applies to all approaches of therapy

In this way you will learn how all change requires you to give up something, and how that could hinder or even block your change process. You will understand three types of blocks and how to explore them further in therapy.

The three types of blocks to change are:

- Loss of emotional and material benefits as a consequence of change.
- Facing challenges during the transition.
- Loss of self-identity.

If your friend complains that he keeps getting into unhealthy relationships, and you respond by saying, "I know you want to change, but you don't really want to," you're likely to be met with a lukewarm response to say the least. However, often when you want to change, it is easy to be so focused on changing that you disregard what you could be losing, in terms of both your identity and your current benefits. For example, if your friend were to explore his relationship style he might find change is difficult for a number of reasons: Perhaps the familiarity of unhealthy relationships, he doesn't don't want to be alone, and the excitement these relationships can generate.

In therapy, you may have a clear sight of what needs to change, or you may discover it as the process unfolds, but even if you are in the darkest of positions, you can usually find something that could keep you from changing if you look hard enough. This is most starkly demonstrated when people in captivity who are abused or maltreated can, even after becoming free, find the change very difficult. They may have sympathy for their abusers, or even a need to be in their captive environment, regardless of the perceived benefits of leaving (changing) their situation. Their transition from captivity to being free is painful.

Here, are some examples of how the desirable benefits of no change can interfere with, or even completely block, change:

- If you give up on an unhealthy relationship, you'll be alone and won't have the good parts of the relationship.
- If you want a healthy lifestyle, you'll have to give up on daily desserts.
- If you want a job, you'll have to give up freedom to dictate how you spend the day.

125

- If you cut all ties to your caregivers because of abuse, there will never be the possibility of having the parents that you long for deep down.

Any change involves loss. The loss can be so vast it can be like demolishing a big part of your identity. With your loss and the difficulty of transitioning to a new version of you can come many feelings, such as fear, sadness, emptiness, or even an "existential nausea" which can be triggered as a result of being responsible for your own life.

A major challenge you and your therapist may face is when the downsides of change remain out of sight, even buried very deep inside you. I really recommend exploring change proactively, especially when the process feels like it is stagnating, so that any blocks are consciously worked upon.

If you do find reason(s) why change may be difficult, or you find that you're inadvertently blocking it, then you can congratulate yourself for finding out. Reasons for not wanting to change are nothing to be ashamed of; you can practice acceptance, and work with it rather than go into conflict with it. From there, change is possible.

Now let's look at the three types of challenge that change can bring: The loss of advantage, the challenge of transition, and the change of identity. You can use these three categories to reflect upon your own circumstances and, if appropriate, explore in therapy.

The gain of no change

Sometimes, an existing problem and its associated symptoms can have significant advantages which are sometimes called *secondary gains,* or even the less helpful term *self-sabotage or resistance*. Advantages could include monetary benefits, having needs met, personal attention, or to avoid situations that you don't like. In all cases, the problem is reinforced because of the secondary gain.

Here are some examples of the advantage of "no change":

> Joe was scared of wasps but it was nice that his wife understood his fear, cared for him and sorted it out. He gained personal attention.

> Samuel had a historical difficulty with eating food, but he also hated going to school. He knew he could avoid the worst teachers by blaming it on food issues and lack of energy. If he got better, how would he able to excuse himself?

> Narinder was afraid to get close to people. He had always done things on his own and had the persona of being an individual, an outsider, or a rebel. If he

dropped his persona of being an outsider, he ran the risk of being hurt by people as well as not feeling special.

Harry was anxious about socialising; he vowed he would do it only once he lost 12 pounds. If socialising is a fear, then the incentive to lose weight diminishes. Unknown to Harry this contributed to him not losing weight.

Margaret feels her husband won't leave her side if she continues to feel depressed or suicidal. Margaret gets her emotional needs met.

Jack gets a lot of care in therapy; if he gets better, he won't be able to get the care he wants.

The pain of change

Change may require you to face the difficulties that will be presented during the therapeutic process, which include making life decisions, facing truths, facing fearful situations, saying good bye, or experiencing emotions.

Here are some examples:

If I start public speaking and get it wrong, I'll feel ashamed and may not be able to do it. The risk of feeling shame is the pain of change.

If I go to therapy, I won't be able to hide (suppress) my thoughts and feelings any longer. I'll have to face my truth. The pain is to own the truth.

I may get myself and my family into trouble if I talk about my brother abusing me. The pain is the risk of disclosure.

If I leave my partner I will have to feel enormous guilt during the process. The pain is the guilt.

So not only look at what you lose but also the challenges and obstacles that lie in your path towards making the change. By airing these challenges in therapy they can be explored further.

The loss of you

Change can also include losing parts of your identity. It can mean saying goodbye to the parts of you that hurt or that are angry, or it may be loss of beliefs which meant so much to you.

An example, the loss of identity can be experienced by some caregivers when their child leaves home for the first time. Not only do they experience the pain of being apart from a loved one, it can also be a big change in their identity. The caregiver is faced with the loss of their role, that of being a constant in their child's life, as well as the loneliness that comes from the change. Needless to say, not all caregivers experience the separation in this way.

Here are some examples of identity or role changes that may be faced during therapeutic change:

> I know who I am now. If I change, who am I going to be? And what am I going to do? I am freaked out by it.

> I was so angry and hurt by my uncle and how he treated my mum. Now that I've let go of that anger, I feel empty and don't have a purpose.

> I have wasted so many years caring for others, but I never paid myself much attention. I feel so sad that I've wasted so much precious time. I don't know what I'll do now.

> Who will I be if I'm not alone anymore?

> I did so much for myself to get to where I am. Now that I am letting people in, it feels good but also like I've lost a friend inside—a friend I could count on even when I was lonely.

> I get into a rage when my partner disappears and goes out with his friends. If I went out with friends too, I would have to accept that we are two separate people, not just "one." It would feel sad and scary.

One way of looking at this kind of loss is to understand that the old parts are still a part of you; you can revisit those parts anytime, without the intensity of their hurt; they become scars rather than wounds. But regardless, the loss of the old parts of "you" may also need to be grieved for in the process of change.

In this way I have explained how the gains of no change can hold back your change process. By giving yourself space to discover and explore these dynamics in therapy you can gain a fuller picture of the things that stand in the way of your change, and what you may want to work on. By understanding the full picture, you can then answer, "Are you sure you want change?" Whether the answer is "yes but" or "no" you can work on accepting it, and that in itself can be the beginning of change.

Exercises
Self-Reflection

1. Think historically about things you have had to change in your life. Identify things you have been able to overcome versus those you were unable to.

2. Why do you think you were able to overcome or not overcome those "change" challenges?

3. Identify what you would lose, fear, or benefit from by not changing in therapy.

    a. Do you believe those things may make change difficult?

    b. Is it worth exploring further in therapy?

4. Consider whether you still want change. Why?

5. Reflect on how you wish to work on those change obstacles in therapy or on your own.

Quiz

1. What are the three ways in which change can be difficult or blocked? How do they differ?

2. Give an example of each type of block to change.

Way 9: Put it all together by understanding your story

Condensed idea: Take a step back in order to understand significant themes and patterns in your life and how they inter-relate with your current problems. Develop a narrative or story about your life and why you are the way you are today. By understanding how you work you can recognise what has contributed to your current difficulties.

Approach variation: Applies to all therapies but, in particular, long term therapy because you will explore in much more depth your story and how it shaped and impacted you. Insight-oriented therapies emphasise how your past and your current problems relate and even suggest sources of difficulties.

This way is about putting what you're aware of together and building a fuller understanding of why you are the way you are. By developing a story of you, you can gain significant insight or "light bulb" moments into what is going on for you, and what needs attention in order for you to direct your life now.

In this way you will learn:

- How building a story of why you are the way you are contributes to answering "why" questions.

- How sources of difficulty often link to problems experienced now.

- Strategies for becoming more insightful in therapy.

- How to recognise possible unifying theme(s) which hold you back in life.

At the beginning, unless it's a specific life event, confusion may reign over your problems—a mist over something, hiding it from view. Your problems may seem illogical, like being struck down with an illness without a reason or a "cure."

However, bring in enough insight and everything will begin to make sense; "you" will make sense, your truth will emerge, and you will be able to tell your story. What appears illogical will have logic. There is virtually always a reason for difficulties, and when there is not, you can work with what you do know.

Building a picture

Often clients seek answers to questions either explicitly or implicitly. Here are some examples of questions that may be asked during therapy:

- Why do I feel down?

- Why do I feel anxious when talking about myself?

- Why do I find it difficult to change?

- Why am I angry at the therapist?

- What purpose did my addiction serve?

- Why did my uncle abuse me?

- Why do I feel guilty saying "no?"

- Why am I scared that the therapist will think I am making things up?

- Why do I find it difficult to share what I feel about the therapist?

- Why do I have panic attacks in work meetings?

- … Add any number of "why" questions.

Here is an example where Joe feels stuck, because he doesn't understand his anger:

> *Joe had been in therapy for six months. He felt "rage" whenever he felt deceived by others. He would talk about what happened and about what he felt, but nothing that came out of therapy changed him. He was frustrated that although he had understood the dynamic of feeling that people were trying to dominate him, it only triggered more vengeful anger inside him. He would often exclaim, "This does not make sense!" He tried logically thinking about "everyone's entitled to an opinion," or "I can't control others, only influence them," but his pattern was ingrained and continued. It was as if something was missing from view, but he didn't know what.*

As you take the therapist on a journey inside your experiences you can start to gain an understanding of what's wrong—the underlying patterns and beliefs that contribute to the problem you are working on. You'll understand the purpose they served and how they hinder your life goals now. In short you'll understand your truth. Depending on what you're trying to figure out you cannot usually just arrive at an answer or an insight without expanding your awareness through the therapeutic process (See Way 7: Understand yourself through awareness).

For example, Joe spent six months understanding his feelings of anger and where they may have originated from, and then taking time to process his feelings, and understand the source(s) of his pain.

> *Although there a lot of nuances in Joe's story he came to an understanding of "how" and "why" from talking about his hostile parental environment. He realised that during his childhood he had had no personal power, and felt his father and mother preferring his siblings to him. He was able to bring out his*

truth, and realise that his true "source" of pain was in the theme of being "belittled" while growing up.

By understanding this story, and that the patterns of the past continued to apply now, he was able to get to a point where he could differentiate between "past" and "present" feelings. Joe continued to work on his feelings and over time he was able to reduce the frequency and intensity of anger whenever he felt deceived.

At other times what's wrong comes out from nowhere, you're in the midst of exploring events and you encounter a sudden flash of insight. Here Jenny describes her problem and stumbles upon an insight.

[Jenny] Whenever I get into a conflict with someone, I stick up for myself, and then I feel sorry for them as if I've done something wrong. I just want things to be okay and then I say "sorry," even though I don't feel I've done anything wrong. I do this so much. I even remember with my dad, whenever I didn't go along with what he said, he would sulk for days not talking to me … it was my mum who said to me, you need to sort it out and say sorry to dad. I always ended up saying sorry….. [A-ha…]

Jenny has joined the dots and come to a realisation that because of her own past experiences of having to say sorry, she continued to do so in the present. The reoccurring pattern of "It must be my fault" came to the fore and she could relate that to a number of relational difficulties as an adult.

Building an understanding of patterns in life, and why these patterns began can be likened to trying to complete a complex and multidimensional jigsaw puzzle. It's a puzzle no one really gets to totally complete, just like learning any complex subject never finishes, but with enough of the pieces in place you can have a pretty good idea of what the picture represents. Obviously, with more pieces, you will gain a deeper understanding, but as long as you develop the appropriate areas of the jigsaw, you'll be moving your process along. With insight you come to understand why you are the way you are, sort out what's useful, and thus what change you want to work on.

Strategies for building insight

So how do you find and place the jigsaw pieces in practice? In many cases as you've seen from the examples here insights just happen from "doing" therapy and therefore no new learning is needed.

However, if you're curious or facing challenges in your process, you can reflect on whether you need to develop more of an insight-oriented mindset. If you're not discovering new things about yourself, and you want to change, that could be a sign that you need to become more insight focused.

Here are some signs that you may need to develop more of an insight-oriented mindset:

- You're not able to explain why you are the way you are.

- There are pieces of your life you don't understand.

- You don't understand how your life experiences contribute to your problem.

- Your problem relates to things that you cannot control, yet you're stuck or looping around trying to control external factors, such as family behaviours.

- You are not making any progress and feel stuck.

- You use therapy more for venting about others and events, rather than turning inwards to look at yourself.

Regardless of your unique experiences and circumstances you'll often find that underlying historical difficulties and life experiences connect in some way to problems you're experiencing in the here and now. When I talk about difficulties, quite often people assume these are very apparent difficulties, like traumatic experiences, divorce or grief, but difficulties can also be subtle in nature. For example, a difficulty could relate having everything done for you, or not being given the freedom to learn. These could all be classed as "difficulties" if they relate to your current problems.

Overall historical difficulties can usually be categorised as:

- Not experiencing enough empathy or acceptance.

- Lack of an emotional role models to make it safe for you to have an emotional world.

- Relational difficulties with caregivers and family.

- Being controlled, including over protection. For example, a time when you were not able to learn to help yourself.

- Traumatic life experiences.

- Living in a hostile environment of blame and criticism.

- Lack of belonging to a group, including family.

- Fear and shame-based feelings.

- Not being validated as an individual self.

- Being neglected. Neglect can often feel normal, but can be insidious.

- Life events such as divorce, bereavement, or work stress.

Overall, other than just trusting the process doing therapy and using the ways in this book, particularly using awareness (Way 7: Understand yourself through awareness), there are two additional ways in which you can start to become more insight focused.

Linking past to present (and vice versa)

You'll find that by understanding sources of difficulty in the past you'll be able to link them to your current problems, or you'll find that your current problems relate to your past experiences. In Chapter 3: Tool #3: Join the dots, I provide some techniques on how to join the dots.

Taking a step back

Another key to being insightful is to take a step back from time to time and you ask yourself, "Why would it make sense for me to be the way I am? How does my suffering impact my life?" and "Where else have I seen these patterns of difficulty before?" In Chapter 3: Tools #4: Reflection I provide some techniques on how to be more reflective.

In the remainder of this section you'll learn about common sources of insights with examples. You can then reflect on whether there are any areas which resonate with you, and so would like to focus on in therapy. Insights can come from:

- Life learnings and experiences
- Relational experiences
- Conflicting feelings towards change
- Association.
- Examining new or existing memories.

Insights based on life learnings

What you learn in life can be something to explore in order to determine how it has contributed to your current problem(s).

Here are some simple examples of how insights about learnt experiences from the past could shape your *limiting* beliefs (those beliefs that way how we see ourselves and others) and manifest as difficulties in the here and now (read either left to right or right to left). Remember you will have to work through your own unique experiences, so don't use these unless something resonates.

Learnt experience	Limiting beliefs in the here and now	Insights/difficulties now
I could not ask for help so had to help myself	*I must be self-sufficient* *No one will come if I need help*	*Keeping people away* *Hard to develop meaningful relationships*
I cannot decide anything unless my father approves it	*I'm helpless to help myself* *I want other people to tell me what to do in life*	*Cannot make own life decisions without help* *Passivity and helplessness*
Home is scary because you get blamed and told you're bad a lot	I can't take risks Making mistakes is bad	Dampened feelings I want people to tell me what to do in life (fearful of using your own voice)
I always perform poorly e.g., school, sport, having friends, being social	I don't belong I am not as good as others Feel helpless to help myself	Anxiety Seeks comfort over change (avoids rejection) Perfectionism
My family neglected me	No one cares I can't move on until my family says sorry	Difficulty trusting relationship Stagnation in life

When you try to figure out your underlying limiting beliefs, they can be hidden from view because it's not a thought pattern that says, for example, "I need to be self-sufficient." You'll need to explore your feelings, behaviours and history to experience or work out any limiting beliefs. Often a question like "What are your feelings saying?" can be a good starting point.

Life learning and limiting beliefs are restrictive when they contribute to your problem and prevent you from achieving what you want in life. Of course, historical learning and beliefs do not necessarily mean they are problematic, ultimately you have to decide.

Life learnings and limiting beliefs can often be seen in a positive light too (or silver linings):

- My need to control and be perfect allowed me to be self-sufficient and so leave toxic relationships behind.

- My past gives me a purpose in life. For example, I can channel my anger towards those who bullied me by supporting others suffering similar problems.

- Because of my strict childhood routine I learnt to have discipline in life.

- My difficult childhood taught me to read people at work and what they might be thinking.

Insights based on relationships

Relational themes can often be traced back to early childhood, based on experiences with caregivers, family and your environment. How you experienced relationships in the early years can become a theme that follows into adult relationships too (sometimes called attachment style). This is a reason why I suggest that if you have relational problems, explore them by comparing how you feel about the therapist too.

Regardless of how or whether you can trace these themes in your development, they may include:

- Distrust of relationships. You tend to keep a distance from or feel anxious about relationships.
- Indifference to relationships. A push-pull style where you want deeper relationship and then don't want the relationship.
- Dependant relationships. Where you allow others to be more important and take responsibility for you.
- Misanthropic relational style. Where you don't like other people.

Here is an example of Musa becoming aware of the relational patterns he learnt growing up:

> *Musa was in therapy and talked for a number of weeks about his difficulties in relationships, in particular his mother being emotionally unavailable to him. It was only through exploring his relationship, in particular about how he felt pity, rather than a heartfelt want or "missing," that he realised his behaviour in other relationships too. His way of developing relationships as an adult was to "pity" them and be the rescuer, rather than because of a heartfelt connection. This "pity" feeling was what he sought or thought what was expected from him, rather than deeper connection and love. He had to*

relearn how to experience heartfelt feelings without needing to rely on being an emotional crutch for others.

Insights based on blocks to change

When looking at patterns in life it can often be useful, particularly if you're struggling, to understand why it could be difficult to change because of what you would lose. Whenever you change you do lose something, whether it's a relationship, having less free time, or dropping the hope of having caregivers who care. So exploring the loss can be as important, if not more important, than looking at the change you want. See Way 8: Consider what makes change undesirable.

Insights through association

By seeing your life as a timeline from now to the past you can link patterns of experiences of thoughts, beliefs, images, feelings or even body sensations to similar past experiences.

Here is an example of how someone may come to develop new insights through linking similar feelings and situations from one event to another.

> *During the week I noticed something that I hadn't really thought about before. I really noticed that when I am in a silent room and there are people outside who are laughing, people having fun, my heart automatically sinks, and I get a tinge of sadness and anger together. I have always felt that way but did not think about it before...it's something familiar that I hadn't understood before {later he became more insightful...}.. I can see now as a child how I felt lonely; I would stand in a corner or sit quietly, and no one would come to ask me if I wanted to join in. I felt lonely, and rubbish. Am I still waiting for someone to come and rescue me?*

Here the sinking heart feelings, sadness and anger become associated with past feelings and experiences, simply by sitting with the feeling and letting the mind associate it with previous similar feelings (See also Chapter 3: Tool #3: Join the dots).

Insights from new or recalled memories

As you explore your feelings and open up, new links and associations form in your mind, which can bring up new memories that you had either forgotten or did not realise had happened. Memories and images of events can provide a window into the way you were, what you learnt and what you're still carrying inside.

It can also be the case, such as with adverse childhood experiences, that you encounter suppressed or traumatic memories you had no idea about. Although they could be distressing they are likely to be an important part of the work you do with the therapist. If you experience these types of memories speak to your therapist if you're ready.

Unifying your themes – the helicopter view

Once you develop a good understanding of your story, your patterns, why you are the way you are, and how these relate to your difficulties, you can begin to look at yourself from a higher vantage point. You can now ask what is holding you back against what you want or need (See also Chapter 3: Tool #8: Express your needs). You may find that all your patterns and themes come down to one base belief or feeling which is holding you back.

Here is an example of how Musa came to understand the unifying theme that held him back in life:

> *Musa had been having relationship difficulties with a push-pull style of relating, where he would want relationships and then not want them. He had grown up being controlled and made to feel guilt for going against his parents' wishes. Overall he had felt unsafe from their harsh judgement and criticism. He felt he was loved conditionally and lived in an unsafe environment where "boys" had to be strong and feelings were not allowed.*
>
> *He worked out that the limiting beliefs which stopped him connecting with his partner were "don't be vulnerable" and "don't trust relationships," and underpinning this was his unifying life belief that "no one really cares."*
>
> *He could now understand how these beliefs limited his ability to have a fulfilling relationship. His reluctance to show feelings conflicted with being able to establish a deeper relationship because it was a prerequisite for him to feel cared for as an adult. He would work on that conflict in therapy. Eventually he would come to take responsibility for developing the relationship he wanted. He now knew deep down that no one else could do it for him.*
>
> *His unifying belief "No one cares" now changed more to "I have to do my share of trying to get the care I need." It does not mean his older beliefs did not come back along with his sad feelings, but he accepted that as being part of life, and in time those low points became less frequent and less intense.*

Now you, too, can look at the underlying beliefs you may have in your life that may be holding you back and underlying your difficulties so that you can work on them.

Exercises

Self-Reflection

1. Explore the types of emotional, behavioural and thinking patterns you've frequently experienced in your life. See categories of difficulties above for ideas.

- o Emotional patterns. For example, lack of receiving emotional needs, feeling worried or being validated
- o Relational patterns. Secure, anxious or untrusting relationship patterns
- o Social patterns. For example, neglect, lack of friends, social networks.
- o Behaviours. For example, avoiding conflict, engaging in aggression or addiction.
2. How do these patterns relate to your problems now?
3. Do you have a unifying, limiting belief that holds you back in life? What is the one thing that underlines all your difficulties?

Activity

1. As you look across all your life what have been your major life themes?
2. Write a short autobiography.
3. Are their things you have learnt that hold you back?
    a. Write down a set of beliefs which have moulded your life and continue to mould your life.
    b. Write down what learnings or beliefs have been helpful or no longer serve you.
4. Write how you would like your story to unfold.
5. Ask someone you trust for feedback on what they believe holds you back.
6. Work out if there is a single unifying missing need or belief that causes you the most difficulty.

Resources

1. Chapter 3 - Tool #2: Reflection
2. Chapter 3 - Tool #3: Join the dots
3. Chapter 3 – Tool #5: Therapeutic processing
4. Way 8: Consider what makes change undesirable

Quiz

1. Name three types of insight that can occur in therapy?
2. What can you do to help someone become more insightful?

Way 10: Peel back the layers

"Homecoming means having a reunion with parts of you you've missed, avoided, disliked or exiled. Bring yourself back home and then you can really celebrate homecoming"

Condensed Idea: Brings in all parts of your personality and go as deeply as possible into exploring these parts from multiple perspectives including your own judgements of them. By bringing all your parts together as a whole, you become your authentic self.

Approach variation: Applies to all therapies but in particular long term therapy because you're likely to have more time to explore more parts of your personality.

Who you are, your experiences, your identity, your roles and your history can be seen as having both breadth and depth. The whole of you can be viewed metaphorically as an onion with multiple layers, and within its core lies your most vulnerable and authentic self. In therapy, particularly longer term therapy involving deep-rooted problems, you may need to peel back the layers to reveal more of yourself, while simultaneously working with your feelings. Through that process you can make contact with parts of you that have been left behind hurt, disliked or avoided, or because you did not know were there.

In this way, I will take you through the most important things you can learn to help you peel back the layers; becoming vulnerable, taking down your masks, and understanding your personas, as well as exploring parts that you are hiding from or disconnected from. From this vantage point you can look at all your parts, understand what they mean and bring them together as an authentic whole.

Terms used in this way

Parts are a way of labelling aspects of your personality, identity, and life stages. For example, parts could include inner child, the good daughter, the free child, the envious or dark parts. Parts can provide a useful way of exploring the personality and understanding how they relate to one another. For example, my caring part dislikes the envious part of me.

Masks are a type of part used to hide elements of your personality. We all wear masks as a normal part of life because not all parts are appropriate or needed for all settings. Masks are also part of your personality, but they could equally be false, or hide parts of your true self, thus masking off your difficulties. For example, a "joker" persona can be used to mask the fact that you're in a dark place, or a "puritanical" mask can be used to hide disowning your sensual part. Through therapeutic exploration you can see how all parts, masks and personas function together.

Going deeper

Clients can often be confused when peeling back the layers. However, if you focus on ways such as Way 5: Allow feeling and watch what hinders them, and Way 7: Understand yourself through awareness, and the ideas here—particularly on vulnerability—you should be able to peel back and reveal more parts of you, and explore deeper your own judgements about yourself.

To kick start the process of peeling back the layers, I recommend making a mental note of anything you leave out of the room that feels difficult or icky, or a part of your personality that you're fearful of talking about, then use that, if you're ready, as a source for reflection. Another suggestion is to focus on your life events and experiences, rather than only analysing your story of how you are the way you are, because therapy is an experience, and too much analysis can also lead to paralysing the process (thus the term analysis is paralysis).

Contrary to popular belief, going deeper into feelings is not about making you cry or having to feel pain. Everyone experiences depth individually: for some it's about insight and completing their understanding (Way 8: Put it all together by understanding your story), for others it's about allowing all parts to be explored— even those they don't like—to allow them to be free, made whole and eventually accepted as authentic parts of you (Way 12: Weave in ideas of acceptance and responsibility).

Of course, you may encounter painful feelings, difficult emotions and even suppressed or forgotten memories. Looking deeply and broadly into your personality will require a good relationship with the therapist, as he/she provides the foundation and environment which allow you to do the work. The quality of the relationship comes to the fore when working in depth exploring the deepest parts of your personality.

Sometimes people can have inner blocks or protective layers that they are not aware of which may need to be understood in order to get to deeper layers. If you're struggling to reveal more parts of yourself it's something to talk to the therapist about. One strategy is to talk about the protective parts of you that prohibit you from going further.

Let's look at a condensed example of peeling back the layers. Andrew generally puts on a mask of having "nothing wrong" so has to work hard to peel back the layers.

> Andrew: I have been having some dark thoughts and have been losing interest in the last few months. I don't know why. I am not the person I was. Things have not been that good; work is a bit shaky, my sister-in-law died five months back, and then a few weeks back my son had a work accident, luckily he was okay.

Therapist: Ohh. That's a lot.

Andrew: Yeah, it was but it's okay now. I don't understand why I'm still struggling with these thoughts or why it's still happening.

Therapist: It's hard to see what's happening.

Andrew: Well I do have trouble with my son, he is quiet difficult. But he's a good kid. He's okay now. I do feel guilty sometimes about me being his dad. I blame myself about the fact that I left his mum and moved on and had another family [pauses for a minute]. Well what do we do now?

Therapist: Well, I notice you want to get it all fixed, which is understandable. I wonder if it's ok to stay with the feelings you were talking about and see what happens...? [pause for a minute].

Andrew: Well I do get impatient a lot. I see that in my son too. Maybe that's my problem [smiles and pauses]. Everything has to be done quick. Whenever I tell him off for doing something without thinking he just says, "Well, I'm like you then aren't I?"

Therapist: He feels like you.

Andrew: [His facial expression changes from smiling to sadness]. Yes I am full of guilt, I wanted to stop this with me. I hate the fact that I have given him something of me. Something I didn't want. I hate myself for it [getting angry]. I wanted to end it with me and now my son has it. I am such bad parent!

In this example, you can see how the client peeled back the layers going from stating his symptoms and their impact, turning to the therapist for answers, and then eventually going metaphorically downstairs into the basement of his feelings. Here, he started to express more of his anger at himself for not being there for his son, and to blame himself for passing on something "bad", like a disease to him. So within that process he went from "I feel sad and this is the problem it creates," to turning to his own judgement of himself for being bad, and the guilt of "passing it on" to his son.

Andrew loathed the impatient part of himself and so that part could not be allowed to come into awareness—to be explored, understood, and for the anger heard. The impatient part of him and its purpose could be understood out in the open: when and why it serves him, when it does not serve him and so on. In this process he took down the mask of "nothing wrong" to let authentic feelings rise and be shown in the room. He went from displaying his social norm of being okay and in control, to being vulnerable. He surprised himself by the feelings he had deeper down. Perhaps later on he will come to realise why he has the mask of "nothing wrong", why he holds on to impatience, and why he loathes this part of himself so much, that he regrets passing it on "biologically" to his son.

So by working on taking down your masks in the therapy room and allowing your most authentic self to be seen by you and the therapist, you can separate your true self and the parts that serve you from those that don't. Metaphorically it's a bit like collecting pieces of a broken cup in a cloudy tank in order to reconstruct it. First you have to put your hands in to the tank and feel around to see what's there, what fits, and what does not. You may find parts, debris or pieces of rock that look like they are part of the cup but on closer examination they are not and you discard them. After a while, the pieces start to fit and the cup becomes more recognisable as a whole. The pieces are now constructed and although it's not the perfect cup, and it doesn't look like you thought it would, its ok, it is what it is and that's okay (See Way 12: Weave in ideas of acceptance and responsibility).

Courage to be vulnerable
"Embarrassment is the feeling that I did something wrong; Shame is the feeling that I am wrong" (Brene Brown)

What do you imagine it's like to be courageous? Perhaps you think of fighting in a war, a parachute jump, or public speaking. These are all very courageous activities, particularly if those things scare you, but there is another type of courage that is internal: that of overcoming an internal struggle to be able to reveal and talk about parts of yourself that you find difficult or even shameful to explore. These parts may represent behaviours, memories or what you believe about yourself; they are typically deeper feelings. You may find it hard to talk about having an affair, spending time in prison, feeling guilty for being a "bad" daughter, being envious or of having obsessional thoughts. Courage of this sort, if you're ready, is the inner courage of the heart, to allow the authentic parts of you to finally breathe and be allowed into existence. It can be the key to unlocking your process of healing.

Parts can remain hidden from you and from others because of fears of their acceptability if exposed, even to yourself. For example, you may have developed a protective wall to keep people away from your personal life because you experienced personal matters being continually being used against you; so to fit in, you've given up revealing any of your personal life, even what you did at the weekend, or your hobbies. You can call this the "suspicious" part of you. But you have to ask how this serving you now. This wall may have been useful in stopping further hurt at the time, but is it useful that you're hiding so much of yourself, including from friends and family?

Here are a few examples of how vulnerability may sound like in the room. The first example is a way of moving away from being vulnerable and delving too far into your actual hurt; instead, you seek to focus in on "wishing the feeling away" by trying to find logical solutions to fix the feelings:

> "My mind is so irrational. I get angry so quickly when someone does not include me or ask me a question or ask me how I am. I lash out in anger and it takes me a while to recover. I feel bad that I get angry, so I end up apologising. This pushes people away so I just need to think differently. It's no one else's responsibility to care about me, it's not good, and my reactions are over the top. I am listening to a lot of meditation exercises just to balance myself."

In the second example, a client is allowing himself to be vulnerable by exploring how he really feels deep inside when anger appears:

> "There is something I wanted to talk to you about for a while. I just find it really difficult to say because it feels so irrational and not normal. You know when I was saying I felt hurt when my friend does not seem to care about me? It reminds me of how… well, of how I have never—I can't believe I'm saying this out loud—truly been part of anything. I don't feel heard, and I just feel invisible all the time. I was controlled by my family and the church, and I was never allowed opinions. I just didn't matter to anyone. No one accepted me and I was bullied at school for years. I try and I try, but deep down, it feels that people see something defective in me, inferior or not worth it. I just end up being a listener but it hurts real badly because no one seems to care about me. It's almost as if I don't exist."

Sometimes, you may find revealing anything about yourself can be so deeply entrenched, that even if you wanted to share more, you cannot, it's as though you are fighting your mind and body which has other ideas about you even attempting to share.

> Julie explained how it felt to her any time she had to confront her feelings. First, a strong feeling would appear in her gut. It felt scary, like a numbness. It felt so overwhelming that her mind would go blank and then she felt that she had to escape the situation and distract herself by doing something different. She said she tried to stay with the feelings but her mind would shut down on her behalf.

Being vulnerable is showing up, facing the feelings and fears, letting go of inner protections, allowing yourself to be free, and showing your human fragility. This, in itself, can be a powerful therapeutic agent for change.

Self-reflection (vulnerability)

1. When was the last time you felt vulnerable?
2. When was the last time you were vulnerable in front of others? What happened?
3. How does vulnerability feel for you? How vulnerable do you allow yourself to be?
4. When are you the most vulnerable?
5. Are you feeling okay about being vulnerable or do you feel a bit scared?
6. Would you like to be more vulnerable in therapy or within relationships? If so, in what way?
7. Are there things you feel ashamed about? That you would not want to disclose to the therapist? Why? Are they related to your goals?
8. Do you need help being vulnerable? Can you broach being more vulnerable by just talking about your feelings of vulnerability with the therapist?
9. If you want to work on vulnerability, develop a hierarchy of vulnerability. Draw up a list of vulnerability tasks based on easiest to worst so you can practice vulnerability. For example, an easier task may be sharing that you found something difficult, while a more challenging one could be sharing what you don't like about your body.
10. What is the worst that could happen if you were vulnerable with the therapist? Or with others?
11. Do you feel ashamed that you are fearful of being vulnerable? That's okay; take it in small doses or stages. You may not need or be ready to be more vulnerable until you feel safe enough with the therapist.

Unmask the self

We all put on masks. They help us fit in and stay safe in multiple situations. Being in therapy is an opportunity to work on understanding your masks, removing them and baring all parts of you, including any that the masks hide. You may feel shame, fear or even disgust at yourself, but by being out in the open without your masks, you can work on the problem you are experiencing and show all sides, including your darker side, which is causing inner conflicts and difficulties.

Here is a narrative of someone who had not been ready to show all of himself to the therapist:

> For a number of sessions, Dave had taken charge in therapy and worked efficiently through his issues, finding solutions and answers. However, it was only when he let go of the mask of "always be productive" that the therapist got to know and understand him more. Deep down, he felt a need to hide that part of him that felt "depressed" and "not understood". He used the mask as a way of covering up his feeling, because no one likes someone who "doesn't do things". He was presenting part of himself, rather than the whole. He began showing more of who he was rather than what he thought he should be.

So what masks can you have? The answer is any that you feel exist in you: the good client, the appeaser or pleaser, joker, hero/anti- hero, formal, professional, controller, romantic and independent/self-sufficient. Masks are used to help you fit into your surroundings and so are a normal social occurrence; they can be part of your self-expression. Certain masks are appropriate at certain times, so they aren't inherently wrong. For example, at work you need to wear the controller mask, at a social event you could wear the joker mask. Certain masks aren't appropriate for certain settings, for example you wouldn't wear the joker mask during a formal business presentation. Not all masks or even any masks are fake, they express parts of who you are.

However, by allowing these masks to be understood and to be taken down in therapy you can get to know their purpose better, to understand what serves you well and what does not. The problem with masks is that they can be tiring to wear, particularly if you never get to take them down, or they are false, or they deny the authentic parts of you. By understanding how your masks work, and by taking them down, you can work on healing parts of you which you may have deemed unworthy

If the mask's purpose is to hide parts of you, then the work will involve becoming more aware of the mask, because it is probably something you once needed—or perhaps still serves a purpose—rather than something to disconnect from, suppress or disavow.

Here a few simple examples of how a mask may operate:

- "Puritanical" masks the sensual part of you.
- "Good daughter" masks the authentic part that wants to be a "free chid".
- "Joker" hides you having to share personal parts.
- "Righteous" hides the deep-seated parts which no one cares about or loves.
- "Funny" in therapy hides your deeper emotions from the therapist.

As well as using masks to hide authentic parts of you, masks can also be used as a compensation for other difficult feelings or unmet needs. For example, you may put on a mask of "ruthlessness", but deeper down it is masking parts of you that felt no love. By being ruthless the feeling of power actually compensates for the feeling of being loved. It's the second best option.

Self-reflection (masks)

1. Do you feel you can be you? Reflect on differences between work, family, friends, therapy or other settings. Note: Carrying multiple personas (or masks) is a normal way for us to be. We may present ourselves very differently depending on the situation.
2. Ideally what type of persona(s) or parts would you like to show most of the time?

3. If you feel you can't be you a lot of the time, reflect on the reasons why.
4. What persona(s) do you carry in therapy or in various settings? Here are a few ideas:
    a. The good client, The appeaser or pleaser, victim, joker, hero/antihero, assertive, angry, emotional, shy, controlled, romantic, independent/self-sufficient.

Scenario: Watch for the "good client" mask

Therapy may make you feel an internal pressure to perform well. But therapy isn't an exam or an interview where your performance will be judged, or you'll necessarily achieve the best outcome. If you try to perform well by saying or doing what you think the therapist requires from you, then it could hinder your process.

Being "a good client" is the equivalent of wearing a mask, showing a side of you, while hiding others. For example, if you feel a need to please the therapist for fear they will "dump" you, it is easy to see how it will hide the vulnerable parts of you that you're fearful of showing.

If you have become aware of feeling you need to be a good client, then it's an opportunity to explore in therapy. You can reflect on what the need is to be seen as "good", and see if it links to your difficulties. Usually, at the heart of this need lies fear, the fear of being seen as you are, being judged or rejected.

Of course, therapy relies on your engagement to want to work on yourself, but therapy does not intrinsically require a particular standard or ideal for you to satisfy your role. It's about working with you as you are, including wanting to be a good client. If you're busy trying to be good, then try to be the bad client.

Self-reflection (the good-client mask)

1. Do you feel a need to please the therapist?
2. In what situations in your history have you had to please people, and why?
3. What were the benefits of being good and pleasing others?
4. What are the downsides of being the "good client" or pleasing others?
5. Are there parts of you that would seem "bad" or "unacceptable" if you were to take down the "good client" mask? Which parts?

Work with your parts

Parts are fragments of your whole personality, identity and history. Examples include child parts, envious part, Asian (cultural) part or neglected parts. Parts can be a useful way of exploring yourself and understanding conflicts within. A conflict occurs when parts oppose each other, for example, a part of you wants to socialise but a part of you wants to save money.

By becoming more vulnerable and unmasking yourself in the safe place of therapy theses parts of you come into your awareness. When you do this you will likely realise what their purpose is, their story and how they relate to your difficulties. By healing, assembling and putting parts of you together you can become a whole. From that point acceptance becomes a possibility (See way 12: Weave in ideas of acceptance and responsibility).

The parts you find more difficult to disclose may be very important to your recovery. By embracing the darker or more difficult parts, you have the opportunity to resolve any conflicts and feelings that are associated with them, or that have caused you problems. Getting to that point is a process which may involve working on other areas first, such as vulnerability and your relationship with criticism and shame. Some of the parts that people may find difficult to share include:

- Hate, rage and murderous fantasies
- Envy and jealousy
- Darker dreams and fantasies
- Secrets
- Affairs
- Sexual addictions and harmful sexual behaviours
- Gender, sexuality and identity issues
- Sexual performance issues
- Taboo problems including incest
- Previous criminality
- Love or eroticism towards the therapist
- Suicidal thoughts
- Self-harming
- Difficult behaviours such as stalking or partaking in dangerous or risky behaviours
- Controlling behaviour of people and partners
- Violent behaviours
- Criminal activity
- Family secrets
- Online offending

As long as your disclosure is not seriously harmful to yourself or to others (See Chapter 1 Disclosure), you may find a lot more doors open up in your therapy. Regardless of outside social norms or expectations, therapy is an opportunity to work though the things in your life that you feel you need to be open about. In embracing feelings about darker parts you, there can be light.

Disconnected parts

Parts can remain disconnected from you, on the periphery of your awareness or completely out of sight as they were for Clare.

> *Clare was a survivor of childhood trauma. She had witnessed the death of her father at the age of five and since then had led a chaotic life engaging in risky behaviours because she felt worthless. She often wanted to nullify her existence and used drugs to numb herself out. She was used to staying in bad relationships where she suffered physical, emotional and sexual abuse.*
>
> *Whenever she talked about her past and what had happened, it was for short periods, and it felt like they were distant stories that happened to someone else, not her. It felt like she was trying to push a float underwater to stay with the difficult parts of her life, but whenever that happened, she would unconsciously go back to talking about the everyday problems and how they could be handled. The float would rise to the top.*
>
> *It was only when the therapist pointed out to her that he wanted to know her in a deeper way that she began gradually, over a year, to talk about the difficult parts of her feelings: pain, anger and loss. The loss of her father, the self-blame for not escaping her abuse, and her wish that she had died not her dad. The deeper healing process had begun. Although she had managed to stay clear of these feelings in therapy and in life by focusing on life goals, she was now learning to embrace the difficult feelings in order to heal. This focus was needed because, unconsciously, her mind was protecting her, as it had done in the past, through fear and panic. However, these feelings had lain dormant until she bravely faced the process of healing.*

Through the therapeutic process she came to uncover the parts of her that were previously out of reach, lost and avoided. The parts of her that felt "guilty" to be alive and the "promiscuous" parts of her she felt ashamed of were allowed to be experienced.

Not all parts come to awareness easily, it's a process, and the more you try to focus in on deeper feelings towards yourself, your worth and your experiences, the more likely any disconnected parts come into view. Bring all your parts home.

Differentiate between the real parts and the idealised parts

You can see yourself or individual parts of you in two different ways: the real-self (or authentic true self) is who you truly are, and an ideal-self is who feel you "should" be. The ideal can present as a goal such as getting a promotion, losing weight, or it can present as an internal ideal, such as being serene and not losing your temper. Having an ideal-self is a natural form of forwarding yourself in life, based on desires and goals.

However, because of life experiences, outside pressures, and the need for social acceptance, you can forget the real-self in favour of an ideal self because parts of your real-self become unacceptable or shameful. You feel there is a fundamental flaw in the real-self because you feel strongly that you "should be" living up to the ideal, even though it may be unrealistic, impossible or just not you.

Here are a few examples that signify the partial loss of the real self in favour of an illusionary ideal self. In this first example, the ideal almost takes over the true self:

> Sabine grew up feeling weak. She was bullied throughout school life, her studies were affected and she did not fit in to any group. During adolescence, she would often fantasise about being someone else, perhaps a traveller around the world, part of the "cool" group, or a great artist. None of those things were true in reality. But in her mind, and in the world, she presented "as-if," she actually was some of those things. She would continue to be false to people even as she got older. She would pretend that she had a "glamorous" lifestyle and hobbies. This was all an act, even though it still felt real. She could hide her real self not only from others but from herself too.

Sabine believed her true self to be deficient and unlovable, just as others had treated her. The ideal becomes the person she felt she "should" be rather than was. There is a clear distancing of her true self, perhaps based on feelings of self-loathing, where the true parts of her are exiled into a place that cannot be found; banished as being too shameful. Her life learnings and social conditions gave birth to the ideal-self to protect her from being an outsider who did not belong. The false-self became so embedded in her personality that it carried on into her adulthood, making the true parts of her harder to reach. The issue here is that she had lost herself in favour of an ideal.

In the following example, Harry pushes away his real-self in favour for being liked and not having to take responsibility for his own life:

> Harry had grown up in an environment where he was never trusted to make his own decisions. He was not allowed to perform activities or take part in new experiences because he was deemed too "fragile and weak" by his caregivers. He learnt to feel not safe enough to learn from his own mistakes. He compensated for this by always trying to fit in by being a "good boy" for his parents. He may not have been good at things his peers were, but he was good at being good.
>
> Now, as an adult, he was afraid of saying what he felt, giving opinions and making a decision. Whenever he had to make a decision he would call his dad in case he got it wrong. When meeting people, he always put on a big smile; after all, "no one likes someone who is miserable," he said. Harry

believed that he needed to put on the fake smile in order to fit in and be accepted. He had learnt to be "good" while growing up and letting everyone else do the talking, and so he would not be put in the "spotlight" of life. His true self was largely hidden from the world; no one knew how low and sometimes angry he felt in secret. All this led to him feeling helpless, frozen and unable to make the simplest of decisions. He had learned not to trust himself and therefore was not in a position to take responsibility for his life. All this pretending was just so exhausting.

In the following example, Max had set his ideal so high that he "should not" fail:

Max's ideal self-image was based around being academically excellent. He worked hard, attending classes and completing work on time; most of the time he was used to being top of the class. Max felt good because he lived up to his ideal. However, when his studies begun to suffer after a road traffic accident, he felt he was a loser and was letting everyone down. He sank into deep sorrow as he found himself middling, no longer top of the class. The mismatch between his ideal and his truth caused him so much anxiety that he felt he would rather not submit any work and fail, rather than do his personal best. He ended up leaving the course abruptly because he couldn't face being just good enough.

All these examples show how the authentic or true self can be replaced by an ideal self in response to life's situation, which can affect you in psychologically damaging ways. The ideal in these cases completely replaces a gentler version of "I would like to" with a tyrannical "I must, otherwise I am unacceptable." This unacceptability represents a dictator despising the real you for not being the ideal.

You can check out if there are any unrealistic ideals in your language. Phrases like "I should be" or "I ought to be," may, under careful scrutiny, reveal your harsh ideals. Here are some examples of "should" statements which represent ideals that are unrealistic or "tyrannical":

- I should not make mistakes.
- I should not get angry.
- I should not be weak.
- I should always be happy in front of people.
- I should not say anything negative about people.
- I should be a size 8 (size 14 now).
- I should always be good at anything I do.
- I ought to be wealthier by now (in comparison to Elon Musk!).

Demands in this context can feel tyrannical or like a dictator insisting on the "wrongness" of who you are, unless you meet the demands of an ideal. You are the judge and jury, there is no room for manoeuvre to a reasonable ground so the true self is exiled and held for ransom unless the ideal is met.

The true self may need to be uncovered in the therapy room first because change can only truly happen if the true or real self can be revealed, understood and accepted. Living in the reality of your truth, rather than the ideal is at the heart of the therapeutic process. This does not mean the false parts are wholly false—they may be an expression of you or what you would like, but when they dominate, hiding the real you, your feelings and needs, it can be damaging.

Therapy in this case can be seen as a unification process of the whole (sometimes called holism), by revealing yourself, being vulnerable, taking off the masks, finding disconnected parts and examining their meaning. You may find a way to live not based on an ideal or perfection, but by living with the whole of you as you are, in your truth, directing your life from that point, and in doing so finding a path to emotional health.

You are *you* regardless of what your mind may do to protect you from pain by offering up ideals and masks, or by breaking off parts into an unreachable void. There is only one of you and there is only one of me, and no one can be anyone else. Bring together your parts as a whole, heal and recover your authentic self. Bring yourself home.

Self-reflection (idealisation)

1. Look in the mirror. How do you see yourself?
2. Close your eyes, take a few breaths and get in touch with your own perception of your true-self.
   a. What do you think of your body?
   b. What do you like about yourself?
   c. What don't you like about yourself?
3. Do you feel a dislike of any part of yourself? Why? How does it make you feel?
4. Close your eyes, take a few breaths and then let your mind go to an ideal you, in the future.
   a. What does it look like? Get in touch with your own ideal concept.
   b. Think about your inner ideals (e.g. becoming calmer) as well as outer ideals like job, relationships, and career.
   c. What will you have to do to achieve your ideal? Is your ideal realistic?
5. What do you notice about the true and ideal "you" that you have envisioned?
6. Can you differentiate between "you" and your "ideal"?
7. Does the ideal serve or hinder you? How?

8. Write down any "should" or "ought to" statements you are known to make. Are they realistic or false ideals?
9. How do you judge your true self? For example, is it gentle like comparing yourself to a friend or a child, or does it feel harsh and hard?
10. How do you think your true self and ideal-self have developed and why?
11. What change would you like to make now?

Exercises
Self-reflection (parts)

1. Are there parts of you which you find difficult to talk about? Do you understand why?
2. Are there parts of you that you don't show to the therapist? Examples are: funny, apathetic, impatient, or resentful.
3. Which parts of you compensate for other parts? For example, feeling in control at work could compensate for having no control in your relationship.
4. Do you have parts which need to be healed or are wounded?

Self-reflection (disconnected parts)

5. Are there difficult parts of your life experiences that you find hard to talk about or admit to yourself?
6. How much do you talk about things that were missing from your past?
7. Do you think any of the things you find difficult to embrace are related to the problems you are experiencing?

Activities

1. Use Appendix G Johari window to label the parts of you that you and your therapist know about, and those parts that the therapist does not know about you yet.
2. Understand whether the parts that you have not shown your therapist would be useful to explore or contribute to your problem.
3. Describe the feelings these hidden parts of you emote.

Quiz

1. What are the benefits of being vulnerable?
2. What do we mean by parts?
3. Name the types of mask people can people wear. When can they be useful?
4. What difficulties can we can experience if we wear masks?
5. What can be the consequences of wearing masks for too long?
6. What do we mean by disconnected parts?
7. What do we mean by idealised parts?
8. How do you differentiate between the authentic and the inauthentic self?

9. Why can revealing parts to a therapist be difficult?
10. What do you think wholeness or integration of parts means?
11. Why can wholeness be difficult?
12. Why can wholeness be an important part of the process?

Way 11: Seek your truth and then seek "the" truth

"If thinking is easy then feel; if feeling is easy then think"

Condensed idea: Check your thoughts and feelings to see if they are based on reality. Work on adjusting any inaccurate assumptions you find over time.

Approach variation: Applies to all therapies, but cognitive-behavioural and solution-focused therapies emphasise rational thinking as part of their theoretical approach.

During your therapy, you may be doing your utmost to share feelings, develop awareness and understand your story. This process can take time, because you're not only trying to understanding yourself and your truth, but also working on what inhibits you when expressing your true feelings.

However, feelings that were previously dampened down, minimised or ignored eventually come to the fore. As much as that process can be crucial to your recovery and healing, it is important to learn that both your feelings and thoughts, while they represent your truth, do not necessarily represent the whole truth or "the" truth out there in the world. In short, both feelings and thoughts can misrepresent reality in a way which doesn't serve you.

In this way you will understand why your truth and reality can differ, and how they could cause difficulties in therapy, as well as in life, unless explored and rationalised. This way does not imply that you should invalidate your feelings. If your car is overheating it is overheating, and if you're angry you are angry—that is the truth in that moment. However, modifying the intensity of your feelings also comes about as a result of changes in perception, embracing feelings, unlearning and reality testing your thoughts.

Why we can make false assumptions

So why can feelings be true, but also not be true? Simply put, the basis of our feelings and thoughts can be influenced by past experiences rather than reality: what we learnt or what hurt us.

Imagine you were going on a walk and encountered an animal you've never seen before, walking towards you on the loose. You don't have time to stop and think, so your mind reacts quickly based on an assessment of the danger. You can't stop and spend time on assessing, thinking "let me see, what do I know about this animal? Is it really a danger?" Our past threats and experiences provide our minds with data for assessing danger quickly based on feelings. This is a crucial survival tool we possess, without which I doubt if I would even be able to write these words for you to read.

However, for all the praise we give our minds in helping us survive, it is not "smart" enough to quickly discern between learnt, triggered threats and the reality of the present situation. Ideally, the mind would be able to inform you in rapid time the truth of a situation, i.e. a risk asssesment based on reality which can be expressed as "I've seen this threatening situation before, but wait, do not to worry about it now because this situation appears safe".

This reactive process may come out not only in daily life, but also with regard to the therapist and your process of therapy. Here is an example of how a client reacted to their own feeling without checking all perspectives, thus abruptly ending therapy.

> Jim was always stressed at home, and he wondered why he became antagonistic when he felt he was being challenged by people—by their opinions and views. He described it as something he could not tolerate, and he would become belligerent if he did not get his way. But behind the feelings was a sense of "feeling ashamed to get things wrong," which was causing fractures in his relationship and his own self-worth.
>
> These feelings also came out five months into therapy when his therapist charged him a cancellation fee for a session, in accordance with their contract. He said to the therapist, "Well, I'm not paying that. I don't think it's fair; it's not my fault! I'm not carrying on then."
>
> If Jim were to explore his feelings, he may have linked them to the problems he was exploring, which in turn would have given him a "live" way of looking under the cover of the issue. However, the decision to quit therapy robbed him of a chance to reality test the feelings (See Way 20: Don't walk away from therapy without talking to the therapist). Were his feelings based on reality or were they based on past learning (threats) in his life?
>
> A good therapist would have been able to accept his feelings as valid, and would have worked with Jim. That is not to say that Jim was not free to end therapy, but it's also an opportunity to heal something which, on the surface, appears to be very similar to the problem he wanted to work on.

In the following example Alison relates to how she felt at a party with friends. In this case she changed her own subjective truth through a process of truth seeking by bringing in other perspectives:

> "I was out with my friends and I went to the bathroom. I returned and all my friends had moved to a different table as a prank. But when I came back, I felt really angry and shouted at everyone; I thought it was really mean. The feelings were overwhelming and confusing at the same time.
>
> Later on in the session she linked her feelings to this insight:

> *"The feeling I had over the weekend was as if I was back at school with people laughing at me or ignoring me. I felt so alone and angry. I went home and thought, what is the point of me trying anymore?"*

> *Once she had taken a step back, she brought in other perspectives which were missing, that her friends were considerate of her feelings, which balanced her feeling her friends were "mean girls".*

> *"You know they do care, they are always there for me when I need them. They were just fooling around after drinking. I just could not see the funny side, and they did all say sorry [pauses]. I'm not over stuff from my past am I?"*

In another example, Jo came to a couple of sessions of therapy, but decided the therapist was not for her. It appears that she made this decision without checking out her feelings.

> *I felt the therapist staring at me, it felt hard. I didn't know what to say. It felt as if the therapist was judging me. He must have been thinking about how terrible I was at therapy when he could be working with others who have it worse.*

This could have been an opportunity to build the relationship, check out her feelings and assess whether they related to her problems. Perhaps if further reflection had occurred, Alison would have received the insight that the therapist really wanted to help, was accepting, and welcomed her feeling the way she did. Of course, the therapist may not have been the right one, but no room was given for that to be explored and validated. Her assessment to leave was based on her subjective feelings rather than validated reality.

I recommend anytime you have strong feelings towards your therapist or therapy to express them, but also be open to exploring them once they have subsided. These examples show how feelings and thoughts may or may not be absolutely true, because of learnt experiences.

So what's the answer to this dichotomy in practice: My feelings maybe true, yet may not be absolutely true? Maintain a balance between respecting your feelings, exploring them and also testing out their logic. Therapy is a safe place in which to explore and reality-test feelings and thoughts, and to bring in new understanding. So first, have your feelings, that is what therapy and therapists are there for. However, also understand that this is an opportunity understand the feelings further, to assess whether they relate to your problems, are completely valid or no longer serve you.

For an introduction to reality-testing thoughts and feelings through rational thinking see Chapter 3: Tool #6: Rational thinking.

Exercises

Self-Reflection

1. Have you ever experienced thoughts or feelings that were based on assumptions you found were not quite true? For example, on what someone said or did?
2. Do you find it easy to deal with conflict? Why?
3. Do you believe your therapist will be able to accept your feelings about them and work with them?
4. Do you generally find it easy or difficult to think logically, taking in all evidence before judging a situation? Or are you more prone to react fast? Do you reflect on fast feeling-based reactions after the event?
5. What thoughts, feelings and actions do you tend to react fast with? Is there a pattern associated with reacting fast, for example, authority, loss of control, being ignored, cannot find the right kitchen tools?

Activity

1. Do you have any thoughts or feelings about the therapist or about people with whom you can check out in reality, for example, with a partner or friend you feel safe with?

Resources

1. Chapter 3 – Essential tools that make therapy work (Chapter 3: Tool #6: Rational Thinking)

Quiz

1. Why can subjective and absolute truth be different?
2. How can you use rational thinking to differentiate between subjective and absolute truth?

Way 12: Weave in ideas of acceptance and responsibility

"You can have hope, you can have dreams. But if what you hope for doesn't happen, do you want to move forward or stay tied to the past?"

Condensed idea: Change happens as you move towards accepting yourself and taking responsibility for your life. Therefore, learn to weave these ideas into your therapeutic process.

Approach Variations: *Applies to all approaches of therapy*

In this way, you will learn the relationship between acceptance, responsibility and change. You will learn:

- What acceptance is and how it can help.
- Types of acceptance: self-acceptance, situational acceptance and acceptance of loss.
- Reasons why acceptance can be a difficult.
- Strategies for becoming more accepting.
- How to use acceptance in therapy.
- How self-responsibility and acceptance can link to catalyse change.
- How change can manifest in therapy.

Acceptance is the acknowledgement of reality. It is a *process* of letting go of a belief that anything could be different, whether it's about yourself or about situations— past, present or pending. Acceptance isn't giving up on change or approval of situations, it is a process of working on reducing your suffering in relation to whatever is causing it.

Acceptance is not something that needs to be forced or made a goal of, because acceptance may be a consequence of the natural unfolding process of therapy, which could include areas of non-acceptance. For example, you may have experienced adverse neglect and abuse, and you're not—or may never be—ready. Acceptance should not be seen as a doctrine that you must move towards, bypassing what you really feel and believe (Way 6: Allow feelings and watch what hinders them). If you don't accept, or aren't ready to turn towards acceptance, you can accept that too.

However, if you believe you're ready to actively work towards acceptance then read on. Here is an example of something you may be familiar with, to demonstrate how non-acceptance could be detrimental. The same principles apply regardless of the severity or forms of suffering described in this way, and regardless of whether they are situational, the result of a loss, or about yourself.

> *Imagine that you are running late for an important business presentation. Traffic is going at a snail's pace due to roadworks, and the traffic lights are*

against you. If you get aggressive towards the drivers and the workmen, it isn't going to get you to work faster, it will just get you stressed and upset. However, if you learned to accept the situation, you'd be resolved to working within it, and have more mental space in which to efficiently navigate yourself to work quicker. You accept the situation as being out of your control. By being less stressed you're also in a better position to do the best you can when you arrive for your work meeting, perhaps even making a joke about it when you begin your presentation.

This example demonstrates how any type of non-acceptance can consist of two types of suffering. The primary suffering— in this case, that of being late—and the secondary suffering, that of being stressed and its consequences.

In this way, quite often I use the term *loosen the grip* or *let go of* rather than *acceptance* because the label of acceptance can imply, even though it does not mean it, approval, or forgiveness of actions. Neither acceptance nor forgiveness approves of bad actions. Approval or forgiveness, either of self or others, may be a part of your process, but I do not want to imply that those things are a must for healing either. Another reason for using these terms is to show that acceptance is not binary, you don't either accept or not accept; acceptance can be seen as anywhere between these opposites. There are degrees of acceptance which may vary over time.

So in therapy, if it makes sense, you can apply the idea of "loosening the grip" to anything you cannot control or influence because there is nothing more you can do. "It is what it is" is an oft-quoted phrase which means while you don't approve or think the situation is healthy, you understand that you cannot do anything more because you cannot control or influence the situation any further.

That is not to say loosening the grip is easy: it's a process, and certainly a part of that process will be to sit with the uncomfortable feelings, giving them space and time to be experienced. It's for you to work out based on your unique set of circumstances and beliefs whether acceptance is an appropriate path for you, as well as the degree of acceptance you are willing to afford.

Scenario: Self-acceptance

At some point in the process, you may start to feel more accepting of yourself as you are, whether it's certain parts of you, your past or the present situation. When you become more self-accepting, you embrace all or parts of you, not just the bits that you or others like, but all parts of you unconditionally and completely. Self-acceptance can include how you feel about your body, a past mistake, parts you feel ashamed of—literally anything that drives your mental representation of who you are.

It does not mean that you don't want further change in yourself—it is not a resignation letter—it means that you recognise your constraints, strengths, weaknesses and even the darker parts of yourself as your truth. The knowledge of any limitations does not interfere with your ability to accept yourself, warts and all. With self-acceptance, you see the reality of yourself, and work with—rather than against—yourself. You develop self-understanding, care, and compassion towards yourself absolutely and unconditionally.

Self-acceptance—just like acceptance in general—should not be mistaken for approval. Approval may go hand-in-hand with attaining self-acceptance, but it's not a necessary condition. You don't approve of errors you have made or things you could have done differently, but rather accept them as being part of you. Acceptance can have a "that's me" or "it's who I am" quality to it; it embraces who and what you are without resorting to self-attack or losing yourself to masks and ideals which are far removed from your authentic self.

When it comes to acceptance of your errors, you see things as a whole, and find an empathic balance between taking your fair share of responsibility and recognising other perspectives, because in reality it's unlikely if you look deeply, that you were either solely or completely responsible for a particular matter. With acceptance you look towards yourself not as right, wrong, good or bad but as shades of grey. By accepting your errors and, if you can, resolving not to make the same mistake again, you set your heart free from shackles that keep you bound.

From a therapeutic perspective, self-acceptance is regarded by many as a cornerstone in the change process, sometimes called the *paradox of change* which states that change can only occur as acceptance begins. Regardless of any theoretical arguments for acceptance, it is clear to see how judging yourself less can lead to less mental pressure and liking yourself more. How you actually get to acceptance is a process, not through any words you say, but a felt response and an internally held belief. It can take many iterations of working on various parts of yourself before you feel deep down that you can accept yourself partially or wholly. And of course, if you can't, or don't want to, you can accept that too!

Acceptance of parts

In Way 10: Peel back the layers, I introduced a way of describing parts of your personality and differentiating those that are authentic versus false ones. Acceptance of parts of yourself, is something to work on in order to deliver further self-acceptance. Here is an example of Josephine getting in touch with an authentic part, and beginning the journey of self-acceptance.

> *Josephine had worked on understanding her need to appear grandiose in*
> *front of others and on understanding why it was there, the purpose it served*

and how it was not an authentic part of her—it was an illusion that kept her from surviving her upbringing because she felt small and without capability. It was not who she really was, even though it did feel like it at times. Instead she turned her attention and feelings towards her authentic self, the girl that "did not belong", who was rejected and felt not good enough.

It hurt a lot for the next few months, but her self-understanding and self-care increased over time. She lay in her bed nurturing her wounds and said "It's okay, I'm here for you now." Rather than that part of her being hidden or rejected, she began the process of accepting it, and in doing so becoming less grandiose.

Scenario: Acceptance of situations

Imagine a frustrating or difficult circumstance, such as being in a long queue, being late for work, or seeing a friend struggle in a toxic relationship. Your relationship with these circumstances could be one of anger, tension or worry. However, if you were to achieve some degree of acceptance of the situation—it is happening and it is frustrating but you cannot control it—you may be able to find a way to reduce your stress. It does not mean you approve of being in a long queue, or being late for work, it simply means you let go of wanting the situation to be different, you understand it is not under your control or influence, so you can either suffer further or you can work towards loosening the grip it has on you.

Metaphorically, non-acceptance is like holding a harness you're pulling on really hard, getting cuts, blisters and sores, but then you realise you don't need to pull so hard because in reality, using that extra strength does not actually help you, so you resolve over time to gradually loosen the grip so that it feels more comfortable. You don't necessarily stop holding the harness, although that is an option, it's just that you realise there is little value in pulling so hard.

Here are a few more examples where the process of acceptance can take away frustrations and distress:

- I will need to spend time and money on therapy. If I accept that fact, I will be less impatient and give myself space to recover.
- I am not having a good night out. If I accept that fact, I will feel less sad and frustrated. I may even end up having a better time.
- I have lost my job. If I accept that fact, then I'll feel better and so can focus more on my plans.

It's not that you like what's happened, but because you can't control these situations you may well decide you'll be better off working on a process of accepting the situation.

Scenario: Acceptance of loss

Losses occur in life, and come in many forms. A loss can relate to any kind of external or inner change, for example a bereavement, the end of a relationship, realising the loss of childhood, loss of a possession, your identity, an idea or held belief.

Acceptance of loss can be seen as a process of coming to terms with reality and resolving to live within it. Just like all forms of acceptance, it does not take away the difficulty, but can diminish the surrounding intensity of emotions that cause suffering, whether it's shock, guilt, denial, frustration, or blame.

Here is Harry's idea of loss, that of having a good enough mother:

> Harry was an only child and was now an adult with his own family. He came to therapy to explore feelings of low mood. Therapy quickly turned to his own childhood and questions of whether there was something underlying his low feelings. When he explored his experiences over a number of months, he came to realise that he lived with a stern and emotionally unavailable mother. She demanded the best from him and when he did not meet expectations, he would feel her energy of disappointment and would often be told to "go away". Over a six month period he realised how much of his life decisions were based on trying to please his mum, whether it was work, relationships or spending time with her.

This was the moment he shifted towards accepting the reality of his relationship with his mum:

> He took a deep sigh and put his head down pushing his hair back and said with a forced smile coming from the corner of mouth, "maybe all I wanted was her to hug me?" He looked up towards me as blood rushed to his face and his eyes became swollen, holding back his tears he asked me "it's never going to happen now is it?" I looked back at him, feeling the moment with him in slow time. At that point he realised deep down the true nature of his relationship, and so begun the process of grieving; that is working towards accepting the reality that she was unlikely to be the mum he wanted.

> He worked on his feelings over a period of time and resolved, at least for the time being to accept there would always be part of him that wanted her approval, and so honoured his feelings rather than ignoring them. But through acceptance he had loosened the grip on his strong need for his mum's approval, and instead turned towards directing his own life, not just as a way of pleasing his mother, but pleasing himself too.

If acceptance is about living in truth, then it must also extend to whether or not you accept something. Because acceptance is a process that involves feelings and beliefs, it is an error to simply state "I accept x", when in reality once explored you realise deep down you don't actually. You can only really accept if you believe it deep down. Harry was courageously able to recognise that parts of him still wanted his mum's approval, and another part of him knew deep down it was not likely to be met. Inside this truth he was able to separate his own needs from those that were directed towards pleasing in mum. Not only did he start to please himself more, but now he consciously knew when he wanted to please his mum. He accepted that he could not completely switch off his need.

Non acceptance as acceptance

In some cases, the pain may be too great to let go even a small amount, and that is okay too. It's not mandatory to loosen the grip in order to get what you need out of therapy, but it is a consideration. You can see letting go as a continuum between the harnesses held with a vice-like grip to being totally dropped. You should not feel pressurised to have to "let go" when you're not ready. You can accept the non-acceptance.

Sometimes, people convert the energy of their pain into a worthwhile cause. For example, many parents who have suffered a child's death may divert some of that pain towards meaningful work to prevent what happened to their child from happening to others. Some of the energy of suffering moves through them into another destination.

Reasons acceptance can be difficult

The path of acceptance is not usually plain sailing, you may be working on experiences that have, or continue to be, extremely distressing. If you're finding it difficult to gain a degree of acceptance, you can explore your reasons in therapy. In most situations you'll find your reasons fall into a few of the areas below:

- You're not ready.
- You would feel guilty, disloyal or bad for accepting.
- Acceptance would feel like giving in or disrespecting someone's existence and your relationship with them.
- You judge yourself based on certain behaviours e.g. addiction, rather than the whole of you that has many other qualities.
- You attack yourself or do not treat yourself as well as you would do others.
- Your standards of what you "should be like" are very high and almost unattainable.
- You hold unexplored negative emotions towards parts of you, such as a bullied part, or a darker part of you where you feel shame or guilt.
- You have grown up in environments that were harsh, oppressive or critical.
- Caregivers did not communicate a message that you were okay and acceptable regardless of your behaviours or achievements.

- You would have to let go of your identity of holding on to a state of non-acceptance (See Way 8: Consider what makes change undesirable).

Strategies for becoming more accepting

Although acceptance is a process you may go through in therapy, here are some strategies to help you during that process.

Understand how non-acceptance impacts your wellbeing

Get in touch with your feelings by tuning in and experiencing your suffering. Understand fully how being emotionally attached to what causes you pain affects you not only in the moment, but on a day-to-day basis, whether it's in your relationships, your direction in life or in being calm and free. Ask the 'wise' part of you to advise what course of action to take.

Watch out for self-attack

You can be curious about the way you treat yourself, your language and actions. First you need to catch these thoughts and then you can, through a process, adjust them to something kinder, less harsh and reality based. Sometimes people use self-affirmations to begin the self-acceptance process. For example, "I am okay as I am", or "I can be kind to myself" which are repeated as a way of consciously building up ideas of acceptance.

Bring in the all perspectives

Try and see the reality of the situation fully. Rather than seeing circumstances, people and yourself as completely right or wrong, allow all perspectives to enter your consciousness so you can get the fullest picture. Explore in as much depth as possible in therapy.

Imagine if it were happening to a loved one

If it were happening to a loved one or a friend imagine what you would say, feel like or do to reassure them. Now try to direct this compassionate mindset toward yourself. If you find you cannot do this for yourself or others, work on that in therapy and ask yourself why you or others don't deserve compassion.

Practice mindfulness

Mindfulness is the practice of being present in reality. It can be used as an exercise to practise loosening the grip, to obtain mental space between whatever is happening, rather than being taken away by the waves of thoughts and feelings. The next time you are in a frustrating situation you cannot control, see if any usual feelings of frustration or worry can be turned down a notch, simply by focusing in on the senses such as sight, smell, or sound, in the moment, and then allowing your thoughts to come and go as you focus your mind on your breath.

There are many good teaching resources on YouTube for mindfulness. I suggest a search for "Jon Kabat-Zinn."

Applying acceptance in the room

As I have described here, acceptance is the cornerstone of change in therapy, and if therapy, in essence, is about living in your truth, then acceptance is an implicit theme in therapy regardless of whether it is explicitly stated. Not that it's a goal, but it's a significant part of easing worry and pain, even if it is not apparent. In addition, there are three specific uses of acceptance that frequently occur in therapy (obviously there are many others, but that will depend on you and your unique circumstances):

Gaining mental space

Acceptance can be used to give you space from experiences in the room whenever you feel overwhelmed, confused, stuck, disappointed or anxious. For example, if you're disappointed that therapy won't be a quick fix, you can work on realising that there isn't more you can do in the moment, and try to let go of the belief that you can be healed instantly.

Ideas of acceptance can be weaved in whenever you get to a point of feeling this is "too much" and when that extra pressure is not helping. Therapy can be hard work and intense; you can work to reduce its intensity by practising acceptance as one way of reducing your suffering. Keep safe and speak to the therapist if things become overwhelming in the room. The therapist may be able to use interventions such as guided visualisation or mindfulness to help you.

How much change is enough

How much change do you need to make and when is it enough to end therapy? The answer is, of course, when you feel it's enough. For some *enough* is easily recognisable, but for others it can feel uncertain. Confusion on how much change is enough can happen because of concern that you will relapse or that there may be more work to do (See Way 14: Use your feelings about endings in therapy).

The truth is that wherever you are in the process you can never come to the end of personal development, and therefore to the end of change. It is unrealistic to soothe all wounds and ghosts of the past and reaffirm your life anew. No one can escape their past and its accompanying scars, after all, your past is a part of you. So at some point you have to decide—at least for the time being—when it is time to accept the end of therapy by saying this is "good enough" change. After all, life is for living not just development and growth.

Letting go of the need to let go

Letting go is not an absolute or a panacea for change (it certainly can help!) so making a decision not to accept is a form of acceptance too. Rather than trying to change, you accept being okay with not letting go, so there is less of an internal struggle. Although you may never let go, you live within that as your personal reality. That is the practice of acceptance.

Examples where acceptance can be weaved in
Where acceptance fits into your therapy, or whether it indeed does, will depend on you and the specific content you bring to therapy. Here are some examples of where acceptance could be weaved into your therapy:

- Past behaviours and choices.
- Getting other people to change.
- Getting family to care.
- Others giving you approval.
- Others judging you unfairly.
- A difficult relationship.
- Past experiences you cannot change.
- Letting go of a need to let go.
- Whatever you deem a failing, e.g. a rejection.
- Being wrong.
- Perceived or relative weaknesses.

For each of these examples, the specific nature of acceptance will be unique to you.

Self-responsibility

Although self-responsibility and acceptance are not usually linked together as part of change, in my experience they go hand in hand. Self-responsibility comes as you begin accepting that only you can make the change, whether it's how you feel about the past, about relationships or about your future direction. Therefore, self-responsibility is a process of accepting how life is, and that only you can be responsible for yours. Of course, this does not mean you won't be supported by others—friends, family or a good teacher—or that you need to be an island to yourself, it simply means actively deciding to take more responsibility for your life.

If that lands inside you as being true, then it's not difficult to see how it could make change possible, whether it's engaging in therapy, finding a relationship or developing yourself. You relinquish any misgivings about others being able to direct your life, including inner change in therapy. Responsibility does not mean you *must* make changes either, because when you actively make a decision *not* to change you are taking responsibility for your life, you are the captain of your ship, rather than its passenger. You enter the main arena of life and decide that this is the way you're going to stand.

Accepting self-responsibility may also induce a sense of fear and trepidation as you realise only you can be responsible for your life and therefore the decisions you make. This, too, can be experienced as a loss, going from feeling less responsible to feeling more so. So exploring the theme of responsibility alongside acceptance could be beneficial in therapy, in particular exploring how you perceive the idea of self-responsibility and whether you want to work on it.

Here are some areas you could explore:

- Which parts within you and your life can you control, cannot control, or can only influence?
- Whether taking more self-responsibility could help or hinder your process and life goals.
- Whether there are any underlying fears linked with taking more self-responsibility.
- Whether you accept in yourself the level of responsibility you take for life (including whether you take too much responsibility for others).
- Whether you take too much self-responsibility. For example, due to self-sufficiency you don't relinquish responsibility, your role is built around being responsible, or you rarely move out of the mode of responsibility.

How change happens

When it comes to change, the widely held belief is that accepting yourself and your truth is a catalyst for change. This usually happens as part of the natural unfolding process in therapy, rather than being an explicit aim. But how does change manifest itself in the room? Often, clients can be confused because therapy does not appear to be doing much, so it can be beneficial to explain how change could land in practice.

Therapists often talk about the client's "mind shift" or "shift" that brings about some change in relation to events, yourself, relationships and the world, which in turn provides a continuous loop which can help you resolve inner conflicts, and allows you to feel more settled in your mind and body.

Shifts come in many varieties—small, subtle, unnoticeable or large. Usually, shifts are small, hardly even noticeable, but these add up over time, and in many cases, you can feel better and do not know exactly why or what has happened. Therefore, the shift in the process can, at times, seem mysterious.

Shifts can often come as a surprise out of the blue. Here are some excerpts of how clients felt and described their shift. In this example, the shift comes as a surprise that doesn't really make any sense:

> John had found daily life hard to manage after the death of his brother. He spent four sessions in the darkness of pain, guilt and not wanting to accept his brother's death. On the fifth session, he came in, sat down, and said, "You know what? I feel a bit better but I don't really know why. I don't know

why. What's happened?" It wasn't that he felt he had completely accepted the loss, but given the darkness he was in, it was almost a shock to him that he could, in fact, feel better able to function in life without knowing what he had actually done! But what he did was to be himself as he was: someone grieving a huge loss.

In another case, a client had worked over a year on her deep problems of rejection and abandonment from caregivers:

"I don't know what has happened really, but I feel like I'm in a better place. Before, I used to feel so angry and sad being rejected or not cared about in groups, but now, although nothing has really changed, I feel I am stronger inside, and those intense hurt feelings don't feel as strong anymore. I could not have imagined that therapy on its own would be enough."

Other times, a sudden insight, a "light bulb or "A-ha" moments can be a direct catalyst for change:

"Whenever I get into a conflict with someone, I stick up for myself, and then I feel sorry for them as if I've done something wrong. I just want things to be okay and then I say 'sorry', even though I don't feel I've done anything wrong. I do this so much. I even remember with my dad, whenever I didn't go along with what he said, he would sulk for days not talking to me and always... it was my mum who said to me, you need to sort it out and say sorry to dad. I always ended up saying sorry....." [A-ha...]

In these examples, it does not mean that nothing happened prior, because under the covers lots may have been whirring inside, causing these moments of change (see Chapter 6: Understanding the therapy process, for more background into the elements of change).

Another reason why change may sneak up on you like this is that small perceptual changes occur without being acknowledged. So for example, feeling empowered in therapy, taking more time for yourself, having less guilt, sharing feelings, and talking more to your partner all provide small but incremental changes that add up.

In this way, I hope I have provided enough perspective for you to weave in ideas of acceptance and responsibility into your process, so you can use them to clearly identify the source(s) of suffering that non-acceptance can bring. If you can become aware of that, then you can make a decision on whether acceptance is something you want to aim towards. Regardless of whether you accept or not, change is always possible.

Self-Reflection (Self-Acceptance)

1. Are there parts of yourself that you accept? Are there parts you don't accept?
2. Why do you feel it is hard to accept some or all parts of you?
3. How did non-acceptance come about? Consider your history, the environment and external pressures.
4. What do you need in order to accept parts of you as you are, rather than adhering to an ideal?
5. What needs to change for you to feel or experience acceptance?

Self-Reflection (Situational Acceptance)

1. Are there situations, past, present—or that will happen in the future—that you would like to be able to accept more?
2. Have you suffered losses that you would like to let go of more?
3. Why do you feel it is hard to accept some of these situations or losses?
4. What needs to change for you to accept these experiences more? Even by 5%?

Self-Reflection (Responsibility)

1. Historically, which areas did you feel you could take responsibility for?
2. What areas would you have liked to take more responsibility for?
3. What shaped or determined your level of self-responsibility?
4. Do you feel you should have been given more or less responsibility growing up? If so in what areas?
5. What aspects of your life do you feel you can take responsibility for now? And what aspects don't you feel you can? What are your reasons?
6. What would happen if someone else took responsibility for your life?
   a. Imagine what it would be like in 5, 10, 20 years.

Self-Reflection (On change)

1. Do you understand why therapy is more than just talking?
2. Do you have examples of when you felt changed inside but you didn't know why?
3. Do you have examples of when you had a sudden "insight" into life or therapy?
4. Do you have any examples of "insight" which took a lot of time to obtain, for example, because the understanding had to sink deeper inside you?
5. What patterns in your life would you like to change? Think about relationships, including with yourself, as well as your behaviours and activities.

Activities

1. Write a diary of emotions rooted in the past that cause you suffering in the present.
2. For these emotions write about how they impact your life now.
3. Is acceptance a path you wish to head towards?
4. Write a diary that tells a story of what you learnt or did not learn about taking responsibility.

Quiz

1. What are the benefits of acceptance?
2. Does acceptance require approval?
3. Why is it beneficial to see acceptance as a process rather than an affirmation?
4. How can you use acceptance to decrease worry about getting better quickly?
5. What is the paradox of change? Why is it a paradox?
6. Name two practices you can implement to become more accepting.
7. What can you do if you don't accept?
8. Can therapy work without acceptance?
9. Why can change happen without knowing why it has happened?
10. What could be a disadvantages to acceptance? (Hint: Inner blocks)

Way 13: Put what you learn into action

Condensed Idea: If you realise what you need to do in order to change things in you or your life then consider whether you are doing enough to realise that change outside of therapy.

Approach Variations: Applies to all approaches of therapy. Cognitive-behavioural and solution-focused therapies tend to emphasise activity as part of their approach.

In this short way you will learn the importance of applying what you learn outside the therapy room. It can be essential depending on what you're working on in targeting external tasks, activities and goals alongside the work you do in therapy. This can have the effect of catalysing your process because you can begin to build confidence in being able to overcome difficulties and achieve life goals.

Here is a possible consequence of not taking action from your learning in therapy:

> Hussan had been coming to therapy for some time. He felt he had understood himself better and had come to peace in respect of his difficult feelings for his mother who had caused him to feel worthless through neglect.

> Hussan had learnt that part of him was still feeling neglected, and what he really needed was more attention and care. But he had not put into practice any way in which he could have a chance of receiving care. He continued to devote time to work, but did little if anything to develop the relationships he craved for.

Hassan become aware of his inactivity outside of therapy and began taking steps:

> In the next session, Hussan appeared to be taking a small but important steps towards what he really needed, he said, "After last week, I started putting myself out there more. I allowed myself to chat with people. I even messaged someone I see at the gym a lot and asked him how a meeting went with his manager. It felt good—baby steps, as they say."

In therapy, you're learning about yourself and what you need, and that may require taking action outside of the therapeutic process. If it's a relationship you need, you can start to focus on being relational; if you want to have more passion towards work, you can start devising a plan to get you there, and if you feel insecure about your relationship, it may be time to talk.

Taking action doesn't just mean visible action, it could mean consciously trying to have a different frame of mind. For example, being more aware of feelings or being kinder to yourself.

Here are some examples of putting what you learn or need into action:

- If you're anxious about doing things on your own, take a small step by sitting in a coffee shop with a coffee and a laptop.
- If you want friendships, join an events group where you share the same interests as the members.
- If you want to improve your relationship with your partner, talk more about your feelings with them (see Chapter 3: Tool #10: Empathic Interpersonal Skills).
- If you want a hobby, pick one and try it.
- If you are overstretched, plan some self-care (see Chapter 3: Tool #13).
- If you tend not to hold boundaries, learn to be more assertive.
- If you want to be more vulnerable, start sharing deeper feelings (safely of course!)
- If you want to overcome a fear of birds then you'll need to set yourself some exposure tasks (with the therapist's help).

If you find there is something blocking you from putting something you have learned or something that you need into action then talk to your therapist to understand it more (also see Way 8: Consider what makes change undesirable). For example, is it a fear of the consequences or do you just need help coming up with tasks to apply? Remember, you don't have to take big steps, just take the steps you can safely make.

Taking action is a way of taking responsibility for yourself, by being the good parent that teaches you to look after yourself. So focus on putting things you've learnt into action—when you're ready of course.

Exercises

Self-Reflection

1. Is there anything you've learnt in therapy that you may need to put into action?
2. What are your needs in life? Do you need to work on them outside of therapy?
   - *Needs can be basic survival, food and water, socialising, belonging, friends, life partner, love and care, having a passion or a purpose. (See Chapter 3: Tool #8 Express your needs).*
3. Now, write about your action-based goals. You can start from easiest and work towards the hardest if it helps.

Quiz

1. Jake had suffered a trauma of being assaulted by a number of people at a party. As a result he had to take time off work. He had overcome his primary anxiety over three months of therapy. However, he still felt unsafe to go back to work because his route took him past the location where he was assaulted. He had

also cut himself off from friends because he felt they did not help him during the assault.

    a.   What small actions could you suggest that Jake could take to help himself outside of therapy?

Way 14: Use your feelings about endings

"Endings aren't separate to therapy; they are part of it"

Condensed idea: Endings are as inevitable as beginnings. Talking about endings during therapy can be beneficial, especially if you have concerns about the end or are curious to discover whether experiences of endings relate to your therapeutic work. If you feel safe set time aside to have an ending.

Approach Variations: Applies to all approaches of therapy. You may need a longer ending process with long term therapy. With short term therapy you may not have the time to focus in on all feelings about endings, but you can still allow some time. In group therapy, members are likely to appreciate you talking to them about your feelings and to say goodbye when either you or the group ends. In couples therapy and family therapy endings may involve the end of relationships with others too.

In reading this way, perspectives in favour of having an ending time with the therapist are given. However, you should only do this if you're ready, feel safe and importantly, if you wish to. You are free to choose how to end.

As soon as therapy begins, there will eventually be an ending. In this way you will learn about the therapeutic potential of endings, when to end, and various perspectives on client-and therapist-initiated endings.

In this way you will learn:

- How endings can be therapeutic.
- Several perspectives on the question of "when to end?"
- What you can reflect upon during the ending phase.
- Perspectives on whether to end silently or not.
- Perspectives on therapists initiating the ending.
- Perspectives on dependency on the therapist or therapy.

For perspectives on client initiated endings see Way 20: Don't walk away without talking to the therapist.

Endings as therapy

What if you had to stop a really good film before the ending?
What if you listened to your favourite piece of music and stopped it in the middle?
What if you watched an exciting sporting competition but never knew the result?
How would you feel?

Now. How would you feel..
If you never got to say what you wanted to say to someone you cared about?
If you never got to say how someone hurt you?

If you never got to say goodbye to a friend?
If you never got to say goodbye to someone who supported you?
If someone you loved said they wanted to say something important, but never got a chance?

Would it bother you? For many people the answer is yes because these situations are all to do with having feelings, and facing issues or concerns. But for others the thought of endings can be painful, scary and an anxiety-inducing experience. Ending may be embraced, or avoided, feelings expressed or left unsaid; either way endings will happen whether or not we choose to experience them directly.

The prospect of ending, whether imagined or initiated by you or your therapist can bring to the surface a variety of feelings. Here are some possible feelings as you contemplate endings:

- I will know when to end.
- I'll feel indifferent to ending.
- I'm anxious the therapist is going to dump me.
- I didn't like what the therapist said so I'm going to end it (whether imagined or followed through).
- I want to leave but I don't know how.
- I don't know what I'll do without therapy. I'll really miss it.
- I don't want this relationship to end. I'll really miss my therapist.
- I don't know if I'll get more from staying or from leaving.
- Should I leave this therapist and try another?
- I would feel guilty for leaving, especially after all the work we've done.
- I don't want to leave my therapist because they'll be losing an income stream.
- I am scared of losing my therapist. Last time they were late, I nearly had a panic attack.

Therapists are typically taught to keep endings in mind during the process so that they can be aware of your needs, and so that you are ready for it when it arrives. However, you can also help yourself by airing your feelings about endings during the process, or when you're thinking about initiating the ending. Feelings about endings can interfere with your process and / or they can be used as an opportunity to catalyse it. For example, if you imagine the therapist is going to "dump" you, it could be a hindrance in therapy because you aren't able to be yourself, or it could be an opportunity for exploration if you're struggling to find your authentic voice.

Endings are not separate to therapy: they <u>are</u> therapy. Your feelings, or even lack of feelings, and how they relate to your past can all be used therapeutically. Thinking about endings is also a way of determining whether you are really ready to end.

Experiences of endings

Your life experiences of endings can also be another therapeutic source to explore. You can reflect upon your experiences of endings and how you have dealt with them.

Here are some examples of life experiences related to endings:

- My husband left me and my children for my friend.
- I had a miscarriage. This is my fifth.
- We lost our family home.
- I usually slip away quietly at the end of a training course and don't like to say goodbye.
- I have lost all my family and friends now. I am the only one left.
- My father abandoned me when I needed him.
- I always say goodbye after meeting people at the end of a training course and make sure I take some contact details.
- I can end easily, sometimes I think too easily, without much reflection, even after years of knowing someone.
- My two brothers died in the space of six months.
- I am used to people leaving me.
- My friend passed away and I wasn't allowed to attend their funeral. I vowed never to have a best friend again.
- I've left the life of a bachelor behind.
- I saw my dog get run over and he died in my hands.
- I loved to dance but after my injury I couldn't dance again.

By reflecting upon your experiences of endings, you can understand what they mean to you: your underlying beliefs, and how you would have liked endings to happen, including therapy. It is not necessary to have a particular concern about endings, but it may increase your self-understanding about how you work and why.

When is it time to end?

A common theme linked with endings is not knowing if it is the right time to end. Sometimes you end for rational, well thought-out reasons, such as you don't feel the therapist is right for you, you feel worse or you're just not ready for therapy. Whenever you decide to end therapy, regardless of the reasons, you can reflect on your reasons or talk with the therapist (See Way 20: Don't walk away from therapy without talking to the therapist).

But when is it time to end in the recovery phase of therapy? You know you have improved, even beyond what you thought achievable, but you can still be left feeling confused, guilty, or even anxious about whether to continue or to end.

Sometimes it can be about the transition out of a good relationship, or you feel you may still need the therapist; after all, what if your problem or symptoms return? Other times, it could be that you'll miss having a space in which to be heard.

I would suggest giving yourself time and space to work through these feelings, ideally with the therapist, and then eventually you will be able to answer the question of whether you are ready to end or not.

A common strategy used to test out whether you are ready to end, is to allow more time between sessions, reducing session frequency and taking a break for a few weeks. If you're worried about needing the therapist you can ask about their policy if you need to return. You're likely to find that therapists, particularly in private practice, will welcome you back as long as they have availability.

Ultimately, if you're not sure, or you have strong feelings about the ending, then that can be a sign you're not ready and need to do more work before making the decision to end.

The end

If you're ready and feel safe I recommend a defined ending stage with the therapist, regardless of whether you or the therapist initiates it. The ending stage could be for five minutes, a single session or many sessions over months. If you're not used to experiencing endings, or are used to bad endings, this is a chance to change that history. An ending can be therapeutic, because it's an opportunity to say what you feel, what the ending meant and to gain closure.

Here is an example of feelings experienced towards the end:

> I feel excited, nervous, happy, and a little sad, but because of therapy I can cope with them. I'm a little sad because it feels like I'm losing a friend. I'm nervous because I don't know what the future holds. I'm also happy that my leaps and gains are far more than I could have ever hoped for. It's time to trust myself and try on my own. It's the beginning of a new chapter for me.

Here are some ideas for reflection during the ending stage of therapy:

- Your readiness to allay any concerns you may have about ending.
- Your journey, such as highlights, lowlights and turning points.
- What you found useful or not during the process.
- Your previous experiences of endings in contrast to therapy ending.
- What if feels like to end the relationship with the therapist.
- What your plans are after therapy.
- What your learnings were during the process.
- What else you would like to work on.

- How you like to end things.
- What this way of ending feels like.

Endings, especially if you have a strong relationship with your therapist can be emotion filled. However, by the end you should be ready to move to your next stage, either in life or even to another therapist. If you feel like it's a milestone then celebrating the ending together can be a gift.

Scenario: Client ending silently

You can end silently if you wish, without talking about endings. It is not that uncommon for people to stay silent about their plan to end, even if it feels like they have achieved their aims.

Here is a way of understanding silent endings from a therapist's perspective:

> A client had been seeing me for a number of months. I felt the relationship to be good and he said that he was starting to feel better; it felt like an ending could be on the horizon.
>
> For a number of weeks he sent me a text messages asking to rearrange planned sessions to which I replied with possible options. However, I noticed after a few weeks, there were longer time spaces between messages and eventually, after a few times trying to arrange a session, messages stopped coming in altogether. He ended silently; the messages just stopped coming.
>
> From my perspective, he has autonomy and freedom to choose the ending. It is what he needed at the time—he got what he needed and ended silently, I wished him the best in my heart. I also wondered why he felt the need to silently end. I reflected on the multiple losses he had suffered in his family recently and whether they linked to not wanting another ending, however positive. I would never know for sure. I also wondered whether he had ever felt a need to end, or even whether he had good role models that showed him a good "goodbye".
>
> The other part of me wondered whether it would have been something to explore, as part of his process. His need was to end in the way he did; as a therapist, this wasn't about my needs.

This example demonstrates two differing perspectives: a reason for ending silently and a reason for working actively towards an ending. Maybe the client felt he did not want to go through another ending given the losses he had suffered, and the therapist wondering whether a process of ending could have been another way of mourning the losses, or experiencing a better ending in order to celebrate and say goodbye.

There is no right or wrong answer, it's about what you need. You decide.

Scenario: Therapist ending

If a therapist ends with you they should be able to justify it and give enough time for a graceful end. Endings can surface feelings, such as frustration, rejection and sadness, and the therapist should be able to work with your feelings in relation to the prospect of ending.

In this example, a client has expressed anger towards the therapist for the ending:

> Client: I'm angry with you for ending therapy. It feels like you've given up on me.

> Therapist: I'm glad you feel safe enough to share your feelings and for letting me know you're not happy with me. What I am hearing is you are feeling rejected by me. But I promise you, that's not the case. If I were to keep you here in therapy, and I can't help you, I would not be doing the right thing. I care because I want you to get the right support. With your PTSD, I believe someone who specialises in this would be able to help you more at this stage. Does that make sense?

Naturally there could be plenty more to explore about the ending, such as the feeling of being "given up on". Good therapists, time willing, would help you work through those feelings when they end therapy.

Of course, if a therapist has ended abruptly, say through an email, that is not acceptable professional practice unless there has been a force majeure incident. Sudden endings by the therapist are usually rare but I do hear of them; I recommend you talk to your therapist if you are worried that they will abruptly end with you.

If you are in distress due an abrupt ending, seek further support (See Way 21: Get help from outside therapy if needed).

Scenario: Dependency on therapy

There are all sorts of dependencies such as chemical substance, an addictive or toxic relationship, a hobby or work. Clearly, dependency can get out of hand when you are controlled by the dependence. But what about dependency on therapy and even the therapist?

Contrary to popular belief, it is perfectly acceptable for you to feel transitory dependence on therapy and the therapist. You may feel that therapy is where you feel most cared for and understood, and you may feel the relief and reward of coming to therapy.

Consider the following statements from clients:

"Therapy is all I have right now. I don't have any support, friends, or family; I'm alone. I really need this... I'm so glad I have got you..."

"I am using the therapist in my mind outside of therapy for support and inner dialogue...I am glad to have them as an inner resource for support"

"[Inner voice] ... I feel so cared for by you... I wish I could be with you more. I love being near you... I can't think of anywhere else I'd rather be."

All these feelings are valid, after all, therapy is a place for you to draw out your feelings, needs, and desires in whatever shape or form you choose. So although dependence may be there for you, unlike an addictive substance, it does not have to be one that controls you. Therapy will come to an end, and you'll want to be able to safely withdraw from it when the time is right.

If your dependence feels very strong, perhaps based on emotions and/or an attraction; you feel you need them more and more, and are worried about the effects of ending, I recommend speaking to the therapist. If you cannot speak to the therapist you can seek further support (See Way 19 and Chapter 5: "Love in the room").

Ultimately, unless the therapist initiates the end, you're free to choose to end—for the reasons you believe are right and in a manner which you feel is suitable. You should not feel you must have a formal ending—one in which you say goodbye. It's not uncommon for clients to decide to leave without really saying why or to feel they need a formal ending.

Exercises

Self-Reflection

1. Are endings important to you at all? Do endings worry you?
2. How have endings been for you in the past, for example, work, school, university, relationships, partners, friends, bereavement, and loss of any sort?
3. Have you had bad endings?
4. If you meet a new group of people in a workshop, event or in training for a few days or weeks, how do you generally say goodbye?
5. What would a good ending look like for you?
6. What are your thoughts and feelings about your relationship with the therapist? Would it be difficult to end?
7. Would you like to end silently or experience the ending?
8. What would you like to talk about or do during your ending with the therapist?
9. If you are struggling to end even though you have met your goals, what are the reasons? Possible reasons include:
    a. You really like having a safe place to talk.

b. You feel like you would be alone or more alone without the relationship with the therapist.
c. You feel anxious that problems have not been resolved yet and wonder what you will do if they come back.
d. The relationship with the therapist is strong and you would miss it.
e. You find it hard to tell the therapist for fear of upsetting them or being criticised for leaving.
f. Dependence or love attraction to the therapist (See Chapter 5: "Love in the room").

Way 15: Don't let things stay stuck without taking action

Condensed idea: If you feel stuck or feel that therapy is not helping, use those feelings to take action. If you know why you are stuck in therapy then consider what you need in order to move forward.

Approach Variations: *Applies to all approaches of therapy*

What do you do when you feel the therapeutic process is stuck or stagnating? You may experience stagnation after some time with the therapist or at various stages, even right from the beginning. You may even be aware of the reason why you're stuck, but feel powerless to take action because you don't know what to do. In most cases the therapist may already be aware of the stagnation and will be helping you in their own way, but as with all these ways you can take action too.

In this way you will learn to identify signs of feeling stuck and strategies to reinvigorate your process, even if that means bringing therapy to an end.

If you feel stuck and would like to leave therapy but can't bring yourself to leave or talk to the therapist I recommend seeking further support (Way 21: Seek support outside therapy if needed).

Signs of stagnation

A sign that things are stagnating is when you feel that nothing is progressing, even after months of therapy, and you appear to be looping around similar content without insight or without experiencing a change. You have stopped learning and therapy feels flat, without energy or vitality; therapy could even be boring for you. On the other hand, you may still like going to therapy, and get a temporary release, but it's not producing the change you long for. It can feel easy, but you're stuck, nonetheless. You may even be using new techniques and tools, but nothing whirs inside you and you don't appear to be getting anywhere with it. It can feel like you're in a forest where no matter what direction you travel, it leads to the same point. When this happens it can be tempting to end therapy.

It is very difficult to give absolute guidance on how long it's okay to feel stuck in the hope that something may change. After all, even if you have felt stuck for many months or more, you could be just one session away from feeling less stuck and even getting a small or substantial breakthrough. Clients can feel stuck for a long time and eventually movement can happen, so there is no way for the amount of time to stay with the feeling of stagnation or when to leave. It is very difficult to give definitive advice on, other than if you are feeling that way, take some time to reflect upon it and take action.

Stagnation need not be seen as the end, especially because it can bring in new material and insight through exploring the nature of the stagnation itself. If you can pinpoint the source(s) of "stuckness", the underlying feelings and what has happened—or is happening—to bring it about, it could be a turning point in your journey. Understanding "stuckness" can open new doors.

Ultimately, on a path towards growth and healing, stagnation may be one of the many themes that underlie your difficulties. Therefore the feeling of being stuck should be embraced just as you can embrace other feelings, such as anger or guilt, to explore them rather than ignore them, as something that is wrong. However, left out of the room and out of your awareness, it can become the elephant in the room, unspoken but doing a lot to block your progress.

Therefore your stagnation becomes an important part of the therapeutic process, not a separate process. Telling the therapist you feel stuck may well be all you need to do to gain momentum in your process.

Strategies for working on stagnation

The reasons for feeling stuck are unique to you. Much of the work on exploring being stuck will require you to reflect inside yourself, your life and the relationship you have with the therapist. Although much of this book is geared around keeping your process going, and by implication not stagnating, here are some additional strategies for working with the feeling of stagnation.

Use the therapist

Talk to the therapist about your stuck feelings if you feel safe and are ready.

You can ask for a review of the progress against your aims and difficulties (Way 4: Use the therapist as a resource). You can use the review as a way of giving feedback to what you feel is missing and what you feel you need from the therapist. For example, you may feel you want more direction or even less direction, help with focusing the session or perhaps there are obstacles to you feeling safe and free in the relationship.

You can also ask the therapist what they feel about the process. Many therapists use their feelings about the process and the relationship to help you. For example, a therapist may feel they would like to know more of you, rather than just day-to-day activities, to get a sense of what is going on inside you. Others may reflect the question back to help you to consider the process more.

If you feel you would find it too difficult to talk about your feelings face to face, consider writing down your thoughts. You can send this to your therapist prior via secure email/message or take it with you to a session.

Explore the theme of "stuckness"

Relate stagnation to life in general and see if there are any similarities. For example, do you feel other parts of your life, such as work or relationships are stagnating? You can explore the nature of the stagnation, how and when it occurred, what is missing and why you feel it is occurring. If you find your life is stagnating or you have been through periods of historical stagnation then it may be well worth reflecting on, and drawing comparisons in the room. You can also relate feeling stuck to any similarities that come up from childhood, for example, lack of freedom, boredom, or lack of direction.

You can also use metaphors and imagery to express in as much detail as possible how "stuckness" feels. You can use pictures, drawings, and even stories to describe how you see stagnation (See Chapter 3: Tool #7: Stories and metaphors). For example, you may relate stagnation to a plant that is not growing. By doing this type of expressive work you may be able to get closer to your underlying feelings (See Chapter 3: Tool #9: Expose underlying feelings) and what's missing.

Another way of exploring stagnation is by reflecting on how you relate to it in therapy. For example, do you flow with it, get frustrated or even angry? Do you see it as part of the process or separate from it? Or did you expect it to happen as it's the norm in life and therapy?

Evaluate sources of "stuckness"
When evaluating the sources of "stuckness" you should not only look at yourself, but also consider whether it could be to do with the therapist too.

In evaluating the therapist, I would recommend going back to reflecting on their relational fit and whether or not you feel safe, and at ease within the relationship. You can use the EPAIY-S to assess whether the therapist is exhibiting good relational qualities. (See Way 2: Find the right therapist and approach).

In evaluating yourself, you can look at how you apply yourself in therapy, and whether there is something you could change in your approach to it (See all the ways, but in particular Ways 5 – 13, 16 and 17). For example, become more vulnerable, feelings-focused, or show more parts of your personality. I also recommend that you reflect on whether you have parts that are not ready to change and whether that contributes to or is causing the stagnation (see Way 8: Consider what makes change undesirable).

Alternatively, you may already be consciously aware of the possible reasons for why therapy is stuck. For example:

- Attraction or emotional dependency on the therapist (See Chapter 5: Love in the room).

- Difficulty sharing important information related to your problem.

- You want to be a good client and not disagree with the therapist (See Way 10).

- There is an issue within the relationship. For example, a silent relational rupture based on a disagreement, hurt feelings, anger, or based on feeling criticised (See Way 20).

Whatever you find or already know, if you feel safe and are ready, then you can explore what you know in therapy.

I hope the ways in this book will help you become unstuck, so do your fair share in therapy to keep your journey moving, however, that does not mean doing your "unfair share". If you have tried everything suggested, but something is still missing, you can think about leaving therapy. You have the right to end therapy and find someone else. If you do decide to end, you can explore your reasons for leaving your previous therapist with your current one and/or when beginning with the next therapist. Therapy is a journey, so you may encounter a number of therapists along the way. Moving on should be seen as a stepping stone rather than a failure.

Exercises

Self-reflection

1. How long have you felt stuck in the process? Can you talk to the therapist? Is it a relational issue?

2. Does the feeling of being stuck seem familiar to past experiences, for example, those from childhood or in your current life?

3. What are the source(s) of "stuckness"? You may want to write in a journal, use art or have an internal dialogue to understand it better. For example, does it relate to:

    a. Lack of hope or meaning?

    b. Difficulty being vulnerable or showing all sides of yourself?

    c. Feeling safe and trusting the therapist?

    d. Feeling that the therapist judges you?

    e. Feeling the need to perform and be the "good client"?

    f. Are you worried about being vulnerable or getting into trouble?

    Look at the quick start guide at the beginning to scan the ways for other ideas.

4. What can the therapist do to help you? For example, be more directive or use several interventions.

Quiz

1. Name three reasons why stagnation may occur.

2. Name three strategies for working with stagnation.

Way 16: Do your fair share in building a good relationship

"Swimmers learn within the safe container of a pool; clients learn within the safe container of a good therapeutic relationship."

Condensed Idea: You can do your fair share in building a good relationship with the therapist. But building a good therapeutic relationship is different to how you build other relationships.

Approach Variations: *Applies to all approaches of therapy.*

There is a consensus in the therapy world that a good therapeutic relationship is a vital foundation for change, otherwise, you could be on shaky ground. Given the relationship is so important to the outcome, you can do your fair share in building and keeping your relationship on track.

However, building a relationship in therapy is unlike building relationships in life. It does not mean catering for the therapist's needs or getting to know them better. Your fair share involves talking to them about anything that interferes with you feeling safe or trusting the therapist, and, if possible it involves being ready to forge a meaningful therapeutic relationship with them.

In this way your will learn about:

- Strategies for building the relationship.
- Whether the therapeutic relationship can be meaningful.
- Example relational concerns.
- Ways to approach the therapist about relational concerns and conflicts.

Strategies for building the relationship

Regardless of the type or modality of therapy, your therapist will very likely be working on building the relationship with you. Therapists know that if you feel genuinely accepted and understood it can lead to a good relationship being formed and thus provide the best environment in which to explore your innermost thoughts, feelings, pain and fears. Just like any other relationship, you will not want to share deeper feelings if you don't feel safe in the relationship. Similarly, trust and safety in the therapeutic relationship are qualities which usually build over time.

Building a good relationship does not mean being a "good client" (See Way 10: Peel back the layers), doing more than your fair share where you ignore or take responsibility for poor practice (See Way 19: Watch out for inefficient or poor therapy), or accept everything they say. It's more about telling them what you need, what makes you feel unsafe and what interferes with your therapy.

You can do your fair share in developing the relationship by:

- Working on accepting their empathy and care when there is no inherent reason not to. Of course, if you can't accept their empathy, talk to them about it.
- Telling the therapist they are not giving you what you need in sessions. For example, more direction, focus, silence or even help using therapy (Note many therapists may help you focus in on the questions rather than answering them directly).
- Talking about and clearing any relational blocks you have with the therapist (See below as well as Way 20: Don't walk away from therapy without talking to the therapist).
- Talking about any strong feelings you have, whether anger, dependency or love towards them that interferes with your process of recovery or may lead to you experiencing a difficult or harmful end to therapy (See Chapter 5 – Love in the room and Way 14: Use your feelings about endings).
- Notice anything that interferes with you feeling the relationship is meaningful. For example, you may not be able to believe your therapist's care is genuine when they are being paid (see below for a perspective).

If the therapist is doing a good job, you feel they are helping and you appreciate it, you don't have to wait, you can tell them. They can receive feedback about your relational experience and what is or is not helping you, rather than them making assumptions. But remember you are not there for them, but if you feel it, it can only reinforce your relationship. Therapists are human, they are not impervious to a bit of appreciation.

Just because you don't have a deep or caring therapeutic relationship with the therapist does not mean that therapy will not be useful. A different way of looking at the suitability of the relationship is when there's nothing consciously interfering with your process, and they meet the EPAIY-S competence criteria (See Way 2: Find the right therapist and approach). If you feel there is something missing, talking about it can be a good way of building the relationship because you're being relational, transparent and genuine within it.

Can the relationship be meaningful?

In my experience many clients have problems recognising the therapeutic relationship as a caring or meaningful one. Usually it's to do with therapy being their job, money changing hands, the one-way nature of the relationship as well as its well-ordered boundaries.

You may feel the therapist is paid to care, pretends to care, or because they have other clients, you wonder how they could care about you. The truth is, the therapist is usually paid and will most likely have other clients. Ultimately, therapists are human and will have expenses and bills to pay, like most other people.

One way of reflecting on this concern is based on your own experiences. Are there people you have cared for where you were paid? Is it possible to care for many people simultaneously? Like friends, family, or clients? Can you "fake" care? An oft-quoted phrase in the counselling world is, "You pay me for my time, but my care is free," because you can't force someone to care by paying them; humans simply don't work that way.

If you feel the therapist cares, maybe it is because they do and they have a lot of passion and heart in working with you, so feel free to allow yourself to feel the care. If you have doubts about their care, talk to them and see what comes up. You can use this as a springboard in your healing. Forging a meaningful relationship can be just what you need to heal.

Scenario: Exploring relational concerns and conflicts with the therapist

If you're experiencing safety or even care with your therapist, congratulations; this is the result of the work you have done with the therapist. You have allowed the therapeutic alliance to be built, you should feel proud of this achievement.

However, if there are some relational concerns which are interfering with you feeling safe, or trusting them, you should consider disclosing how you feel to them.

Examples of client's relational concerns

At some stage in the therapy relationship, particularly if it is long-lasting, you are likely to experience some feelings and moments of anger, hurt, anxiety, disrespect or other negative emotions towards the therapist, or you may perceive your feelings being minimized. However, as with nearly everything described in this book, nothing is negative in a strategic sense; it's all grist for the mill and an opportunity for you to learn more about yourself as well as build the relationship. Here are feelings I often encounter with people in *therapy coaching*.

- I felt the therapist minimised my feelings by offering suggestions for why I feel this way when all I wanted was to be heard and understood.
- I feel my therapist is not in tune with me and interrupts my train of thought, blocking what I want to talk about.
- My therapist keeps changing the time of my appointments at short notice.
- I found out that my therapist is a trainee and I think she should have told me at the beginning.
- I worry about whether my therapist is good enough.
- My therapist often doesn't say anything and waits for me to speak. The long silences make me feel uncomfortable.
- My therapist used to shake my hand but now doesn't.
- I would feel better if my therapist would give me a hug sometimes, but he won't.

- My therapist said I could message him twice a week but now he's told me to stop.
- I don't understand why my counsellor wants to tape some of my sessions. I don't know if this is normal.
- I feel very uncomfortable because my counsellor takes notes during sessions.
- I read something online about the therapist, and now I can't relax in the same way.
- My therapist is referring me on. I feel she's dumping me and I'm very upset.
- My therapist won't give me any advice although I keep asking her. I expected to be given more help in making decisions.

If you feel something is not right in the relationship, or you're not getting what you need, you have the opportunity to improve it. Even a good therapist can get things wrong and not be aware of it. Equally they can't always know what you're feeling until you tell them. You can take an active part by guarding the relationship, thereby keeping your growth on track. However, if you don't feel safe or ready, that is to be respected too.

Working on relational concerns does not mean accepting unethical or unprofessional practice (See Way 19: Watch out for signs of inefficient, poor or harmful therapy).

Strategies for exploring your concerns

You have the following options for handling relational concerns you have with the therapist.

First, you can do nothing. Have you ever met someone you didn't immediately like or couldn't get on with? It could be that the relationship is in its very early stages; it will take time to grow and then you can review it later. You can keep it in the back of your mind and see if it clears up.

Second, you can talk to your therapist and let them know what you need to feel safer or to connect better with them. Explaining what you want to improve in the relationship is applicable both inside and outside the therapy room, so it's a useful skill to practice regardless.

A good therapist welcomes you sharing feelings about the relationship, even if you may be critical of them. They know they are not perfect and will want to hear, adjust their approach and talk through it with you. They will want to attune (a fancy word for tuning in or being in tune, like a piano!) to your needs and build the relationship. Your feelings are never wrong and equally they can lead to understanding yourself more, learning to assert your needs and learning how your feelings relate to your experiences in life. This does not mean the therapist won't give their perspective, but they do so in the interests of furthering your process.

191

Here are some examples of how you can broach this:

> *"There was something I wanted to talk to you about, but I am a bit nervous of your reaction. Whenever I get into the flow of things, I feel interrupted and what you're saying feels kind of out of tune with what I want to explore. I appreciate you trying to do the best for me, but I just need a bit more space in my mind."*

> *"You said that I am creating a lot of distance in relationships and acting in a way that pushes people away, but when you said it, I perceived my feelings being minimised and I was hurt."*

Improving the relationship may also help your healing:

> *"That was the milestone event for me: asking for what I needed from the therapist. The therapist really cared about my feelings and admitted they did not realise that was something I needed help with. I realised deep down that I can't really expect people to know what I need, so taking responsibility was really empowering. Last night I was sitting in bed with my partner and thinking she must really not like me at the moment because I'm out of work, and she has had to take on more work. I was really getting low about it. I asked her, and she did have concerns about us being able to cope financially, but she assured me she didn't blame me for it. We're getting along a bit better because of it."*

Talking about your feelings about the relationship is not always easy, especially if you're not used to asserting yourself and are nervous about their reaction, for example, feeling fearful of being criticised by the therapist. Even if you're tentative, here are a few ways you may feel safer to segue into talking about your needs in the relationship.

> *"I really find it hard to express what's wrong sometimes. Can you help me with that?"* It may be possible through this dialogue to see if you're ready to share feelings about the therapeutic relationship too.

> Ask for a review: *"Can we review my progress and what I could work on?"*

If you're struggling to share something important you could also consider secure message, email or write what you feel in a diary to read to the therapist.

The third option is, of course, to consider leaving the therapist. You may not be ready to talk about your feelings and needs, or you may not trust the therapist to respond well (a therapist should not be critical of you or blame you). Respecting your feelings is important too: if, at that point, you feel the therapist is not right for you, then that is your truth.

Working with therapy coaching clients, I have to be realistic that there is always a possibility the therapist will not react with care. If this has happened to you, for example, minimising your feelings or not listening to them, then I recommend reading Way 19: Watch out for signs of inefficient, poor or harmful therapy. In this case, you can try and resolve the conflict if you wish, but you have to decide whether it's worthwhile continuing, especially if the feelings are left unresolved and you no longer feel safe to be yourself in therapy (See Way 19 & 20 for further guidance). A more likely philosophical attitude would be something like this:

> *"Well, I tried and I felt really hurt by the therapist that he did not acknowledge my feelings. I know I said it when I was a bit angry, but that's no excuse. After all, I am there to get help. Well, if he was like that, he can't be right for me, and this saves me a lot of time and money. It was just not working for me. I'll bring this up with my next therapist. I hope they can tolerate some feedback."*

If you've given it your best shot and asked for help, but it's still not working for you, you should consider leaving because you have done your fair share in building the relationship. There is little point staying if you've come to a cul-de-sac, taken the time and made the effort to make things work better, but it is still not working. Remember you do still have the option to explore what happened with your next therapist. If such an exchange has left you with emotional wounds, please consider seeking support (Way 21: Get help from outside therapy if needed).

Exercises
Self-Reflection

1. Do you feel your therapist is competent? Why?
2. Does the therapeutic relationship mean something to you?
3. Do you tell people when they have said something that annoys, frustrates, angers or makes you sad?
4. Do you understand why you do, or do not share your feelings? Will you share in certain settings or with certain people more?
5. Are you afraid of sharing your feelings with the therapist? What do you imagine the consequences of doing so would be?
6. Are there moments with the therapist where you felt discomfort, irritation or wished for a different response? Write about why that is.
7. Is there anything you could do to strengthen the relationship?
8. Do you believe the therapist is accepting, caring or empathic?
9. Is there anything missing in the relationship which would help you?

Quiz

1. Name two strategies for building the therapeutic relationship.

2. How could you open up a dialogue with the therapist about a concern you have?
3. What needs of the therapist does the client need to meet, if any? (Hint: contracting).

Way 17: Reflect on whether you're being distant from feelings or getting caught up in them

Condensed Idea: You may be keeping away from feelings without realising it and thus blocking off a major channel of healing. On the other hand you may be getting caught up with feelings blocking off awareness and insight. Use both heart and mind in therapy.

Approach Variations: Applies to all approaches of therapy.

One of the most common themes experienced by therapists is when you keep away from feelings, either from talking about them at a deeper level or experiencing feelings in the room. Most of the time this happens out of your awareness, either because that's just the way you are or because the mind wants to protect you from experiencing difficult feelings. That is not to say it is wrong to stay away from feelings in therapy, because that may be exactly what you need and can be enough. However, be open to the possibility that out of your awareness you may be distancing yourself from expressing or experiencing feelings which could be making your process unnecessarily slower.

The opposite to not experiencing feelings is when you get caught up in the feelings so much that it can feel like you're continually under water, without coming up for air to reflect on your experiences. This, too, may be a very important part of the process, but it could also be blocking you from gaining perspective.

In this way you will learn:

- What distancing from feelings may look like in therapy.
- Some signs to assess whether you're keeping away from feelings.
- How to move towards becoming more feelings focused.
- The various forms in which feelings are usually expressed in therapy.
- What distancing from awareness and rational thinking may look like in therapy.

Scenario: Moving towards feelings

Here is an example: out of awareness, Tom had distanced himself from feelings, but came to realise how it was a pattern in life:

> Tom talked about both his problem and himself in a highly analytical manner. His mind was overloaded with analysing and second guessing-himself. Whether what he was saying was the right thing, why he thought the way he did, and how he wanted me to help him.
>
> At this point I said, "To me it feels like I am missing a sense of who you are, your feelings" Tom paused and then said, "I had a good childhood, but was

bullied at school in rugby for what seemed like just trying hard. I told no one".

He directed his analysis on himself, and after a few sessions came to realise he had always kept himself busy in order to avoid difficult feelings at school, whether it was through an evening job, school work or hobbies. He was able to acknowledge that not only did he not share feelings, he had not experienced them in himself either. He had been keeping away from feelings in the therapy room as he did in life and as he had done at school. Having acknowledged this he could work further on allowing his feelings to enter the room.

You, too, can become aware of distancing yourself from feelings by analysing how you tend to express yourself in the room. It is not possible to be specific in guidance, but here are some entry points into exploring whether you're keeping away from feelings:

- You don't talk much about yourself, or make judgements about yourself.
- You don't talk about how things have affected you in any detail.
- You feel bad about talking about other people that have affected you.
- You tend to vent about others and what happened rather than how you feel about the people involved and the situation.
- You tend to pre-filter what you say in therapy rather than spontaneously talking.
- Whenever something comes up that is difficult, you consciously or unconsciously pull away in favour of other more comfortable material. Because it is unconscious it can be difficult to catch, but your therapist may be able to do so.
- You tend to minimise your feelings.
- You tend not to give examples of what's happening in your life and relationships, rather you talk about your symptoms and the difficulties they present to you.
- You feel numb or empty.

If you feel you're distancing yourself from your feelings and it may be stalling your therapy, you can, of course, talk to your therapist.

Becoming more feelings focused

In Way 6: Allow feelings and watch what hinders them, and in Tool: #1 Therapeutic talk, I give you some ways you can start directing yourself towards expressing feelings as well as assess whether you're distancing yourself from your feelings.

Deeper feelings aren't something you can directly pull out of the bag. Getting to these feelings—especially if you're unaware of them or they are lying dormant, can come about spontaneously or gradually during the process. Generally, all you can do is explore your experiences and let the relational container of therapy do its job.

However, that does not mean you cannot express more feelings by using the language of feelings, giving examples of situations which affected you, and making yourself more vulnerable (See Ways 5-10 in particular).

Forms of expression

When assessing how you express your feelings it can be useful to know about the main forms of expression that frequently occur in therapy. The types of expression described here will help you to reflect upon how you express your feelings, remembering there is no inherent right or wrong way.

Lived in experience. Where your body and voice express your feelings in the room. For example, "I felt so guilty that I could not support her!! I am so bloody useless!" This expresses the feelings where both your voice and your physical presence reflect the strength of the emotion.

Reflective feelings. Where you express feelings in a descriptive way rather than in an experiential way. From the outside it can feel like a narration of a story as an observer rather than feelings that actually happened to you.

No feeling. Another type of feeling, often overlooking is the feeling of numbness, or emptiness, where as hard as you may try you cannot get to a feeling. Through a process you may be able to pierce the numbness to connect with your feelings.

Dormant feelings. Feelings can also come out of the blue, they may have been lying dormant and without you being aware of them at all. Usually it's through the process that you would access any dormant feelings you were unaware of, or you had even forgotten. See Chapter 5 Oliver's journey for an example of how dormant feelings can emerge as you get in touch with your feelings and with what's wrong.

Suppressed feelings. It can also be the case, such as with adverse childhood experiences, that you encounter suppressed or traumatic memories that you had no idea about. Although they could be distressing they are likely to be an important part of the work you do with the therapist.

For many, working on feelings will be at the heart of their therapy, but remember that there is no right or wrong way for you to work on feelings, and just because you don't experience or get to them, it does not mean that your therapy has not been helpful. And contrary to popular belief, it's not about making you cry, it's about knowing what your feelings are about. A fixed view of how you should be in the therapy room isn't useful because of individual differences and your unique experiences.

In the same way you may distance yourself from your feelings, the other side of the spectrum is where you continually remain in a feelings state, venting and reacting to situations, or continually being flooded by waves of emotions which you may even experience through the body. Because you remain so caught up in the feelings you do not have a chance to step back into self-awareness to explore your feelings and their meaning. If you find yourself getting caught up in the feelings and your therapy appears stalled I recommend you develop your awareness and rationalisation skills (Way 7: Understand yourself through awareness and Way 11: Seek your truth and then seek "the" truth) and of course talk to the therapist.

If you're frequently in a state of emotional distress or could be emotionally triggered, your therapist can help you to process your feelings safely. Safe processing means working on feelings without falling into a hole consumed by them, but also without keeping yourself really distant from them. This allows you to experience feelings and develop awareness in parallel. Staying at the edge between feelings and being present in the room with the therapist is a recognised way of healing emotionally charged traumatic memories and experiences.

In general, I would say there is no right or wrong type of expression. However therapy usually consists of differing kinds of expression: talking about how you feel and felt, venting, analysing, reflecting on your feelings, experiencing live feelings and also recognising and working with thoughts. In simple terms, thoughts can influence feelings and vice versa, so all these elements mesh together to enable your healing and growth process.

Exercises

Self-Reflection

1. How do you normally express yourself? For example, do you vent, get swept away by emotion, or are you more analytical and focus on self-understanding?
2. Do you think that you distance yourself from feelings?
3. Do you think you get caught up in your feelings without being able to understand them?
4. How has either talking about feelings or thoughts helped so far?
5. Do you turn inwards (or "look in the mirror") to develop awareness of yourself in relation to what's happening or happened?

Quiz

1. What are the possible reasons clients may avoid feelings in therapy?
2. What do we mean by safe processing?
3. Name two ways in which you can become more feelings focused.
4. Name four forms of feeling based expression.

5. Is there a best way of expressing yourself in therapy? Why?

Way 18: Use essential tools that make therapy work

Condensed idea: At the heart of therapy lie certain enabling tools that are frequently used to make therapy work. These tools may be innate in you, or they may need to be learnt.

Approach Variations: *Applies to all approaches of therapy*

In this way I introduce the most essential tools that make therapy work (Chapter 3: Essential tools which make therapy work), regardless of therapeutic approach or presenting problem(s). While the 21 ways embody the tenets of success in therapy, these essential tools apply aspects of these ways in practice. For example, you can use Tool #9: Expose underlying feelings, across a number of ways, such as to deepen your understanding of your feelings (Way 6 and 10) and to assess whether there are any gains to no change (Way 8).

When it comes to considering the most important tools you can learn in order to make therapy work for you, it will naturally come down to selecting the most important and fundamental ones that align with these ways and thus align with the way therapy works. While there are many tools and techniques a therapist will tailor to your needs, there is a set of important tools which fuel therapy, borne out of theory and experience, which you can use to make therapy work for you.

Some of these tools are so fundamental, they often come naturally. You may already be applying them or discover them as your process unfolds. For example, you may already be used to applying rational thinking to give perspective to your thoughts. On the other hand, some of the tools may not emerge because you didn't know they existed, or rarely apply them, but then they turn out to be absolutely essential to the success of your therapy. Knowing the "art of the possible" when it comes to using therapy effectively can only be a good thing, particularly when you're curious, unsure, stuck or don't know what to say or do. Sometimes, even a small adjustment during therapy can result in big leaps.

Let's jump in and look at a few examples of how the tools (See Chapter 3: Essential tools that make therapy work) can be used:

> "Joe was stuck for words. He did not know what to say. He remembered the tool to share what he felt in the **here and now,** and even though he did not know what to say, he could talk about his stuck feelings."

> "Joe was looping, going from relationship to relationship. He remembered the tool to look at **the big picture** to see if there were any similarities or patterns to help understand what was going on and why."

"Joe spent a lot of time talking about his friend, but he remembered to check in with himself to **talk about impact** in order to ascertain whether he was talking about the impact of the situation on him, rather than focusing on his friend's words, behaviours and actions."

Many of the tools can be used in the live experience of therapy, such as the tools that lead you to express yourself therapeutically, reveal underlying feelings, build awareness, or join the dots. On the other hand, many tools are for use outside of therapy, such as self-care and psychoeducation.

I hope by reading Chapter 3, you will be able to discover, assess and appropriately use these tools to unlock the power potential that makes therapy so effective. If you're unsure about a particular tool, return to Way 4: Use the therapist as a resource.

Note: I use the term *tool* generically. In actually, it may be more of a skill, task or resource. And if a tool is essential that doesn't mean others aren't important; essential tools are the ones commonly used, even if it's not always apparent.

Now go to Chapter 3 and assess whether there is a particular tool that you want to use further.

Way 19: Watch out for signs of inefficient, poor or harmful therapy

Condensed idea: How the therapist communicates and behaves with you is something you can use to determine whether the therapist is working competently and ethically. Competence is therefore more than qualifications, skills, training or experience.

Approach Variations: Applies to all approaches of therapy

Caution: Evaluating competence, especially in the grey areas (see below), is subjective. So when it comes to making a big decision about ending therapy, particularly where you have invested time and are getting something out of it, I recommend talking to the therapist and/or seeking help (See Way 21).

If you have read through other parts of this book, you will already know about the importance of the therapeutic relationship in feeling safe, because it's entwined with the reason why therapy works. For most, the litmus test for relational competence is EPAIY-S (See Way 2: Find the right therapist and approach) and that will be all you need to know to determine the competence of the therapist.

However, confusion, stagnation, relational ruptures and strong feelings can arise during therapy based on how the therapist works with you. These feelings may arise because of what they say, what they don't say, or what they do. Such feelings can interfere with you feeling safe, and confident that you're on the path towards recovery. You may wonder whether you would be better off leaving the therapist and finding another one.

In my experience as a therapy coach, clients check whether the therapist said or did the right thing, not only because they want to determine whether the therapist is competent, but because deep down they want to know whether it's okay for them to feel the way they do. Underlying these feelings is often a sense of not being cared about—or even worse, blamed. In most cases, when clients bring these feelings to the attention of the therapist, they are well-received and strengthen the relationship. After all, therapists can get things wrong without knowing and neither can they know all that you're feeling.

However, just like any other profession it's possible to encounter a therapist who doesn't work with you professionally. Most cases of unprofessional practice could amount to wasted time, effort and money. But there is always a possibility that your experience of therapy is more emotionally harmful, particularly if you're in a vulnerable place or feel strong transitory emotional dependence on the therapist. At this extreme end of the scale, the harm caused by the therapist could set your process back for years.

You can use this way to protect yourself by learning to assess and spot the signs of inefficient, poor or harmful therapeutic practices:

- Why relational qualities of EPAIY-S (Way 2) are so important.
- Understand why assessing competence is not always easy.
- Understand the signs of overt unethical and harmful practices.
- Strategies to protect yourself if you feel strong emotional feelings towards the therapist.

For strategies for resolving issues and conflicts with the therapist see Way 16: Do your fair share in building a good relationship.

If you have a gut feeling something is not quite right in the way your therapist is working with you then I recommend working on those feelings, either in the room or outside of it. In my experience as a therapy coach I have never found exploring these feelings to be anything other than beneficial, even if it's only to clarify and re-establish confidence in the process. There is no such thing as a wrong question.

Competence revisited

Therapist competence is not only about qualifications, standards, skills and experience working with your problem (covered in Way 2: Find the right therapist and approach). It is also as much about *how they are with you and within themselves*. How they are is important because you need to feel safe, and because the relationship is a big part of why therapy works in the first place.

Therapists need to be present, active and empathic with you in order to understand you and to be with you in your process, not just in what you say but importantly in how they receive you in to their awareness. Here is an example of the therapist *not* being present in the room.

> Amy really liked coming to therapy, it gave her a chance to offload about her stresses in work. Quite often she would see Suzie, her therapist half closing her eyes. She didn't mind too much because most of the time she felt heard, and after all she was used to people not listening anyway.

They also need to be mature and balanced so that when challenged, or when they experience your strong feelings, or the process is stalling, it does not push a button within them that takes them away from focusing on your needs, or even cause harm. Here is an example of the therapist's internal "button" being pressed.

> The therapist really wanted to help Ruth, but he felt she would spend so much time talking about daily life that she would never let him in to her deeper feelings. He interrupted her a few times and then said "you're avoiding your feelings", to which she replied "erm. Not sure, nope". The

therapist felt frustration inside his chest and let out "well, how am I supposed to help you, you obviously know best!".

In both cases the therapists had worked unprofessionally. In the last example, therapists through their training, experience and supervision do understand this possibility of their internal buttons being pressed and work with their supervisors and even personal therapy to "clear" internal difficulties that could appear in therapy. However, by being informed you, too, can assess the therapist's behaviours because if you feel unsafe it is likely you'll feel that it interferes, blocks, or in some cases harms your therapy.

Now that you have six overarching principles of good therapy (EPAIY-S), i.e. empathy, presence, assuredness, inner balance, "you" focused and supported (See Way 2), I have further expanded upon specific types of therapist behaviours that are indicators of good practice.

Signs of good practice

- You felt heard, understood, accepted and not judged. Remember, the therapist may challenge by giving their perspective but they still accept and work with your feelings.
- You feel they were present in the room, attentive and followed what you said.
- You felt the therapist was open to you sharing difficult feelings about them, rather than giving defensive responses.
- Generally, they own their limitations and mistakes, and are not afraid sometimes to be vulnerable. Remember, therapists may not always know they've made a mistake.
- You feel seen for who you are rather than only an object of diagnosis, assessment, symptoms, issues and labels. Some therapists may work in a more diagnostic or analytical way; it does not mean they are unprofessional, but it may not be right for you.
- They have inner emotional balance. They work with you even when things become challenging or difficult, which indicates they will not present their insecurities to you, thus providing a "secure canvas" for you to draw on.
- They remain consistent and reliable in their actions. For example, even if you get frustrated with them they help you work with your feelings in an "adult" way rather than a defensive, critical, blaming or angry manner.
- They allow you the freedom to be yourself, to have your own opinions and to make your own decisions. Therapists may say things that are counter to your opinions, particularly about the underlying nature of your difficulties, but it is done in an empathic manner with your interests in mind.
- They end therapy gracefully and if they decide to initiate the ending it is justifiable in your interests.

Grey zone of competence

International variations: In this section I describe working with grey areas that arise in assessing competence. There may be variations in terms of whether some of the examples are considered unethical or not, depending on the country or region you are in. For example, requirements for insurance, self-care and self-development.

Determining competence or good practice is not always easy to assess in the grey zone because of four reasons:

- The therapist cannot be perfect, only good-enough, so they can get things wrong, sometimes without knowing it, and therefore without knowing its impact on you.
- What you may regard as "good" or "bad" may differ to someone else's definition. Therefore feelings of safety can be subjective based on how you gel with the therapist overall, rather than thinking of a therapist as either employing good or bad practices.
- A few low-level instances of poor practice do not necessarily mean that overall, they are not competent or good for you.
- Just because a therapist works in a way which you do not like does not mean it is unprofessional either. For example, a therapist who works in ways that are more challenging than you would like isn't necessarily unprofessional.

Because of these considerations in what I call the grey zone of competence, only you can decide whether to challenge or continue with a therapist who has done something "wrong". Use your own feelings and ask yourself whether your relationship can be kept on track (Way 16) and whether any conflicting feelings can be overcome. In making a decision, you also need to consider whether you have been getting something out of therapy overall. Ultimately, you need to feel safe in order to share and to have a good relationship with the therapist. If, after having tried to clear any interference, it's not working, you will need to decide whether to continue or not.

Here is an example in the grey zone which happened to me.

> I had been working with my therapist for number of sessions and valued the work that was being done. After a few sessions my therapist forewarned me that he was on standby because his partner was expecting a child so may need to cancel if it happened. {Note: therapists don't usually disclose too much personal detail, but I suspect he had to in case he had to end the session abruptly}.
>
> A few weeks passed and I told him I was excited about a job interview. The next session I returned eagerly to share my good news, but noticed my therapist was looking tired and distracted. I didn't think too much of it, but

underneath I also wanted him to remember and ask me about my interview. I challenged him on it and said, "You've taught me to share feelings, and if I was to share today, I would say I was disappointed that you didn't ask me about my job interview, and that you look a bit distracted". He replied back, "and if you were to share, I would say I've had a few sleepless nights because of the new born baby".

I was happy with his openness and his reasons. Of course being tired is not professional practice, but because I was getting something out of therapy, it was a one off, and the therapist was honest rather than defensive, so it did not become an obstacle. I did not feel it interfered with my therapy, in fact it strengthened the therapy because I practiced sharing feelings and had an adult conversation about them. However, I can imagine that if my therapist did not openly accept my feelings, it could have been a different outcome, especially if it had stopped me feeling safe.

As a therapist I, too, can confess that occasionally I have got things wrong in my practice. Examples include losing my keys for the office, double booking a room with another therapist, being a bit hasty at the end of a session, forgetting to follow up an email, getting scheduled times wrong, feeling more sluggish than normal, and not turning off my phone. However, these mistakes were one off occurrences over a period of 10 years. Further, where I know about them, I always own my mistakes, and allow clients to express their feelings. Of course, I apologise and try to remedy the error where possible too. This also makes me wonder whether I have made other mistakes, but clients were too polite to tell me.

This type of judgement on "good" or "bad" can be compared with other relationships too. You may have frustrations or feel let down by people, but you can focus on the intent and the extent that you value the overall relationship. Wrong behaviours do not always mean you don't get anything from the relationship or you don't want to see them again. Of course, the opposite may be true.

Here is a list of the most frequently occurring unprofessional behaviours with possible circumstances under which you *may wish* to consider giving the therapist the benefit of the doubt. If you feel safe and its affecting you then talk to the therapist about the issue to see if it can be cleared up to an extent that it doesn't interfere with your therapeutic goals. Use these examples as indicative rather than definitive because only you can judge how you feel inside, and whether it will impact your therapeutic aims.

If these behaviours are a matter of course, or more severe in nature then they fall into what I would call overt unethical practice (see next section). In considering these experiences you should also look at how much you're getting from therapy overall.

Your experience of the therapist	Possible Exceptions
They seem mentally tired, distracted or preoccupied when you're talking to them.	As long as this happens as a one off. If this is a single session or short-term therapy it is going be a more significant issue.
They don't appear to fully understand where you're coming from.	As long as this happens infrequently or is a one off.
They don't own their errors. For example, being late or forgetting you have told them something significant before.	As long as this happens infrequently or is a one off. As long as they are not blaming or critical of you As long as they own the obvious error when you tell them.
Their boundaries are not clear or surprise you when they are brought up.	It depends on the boundary being breached. For example, you may wish to overlook a single session ending early or beginning late. See overt unethical practice below for unacceptable breaches of boundary. For example, also being in a friendship or business relationship.
They interrupt you more than you would like.	Therapists may interrupt you to help you focus in on particular feelings or provide interpretations of your experiences. As long as they do not continue to interrupt when you ask them not to. As long as they are not criticising or blaming you.
It appears, at least to you they are pathologising you as an object of assessment rather than with empathy and acceptance	As long as this happens infrequently or is a one off. As long as they cease the practice when

Your experience of the therapist	Possible Exceptions
	you ask them not to.

Remember therapists may work in a more analytical diagnostic ways or use assessment tools so it can be subjective. Nonetheless, you may wish to consider whether it is the right approach for you. |
| They use touch as part of a therapeutic technique without your permission. Some therapies use touch but it must be permissive and not a surprise to you. | As long as this is not sensual in nature.

As long as it does not reoccur if you have requested not to touch. |
| The therapist appears more interested in hearing the details of what happened to you. For example, the details of abuse or traumatic events rather than in helping you. | As long as it does not reoccur if you have stated that you don't want to go further into detail.

Content of event may need to be explored. They must be able to justify it. |
| They offer advice. | As long as it's only about how you came to be the way you are, or they are signposting supporting services.

As long as it's not for significant life decisions such as work or partner choices.

If the advice is offered as a suggestion or a concern rather than recommendation or a definite. |
| It appears to you that they are intruding with questions into your life and events. | As long as this happens infrequently or is a one off.

As long as it does not reoccur if you have stated you don't want to go further into details. |
| They seem disinterested and spend most of the time passively listening or nodding their head. | Some therapies can be less directive and so the style may not be what you need. |

Your experience of the therapist	Possible Exceptions
	As long as you're getting something out of therapy. Of course it could be they are truly disinterested which can be reviewed with them and you will need to make a decision based on your feelings.
They tend to set the agenda. That is, they focus of the therapy session and the content.	As long as it's in agreement with you and can be justified. As long as it does not continually reoccur if you have stated and agreed that you want to set the agenda more.
They spend a fair amount of time talking about general things in life (not personal disclosure) rather than anything therapeutic.	As long as it can be justified. For example, to develop rapport or humanise the relationship. As long as it does not continue if you have agreed to work in a different way.
Therapy is flat or stagnating, even after many months.	Therapists work in many different ways and may be able to justify their way of working. Ask them for a rationale for their way of working. As long as you're able to openly talk about it and agree a way forward.
The therapist doesn't publish or agree a verbal contract with you such as payment, times, confidentiality.	As long as its rectified when asked for.
The session is interrupted.	Only if it could not have been foreseen and is a one-off instance. For example, someone unexpected knocks on the door in an office space or in an emergency.
Watches the clock a lot.	Therapists may look towards the clock a few times, particularly towards the ending but if they fixate on it then they are not being present with you.

Your experience of the therapist	Possible Exceptions
	Only if it's a one off and the issue can be cleared up.
They didn't give notice for being on holiday.	Only if it's a one off and the issue can be cleared up or it does not impact you.

Scenario: Working through feelings about "grey areas" of practice
Pete's therapist kept on interrupting him in a session. Pete could feel an anger brewing inside him. He tried to calm himself and be controlled. Inside he felt just like he had always been treated—as an object, someone to be talked at, rather than to be listened to. He carried on therapy ignoring his feelings as he had always done.

Whenever you encounter some conflict in therapy with the therapist, it should be seen as an opportunity to find your voice and bring out your feelings in the room. Many people struggle with saying what they feel, want and need, so it's an opportunity to be your authentic self.

As I have described in the Way 11: Seek your truth and then seek "the" truth, I recommend working through your thoughts and feelings and checking out their validity. In doing this you are determining whether your feelings are truly true, or whether there are multiple truths, including that of the therapist. On the flip side you can also check that you are not dampening down or minimising your own feelings and needs, which can lead you to assume you are wrong and the therapist is right.

Here is an example where the therapist has validated and empathised with the client's feelings towards them (an example of good practice), but also used them therapeutically.

> As Andrew was talking, he noticed his therapist looking at the clock hanging on the wall behind him a couple of times during the session. Andrew became very angry about this.
>
> Andrew: [shouting] "Why are you looking at the clock?!"
>
> *<In the following statement the therapist shares feelings which Andrew may not have been aware of.>*
>
> Therapist: I look towards the clock near the end to check how much time we have. I feel that I'm here with you and have heard what you're saying. I'll bear in mind your feelings.

<Now deeper feelings of being angry and what it meant could be explored which may even relate to the problems being worked on.>

Therapist: Andrew, it seemed that you were really angry at me. I was taken aback a bit; shocked...even scared. Anything going on?

Andrew: I didn't like it.

Therapist: You didn't like it?

Andrew: Yeah, I feel embarrassed now. (This is a lead in to working further on the underlying feelings if Andrew wants to).

In this example, what appears to Andrew as the therapist being unprofessional or "wrong" is not only worked through, but also used as a potential source of therapy. For example, Andrew may learn that it's okay to talk about relational issues, or that his anger is directing him to look deeper at his underlying feelings.

Here is another example, where the therapist is clearly being unprofessional. However, the client feels that they did something wrong, because they do not trust their own feelings and boundaries yet:

Client: There was something I wanted to talk about. It's really difficult and scary but I feel I need to say it.

Therapist: Oh, what is it?

Client: Whenever I make an appointment the sessions keep get changed around. Also sometimes I feel you don't want to be here, like you're somewhere else.

Therapist: Yeah, you know it is a busy practice. Been travelling and things just came up. We can try a different time, maybe that will be less disruptive.

Client: No that's fine. It's okay, it just makes me feel uncared for.

Therapist: Well then that's sorted.

Client: I still feel that something is missing.

Therapist: What do you mean? I am here with you and we can sort appointments. I think you're diverting away from your own feelings by focusing on me instead.

Client: Ah OK, I get it, I think you're probably right.

In this example, the therapist bypassed the client's feelings and focused on fixing the problem of session times. However, what needed to be "fixed" was the relationship. When the client stated their feelings, they were not considered, or allowed to be aired. The therapist did not open a dialogue around the client's feelings, perhaps because it pushes their buttons of needing to be "right". The therapist should have been more accepting of the client's feelings and worked with them, regardless of other perspectives. Given the client already tends to dampen down their own feelings, they aren't in a position to trust their feelings or consider whether this is the right therapist for them.

Here is another example where the therapist acted unethically:

> James had been in therapy for nine months because of his sudden breakup with his fiance. He admired the therapist and hung on to every word he said. The therapist, after some months of listening to James, said he should have gotten over this previous relationship by now. Based on the therapist's judgment, James decided to take action and write a letter to his ex in order to gain closure and move on.

> However, even though he did that, he still felt the same way; a deep anguish about his ex. In therapy, he began minimising his feelings towards his ex to try and please the therapist. He felt really bad because he was not getting better. Needless to say this only added more pressure to the situation and blocked him from being able to make the most out of therapy.

Therapy is not about telling you what you should or should not feel, and the example given is to demonstrate what can happen when you are not quite ready to use your feelings. Ultimately, the therapist acted unethically, perhaps out of their own frustration, stating that James should be "over it" by now. In actuality, James was not ready; he needed to find his own way and he needed more time to work on his feelings about the grief around his break up, rather than being concerned about the therapist's assessment that he should be over it by now. His process and feelings were now blocked and not allowed to enter the room. However, if James had trusted or even known his feelings, he could have acknowledged that he felt pressured by the therapist to get better. Following that, he could have decided whether or not to continue with the therapist.

Overt unethical practice

Overt unethical practices are more readily discernible than those in the grey areas. These practices can directly interfere with, stagnate or block your therapy. Some of these practices may also cause you significant harm beyond wasted time and effort. If you feel unsure please seek outside support (Way 21).

International variations: There may be some variations as to whether some of these are considered unethical depending on the country or region you are in.

×   **Pressure tactics and exaggerated claims**
   o   They guarantee they can fix your problems.
   o   They can definitely resolve your problems in a certain number of sessions. Some therapists may give estimates but it is based on experience or evidence.
   o   They try to pressurise you into undergoing therapy with them and/or criticise you for not wanting therapy with them.
   o   They pressure you not to leave therapy. Therapists can suggest you continue in your interests, but they must not force their will on you.
   o   They tell you they are a specialist in working with certain problems but don't have any specialist training or experience.

×   **Poor practices**
   o   When asked, they aren't able to explain their rationale for working with you in a particular way.
   o   They provide definitive life-changing advice. For example, to break up with a partner or leave work.
   o   They spend unnecessary time talking about themselves and their personal life. Therapists may disclose, tell stories and use metaphors, but it should be focused on helping you. They should not be getting their needs met through you, such as talking about their frustrations in life.
   o   They try to force their opinions on you about why you are the way you are, what you must now think, feel or behave like. Because of therapeutic boundaries the therapist may ask for a certain standard of behaviour in the room in order for therapy to be useful, for example not turning up intoxicated.
   o   They do not engage in supervision, have insurance or undertake further development.
   o   The therapist engages in talking about everyday experiences, small talk, humour, events and situations without any therapeutic content. Therapists can talk in this way but there has to be a reason for it, for example, to humanise the process. This type of talk is separate to personal disclosure as it's mostly not personal to them.
   o   The therapist is distracted in the session. For example, intermittent clock watching rather than occasional glances, looking away from you, or frequently forgetting what you say.
   o   Practices gay conversion therapy.

×   **Relational Boundaries**

- o They try to engage in or enter into a dual relationship with you. For example, a romantic or business relationship.
- o Sensual communication. For example, flirting or sensual physical contact. Of course this could be subjective but you will still need to decide whether it is.
- o They work to make you reliant on them emotionally so they can meet their needs through you.
- o They breach confidentiality without any professional rationale. For example, on social media, or leaving the therapy door open.
- o They miss or forget appointments more than once, particularly without owning the error or talking about it.
- o They are aloof and distant. They are treating you like an object without empathy or eye contact. Some therapists may work this way, so ask them if there is a justifiable reason for it.
- o They breach confidentiality of other clients with you. The therapist may refer to cases as a way of helping, but they should not be personalised.
- o They fall asleep during therapy.
- o They use discriminatory language.

× **Unsafe practices**
- o They continuously ask you to recall traumatic memories, phobias or emotional triggers causing you distress, without any guidance on safely processing them.
- o They terminate therapy without notice or without working towards an ending. You may not even be told, and they just disappear. This can be more harmful for some due to the relational bond triggering feelings of rejection and abandonment. Please note that therapists can sometimes be plunged into emergencies like family death, so be open minded until you know better. If you are worried about sudden termination for whatever reasons explore it with your therapist as soon as possible.
- o Unorthodox practices. While therapy is a creative practice it needs to be grounded on some theoretical working assumptions. It is difficult to define "unorthodox practices" because there is so much potential for separate, ethical ways of working, so you should seek advice if you are unsure. An example could be all day therapy or an esoteric practice unrelated to the therapy. Whatever they practice they must be able to reference a body of established counselling or psychotherapy knowledge in order to explain their approach.
- o Outside medical help. The therapist stops you seeking outside medical help, suggesting that medication or medical treatment won't help or will be detrimental to you.

      o   Definitive statements or "answers". Any interpretation or why your experiencing difficulties are offered as suggestions, including what you need to work on to alleviate your difficulties.

      o   Suggesting there is one memory you need to unlock which once discovered will immediately resolve your difficulties.

×   **Inner balance**

      o   They show frustration towards you which could include criticism and blame. For example, asking why you're not better, and accusing you of doing this to yourself.

      o   When you share feelings about the process or the therapist they ignore you or shut down your expression. They often do not validate your feelings.

      o   Continually avoid or refuse to deal with any conflicts between you and them.

      o   They come to therapy intoxicated or continually look tired.

Therapist exploitation

The signs of therapist exploitation are largely very similar to that of any other harmful relationship, where the therapist gains your trust, makes you feel special, and entraps you in a relationship that is toxic.

Here are signs that therapists *could* be moving towards abusing their power in therapy:

- Boundaries are broken. For example, you meet socially as well as for therapy, or they talk a lot about themselves, and their life.
- They appear to favour you rather than others. For example, offering extra time, reduced rates, or even allowing your fees to accrue without payment. Please note therapists may offer free or reduced sessions so that should not be confused with this point.
- They create a dependency on them and isolate you. For example, telling you to call them for no reason, to have more sessions, telling you only they really care, blaming people in your life and giving advice, including cutting off ties with family members and friends.
- They make you feel special, and once they gain your trust in the relationship, they can switch between praise and giving you a feeling of being special, to blame and criticism. They give and take away praise in the relationships rather than being consistent, safe, and reliable in the therapeutic relationship.
- Any sexual activity, including seductive language, such as comments on your body, or a lot of focus on your sexuality and experiences for no apparent reason.
- Threatens you if you leave, or try to make a complaint about them.

- Criminality such as sexual abuse, rape, blackmail, fraud, physical abuse, aggression and violence.

Scenario: Harmful dependence

Tony had been seeing Stephen regularly for over a year working on his problems of childhood trauma and physical abuse. Today when Tony arrived, he pressed the buzzer waiting for the usual six seconds to go inside, but this time the door did not open. He tried and tried again each time growing more alarmed at the lack of no response. His head was filled with noise, his heart raced, he felt the therapist had abandoned him. How would be able to cope now?

In this scenario Tony had developed an emotional bond so strong with his therapist that the thought of their relationship being severed plunged him in to panic. Whenever you have a strong dependent bond, whether emotional, erotic or sexual, you are in a vulnerable position because disruption can trigger off distressing feelings which for some, could put them back years in their recovery.

In this scenario harm could arise in the following situations:

- The therapist ends abruptly. An abrupt ending, whether actively initiated or where the therapist becomes incapable of practice, can trigger painful long-lived feelings.
- The therapist takes advantage of this strong feeling you have of them. An unprofessional therapist can cause harm by abuse of power because of your need for them (see overt unethical practice section above).
- The emotional bond or attraction interferes with or blocks your process from being therapeutic. There is potential that the service no longer serves a therapeutic benefit, but rather it fuels the dependence unless addressed (See Chapter 5: Love in the room)

If you feel this way it does not mean you have done something wrong; these feelings are well-known occurrences in therapy, it simply means you need to be careful that you're working with a good therapist who can provide a safe container in which your feelings can be explored and contingencies can be put in place so that you feel safe.

If you have such a bond with your therapist then you can take charge to protect your safety as far as possible:

- Ask the therapist how they usually do endings.
- Tell the therapist you are worried that the therapy may end mid-flight and cause you distress.
- Ask what would happen in an emergency if they could no longer work with you, even if it were a force majeure incident, so you know how to get continued support.

- If you feel safe and are ready, talk to the therapist about your worries and the deep bond you have with them so it can be explored therapeutically.
- If needed seek outside professional support (Way 21).

I explore this kind of dependence and its therapeutic potential in more detail in Chapter 5: Process themes in therapy: "Love in the room".

Mediation and complaints

The decision to make a complaint can only be yours. However, I do recommend taking some time to reflect on your feelings when making a decision.

To make a complaint, you would usually have to talk to the therapist's employer (if they have one), your insurance provider, or an organisation that governs their therapeutic practice. Many therapists belong to a voluntary membership organisation or must be licensed to practice by the government. If they are then you are likely to have recourse to a complaints process (see Appendix B for major UK therapy membership bodies).

If you would rather not make a complaint you may have the option to seek out a mediation service to try and organise a meeting between you and the therapist (only seek mediators who are licensed/accredited and who are ideally therapists themselves).

The purpose of mediation must be well understood by both parties prior, particularly as you'll have no control over the way the therapist handles the mediation. The purpose of mediation is usually to be able to say what you need to say, including the impact your grievance has had on you, as well as anything you may have appreciated. If you wish, and if mediation goes well, it can allow for you to part ways amicably and gain closure, or it can be used to offload and say what you need to say face to face.

Regardless of whether you choose to complain or enter into a mediation process I recommend you talk with another qualified therapist to reflect on your wounds and grievances so you are clear what you need before you making a decision (See Way 21: Get help from outside therapy if needed).

Exercises
Self-Reflection

1. Has your therapist met competence standards?
   - Do they meet standards of practice (See Way 2)?
   - Do they pass the EPAIY-S litmus test (See Way 2)?
1. How do you normally deal with your feelings and conflicts with others? For example, dampen your feelings down, express them, get emotional, be assertive, avoid feelings, listen to others' feelings more or be diplomatic.

2. Are there any blocks between you and the therapist which stop you trusting or being able to share freely?
3. Is there anything your therapist has said or done that you did not like?
4. Do you have any doubts about the competence of your therapist?
    - If so write down your feelings and why you may be experiencing them?
    - Is it interfering with the relationship and your process?
    - Do you feel reluctant to share because of it?
5. What positive feelings do you have about your therapist? Do those feelings interfere with your therapy? Would they cause distress if things were to end abruptly or gracefully?

Quiz

1. What does EPAIY-S stand for? What do the terms mean?
2. Why are there grey areas when determining good practice?
3. If you experience a strong bond with your therapist, what strategies can you put in place to protect yourself from harm?
4. Name five signs of wholly unethical practice.

Way 20: Don't walk away from therapy without talking to the therapist

"Squeeze every last drop of therapeutic value from your sessions"

Condensed idea: If you've decided to leave, processing your thoughts and feelings with the therapist can lead to new insights and perspectives. It might even catapult your process beyond expectations.

Approach Variations: Applies to all approaches of therapy. In group therapy, members are likely to appreciate you talking to them about your reasons, as well as saying goodbye.

When you initiate an ending with unresolved problems, unless it will cause harm or you're not ready, regardless of the reason for leaving, always work through your feelings, thoughts and decision process with the therapist first.

In this way you will learn about the potential upsides of talking to the therapist whenever you wish to initiate an ending, especially prior to leaving with unresolved concerns. In particular, you will understand how conflicts (sometimes called rupture and repair) in the relationship can—if handled well by both you and the therapist—be of enormous therapeutic value.

You may decide to leave therapy for any number of reasons including:

- You feel worse.
- You're not ready or therapy is not for you.
- You feel the therapist may be thinking badly of you.
- You don't want to be rejected by the therapist, so want to end it first
- You feel you don't deserve to be in therapy any longer.
- You don't feel connected to the therapist.
- There is something intangible you don't like about the therapist.
- You're not improving.
- Your ideal in how you envisaged the therapist and the process to be has not been met.
- You come into contact with new memories and thoughts which you are aren't ready to bring into awareness.
- You don't feel therapy is going to work for you.
- The pace of therapy is too fast or too slow.
- The therapist said or did something you didn't like.
- The process of therapy feels threatening. For example, going to your inner feelings and experiences.
- Life priorities and money.

- Any number of other reasons described in Appendix D – Inventory of client concerns.

The objective in talking about your reasons to end is, of course, to learn something new. By exploring the end you can check out your feelings, see if the relationship can be repaired, check out the therapist's perspective, learn a new way to deal with feelings including endings, and determine whether there is therapeutic value in exploring your reasons.

Talking to the therapist does not take away your decision and your freedom to choose. For example, the therapist may not be right for you or you may feel that their way of working is not suited to you. But by checking out your feelings, it could provide closure or even accelerate your process. If this doesn't yield any benefits you have still learnt to speak about your feelings, and you can end gracefully. If a therapist is critical or does not accept your feelings it obviously confirms your decision to leave, so in that sense even a negative experience can be seen as an acknowledgement that your feelings are in harmony with reality.

Rupture and repair

Rupture is a term in therapy used to describe the underlying strain or breakdown in the relationship between you and the therapist. For the purposes of this section, I extend the definition to include a rupture between you and therapy, which is a felt internal threat from acknowledging your own feelings to yourself and the therapist.

In moments of rupture you can feel threatened by what the therapist does or says, or by the challenge of the therapy process. Ruptures may sit silent and unsaid, or they can burst out in the room through anger. They may even result in you walking out of the room. These ruptures are common in therapy and good therapists know how to work with you when they occur, because they know it can be a breakthrough moment in therapy.

Therapy, by nature, can be a challenging encounter even if you feel comfortable talking about yourself. There is a part of you which you have learnt to keep hidden, sometimes even from yourself, and this can be loosely referred to as the "inner child", which is a symbol of your most important early development in life. This part can feel threatened by the experience of therapy for a wide range of reasons, which you may not even be aware of:

- Feeling less powerful than the therapist. For example, less competent, or you feel they are viewing you through a critical or analytical gaze.
- Vulnerability. The inner part of you is threatened because it is never shown to anyone, let alone a stranger. Your internal parts feel under threat of shame at the thought of being revealed in the room.

- The therapist may say something that pushes a button in you. For example, being belittled, not believed, judged, challenged or put under pressure.
- Due to an injustice. This can come up if you believe the therapist is not being fair or sensitive.
- Loss of control. Experiencing feelings where you say or do something that you regret. You feel you made a mistake and say something you feel you should not have said, either about yourself or the therapist.
- A way of relating. For example, you become uncomfortable when the relationship with the therapist becomes closer. You feel exposed or are fearful that once you reveal the "authentic you" you will be abandoned or rejected. There is part of you that does not feel good enough in the relationship.

These threats can trigger in you the need to take control and power back from the encounter; this may be through abruptly leaving session, ghosting the therapist or even harshly challenging them. Here are some examples of the inner narrative of clients seeking to take control back from the encounter of therapy.

Tim was really silent in therapy. The therapist was tentative in the session; he did not want to rush his client, but he was not attuned to the fact that his client felt really uncomfortable with the long pauses. The client left feedback later by email that the therapist had "freaked him out" by being too silent. Tim did not return to therapy.

David had cancelled sessions outside the 24 hour time limit. On the second occasion, the therapist reminded the client this had happened a few times. However, the client felt a sense of judgement and criticism, even though the therapist was highlighting boundaries. He never returned any messages and terminated three months of therapy.

Tina was feeling increasingly tentative about therapy; as she started to talk more about feelings about her partner and her relationship, the therapist noticed how her breathing would change, words would become slower and she would put a lid on it quickly with phrases like "Relationships are not easy." She decided to end therapy by sending in an email after the session.

In all these cases, these clients did the right thing, which is employing their right to choose. But therapists can make mistakes, and try as they may to reduce the possibilities of rupture, they won't always be able to meet your needs because they can't know everything (See Way 19 for perspectives on therapist mistakes). In Tina's case she was clearly not ready to admit, perhaps even to herself her feelings about her relationship.

After a sudden relational rupture, it is possible that you will end the session immediately, and not return because you feel aggrieved, or because you feel embarrassed by your actions. However, a good therapist will accept your feelings and work with them, and while they may express their own thoughts, including their boundaries, they are there to work in your best interests. Working through the impasse could be the most liberating part of therapy.

Another reason for ending without talking to the therapist is that therapy may be making you feel worse. Therapy is not always a straight line, nor is it a process without difficulties, so you may feel worse before feeling better. Feeling worse in therapy can appear to be self-defeating or hopeless, when in fact, it could be the opposite. For example, you may be edging towards facing feelings you are unaware of or mourning a loss. However, just because you're feeling worse, or if more pain is being experienced, that does not imply that it's healthy either. Talk to your therapist and/or physician if you have concerns about feeling worse.

Therapy is an opportunity to explore, perhaps for the first time, to check out your feelings and assumptions, by telling the therapist what you need or what is missing. Of course, none of this is guaranteed to repair the relationship or lead to further insights, but on the other hand, it may be the most important catalyst for recovery.

So if you are ready and it's safe, don't walk away until you have said what you feel and why you want to leave. Take a risk and say what you don't like, even if you don't know exactly why. Sticking around during the difficult periods to explore reasons for ending—even over a number of sessions—could be just what is needed to take your process to the next level.

If you are concerned about your therapist's professionalism and competence see Way 19: Watch for signs of inefficient, poor or harmful therapy.

Exercises

Self-Reflection

1. How do you normally deal with conflict whether it's with friends, family or at work?

2. Have you sometimes felt, even temporarily, that you wanted to leave therapy? Is that something you can talk to the therapist about?

3. Have you had doubts whether therapy is going to work for you? Is that something you can talk to the therapist about?

4. Do you have any anxieties, fears or feelings in talking about your reasons for initiating the ending? Is that something you can talk to the therapist about?

Way 21: Get help from outside therapy if needed

"Being able to know when to ask for help is a great way to learn"

Condensed idea: Seek professional help outside therapy if you're confused, have questions, concerns, dilemmas or if you are struggling to achieve your goals. This includes concerns you have about the therapist.

Approach Variations: Applies to all approaches of therapy.

International Variation: The availability of further support will depend on the country or region you're in. Seek advice from reputable sources such as a regulatory body, membership body or reputable therapists.

Note: If you feel you're not getting what you need in therapy I also recommend you consult your doctor/physician to way out any undetected underlying medical conditions which may be affecting the way you're feeling. For example, an overactive thyroid may produce symptoms of nervousness, anxiety, and irritability (source: NHS England).

In this book I have revealed the biggest secret to success in therapy, which is that ultimately, only you can make change happen. Therefore by learning to use the instruments of therapy well, i.e. yourself, the therapist and the relationship between you both, you can take charge of your role. I hope in this book I have taught you how to use therapy effectively, efficiently and safely through the 21 ways of learning.

You may have additional questions, concerns or dilemmas which you may also encounter during your journey too. To address this I include professional answers to over 100 questions, concerns and dilemmas I have received from people in therapy (See Chapter 7 – Client topics, questions and concerns).

Although I believe I have covered nearly everything you need to know in order to be successful in your therapy, I am sure some things will come up that are not covered in this book or that require deeper exploration. Of course the therapist will, in most cases, be your first point of call, but if you would like outside help, you have the following options:

- I offer a confidential *therapy coaching* service to help pinpoint and explore sources of difficulty in therapy (see Appendix C for further information).
- You could reach out to another professional therapist. In general they are a friendly bunch and you may be able to set up a session with them to help you process your feelings.
- You could try and make contact with an independent regulator or voluntary body for counselling and psychotherapy to see if anyone is qualified to assist you (see main UK membership bodies in Appendix B).

- If you wish to complain about your therapist, contact the regulatory or voluntary body serving your therapist (See Appendix B). Remember that the membership body can only process a complaint if the therapist is part of their membership.

If you are seeking help from outside therapy, you should be cautious of any advice or guidance from anyone who is not regarded as a qualified therapist in your country or region. I know there are support groups in which people can talk about their experiences of therapy, which are often helpful, but they are not moderated by professional therapists so I recommend caution. Ultimately, whatever you learn from outside sources, use your own judgement to make your own decisions. In therapy, as with life, only you can decide what's right for you.

A major driver for writing this book was to normalise the range of experiences you might encounter in therapy. In that respect you may be curious about the sorts of concerns that I have worked with as a therapy coach; well here is the list:

- Unsure of direction therapy should take.
- Unsure how to make therapy work for you.
- Feeling therapy is not working, blocked or stagnating.
- Don't know whether to remain with or leave the therapist.
- Not sure if the therapist is right for you.
- Not sure if you are using the right type of psychotherapy (counselling, CBT, EMDR, DBT etc.) or what options you have.
- Confused feelings towards the therapist.
- Feeling that no therapist is able to help.
- Continuous cycle of starting / ending therapy.
- Finding it hard or ashamed to say things to the therapist you would like to.
- Feeling a loss/attachment towards the therapist even after ending therapy.
- Feeling abandoned by the therapist.
- Feeling angry/frustrated at the therapist.
- Feeling you're being blamed by the therapist.
- Feeling the therapist is not being open and / or is withholding information.
- Constant thinking about the therapist.
- Emotional and/or therapist abuse, e.g., anger directed towards client.
- Difficult endings in therapy.
- Love and/or sexual attraction.
- Finding it hard to end therapy.
- Detangling feelings between that of a friend and therapist.
- Boundary/ethical issues.

Self-Reflection

1. Do you have concerns about using therapy effectively, efficiently and safely?

2. Are there any themes listed in this section that you are concerned about?
3. Are there any topics of concern not covered in this book?

Do you have any feedback on the material in this book or something you don't understand? Feel free to reach out and make contact ma@paththerapy.co.uk or visit empoweringyourtherapy.com.

Chapter 3 – Essential tools that make therapy work

In this chapter you'll find the most essential tools that make therapy work, regardless of therapeutic approach or presenting problem(s). While the 21 ways embody the tenets of success in therapy, these essential tools apply aspects of these ways in practice. For example, you can use Tool #9: Expose underlying feelings, across a number of ways, such as to deepen your understanding of your feelings (Way 6 and 10) and to assess whether there are any gains to no change (Way 8).

When it comes to considering the most important tools you can learn in order to make therapy work for you, it will naturally come down to selecting the most important and fundamental ones that align with these ways. While there are many tools and techniques a therapist may tailor to your needs, there is a set of common tools which fuel therapy, borne out of theory and experience, which you can use to help make your therapy work.

Tools 1-9 hold the most relevance inside the therapy room while tools 10-15 are there to support your reflection outside of the therapy room. Of course, all tools can be used for developing life skills too.

I hope that by reading this chapter, you will be able to discover, assess and appropriately use these tools. If you're unsure about a particular tool, return to Way 4: Use the therapist as a resource.

Note: I use the term tool *generically. In actuality, it may be a task, skill or resource depending on the context of use.*

Tool #1: Therapeutic talk

Tool summary: Learn the differences between talk and therapeutic talk.

During therapy, you will be communicating with yourself (internally) and the therapist, both verbally and non-verbally. As a natural part of the process, you will be expressing your thoughts and feelings about whatever it is you're working on. However, talking in therapy has some qualities that align more to the healing process. You can use this section to differentiate between talk and therapeutic talk. This is not to say the former is not needed in therapy or that both can easily be differentiated. It can be equally important; however, you can use this skill to assess whether you would want to adjust your generic approach to expressing yourself in therapy.

Tool #1.1: Talk about you

In therapy, there is no right or wrong approach to talking, but most good-enough therapists are likely to be attuned to three particular patterns that may get in the way of them understanding you fully. Remember that therapy is usually about working with the whole of you, so to get to that, you will usually need to go beyond surface thoughts and feelings when talking about yourself.

The first is what I call **talk about anything but you.** This is when you spend a lot of time talking about everyone else or everything else apart from you. It sounds obvious, but if you are talking a lot about others, their lives and feelings, it may be worth taking a step back to recognise why that is happening. It may be very relevant to spend a lot of time talking about others, but therapy on the whole needs to be relevant to you, your life and your problems.

If you feel you are talking a lot about the details of others in general, where it is not related to you, you should spend time reflecting on why that is and share that with the therapist. If this goes on for a while, most therapists are likely to reflect back to you what they are hearing.

Here is an example of a lot of content over long duration that does not, at least on the surface, appear to be related to a particular problem:

> I worked with my friend Joe. We lived together. We got on really well together. He went on to do really well for himself, and he travelled the world.

The second kind of talking is more common, which I call **talking in general terms about yourself.** This is when you talk about things in general, about your life, activities, and events. There could be a lot of detail, which may also be rapid and switch to many different topics, but it barely scratches the surface of what is going on for you under the surface and the problem.

Talking about it may sound like a recap of day-to-day life, situations, and events that happened:

> Over the weekend, I spent time with the family, which was good. I spent a lot of time on my own and watched TV. I caught up with my friends and went for some drinks. I went over the top and drank more than I should. I'm trying to go to the gym more and keep myself busy.

In another example, while the talk is more about your problem, you may spend most of the time talking at a surface level, and talking about what you want and the symptoms, goals and the fundamental issues of your life, rather than getting stuck into looking at working on the problem.

> Kevin came into therapy for an addiction problem. He spent most of the session talking about day-to-day things, such as stress, work and his addiction, as well as his symptoms and triggers. Whenever he did talk about matters that stressed him, he would speak in generalities without going into specific examples and his deeper context, such as his thoughts, beliefs and feelings.

This type of narrative can also feel like a summary of a book being read without experiencing reading the whole book.

The third is what I call **over analysis,** where there is a lot of emphasis on interpretation or analysing yourself. This can also be very useful "grist for the mill" in therapy, but when it dominates most of the time in the room, it could keep you from the experiencing therapy.

An analytical expression may sound something like this:

> "Over the weekend, I felt no one was talking to me. I know it goes back to my childhood because I was bullied. I know it's my critical voice. I just need to accept that [etc.]."

In all these talk types, there is nothing inherently wrong with approaching therapy in this way; after all, it could be what is helpful to you and what you need. Most likely, new doors will naturally begin opening as you and your therapist build the relationship. However, on their own or if they take up all the time in therapy, over a number of sessions without movement, this could mean looking at the reasons why this is happening. In most cases, a good-enough therapist is likely to naturally pick up on this to help you; however, you can self-assess too.

Self-Reflection

- Do you spend a lot of time talking about other things apart from yourself?

- Do you spend a lot of time talking about things at the surface, in general? Does it help you? Is that what you find beneficial? Or would you want to change that approach?
- Do you tend to analyse yourself a lot? Does it interfere with your growth?

Tool #1.2: Talk about impact
"The 'I' is for impact."

You may already know the well-worn cliché of the therapist who continually asks clients, "How does that make you feel?" One of the reasons this comes up a lot is that the therapist is trying to help you focus back on yourself, the "I," which is you in relation to what is being talked about. This is because one of the most common themes within therapy is your self-relationship and in particular your self-judgement. Whenever you are talking, you can talk about the "I" experience by using language such as "I feel," "I felt," or "It impacted me because of xyz."

The "I" experience reveals both sides of what happened and how what happened impacted you. The impact to you can be expressed in relation to your thoughts, beliefs, feelings and images. Here are some examples:

> "I was drinking" changes to "I was drinking and I felt really angry with myself the next day. It took me out for a few days. It just repeats. I can't seem to control it."

> "I distract myself" changes to "I distract myself so I won't have to think about the difficult feelings I have towards my partner."

> "I am losing my job" changes to "...and it's really scary."

> "I had a flashback" changes to "...of the attack and seeing myself getting hurt."

Adding yourself, your feeling and your impact into your talk has the potential to deepen your understanding of events and your situation so you can understand yourself more.

Tool #1.3: Disclose and talk
Talking or disclosing something about yourself, the past, a situation, event, or memory for the first time can mean you are taking an important step in your healing. However, disclosing something important about yourself and your life, while an important step, is not necessarily the same as "working on it" in therapy. When you're working on ingrained and complex feelings, it will usually take more work to make sense of your feelings, bring in perspective and to gain insight before you feel a change within. That does not mean all things have to be talked about further, but you can, with the therapist's help, discern whether there could be more work to be done.

If that is the case, keep expressing feelings. For example, use feelings, join the dots with the past, and look at the content through multiple perspectives. Work through it until you feel you have revealed all your underlying feelings about the disclosure.

Also remember that talking about the same thing repeatedly isn't wrong, often it is right, as it may take many iterations before something changes. Talk to your therapist if you feel concerned you're repeating familiar material.

Here are some examples of disclosure which may need more work to process the thoughts and feelings underlying them:

- I watched my friend getting attacked and felt frozen.
- I lost my uncle; he committed suicide.
- I was physically abused by my neighbour.

One way to elaborating on a disclosure can be to answer "what, why, when" questions about it (See Tool #2: Reflection).

So, in the example of "I watched my friend get attacked," it may be elaborated as:

- What happened?
- Why did it happen? What were the circumstances of the fight?
- How has it impacted you? For example, loss of sleep?
- What are your feelings about it? For example, guilt, anger at yourself for letting a friend down?
- How has your relationship with the friend changed from before to now?

Working on the issue involves not only disclosure of the issue, event, or difficulty, it involves allowing yourself to freely explore all aspects of your feelings and seeing where it leads.

Tool #1.4: Processing vs. Venting
Another aspect of therapeutic talk that may be helpful for you to assess is the difference between venting and processing. Venting is usually a necessary part of therapy, you are talking about life events "as-if" you were inside them as you talk.

Here is an example of someone venting, by focusing in the events and feelings about their children:

> Over the weekend my sons came to see my husband. You know what they ignored me and spoke to their father. I could not believe how rude they were to me. They don't know how hard it has been. Not a word. Don't they know how hard to look after their alcoholic father? Where were they? They are just relieving their guilty consciousness. I'm the villain. I've told them time and time again to share feelings. I'm not having it.

With venting you're in inside the wave of experiences and feelings about matters in life, what happened, what was said or not. However, venting may feel like the same situation different story where you are replaying the experience, like a loop that continues to dominate sessions every week. Here is another example of venting, but the theme is similar to the first i.e. that of disrespect, and being uncared for.

> I got a call from my son the other day. They said whether I wanted to come around and see my granddaughter. I just think "beggars belief" how can he ask that, doesn't he know what I am going through. He thinks I'm just making excuses for not coming. He thinks I'm just angry all the time, but I'm the one who has to deal with their father. Where were they?

You can reflect upon whether venting and being heard is enough and all you need? Or do you want to break that cycle and look inside yourself to effect some inner change? In which case you can use other skills more geared towards processing (See Tool #2 and #3).

If you feel you need to vent and be heard then therapy may be a costly option as there may be other listening services that can offer it. Mostly therapy is geared towards change rather than the being focused on goal of listening and being understood by someone (although that could lead to change). Both go hand in hand in therapy though, although if it's just geared towards you talking and the therapist listening it is not strictly therapy. That does not mean you should discount it because your process may unfold and you may get the inclination to move towards looking deeper within, even if you are focusing on venting at the moment. Talk to the therapist if you have concerns about processing vs. venting.

Tool #2: Reflection

Tool summary: Learn to focus in on a feeling, situation, event, or memory and then stand back and ask questions about it.

Being reflective means you're thinking about your thoughts, beliefs, values, images, emotions and behaviours. You ask questions about them to find out how, what, why, and what they mean. In turn, the reflection process can lead to greater self-awareness and ultimately to change. By reflection, you can learn more about yourself and your needs.

In therapy and in life, you are probably being reflective without even knowing it. Being reflective is an essential skill because it provides a window (reflection) to look inside yourself, which ultimately opens an inner draw bridge to answer "What's wrong?"

How to reflect

You can reflect on anything you feel is relevant to therapy, whether it's a relationship, how you feel about yourself, or why certain behaviours, thoughts or feelings come up.

The starting point into a reflective process is to apply four key questions to whatever it is you are focusing on. You can simply ask, "What happened? How did it happen? Why did it happen? What does it mean? Is it familiar?"

Here is an example of a client reflecting on her anger towards her partner:

What happened?

Anne talked about how she felt a huge amount of anger towards her partner for spending money. She would often go quiet and later end up bursting with anger. At the beginning, she told the story of **what happened**, what was said and her anger towards her partner.

How it happened?

Here is Anne's narrative of how it happened.

Whenever I feel this anger, I don't know what to do with it. I've tried so many times telling him to budget, but it just happens again and again. He promises and then breaks the promise. I try so hard to distract myself. It works sometimes, but then I lash out when he says something stupid. It tips me over the edge. I end up saying sorry and then he promises to do better, but it keeps happening the same way!

Why does it happen?

Now she stepped back from what happened and asked, **why does it happen?**

She described more about what led to the anger. She spoke about how she felt he spends the money on his family and all she seems to be doing in life is firefighting, trying to earn money month after month but never being able to put money aside.

Then she asked the question, **what does it mean?**

I guess I just feel disrespected. Surely, he should know better and not do this. I would make sure I only spent what was needed and leave stuff aside for a rainy day. Why would he do this if he cared? He obviously cares more about his family than me!

In this example, you can see how Anne was able to reflect and thereby understand more, in particular, how she dampens her feelings, feels her partner spends money on his family only, and it makes her feel he just does not care. Of course, this may only be the start of Anne's reflection. For example, why does she hold feelings in, is it rational for her partner to know how she feels, and what can be done to break this cycle?

Tool #3: Join the dots

Tool summary: Look at patterns of commonality of feelings, thoughts, body reactions and behaviours associated with whatever you're working on in therapy.

Joining the dots means linking whatever you are talking about, your feelings, or whatever is occurring in your life to experiences in previous situations or circumstances. Joining the dots refers to finding the missing or similar links, the blank words, pictures or missing parts that give you the ability to arrive at an insight to solve the confusion of "Why?" Joining the dots for most is an activity that just happens as you talk and reflect, but not always. Sometimes, by joining the dots, you can arrive at an insight, which is equivalent to having an "a-ha" or lightbulb moment. In this section, I provide some tips on how you can maximise the possibility of having such moments, even if they are micro variety.

Tool #3.1: Link now and the past

One way of joining the dots is to think about a feeling, thought or bodily reaction and ask yourself the question: "Does that remind me of something? Did you have an experience like that before? When was that?" Here the thoughts, feelings, body sensations and emotions reveal similar events, or memories related to whatever it is you're working on.

Here is an example of linking the now to the past:

> Therapist: When you feel that anxiety, that feeling that you felt when forcing yourself to tell me how you feel—can you tell me more?
>
> Client: Ermm, I felt my heart pounding, I felt my body was pushing me back and I could not speak.
>
> Therapist: So, with those feelings, do you remember a time before when you had those same feelings of a pounding heart and something pushing you?
>
> Client: [pausing as her breath changes] It felt like a memory I have of my dad hitting me, telling me I was a stupid and wouldn't be anyone. He said no one would want me. He physically pushed me back. I felt scared.

In the above example, voluntary memory recall was used to gain an understanding of influencing factors that created that anxiety.

In many cases, the association or links can happen without any voluntary attempt as you are working on something in therapy because the mind automatically associates a feeling or thought with something in the past, sometimes called "involuntary memory." An example may be a smell that reminds you of a particular memory in childhood.

When you are processing memories with the therapist, you may be asked to bring up memories and your thoughts and feelings in a safe way. This type of processing can be used by therapists, particularly when recovering from trauma.

Tool #3.2: Big Picture

Another way of joining the dots, is to take a step back, looking from above at events, thoughts and feelings across time and identifying key themes which led to you be who you are. Again, this may happen naturally; your mind does it anyway as part of a process where your mind finds multiple thoughts and ideas and combines them into an understanding of what is going on and what it means.

In this condensed, more analytical example, you can see how a client associates a number of threads around his feelings towards his wife, which leads him to understand his behaviours more.

> *Mark was unsure why he withdrew in conflicts with his wife. He would shut himself down and numb himself. He could not associate anything of his past with it. He felt hopeless and sad that he could not change, particularly as he loved his wife.*
>
> *He always remembered that he was on the whole allowed to share feelings during his childhood and listen. So, why was he doing that now? There were a number of threads of insight that came out over period of time to explain his "shutdown stance". First, as the youngest in the family, he was often used to others taking the lead to ask him what was wrong; they had always been the one to notice and help him resolve his feelings if he felt "sulky."*
>
> *Second, he realised he did not like conflict as a child. His parents would often say, "He is such as good boy; we've never have any problems with him, no tantrums or arguments." Once he remembered a time when he did get angry at a friend who had broken his toy and remembered how he kept his feelings inside and ran upstairs to his room to cry so not to cause an argument, but he cried himself to sleep.*
>
> *Third, he also had a memory of how he would not want things to go wrong between his parents, because they argued so much. He wanted to keep quiet and hope things would be okay. They didn't end up okay because his parents separated.*
>
> *In all these threads, Mark noticed the commonality between these insights, of being quiet, keeping feelings in, soothing himself and fear of abandonment by his parents. This gave him the insight to understand himself better, and it gave him an idea of why he shut down in conflict. Changing*

and connecting with feelings, rather than his usual numbness, would take time, but he could take baby steps now.

In this example, you can see how the client is beginning to bring in multiple strands of feelings and events in his life that shaped his feelings of going quiet and numbing down, from being praised for being "good," to not having to take self-responsibility in sharing feelings and also having to keep quiet as to not cause his parents to argue. These threads slowly come together to get to a point of understanding himself better and releasing his feelings.

Tool #3.3: You remind me of

Another way of joining the dots is to look at people and ask yourself, who do they remind you of? Sometimes, it may be no one at all. In some forms of therapy, particularly analytical insight-oriented psychotherapy, it is believed that people can remind you of other figures in life. It may be that the therapist reminds you deep down of someone or they stir your feelings in some familiar way. They may remind you of something you missed, needed, wanted or even a negative oppressive symbol too. It may also be gender specific too. For example, if you have had bad experiences with men all your life, it may interfere with you feeling safe. If these feelings come up with the therapist or others in life, they could be worth putting out there to explore with the therapist.

There is nothing wrong with feeling a particular way towards the therapist, it's more about being aware of it and exploring it. Of course if it makes you feel unsafe you either need to work through it, hope it resolves itself organically or consider another therapist.

Tool #4: Here and now

Tool summary: Use whatever it is you are experiencing in the moment as a way of exploring your thoughts and feelings.

The skill of "here and now" refers to tapping into what you are experiencing right now in this moment as it unfolds moment to moment. Let's get straight into it: how are you feeling reading this text right now? Think about it by answering the following.

- What are you thinking? Examples, "I'm intrigued," "I'm bored," or "Nothing particular."

- What are you feeling? Examples, "I feel nothing particular," "I'm excited."

- What is your body doing? Examples, "I'm tense," "I'm relaxed," "I'm hungry."

Here and now can be used to create self-awareness of your experience in the room with the therapist. Using this technique, you can check-in with yourself and if appropriate, share your findings with the therapist. The technique is useful for you to catch your thoughts and feelings as they occur, "live" during the experience of therapy and then reflect and use them to aid your process. Your therapist will be keen to hear what you are experiencing, so feel free to share what you feel may help.

Here are ways in which the skill can be useful in therapy:

- To get back to what you're feeling in mind and body

- To share when appropriate your feelings about your therapist

- To share what you feel about yourself when talking

- To unblock your process if you feel you are looping or can't get any further

- To become aware of your process (See Way 7: Awareness of process)

Here are some examples of "Here and now" feelings:

- My mind is racing. I can't concentrate in the room.

- I'm feeling nervous about being here.

- [towards therapist] What you said made me feel my feelings didn't matter.

- I can't find anything to say.

- I'm frustrated. I don't know what to do or say to make it better.

- I felt a guilty feeling just then talking about my mum.

- My heart is racing.

- I felt an emotion come up but don't know what about.
- I'm talking to fill the silence.

Of course, using "here and now" experiences can also be used outside the therapy room too, including what you think and feel about what others are saying to you.

Tool #5: Therapeutic processing

Tool summary: Difficult material you bring to therapy may need processing to help you feel better.

Therapists often talk about processing, whether it is feelings, thoughts, images, body responses, memories, or emotions. But what does that mean? How do you do that? And how will you be able to recognise the difference between talking on its own vs. talking and processing? What does good "processing" look like?

Keyword: Process. In therapeutic terms, "process" can refer to three separate things: first, the steps and activities that occur during therapy that lead to growth; second, the process that is going on within you, under the surface. Thirdly, in this section, the "process" refers to the characteristics of working therapeutically on whatever comes up so it is understood, reappraised, and even resolved in some way.

If you are talking about something, whether it's a situation, event, memory, or something that you have taken the brave step to disclose, this can be a critical first step and may be the most important step in your recovery. However, saying something out loud is usually just the beginning. Talking about something is not necessarily the same as completely processing it. Processing is to squeeze out all the healing potential, to be wrung dry and metaphorically digested into the mind. For example, revealing a past mistake you feel guilty about is a start, but it won't necessarily enable the strong feelings, thoughts, and beliefs you have about the mistake to be understood, dissipated, accepted, or made less painful. To do so will require processing work with a therapist over time. So, processing in this sense is a mental conversion process, analogous to converting wheat to flour and eventually bread. You will need to combine ingredients to be able to process them and eventually to achieve healing. Identification of ingredients is a start, but it does not make the final product. You "make new" by processing in therapy.

Here is a narrative of someone who is consciously not ready to process:

> Jane had found it really hard to be vulnerable; her feelings were trapped inside. She made the brave step to share feelings. When she did, she did her best by quickly stating that "she found it hard to talk about an affair, and even though she wanted to share more, she could not." It was understandable that was all she felt she could do, but it probably would not be enough to process it. She wished deep down that it was all she needed to do to overcome her difficulty.

Here is a narrative of someone who may not be aware of distancing from feelings and thus processing them:

Kevin came into therapy for an addiction problem. He would spend most of the session talking about day-to day-things, stress, work, and his addiction. He would spend most of the time talking about his symptoms, triggers, and how "if only" he could not drink anymore. Whenever he did talk about matters that stressed him, he would speak in generalities without going into specific examples and his deeper feelings. When he did talk about things, it would be about a situation that made him angry, but he spoke about a lot of things very quickly, moving from one situation to the next. It was clear he had feelings of anger and guilt but because they were not, for reasons unknown, being aired in the room, instead the process was looping rather than moving. So much content was being said, but nothing really had a chance to be explored further, so he remained distant, like reading a book about someone else, not him.

So, what does good processing look like? To process something is to examine it, analyse it, and walk around it from different angles, like you would examine a statue from different angles. By processing through the feelings, the content, and your relationship towards whatever is under examination, you can come to new awareness. In short, you give yourself the time to increase your understanding, to have new insights, or to allow the feelings to pour out. By processing feelings, memories, and thoughts, you have the opportunity to uncover and give them a fresh look, updating details of your memories, joining the dots between the past and now, your understanding and their context. These insights can help you complete the "puzzle" in your story, shifting your narrative about how you feel about yourself in small but different directions. Another way to see processing is that it is like clearing out a messy cupboard that needs reorganisation, checking the folders and files, and filing the files correctly in a way that makes sense to you; this helps you feel that things are in "psychological order".

Here is an example of Jane beginning processing:

Therapist: Can you tell me more about the anxiety you felt when forcing yourself to tell me how you felt?

Client: I felt my heart pounding. It felt my body was pushing me back, and I could not speak.

Therapist. So, with those feelings, do you remember a time before when you had those same feelings of a pounding heart and something pushing you?

Client: [pausing ... hearing her breath change] It felt like a memory I have of my dad hitting me and telling me I was stupid and wouldn't be anyone and no one would want me. He physically pushed me back. I felt scared...

Sometimes, your patterns will be deeply entrenched and there will be good reason for that, whether it's fear of abandonment in relationships or a trauma of the past. These unconscious patterns that impact your life and cause issues can be processed and brought into consciousness. Through processing, memories remain, but the intensity of the pain and hurt could settle to a point where you can function in life.

Self-Reflection

- Are you used to exploring your thoughts and feelings about situations, e.g., to a friend or a partner?
- How much vulnerability do you typically show? Do you share how events affected you? Or do you find it harder to share feelings when you may be perceived to be less in control, weak, vulnerable, or fragile?
- How do you feel when you share feelings or when you've had to share them? Do you feel you avoid or block feelings, find them difficult or even scary?

Tool #6: Rational thinking

Tool summary: When thinking about yourself, the world, people, events and situations, check in and reflect to see whether your conclusions are based on sound evidence, reality and facts rather than assumptions.

Thinking rationally, or being able to assess and use reasoning, is the ability to consider a situation and apply logic, evidence, facts, knowledge and judgement to arrive at a conclusion.

Due to the way human learning occurs, our minds can sometimes learn to make assumptions when it senses certain situations in the world, not necessarily because of the event in hand but more so because of past events, hurts and difficult situations. The distortion in our minds may be hardwired or learnt to protect us from danger, but equally they may no longer serve us. For example, if your mind remembers you being scared when you felt ill abroad, it may try to protect you by causing you anxiety every time you try to travel. Similarly, if you felt like a "failure" when you were young, primarily because of harsh criticism, your mind and body remembers those thoughts and feelings automatically whenever you "fail" at anything now.

Cognitive distortions

Cognitive distortion (derived from cognitive behaviour therapy) is your biased perspectives of situations, yourself and of the world. Here, I have listed the most commonly occurring types of distortions in therapy with examples. There are many others. You can learn about them to assess whether there are any you recognise during your process:

Mindreading is where you guess what someone else is thinking without the facts. For example, thinking your girlfriend is using you and does not care, because she is going out with her friends twice a week. A re-evaluation might be, "Just because my girlfriend has been busy with friends does not mean she does not care. I will cook her dinner tonight to talk to her to see how she really feels."

Reverse-mindreading is where you believe others should be able to read your mind. For example, "Surely, she should know that I want to be hugged. I should not have to tell her." A re-evaluation might be, "We have only just started seeing each other; she does not know what I like. I can ask for what I want."

Black-and-white thinking is where you see things not as shades of grey, but as binary, one or the other, without considering complexity, subtlety, options, other factors and perspectives. You may see people as "good or bad,", "to blame or not to blame."

For example, "I failed my accountancy test. I'm dumb." A re-evaluation could be, "Just because I failed my accountancy test this time does not mean I will fail it again. I was only 10% off, and if I put in a bit more work, there is no reason I can't do this."

Focus on the negative is where you dismiss the positives in favour of one or a few negatives. For example, getting a great performance review but focusing in on one subjective criticism. A re-evaluation could be. "It was great I got feedback from five different people and only one person made a negative criticism. I will go and find out what they meant so I can learn from it. Even if they are holding a grudge, that is their problem; it does not mean it's a negative on me. I got a good review, and it doesn't make a difference to my career anyway."

Catastrophising is where you feel the worst will happen based on a small evidence or likelihood. For example, if you don't work unreasonable hours in a day, then you will be fired, even though others work less than you. Focusing on the positives can be an antidote to this kind of thinking. Re-evaluate to, "I have worked for the company for five years, and the company always appreciates my skills. While it may be possible to be made redundant, which won't be a good feeling, I know I can get a job elsewhere."

Overgeneralization is where you take a few occurrences and magnify them as a general truth. For example, you go on a few dates that don't lead to anything more and believe you will likely always be alone. A re-evaluation may be, "I have only been on a few dates, and it's true I didn't feel a spark; they were not right for me. There are others and plenty of time and opportunity yet."

Personalization is where you take something as a personal fault or you blame yourself when there are plenty of other possibilities. For example, the boss looked annoyed so it must be because of you when there is little evidence to suggest it is the case. A revaluation may be, "Just because the boss looks annoyed, it doesn't mean it is because of me; he might be stressed. He usually says what is on his mind and hasn't said anything to me. Even if he is annoyed, it doesn't mean I am not good at my job. Of course, if he has something that needs improvement, I can take that on board."

Fallacy of fairness is looking at life as though it should always or mostly be fair when in fact, life is not always fair. For example, "It's not fair I lost my job," can be re-evaluated as, "It does not feel fair, but many others in the company lost their job too. It isn't fair, but I guess it was my turn this time. Things aren't always fair."

Shoulds occur often when we break our internal way or expectation. They can be tyrannical because they are insisted upon; otherwise, you feel "not okay" or even bad, shameful or wrong. For example, I should not be ill; I should not feel down in the dumps." This can be re-evaluated as, "I've read about mental health and understand more about why my stresses have made me feel low; I am not Superman! I can seek assistance; maybe a few therapy sessions might help."

My feelings tell me the truth. While feelings exist and you'll have a reason for them, they can also be echoes of previous feelings; therefore, feelings do not always tell you the absolute truth of the moment. For example, "I feel my partner is cheating," may be a strong feeling without a shred of evidence. A re-evaluation may be, "I feel threatened; I've had this feeling before, but there is nothing my partner has done. I do trust her. I'll have to be honest and tell her my feelings. Maybe she can help me."

Always being right involves the idea that being wrong is not an option, so you focus more on being right, rather than focusing on feelings of others or importantly your own inner feelings about not being good enough unless your right. For example, "I must be able to answer a question and if I am unable, I feel I'm not as good as others." This can be re-evaluated as, "Others get it wrong, so I can get it wrong. It's not wrong to say I don't know and to learn from it. No one can possibly know everything in this job."

Self-Reflection

Write down your thoughts and feelings about a time where you felt hurt, angry or sad.
For example, "I thought it was really unfair that my friend did not give me my money back and I had to ask twice. I felt disrespected and not cared about. She is not a good friend. She should have known better."

Reflect on what evidence exists to back up these statements.
For example, "My friend usually does give money back. I've never known her to be unreliable, but she can be forgetful."

What cognitive distortions do you feel exist in your thoughts and feelings?
In the above example: shoulds, fallacy of fairness, black-and-white thinking, and mind reading distortions are present. The distortions include:

- That friends should know better
- That things should always be fair.
- That friend should know they have hurt my feelings by me having to ask several times.
- They are not a good friend.

Now, write down an alternative logic
For example, "It was not nice for my friend to not pay me the money back. However, I do like my friend and is usually reliable, but I feel she has been taking me for granted lately, which can happen sometimes. She is still a good friend. She always is

there for me when I need her. Maybe I need to talk to her and tell her why I didn't like asking several times so it doesn't happen again."

Also see Appendix G – Patterns and rationality for an example.

Tool #7: Stories and metaphors

Our minds allow us to think abstractly and imaginatively to express ideas in novel ways through a combination of language, stories, memories, dreams, metaphors, associations, thoughts, feelings, senses and even intuition. These forms of expression can help open up our internal world and discover who we are and what is wrong.

A metaphor is a figure of speech that makes an indirect or hidden comparison between two things that are unrelated. For example, mist can be seen as a metaphor for confusion or uncertainty. Metaphors for therapeutic change can help to understand your process, your feelings and what is causing your suffering.

Here is an example of a metaphor of healing in therapy.

Open heart surgery

You're born with a heart that is unobstructed and ready for love.

Scars start to be visible from abuse, criticism, trauma, and abandonment. Through time, the heart becomes obstructed, weaker, slower, weary and wounded. The capacity for love diminishes over time. The heart stops feeling like a heart and more like a wooden box.

The wooden box helps us to survive and even stay alive.

Instead of healing, we opt for ways of hiding the hurt, covering up, first putting plaster on the wound, then a bandage and eventually we put the heart in a vault and bury it deep down inside, not to be seen again.

The heart is out of sight from you or anyone else. In this place, your wounds are out of sight and appear healed.

But in the vault of the heart, a virus grows, destroying the heart's mechanism for love, instead creating infections, destroying your immunity. The virus escapes and seeps through as pus from the inside, a leak from the heart's wound.

This virus stays contained for the most part, but over time, the pus seeping through the walls of the vault turns into a rupture of the heart. The rupture brings forward primeval feelings of anger, hate, and deep insecurity to the fore, those feelings left unattended.

You may turn to work, drink or drugs to hide the pain you feel deep down. Where there was once love, it is filled with toxicity and you have no capacity for love any more.

Eventually, no amount of covering up can stop the full force eruption, and the heart cries out its pain in full force.

It needs to be dealt with directly and in the open. The heart is now open for work. Performing open heart surgery is painful work, but at least it enables you to allow for healing to begin.

When you open the vault, you may find the heart is no longer recognisable. You undo the bandage and take off the plasters; it was painful before but now feels even more so. You try to tend to the injury, by cleaning it, leaving it out in the open, and spending time caring for it. The process of caring for your heart can make you feel the hurt you felt when your heart first broke. It will be painful and tender to touch. The process of care takes whatever time it takes, many years sometimes and eventually you start to feel some relief, even if it short-lived. You feel you go one step forward and two steps back.

Once the wound has been treated, you can go in deeper to remove the virus; the trauma of the broken heart lurks further and has spread in to other parts of the body so needs more work. It really hurts and sometimes feels worse than before, and you regret starting this process, but there is hope.

Over time, new thin layers will form over the wound, one day at a time, and eventually, the wound will seal and scar over. The size and type of scar symbolizes your relationship with the wound. If it is small, it will be a small light scar, barely noticeable. If it is big, it may be very tough and cover a bigger part of your body, and it's always visible. The scar is a reminder of your history and what we went through to survive. You remember the pain but now the heart is free to move on and love unobstructed again.

Self-reflection

What story including metaphors would you use to describe your therapeutic journey? Think of the stages you have been through in life and/or the therapeutic process. Here are some ideas for metaphoric story telling you can use to get started. If you wish, submit your metaphors to the empoweringyourtherapy.com and I'll publish them (credits acknowledged).

- The broken heart

- Renovating the house

- Travelling and weather

- Gardening, plants and flowers

- The warrior's journey

- Making food

- Clearing out the attic/cupboard/garage/airing cupboard

- Darkness and light
- Driving in the fog
- The dormant volcano
- Striking oil

Tool #8: Express your needs

"A simple but potent question to ask yourself: What do I need?"

Psychological needs are an extension of our basic survival needs, such as food, warmth, and shelter. Often, in the process of therapy, you'll ask, "What do I need?" or even, "What don't I need?" Your needs, both in life and in therapy, may come to the fore at different stages, and usually the more you come in touch with your truth of what is wrong, deficits in your needs become conscious to you.

Here is a narrative of someone approaching their own needs in life:

> Gerry understood the deeper hurt he felt towards his mum:
>
> "I've had enough of this; she has caused me and my family so much hurt over the years. I know she has an illness, but everyone gave everything. She could at least care about me and what I'm going through. She's always thinking of herself. She keeps hurting me!"
>
> Then he became more aware of his needs and of how to attend to them:
>
> "What about me? I am neglecting my own family and kids and even myself. Everyone's life is put first except mine. I need do what I want to do more, to spend more time with my family."
>
> Gerry decided to focus more on meeting his own needs by living life so that he was doing what he wanted to do and develop deeper relationships with his own family, rather than spending so much time on seeking unobtainable closeness with his mum. His mum was not in a position to give that. He still supported his mum but no longer was tied to the wish that she could be the "mum" he wanted.

It is not uncommon to feel out of touch with your needs, especially at the start of therapy; however, once you get in touch with your feelings and you gain clarity and awareness about your life, you may come to understand what you need more and more. Keep asking, *what do I need?* Whether it's a life purpose, a caring relationship, life projects, or better friends, needs are a source of nutrition for well-being.

Self-Reflection

- What needs were missing in my childhood?
- Do you have the relationships you want with caregivers, family, and friends? Are your needs met? If not, can they be improved or do they need to be obtained somewhere else?

- Do you want a life project or a task to pursue?

- Do you feel a sense of belonging in your family and in your community?

- What needs are missing in your life? How do these relate to your childhood?

Note that needs may include privacy, community, love, work, life projects, passions, and/or relationships.

Tool #9: Expose underlying feelings

Tool summary: Go below the surface of what you're saying by asking: Why is what I am saying bothering me?

In therapy, you'll be sharing experiences which impacted you, whether relationships, situations, or memories. However, behind the content, it's not always easy to get to your deeper feelings. Revealing underlying feelings can be compared to Russian dolls, where you open up one doll to reveal another until you reveal the last one. In this tool, I present three ways to help you reveal underlying feelings.

Why does it upset you?

Here you simply continue to ask questions such as: "Why does it upset you?" or whatever the appropriate question is that would help you go deeper into your feelings on a particular subject.

In the following example, the chain of questions and answers reveals some of the deeper feelings of a situation:

Client: I got angry last night when my partner said that we couldn't buy my dream house.

Therapist: Why did that upset you?

Client: Because I could not get the house.

Therapist: I understand, but why does it upset you?

Client: Because I always wanted my dream house when I was a child.

Therapist: Why does that upset you?

Client: Because I did all this work to achieve it, which she doesn't understand!

Therapist: Why does it upset you that she doesn't understand?

Client: *Because she doesn't care.*

So one of the underlying feelings is not being **cared** about by the partner.

Feeling about habits and addictions

Here are some positive feelings you can get towards a negative habitual behaviour. You can use this card as a cue for talking about the feelings behind a particular behaviour. For example, by looking at the card, you are reminded that eating provides feelings of "reward" and "aliveness." Once these feelings are revealed, they can be explored further in sessions.

Here are some of those positives which may underlie feelings.

Connection	Bonding	Friendship	Belonging	
Freedom	Defiance	Winning	Envied	Look at me
High-Status	Productive	Aliveness	Approval	Joy
I'm manly / womanly	I'm sophisticated	I'm okay	I'm competent	
I won	Victory	Reward		

What attracts you

Sources of feelings can also be found in the environment you're in, whether it's about your therapist, nature, art, music, films, or books. Things that capture our attention (negative or positive), or reveal unexpected emotions, can be a reflection of what you're feeling inside, much like a mirror to your inner self.

These feelings can often reveal something if explored in therapy. For example, an unmet need, a fear, or life calling. Here are some examples:

> I was watching a nature programme last week about a family of penguins and how they were fighting for survival, and the mother sacrificed one of her children to save the other. This brought up huge emotions in me.

> I was in the garden, looking at the flower but I was so captured by the bees in the garden, how busy they were and flying away. I was drawn to them I could not stop looking.

> I can't wait to meet my therapist. I am drawn to him and want to be with him all the time. He's like the father I never had.

> I saw a girl on the dance floor. I was felt so embarrassed for her, I went bright red.

Tool #10: Empathic interpersonal skills

Tool summary: Learn to develop empathic interpersonal skills and use them to develop deeper connections with people in your life.

Regardless of the problem you may have, you may come to realise during the process that there are relational difficulties going on, not just between you and others but also within yourself. If you are keen to develop deeper and better relationships, then I would recommend, unless you are already practicing this, to learn empathic interpersonal skills and to apply them to yourself and other relationships in your life.

The core empathic interpersonal skills consist of empathy, understanding, boundaries, and vulnerability.

You can use these skills to develop better relationships a well as within individual, group, family and couples therapy.

Boundaries. Boundaries represent fences in your own mind that if infiltrated, can cause you to not feel good about yourself. Boundaries can represent what you feel is "okay" for people to say to you, or what you are prepared to do. Boundaries may be flexible in that they may be adjusted over time. They may vary based on different people or in particular contexts, but they exist nonetheless.

Examples of boundary points are:

- I don't like it when people say, "I'm ugly."
- I don't mind sharing a taxi with a friend, but I am not prepared to pay for it all.
- She was in his face shouting. That's not cool.
- I don't mind taking turns paying for dinner.
- It does not feel good for my therapist to hug me.

Boundaries are important because they are what you need to feel safe inside, and to maintain self-respect. Without which, your feelings can be squashed, you can be taken for granted, and lose a sense of yourself, the "I" in you.

Empathy. Empathy is to understand the other person or person(s) "as-if" you are living within the other person's world. The "as-if" is important because in understanding the other, you are not losing you; you still have the "I" which is you, so you don't go down fall into the dark hole with the other. Empathy is important to establish a feeling of connection between people and nature itself, it builds trust, friendship and care. Empathy is fundamentally more about presence and understanding, aimed at sitting with the feelings and words rather than moving away from them hurriedly or trying to fix feelings. Empathy may not consist of any or many words, but behind it you will be sending out signals of understanding, care and concern for the other. To understand why things make sense for the other, rather than disappearing in your own head to rush to fix it.

Some inflated examples of how empathy does not sound:

> Friend 1: I lost my father yesterday.

> You: Sorry to hear that [little pause]. Do you need to see someone for that? OR

> You: Sorry to hear that. I lost my father a few weeks back. You'll get over it too.

A more empathic type of responding would be:

> You: Sorry to hear that. [Pause while connecting, feeling and waiting]

> Friend: Thanks, I don't know what I am going to do. I have no one now.

> You: [expresses feelings] that's a big change. It sounds scary.

In the later example, you have held off wishing your friends feelings away, but rather have stayed with their feelings. You didn't say, "You'll get over it in time." You have allowed the friend to have their feelings to describe what it feels like for them in the moment, i.e. they "have no one now."

Emotional vulnerability. Vulnerability is the disclosure of anything that feels difficult or scary to say aloud. The difficulty may be a feeling of being rejected, shame, insecurity, or just something you're not used to doing. To share feels like a scary risk inside even though the risk may actually be in rational terms minimal. Through time, as you practice vulnerability these fears may quieten down.

Examples:

- I'm scared I will lose you.
- Can you help me?
- I love you.
- I did something wrong.
- I miss you.
- {Shedding tears}

Crying is the shedding of tears from tear ducts in the eyes when encountering feelings or in distress. There are four distortions or myths about crying. First, that people should not cry and when doing so, they must be stopped. Second, crying is all you need to heal. Third, if you don't cry, you're not going to get better. Fourth, people must not show weakness by crying, e.g., boys don't cry. If someone cries, it shows vulnerability, which could be a good sign of healing, and importantly, a chance to practice vulnerability and deepen connections. By using empathy, you can "stay with" rather than "fix" or "turn away" from it.

Applying these relational dimensions, empathy, vulnerability and boundaries, in your most important relationships, is an essential skill you can learn because it is hardly ever taught and can often be missing when it comes to relational difficulties. In practicing them, you can role play them with the therapist or talk about any difficulties that block you from being able to use them.

So, the next time someone opens up to you, sit with their feelings, understand their world and be present and understand why they feel that way. Don't try and fix it, at least to begin with. Similarly, next time you feel something that would make you vulnerable, see if you can share it in a safe relationship and allow the other to reciprocally receive your feelings. If they don't know how, perhaps you can teach them. There is of course no guarantee that others will be able to take time to offer you empathy and understanding. If they are not able to, then it's not your fault; you have tried.

Self-Reflection

- For your main relationship(s), think: Do I really take time to understand their world? What they are saying? Why it's important to them?
- Do you tend to try and fix things? Why? What would happen if you took the time first to understand and offer empathy before trying to fix things?
- Do you feel others offer you empathy, time and understanding when you need it?
- If you feel safe practice the skills of empathy, vulnerability and understanding with people around you, or the therapist.
- In safe relationships, try being vulnerable and sharing feelings you would not normally share.

Tool #11: Expressive material

If you're stuck for ideas or looking to reinvigorate the process, here are some topics you may want to reflect on if relevant to your therapy. Talking about being "stuck" about what to say with your therapist may also be beneficial. You don't need to talk about any or all these, but choose any that you resonate with.

- Use a journal between session and use that as input into therapy (Tool #12: Dear diary)
- Describe dreams and what they mean to you
- What you are thinking or feeling in the "here and now"
- What stops you from sharing particular things (if you are aware of anything that you're not ready to share)?
- Fantasies and wishes
- Stories, art or films that resonate or make you feel something
- What you want or need
- What you think or feel about yourself
- Relationships and how you experience them
- Childhood impact and how it influenced you
- Memories and events
- Feelings about being in therapy and the process
- How you experience the therapist and whether they are part of your internal headspace or not
- Qualities you like about yourself
- Wishes for the future
- Your family and role
- Your personal beliefs or worldview

Tool #12: Dear diary

In between sessions, you may have a lot on your mind, including emotions and thoughts. In other cases, you may feel empty. Using expressive techniques, such as a diary, drawing and colouring or completing homework tasks (those tasks suggested by the therapist) can provide another safe way to express emotions and thoughts without judgement. Many find this type activity a way of processing feelings.

Here are some ways in which "dear diary" can be used:

- To document triggers or events that caused emotional or mental distress. You can identify what was going on before, during and after the event. This can be useful to identify patterns of feelings particular if you don't know what specifically causes the triggers.
- Key points and reflections that came out from your therapy session.
- To express difficult thoughts, feelings and concerns you want to express to the therapist but are not ready yet.
- To draw a timeline of your life so far to identify standout times in life, whether good, bad or indifferent. You can split the timeline into themes such as family, friends, partner(s), education, or work.
- A narrative of your life story. You can complete this in parallel to therapy.
- To have a dialogue or conversation with conflicting parts of yourself. You can think of parts as subpersonalities that have different viewpoints and you create a dialogue to and fro between the different parts to negotiate the conflict. The parts in conflict can be any number not just two, such as the wise part.
  - For example, part of you may be wanting a change to a healthier life style and another part does not. Instead it wants to retain your unhealthy habits. You can write a dialogue between the two to negotiate the conflict inside and in preparation for therapy.
  - Another example of a dialogue could be between part of you that wants to share something difficult with the therapist and the other does not want.
- When feeling confused about something in therapy, including whether the therapist is right for you or you are thinking of leaving, journal your feelings, needs, and fears. You can write an internal dialogue to determine what is creating the confusion. This will help you release and get in touch with your feelings rather than dampen them down.
- Express what you feel about therapy and the therapist.
  - What you like / don't like?
  - What could be improved?
  - What you feel the therapist does well or not so well
  - Are there any relational difficulties?

Tool #13: Self-care

When Pandora's box of emotion starts coming out and all you want to do is to heal and improve quickly, it is tempting to put as much of your time and energy into healing as possible. You may start reading more, thinking more, going to therapy, but find that everything else in your life gets left behind including important relationships and your own self-care.

Self-care is about taking any actions to care for yourself and for your emotional and physical health. Although it's a simple concept, it's something very often overlooked. Good self-care is key to improved mood and reduced anxiety. It's also key to a good relationship with yourself and with others.

Because therapy can make you feel worse before feeling better, self-care may be even more important. Signs that you need more self-care include feeling rundown and tired, having difficulty concentrating, sleeping and not feeling right. You may find yourself feeling angrier and your moods change more than you expect, or it may be that you feel more sadness. You're just feeling more "off" than normal. Here are some examples of self-care activities for you to consider:

- Take a break or a holiday
- Engage with safe interests that do not cause stress, such as friends, and hobbies
- Maintain a healthy diet and exercise
- Balance work and life. Don't overextend yourself by listening to your mind and body
- Restful or relaxing activities, such as reading, take a bath, playing with an animal, listening to music, draw, watch a film, go to a theatre, and practice mindfulness
- Have a healthy sleep regimen
- Engage in your main relationships such as with your partner or family
- Accept help from others to ease the burden
- Allow others to offer you empathy and understanding
- Taking care physically; dressing, or grooming to look your best
- Treats and celebrations such as birthdays or a reward at the end of the month
- Keeping boundaries (see Tool #10: Empathic Interpersonal Skills) to keep you from feeling used or disrespected

What self-care activities could you engage in?

Tool #14: Psychoeducation

Psychoeducation helps people going through psychological issues understand their difficulties through education and support. By understanding your problems and difficulties it can instil hope because your problem(s) are not seen as unique and can be overcome. Knowing the biological, social and psychological nature of problems can help you feel there is not something "mental or crazy" about you. There are reasons for your difficulties and others have managed or overcome similar problems.

Psychoeducation also supports families and friends so they can have their own care, understand the problems you are experiencing and what they can do to best support you. Supporting your wider family and people who you are close to can help them accept the situation, particularly as families can fall into the trap of "blaming" themselves and others, rather than accepting the situation. The people who support you can have an outlet to share feelings, and to find ways of supporting you appropriately. In many cases support may simply be to allow you time and space to work on whatever you are going through.

The resources may be delivered online, or by a service provider. It may include:

- Describing mental health issues and understanding the causal factors and treatment options (e.g. depression, fear and phobias)
- How mental health problems can impact life
- Pros and cons of medication (Must come from a doctor)
- Information for family and anyone supporting you
- Self-help strategies to help you manage your symptoms
- Support groups (Non therapeutic) so people with similar problems can develop connections with others and to provide reciprocal support (see Appendix B for support groups)

Resources

Here are some reputable resources for psychoeducation:

NHS UK (https://www.nhs.uk/conditions/stress-anxiety-depression/)

MIND UK (https://www.mind.org.uk/information-support/)

PSYCHOLOGY TOOLS (https://www.psychologytools.com/category/psychoeducation/)

BLACK DOG (https://www.blackdoginstitute.org.au)

Tool #15: Inner child dialogue

The inner child can be seen as a part (or sub personality) of you. It provides a reference point to your child's experiences, feelings, and behaviours.

Because most would agree that childhood is a powerful source of who we are now and what we have learnt, a common intervention used by therapists is to help you bring out these feelings in therapy by referring back to your inner child experiences, including unmet needs, hurts, and difficulties. Working with your inner child can provide a way to allow early feelings to be aired, understood, processed, and healed.

You can use the inner child as a reference point in your expression with the therapist and to help you peel back the layers (Way 10). For example, you may say "my child part wants to hide away and numb itself out" or "it feels unloved." Of course, child feelings are a part of you and are not separate, but this allows you to relationally connect to the child feelings, whether it's feeling hurt, neglected, free, or overprotected.

You can have a dialogue with the child as a form of self-therapy or something to read out in the therapy room. Here you soothe your inner child or give your inner child advice in a way that represents how a good, caring, and wise parent would.

Here is a letter from the adult to their inner child who had suffered abuse.

To Steven

I know you are scared and that you haven't told me everything but I know enough, I think, to tell you some things. First of all, please believe me when I tell you how I am proud of the things you survived, to have been through even the bits that you have allowed me to remember and still be fighting is a magical thing.

I know you feel bad about that happened, and that you feel that you were to blame in some way for what was done to you and what happened to Dad but it was not your fault. I know that you done believe this but it is true, it wasn't your fault.

There was nothing you could have done to prevent it, nothing you could have done to keep the family together. I know that it has left you feeling very scared hat at any moment 'They' will come to get you, to take you away. To take you from what little feelings of security you have left.

I know that the worst is that despite everything you did, and tried to do, you were rejected by the one that should have loved you the most, hurt by the one that should have protected you and betrayed by the one that you should have been able to rely on. Despite everything you did she didn't love you, still doesn't, but that too is not your fault.

All of this, all of the things you blame yourself for, the things you think you did wrong, the things you feel you should have done but didn't, the things you failed at, none of this was your fault.

I know that this is difficult for you to see but it is not because of you that she hurt you, that she didn't love you. You have done everything that you could, and things that you should never have been made to do, but nothing you could have done would have been good enough for her and nothing that you could have done would have prevented her hurting you, doing the things she did to you.

Because she never wanted you, because she never, couldn't, love you like a mother should. Because she never cared for you or about you doesn't mean that nobody can ever love you want you or care for you.

Steven, please try to believe that you are more than good enough.

And I am proud of what you did, what you managed to achieve and any failings and dreams that we failed to achieve are my fault and not yours.

And I am sorry that I have been unable to let you be the person you deserve to be.

By Steven Payton: Somersetsurvivors.org

Chapter 4 – Oliver's journey

Many a time with clients, I have been asked, particularly as therapy begins or a block appears, "What is it like for other clients who have experienced this process?" Behind that question is the feeling that they are in the dark and don't know what they need to do to move the process forward, whether it is correct, what more they can do, how it will work, and most importantly, how they can make it work.

In this chapter, I bring to life the healing and growth process for a client named "Oliver" who is struggling with problems he experiences as "sadness and low moods." I demonstrate his process narrated from a therapist's perspective in order to help you understand the dynamics of therapy, how it works under the covers and the types of thinking and feeling that go on between the client and the therapist's inner world. You'll also notice during the process how the therapist uses his own feelings and self-knowledge to help the client.

As you read through this slowly, notice how you feel inside and whether something expressed feels familiar. Perhaps make a note or two and complete the reflection exercise at the end. Remember, the case shown should be used to educate and inspire your own process by helping you reflect and expand your understanding of it, rather than to prescribe how your individual process needs to be.

The example that follows is based on the humanistic school of therapy. For examples of therapy from analytical insight oriented, cognitive behavioural, solution-focused and integrative schools, see Appendix F.

Oliver's problem

Oliver is a white male, with red hair, age 19 and about 6 foot 3 inches. He would always be in casual clothes and as soon as he entered the building he would smile at everyone and sit in the same chair, on the far right, waiting to be called in. The one thing that Oliver would regularly change was his hair, both hair on his face and head. For him this symbolised his love for Samurai, but as I got to know him, I noticed that he used his appearance to represent how he was feeling.

On our first session Oliver explained that he had come to therapy because he had been feeling down and just really sad, and he wasn't sure why. He told me he had never had therapy before and was really nervous. He thought he might try one session and then possibly will go to see the doctor for some anti-depressants.

In his family home he lives with Mum, Dad and a younger sister who is 14 years old, whom he is particularly close to. When he started therapy Oliver was in the last year of college and was attending the 6th form from his secondary school. His family had moved to a different borough. He found the move hard as he was now far away from his social circle of friends so felt very isolated.

As he entered my room I greeted him and he asked me how I was. That struck me, I felt cared for by him, it felt generous coming from someone in emotional distress who was coming from my help. I also noted that he mentioned he wasn't a very likeable person, but I didn't experience him as such, my experience on the first session was of someone who came across as intelligent, funny warm and caring. This made me wonder about the apparent mismatch. In this case, Oliver presents his ideal of being likeable, which is a mismatch with how he really feels inside, which is lonely and sad.

During our first couple of sessions Oliver explained that his life felt mundane, lonely, boring and at a standstill; he wanted to understand why he felt like this. He kept saying "I just want something more, but I don't know what," I had noted that he looked like a lost little boy, hunched over in his seat, rocking himself. This would become a familiar sight in our sessions.

Oliver told me that he was experiencing confusion, loneliness and helplessness, but had no clear understanding of why he was feeling like this. He was not able to give meaning to his current thoughts, feelings and reactions, this was making him anxious and vulnerable. I felt how having no sense of what is going on must be confusing.

Oliver struck me as someone who had led quite a sheltered life, and lives life with real caution and fear. I would hope that by doing therapy Oliver would feel understood and safe to explore his inner world, unveil the hidden and lost stuff, and feel safe to unlock himself from being or not being a certain way.

From the beginning Oliver was very committed to his sessions, in which, overtime, he worked through some difficult and deep rooted issues. But it would not be easy.

Stuck in my room

In the first sessions I got to know about Oliver's life and how he was struggling with the routine of daily life, and felt confused and empty, but was sure of one thing - he wanted to escape, and escape fast. This led to exploring what the term "escape "meant. He was looking forward to going to Asia and leaving for university. He said "It's my ticket out of here".

> "It's the only thing that doesn't weigh me down; it's my ticket out of here," he said.

Oliver said that he was the calm and logical one of his family and friends, the person who looked after others and took time to listen to their problems.

> "What's the point of moping around, look at me? I'm becoming a moaner, and no one likes that."

"I'll always try to make someone else feel better, because I'm fine."

Oliver seemed to have a self-belief and acceptance of who he really was: the person who could make others feel better, that people in his life didn't like anyone who was a moaner and that his role was of the calm logical person in his environment, and yet he urgently wanted to escape, he was feeling down and empty, and needed to talk. I wondered if this was part of the incongruence in his life.

This made me think of self-worth, where we feel more worthy when we become the person we perceive caretakers want us to be, even if it is not genuinely who we are, which are the ways we must follow in order to serve the perceived expectations and preferences of significant others. Was Oliver's understanding of who he thinks he ought to be based on others' expectations, adding to the confusion and tension in his life? A tension expressed as:

> "I feel so confused right now, but I don't know what about. I have a good life, what have I got to really complain about? I just want to get away?".

Oliver spoke a lot about his friendship circle and always being the friend who listened to others and their issues. He felt he genuinely cared for people and wanted to look after them. He felt he had time for others but desired to get some of that time back for himself too.

> "I have a lot of time for people...but sometimes I wish they would ask me something."

He had a desire to be liked and care for others. He seemed to take on the role of "listener" in the group, which gave him a sense of belonging and fit his belief about himself and who he is.

The more he talked about his life with me and about his relationships, I noted the angrier and more frustrated Oliver seemed to get, but he seemed very uneasy to express anger.

I used it as a guide to help me connect at a more empathic level with Oliver. He continued to talk about his desire for more exciting things to happen to him, but over and over we would come back to anger and frustration, which is when he seemed to immediately shut down. This appeared to be another condition of worth. Oliver told me how since he was little anger frightened him, because something bad always happened. He said anger was an unfamiliar concept.

Shadow of fear

He talked about his parents and their volatile relationship. He said you never knew how bad an argument would be - it was so scary "that I would nearly wet myself." My response was "that it sounded really scary." I felt it, and let him know how traumatic that must have been.

Oliver told me that lots of things scared him: confrontation, aggression of any kind – he even found asking another person a question, especially an adult, really terrifying. He was afraid how they would react, what would happen next. He said that "it is the only time I'm not "numb", when I get "scared"." Oliver told me that he sometimes overcompensates his behaviour to be liked, and will go out of his way to please, so not to make someone upset or hurt their feelings - even if his hurt.

Oliver talked a lot about the "safe haven" of his room, where he spent most of his

Therapist - Sounds like your world can be scary, lonely and really confusing and yet you give a lot of your time to listening and helping others. I just want you to know that I was listening to you today and I was really touched by what I heard.

Oliver - I don't usually get that.

Therapist - It's a new experience.

Oliver - No one really listens or cares….it's err…hard….I feel like I'm going to burden you with my rubbish.

Therapist - You feel like it will all be too much for me.

Oliver - Yeah, what if I'm not really good?, like a normal kind of person, what if I'm not that interesting, what if you're bored of me….I guess it's your job to like everyone and just listen.

Therapist - You feel like you won't be good enough as a client in here for me, and that I might get bored but that I have to listen….but maybe Oliver I want to listen because I find what you have to say important, and if something does come up that makes me uncomfortable or doesn't feel right I would share that with you, just like you are sharing with me.

Oliver – Thanks…in here it's easier being me than it is outside.

time writing, playing music according to his mood, which was usually down, but he felt he was 'My bedroom is a safe place to be where no one can hurt me; therefore I like to be in my room". It's a place where he could cry and feel down and save the "pretend face" for the outside world, as he didn't feel worthy or deserving of any more than he already had.

Pleased to meet you

As I listened to Oliver I tried to put myself in his shoes. I was feeling this huge amount of confusion and frustration, but also this sense of loneliness, of someone who is really missed in life and not seen enough. I offered an empathic response.

Therapist - *Sounds like your world can be scary, lonely and really confusing and yet you give a lot of your time to listening and helping others. I just want you to know that I was listening to you today and I was really touched by what I heard.*

Oliver - *I don't usually get that.*

Therapist - *It's a new experience.*

Oliver - *No one really listens or cares….it's err…hard….I feel like I'm going to burden you with my rubbish.*

Therapist - *You feel like it will all be too much for me.*

Oliver - *Yeah, what if I'm not really good?, like a normal kind of person, what if I'm not that interesting, what if you're bored of me….I guess it's your job to like everyone and just listen.*

Therapist - *You feel like you won't be good enough as a client in here for me, and that I might get bored but that I have to listen….but maybe Oliver I want to listen because I find what you have to say important, and if something does come up that makes me uncomfortable or doesn't feel right I would hope that I would share that with you, just like you are sharing with me.*

Oliver – *Thanks…in here it's easier being me than it is outside.*

Access to feelings

By being able to share my experience of him, Oliver was able to tap into painful feelings. He was also able to access that a lot was deep-rooted into his early childhood, memories and feelings he had pushed so far down that he physically stopped feeling anything and walked around in a state of numbness. He felt that the weight of those memories and perhaps suppressed emotions were weighing him down and that his home life had forced him to live in a state of denial and fear, to always be good, always do the right thing, never argue or question anything even if he had strong opinions about it. His sense of self of "never rocking the boat" was no longer making sense, which disturbed him; he wanted a change, yet was still afraid, but was now more aware than before that something was missing from his world. This is the process of a new awareness, looking at your world with more understanding and realising that there are some needs that haven't been attended to.

Later he talked about more feelings that had shaped his world.

Oliver - *When I was in school I was bullied because I'm ginger…I didn't want to be* *like me anymore so I tried to be like my friend John - he's tough, sarcastic and really funny. I never reacted to the bullying, pretended it didn't hurt, always pretended....my life became the perfect act from when I was 12.*

Therapist - *It was easier to be like John than yourself; they could hurt you less if you pretended...*

Oliver - *But I guess I never stopped pretending and now I don't know who I am.*

Therapist - *You just don't know who you are anymore...*

I felt a great deal of warmth from Oliver and listened with great enthusiasm, but at the start he talked more about the routine than about himself and this left me feeling quite disconnected from him and sometimes even bored, which made me feel kind of guilty as he was talking about his "boring life" and there I was sitting listening to his life feeling "bored". I felt something was missing between us and a lot of it had to do with me not telling him how I genuinely felt, which I understood was blocking our therapeutic process. How could I expect Oliver to be transparent when I was struggling or even doubting myself? It would not be okay or even ethical to ignore this. I wanted to share my feelings but felt fear of upsetting him, or even that it would hurt our relationship.

Things changed for Oliver and I when I was able to share my feelings about my experience of him:

Therapist- *Oliver, sometimes when I'm listening, I feel as though I'm getting to know what your daily routine and schedule is like. I feel like I'm missing you or hearing how you really feel about things. I guess I just wanted to let you know what was going on for me.*

Oliver- *No one ever really asks how I feel, I usually just listen... I don't know how I feel...I haven't...well, felt anything in a long time.*

Therapist- *So it's been a long time since you felt something.*

Oliver- *Yeah...most of the time I feel numb but when I feel angry I feel something, but mostly really scared like something bad's gonna happen, but I don't know what, but... I .... (Holding himself)...I feel a little scared now...*

I was aware that at times he told me part of his story, but I was always aware not to rush this development or feel like I should be doing more to understand him quicker allowing him to find his way.

There were times when Oliver implied that he needed advice, but with careful reflection and silence he was able to process his own feelings. Sometimes, after he finished speaking he would say "maybe that doesn't make sense." To let him know I heard what he was saying I would either reflect back or say if it didn't.

At the beginning, Oliver tried to do and say the right things based on valuing how others saw him, but later, he started to listen to his inner voice. Although you can never say why this happened, it happened somewhere along the line and through meeting in real terms.

In the 7th session Oliver let me know that not only was he feeling understood but also felt no judgement from me saying "I carried so much shame for wanting my dad to pay attention to me, and for wanting my mum to be nicer and not so mean, [...] this is the only place I am really myself and where I don't feel so tired."

When talking about his mother I would always feel like Oliver wanted to say a bit more but he would stop. However, when I expressed what I was noticing he shared how much fear he had and also a memory on his 13th birthday where his mum had not posted his dads letter triggered an argument which became physical. He said both him and his sister were in the back seat whilst his mum was punching his dad and biting him. He said his sister started crying and he was covering her eyes so she didn't see what was happening.

Even though it was an incident in the past, I had to make him aware of the "confidentiality agreement" between us, and that if I thought he was at risk, that this could be a safeguarding issue and that I would to make sure he was safe but was also clearer on what would happen if action needed to be taken. He went on to tell me his mum is the reason he wants to leave home because of the atmosphere and lack of attention from his dad.

Oliver-I just want to get away, it's horrible, there's no life at home

Therapist-No life...

Oliver-But then I feel bad, I should be a better son, I should help them sort it out so they don't argue.

Therapist-You feel like you should do more to help them, to keep the peace.

Oliver-After that fight my mum told my dad that she hated him and us. She told him she had been having an affair...I was sitting on the stairs listening.

Therapist-That all sounds really, err....I'm not sure I even have the right words to describe how scary that must have all been, and shocking too....

Oliver-*I feel scared thinking about it, it's so bad to think I don't like my mum....I'm her son and I can't believe I'm saying I don't like her.*

Therapist- *You don't like her.*

Oliver- *No I really don't, but I should you know 'cause she my mum, but I don't feel like that...and my dad...even though he says nothing I don't like him either.*

Therapist- *There are two sides, one saying she's my mum I should like her, and I should like my dad, but really I don't like them.*

Oliver- *(in a whisper) Yeah.*

I felt the emotional depth for Oliver, the two sides of him split and such a painful experience, wanting to like his parents but the other side not liking them at all. I tried to respect and hold both feelings Oliver was having equally. Oliver talked about how the very next day after this argument he woke up to complete calm:

Oliver-*It was like the twilight zone, I thought I dreamt the night; they were acting normal, , laughing and chatting...like nothing happened.*

Therapist-*Like it didn't happen.*

Oliver-*That's why I'm never sure about stuff, I feel like I imagine things, one minute it's a nightmare, then I wake up and it's like the bloody Walton's...and I never ask.*

Therapist-*Ask?*

Oliver-*Never ask them why they were arguing, are they ok now. They went from my mum beating my dad, to her making pancakes...so confusing.*

Therapist–*It does sound really confusing, like did that just happen, was it a dream?*

Oliver-*And I get scared that if I ask there will be another fight, and they'll get divorced and then how bad it all will be?*

Therapist-*It's like if I ask, I might make it worse...*

So in these 8 sessions I saw Oliver express a wide range of sometimes conflicting emotions, needs and anxieties. He looked like he was a little boy, carrying this heavy backpack full of pain, fear and anger, and it was weighing him down. I just stayed with him, listening and holding this vulnerability. Oliver recalled "Since the age of four years old, I felt odd but could never explain why." In total that was about 14 years of holding feelings inside, or maybe more. In essence it's always an honour when a client can release emotion and share what they have been holding - did he already feel safe with me? What was moving was the state of Oliver's process and ability to recognise his feelings no matter how confusing I felt I was truly accepting of him in these moments.

It really hurts

Oliver's was revealing a lot about himself and I sensed he was moving him forward and changing how he viewed himself. For so long he had held in his anger, afraid of what would happen if he let it out. He was able to demonstrate anger but not able entirely to own it.

He couldn't understand why he had felt so bored, numb, heavy and empty, and wanted to escape. Sometimes I could detect he wanted immediate answers or resolutions for his hurt. I would reflect back on his journey from day 1 to now and how he was really the expert of his life, that resolution and answers may take time, that it can be a slow process and I would never want to rush his journey.

During the 9th session Oliver told me the following.

Oliver-Last night I wrote my parents a letter, telling them that I feel down and suffocated and want more freedom. I couldn't do it face to face, so I did it this way.

Therapist-Sounds like a really big deal, and the most comfortable way for you.

Oliver-I thought there was going to be a really big argument. I was scared, but then they called me down and said, "We wish you talked to us sooner, we don't want you to feel like that, how can we help?" It wasn't as bad as I thought it would be, but I thought I was going to have a heart attack.

Therapist-Wow, that sounds scary and surprising all at the same time.

Oliver-it wasn't as bad as I thought, they were really understanding, and listened.

This for me felt like a huge step, and I wanted Oliver to know that I knew what a big deal it was for him. This led Oliver to reflect on other aspects of his life that he might want to deal with such as wanting his dad to reach out to him. I felt our relationship was close enough for me to be authentic in my response to Oliver's question.

Therapist- Sounds like you have more to say and question. [Context Oliver said he always put on a front where everything was always ok and perfect, perfect student, perfect friend, perfect son.]

Oliver- It makes me feel empty and alone, I'm so tired, really tired of all this.

Therapist- Sounds exhausting Oliver, like it's enough.

Oliver- How long will it take for me to stop being so scared and just saying what I need to?

Therapist- I wish I could tell you Oliver, but what I hear right now is that it's really scary and tiring and you just want...no sorry...you need more...you need it to stop being like this.

During these sessions Oliver's mum was constantly reminding him how it would look to the world if he didn't do well, and how she would look like a failure. He seemed to agree with his mum and felt guilty that he wasn't living up expectations. I remember being aware of how cross I felt with his mum and a little sad that he felt the need to protect her so much. When I heard him talk about this, it reminded me of the value I had put on external opinions and trying to please others. I wrote in Oliver's notes: "Oliver's feelings are what matter, if he agrees with mum or if he feels guilty - this is where he's at and this is his reality," and I can only work with Oliver's truth.

Although Oliver had expressed not liking his parents, he expressed wanting and needing more attention from them, saying "I want my dad to talk to me about the band he was in, I want my mum to really listen and stop being so mean...Why do I care?..I don't even think I like them goddddd!!!".

Oliver said his usual way of dealing with this kind of frustration was to shutdown, but he wasn't able to do this -"It hurts, everything just hurts...I just want to scream at them and tell them how they've damaged me," he said to me. He was feeling the hurt instead of numbing it, listening to perhaps his inner need, the need to feel and anger, wanting to scream instead of muting his inner voice.

In week 11 Oliver returned to therapy clean shaven which seemed like a big change. When he arrived he seemed really angry, saying "they had a fight last night." He then started to cry, the first lot of tears I had seen. Even now as I type this I hold the image of him hiding his face in his hands and sobbing. To see the tears, with no facial hair for the first time, felt like I was seeing Oliver without his public mask for the first time. "My mum is bitch!!!.....My dad is a coward!!" he shouted out, "I don't want to be nothing like them, closed off, cold, mean or weak, I want to be me, I'm different I'm not like them!! (sigh)". A few moments he look wary of what had occurred - his body language tensed up, clenched fists and tight jawline, he kept looking to the far wall. I felt something was going on, that he was worried, or scared. I felt this powerful urge to be say what I was feeling and seeing. I was feeling the risk would be helpful.

Therapist- Oliver, when I watch you right there, I feel like something is happening but I'm not sure what, but it feels like something...like, I can't believe I just said that out loud and now it's out.

Oliver- That's....that's exactly how I feel, I feel like I have let them down, and I wonder what you're thinking of me and them.

Therapist- When you said it Oliver I felt like a huge burden came off you, I heard it even when you released that deep sigh when you finished, it was out. It felt good to hear your feelings, and though you are worried about what I think about your mum and dad, my concern is you and how you are.

Oliver- It's horrible to say but that's how I feel about them right now.

All the things he had been holding back for years were no longer being ignored, Oliver was becoming aware of his feelings, a move towards becoming his own person, experiencing himself in the present, with immediacy and able to live in his feelings and reactions of the moment. He is unbound from the structure of his past learning. He tastes freedom, with his own subjective truth confronting life as he intends it to be.

It felt important that whilst working with Oliver he needed prizing, warmth, honesty and a safe place to own his voice, a place where he could accept himself and the world around him. What I did not want to do is what a therapist told me once, "yeah it happened but it was a long time ago," this didn't help my process, I felt like a silly child who was moaning about her life who couldn't get over stuff. I felt more shame and it just made me shut down and made me trust the world even less than before. Oliver already felt he had to be a particular way in life to receive acceptance. I wanted him to experience something different from me that I would accept him how he was.

He began to recognise the differences between himself and his family but also the different things he needed to make his life more fulfilling. He felt that he needed to act his age and have some carefree fun and sought support and fun through friends, and not always worry if mum or dad were ok.

I felt really excited at this shift in Oliver. The fact he was thinking about his needs and wants. I did wonder if this was for real, or just a spontaneous development after releasing the burst of anger about mum and dad. Was he riding the high? I reminded myself of dealing with clients in the "here and now", dealing with what's in front of us. And right now Oliver was feeling good about his friendships.

Oliver did go back to the place of anger a session later; He was told to quit therapy by his mum as he was "fine" and didn't need it. He said he felt his anger rise and he just wanted to scream at the top of his lungs, but he said he took a breath and stood up and said "No," with this being the first time he had said "no" so directly. He said not only did he feel shocked that he did it, but his mum looked stunned at what he just said: "she doesn't get to take this away for me, it's mine." I felt like I was witnessing mammoth shifts in Oliver which were having huge impacts to his life. He was moving through his felt experiences.

This "no" led to some tensions at home. He told her what he thought of her and how some of her actions have caused him pain that he has carried for many years, and he didn't want to feel so angry with her anymore. He recalled an early memory where he felt shutdown and scared and was a huge development in his life:

> "It took me ages to remember when I felt myself shut down from the world, but I remember now...I was 8...my mum and dad had a fight, she was punching him. I remember being so scared that I thought I would wet myself (crying), then she grabbed me and my dad was screaming for her to stop...she drove me to shops...and then...(rocking himself)...then she said "I'm having an affair, I don't love your dad, he is horrible, you can't love him either and soon I will divorce him".....that's all she said, then she got out the car and left me in to go and do the shopping....after when we went home it was like nothing had happened, like I dreamt it!!! From then on I have felt scared, I have felt that if I'm bad they will break up and something awful will happen.....now I don't care, maybe it would be for the best, maybe they would be happier apart, and maybe so would I."

This was the moment I remember that all the loss Oliver felt in his life started to surface, the loss of a childhood, two available parents, never seeing how to love or deal with confrontation except in an aggressive or violent way, and the loss of time he felt living in fear of the "unknown". His condition of worth that told him that to be loved he must behave like a good boy and not question things were now changing. He had had started to revise his own internal belief structure because they were not his experiences now.

He felt more confident in what he was feeling, and even sometimes when it felt scary he started to recognise what he felt was important "I love my mum, I want to start to like her again, I want to like my dad and even if they don't get on, I don't want to be like them, I want to be different.". I made a mental note "Oliver seemed so calm and peaceful." He seemed to be accepting his reality for what it was, but making his own path instead of following others.

This is me

As a therapist one of the best and important learnings you can have is to trust the process. Oliver transformed from someone who found it hard to express feelings but could tell me his thoughts, to someone who cried in anger and loss. The path he had been on had been having profound effects on his life and wellbeing; by never opening up he felt empty and numb.

He recognised that he wanted more and something better; he wanted to have more genuine relationships where he was able to be more honest about his feelings and not always hold back because of fear of what might occur - "It's scary and exciting." In friendship groups being himself was a revelation instead of being the "intelligent" or "funny one". He said "I wanted to talk about the Samurai but wasn't sure other people would be interested, but they were! It felt so good, and less tiring to figure who I should be today."

As he got more comfortable being himself, his confidence seemed to go up, especially when it came to dating when he felt comfortable he would ask out ladies he felt attracted to, "I just thought if I don't do it I never will, and she said yes, oh my god."

So much was changing in his life. He was letting his parents get on with their stuff, but he did things with them individually, like seeing a band with his dad. He was thinking of his needs. The growth and wisdom in him felt tremendous.

He was doing things that previously he struggled with such as driving lessons. He felt he could conquer it and by the time we came to finish, he had got his licence. He booked himself on a Samurai re-enactment weekend with his father.

Not only was Oliver looking and speaking more confidently, but I noticed it even in the way he sat in the therapy chair with his shoulders back and head up high. Even his voice seemed more mature.

Around session 19 Oliver could see the end of his journey. He would be leaving for Asia, then to university. Even though he said he felt sad and a little anxious of what might happen if he stopped therapy, we planned to see each other every other week to see how it would feel to be without a session saying "I can see why it's coming to an end, but still it's scary, what if I go back to my old ways?" We planned our ending slowly, as this is what Oliver thought would be the best. He seemed to be doing okay with coming every other week. Life had changed for him - instead of feeling stuck at home he was out "living life".

On session 20 he said his parents had a big row, a verbal disagreement. He said that instead of hiding, he told them to "stop it," and "if you don't want to be together than split up for god sake," he said he was worried his mum was going to get angry with him, but she started crying and said "I think I need help.". Oliver said "They are going to marriage counselling, as long as they do something, they can't keep doing the same old shit."

For Oliver, I had become the person he trusted and was able to say things to that he never thought he would be able to say out loud and someone who got him, saying "I used to walk out here and go…I can't believe I told her that, you were just always here."

The last few words of our ending went as follow.

Oliver- *I learnt a lot, I couldn't have done it alone….remember I wasn't even sure I would last one session.*

Therapist- *I remember, it has been a long road.*

Oliver- *Thanks for sticking by me and helping me find me.*

Therapist- *You know you did it, all that hard work and all… really getting down deep you did it; I was just here with you.*

Oliver- *I'll miss you.*

Therapist- *I'll miss our sessions too.*

Oliver's healing journey

At the beginning of therapy, Oliver felt isolated, lonely and misunderstood. By the end of therapy, he was at a place where I could say he had "a greater degree of independence and a sense of being whole." He seemed confident and had a stronger sense of who he was and what he would accept in his life. As part of the process, you can see how Oliver moved from a fixed view of the world to a more fluid state, where at different stages, Oliver changed his position and understand of his relationships to self, people and the world. For Oliver his life seemed to have a lot of rigidity, and routine governed his life. It sounded oppressive for him, but as he moved through his process, he became more open to experience and more congruent (or in harmony) with his true feelings, e.g., friendship circles expanded and he was more outgoing.

I would say that when Oliver started therapy, he was somewhere around the minimisation stage (see Chapter 6 - Stages of Therapeutic Process) where his feelings were out of awareness. He was open to therapy; he came of his own accord but initially found it hard to talk about himself. He would talk about activities and his daily schedule, but things shifted in our relationship when I was able to be congruent about what I was hearing and listen with empathy and acceptance; instead of placing value on the external messages. He began to listen to his internal voice and give value to that. Instead of sinking into the volatile hole at home, he desired more. He wanted something, "a change." He began to embrace who he was, he reunited with an old friend to gain support but he also escaped his home life, and he faced his anger and loss. He started to ask for what he needed. Once he was able to confront his anger, he began to confront the people who were hurting him. He wanted a new way of being with them. He knew he couldn't change them, but he wanted a change in himself, so he took ownership of his life and began to listen to his feelings and instincts rather than being wary of what someone might say or think of him. Oliver's fear of anger and expressing it changed as he grew to understand he had a right to be angry about the things he was angry about. He learned it is ok to express these feelings, to ask for things, to question things and to need things. He also learned he can change things.

If I had to pass on some wisdom, as many have done for me, in reflection, it would be that the importance of a relationship cannot be underplayed—a relationship that is built on trust, honesty, patience and authenticity, a connection that is unique unlike any other.

I wanted to use an analogy that I had used with Oliver about his therapeutic journey. I imagine Oliver as a Samurai warrior going out to find some stolen treasure, riding his horse through the mountain plains. Every time we got close to our destination, an obstacle would be in the way delaying us, so it was up to Oliver to decide how to get around each obstacle. Whether it was his parents, anger, or loss, he could face it, feel it and trust himself enough to know what was best. Oliver went from being a great warrior to being a great leader and successor of his own life. The journey of the relationship takes more work than dealing with the issue itself. That is the healing process.

Through Oliver, I have now shown how someone's healing journey works. It is not a process to be copied but one I hope will help you understand the significance of relationship, how inner change occurs and how that helps make the changes you want on the outside. I hope you find your heart during your process. In subsequent chapters, I will draw examples from Oliver's journey to explain therapeutic change and its stages.

Self-Reflection

Use these questions to explore your own, as well as Oliver's, therapeutic process.

Note: Since not all that went on could be written, you can try to get a sense of Oliver's journey from your own feelings as your read about him. Feel free to "fill in the blanks," letting your mind wander and imagine what it was like and what went on inside him for his change to happen.

1.   What problem do you believe Oliver was experiencing? Why?

2.   Why do you think he felt confusion?

3. Why was he upset at the start and towards the middle?

4. What inner changes did Oliver experience during the process? (See Chapter 6 "What Changes Inside" for ideas.)

5. What external changes did Oliver experience during the process? External changes are things outside himself that he changed, e.g., change of jobs.

6. Why do you think he changed internally and externally? What changed internally? (See Chapter 6: "What changes exactly?")

7. If you have been in or are in therapy now, how would you answer the questions above with regard to your own experiences?

8. What stage of the process do you feel Oliver was in when he entered therapy? (Decide after reading Chapter 6: "Stages of Therapeutic Process.")

9. Can you recognise particular stages of the process Oliver went through? Why? (Decide after reading Chapter 6: "Stages of Therapeutic Process.")

10. What stage of therapy do you believe you are in? Are there any internal or external changes you are seeking to make? (Decide after reading Chapter 6: "Stages of Therapeutic Process.")

Chapter 5 – Process themes in therapy

A significant part of the work you do with your therapist is to understand what lies beneath your words and actions (i.e. your process). This can occur naturally where you speak and the therapist hears and experiences what you say. You build awareness of your world and so does the therapist.

Awareness can also be used to notice any inconsistencies between what you say and what may be going on deeper inside, or in what you really think and feel. Knowing how you really feel is not always easy as it may be hidden from you and/or the therapist. Understanding what is below the surface of feelings and behaviours is sometimes called "awareness of process" (See Way 7: Understand yourself through awareness).

These process themes or patterns could occur, regardless of your specific problems or what material you bring into therapy. It does not matter if you're talking about grief, guilt, anxiety, or issues in your relationships.

In this chapter, you will find some examples of process which are relevant to the ways in this book. Of course, there are many others, but I hope it gives you a start in understanding the idea of "process," types of process, and so lead you to looking at becoming more aware of your own process. I introduce these themes here, but for a more thorough treatment see my other book "Client perceptions in therapy".

These process themes in this chapter are divided into three categories; those that occur within yourself, between you and the experience of therapy, and between you and the therapist.

If you identify one of these themes or others within you, it can be used as an opening to explore further during therapy. In doing so, you become more self-aware and assess whether it has a part to the play in your difficulties.

Quick Start – Process themes

Here is a list of the themes covered in this chapter to help you decide which ones you want to focus on.

Title	When it could be relevant to explore
I forgot myself	You tend to focus more on others than yourself.
I am my labels	You assume that your psychological difficulties are to do with having a condition (like a disease) more than your unique experiences.

Title	When it could be relevant to explore
But I had a good childhood	You have difficulty seeing how childhood could be relevant to how you are the way you are, or your difficulties. You feel it's difficult to talk about the impact caregivers had on you.
But I'm feeling worse now	You feel worse so you are considering leaving therapy. You are worried that therapy will make you feel worse long term rather than better.
Calm the inner critic	You tend to be harshly critical of yourself
I know	You're stuck in therapy
No time to heal	You have no time for therapy or recovery
I can fix it	You tend to focus on solutions rather than process
It's you, and it has always been you	You're confused on how to effect your own change
As you are	To understand the importance of being yourself in therapy You find it difficult to be yourself in therapy
Love in the room	You feel emotionally or sexually attracted to the therapist
Idealised	You tend to idealise the therapist You tend to see people as either good or bad

Themes in relation to the self

In this section, some of the patterns which occur between you and yourself, and their possible meaning are described. How you relate to yourself and its meaning is critical in understanding who you are and what you need to change. In this sense, it's your "process" in how you feel about the relationship you have with yourself that is under the spotlight. As with all patterns, not all will be applicable to you, but if any resonate, then that is a good opportunity for further self-reflection and potential work with the therapist.

I forgot myself

Socrates was on trial and accused of blasphemy against the gods, inventing new deities and corrupting the youth. The accusers gave such a powerful and moving account of why Socrates should be found guilty. After the end of the accuser's rhetoric, Socrates took a lengthy pause and said:

> "I do not know, men of Athens, how my accusers affected you; as for me, I was almost carried away in spite of myself, so persuasively did they speak. And yet, hardly anything of what they said is true."

Socrates was clearly entranced by the mesmerising account of his misdeeds that even the wise Socrates was taken in; he lost himself and almost believed what the accusers had said was true. He had to get back into his own mind and to his own internal frame of reference to understand that hardly anything said was really true.

This is something that you may also discover in therapy, that aspects of you are lost in the world, outside yourself. Often others become central, and the external world is where you focus your mind more. Whether it's your beliefs, who you are, what to do, decisions, and self-care, they are externally determined rather than by you in relation to the world.

> Lucy had spent most of her life caring for others. She was the eldest of three children. She had been a carer for her mother when she was being beaten by her dad and also had to fill in to care for her siblings. Her father and mother also controlled her and her decisions, because she was not able to do things "like other children." This became her norm to care for others and to need her parents to tell her what to do in life. As a grownup, she sought relationships where she could continue that role and was particularly attracted to ambitious and "righteous" men, who knew how the world worked and what to do. She continued to "go along" with others who understood the world more and she wanted to care for people even though she did not feel cared for by her family or partner. She spent twenty years of marriage in state of being entranced by people and the world. She entered therapy because she had reached a stage where she could not do it

280

anymore, and she did not want to be invisible anymore. She had lost herself and wanted to return to her own mind.

If parts of this resonate for you, you can ask at what expense and whether the way of being is what you want now. This is not to say that continuously caring for others is not the right path, it means that you recognise the impact to you. Communities, relationships, family and groups thrive based on reciprocity, which means you give and you receive. However, if you are the end of the chain and no one is particularly "giving" or championing you, you can feel as if you have dropped off the edge. Therapy is an opportunity to put yourself in centre stage, to see the world in relation to you. This is what "finding yourself" can mean.

Self-Reflection

- Do you feel you give more than you receive? Is that an issue?
- What are you needs, and how do you get them, e.g., care, love, understanding, intimacy and empathy?
- How can you get your needs met, e.g., share more or ask for it?
- What are the obstacles to getting your needs met?
- How much of what you do, understand or believe comes from your own understanding rather than people and the world?

Labels are really useful in life. They help us identify things and what they mean. Without labels, we would have no idea what town we lived in, what food we were buying or what the term "bachelor" means. However, when it comes to labels to define who you are, your problems, and your emotional world, things get more complicated. When we label ourselves in therapy with an assumed or an official mental health diagnosis, it can have the inadvertent potential to mask off or hide your whole being and your fuller experience from being revealed. The label can become an idea of who or what you are, and what it's like to be you, based on preconceptions around the label rather than the real or true you. Labels therefore have the potential to cover up feelings, what life is like for you, your history and memories, and ultimately block off developing a thorough understanding of yourself and what is true for you.

That is not to say labels should not be used in therapy, but they are a starting point for exploration, a possible means to an end, not an end itself. The label should serve you, not the other way around. Just like you cannot judge a book by its cover, the labelling of you and your emotions can, if not checked, communicate misjudgements about you as well as others. Becoming aware of how you use labels can be useful in your process. Look below the label to what the label means and explore it further.

In addition, the label can, if left unchecked, end up becoming a *self-fulfilling prophecy*. For example, if you believe you will never be a swimmer, then it's unlikely you'll try to find out. It is self-fulfilling because you have labelled yourself when in fact it may or may not be true. Even though your feeling is your truth, it is not an objective one, so it narrows down possibilities. Similarly, if you believe "no one likes you," you may develop an anxiety of fear of people, you're reluctant to make the effort to engage and keep a distance which in turn keeps you away from meeting new people. Subsequently, it reinforces the "no one likes you" label.

Keyword: Self-fulfilling prophecy is any held belief that causes, either directly or indirectly, that belief to become true.

Labels may also be a way of hiding what you truly feel about yourself, and instead your find a preferred way (persona) of presenting yourself. For example, you may say, "I am not scared of anything," as you believe that showing your fears would make you a weak person. In actuality, you may be fearless in certain areas but scared in others, and it's what you feel scared about that may be what is relevant to therapy.

Some people may have or want a diagnosis. Examples of labels include autism, bipolar disorder or post-traumatic stress disorder. In therapy, the diagnosis can help the therapist gain an initial understanding and even inform the way they provide therapy, but therapy sees that very much as a starting point and seeks to look behind the label to the whole person because therapy is more about understanding the whole of you – the inner you, your story, feelings, what has shaped you and how that relates to any problems you share. In therapy, the therapist will be recognising you as more than any label or symptom; they will see you as a whole, unique and complex being.

Another way to look at labels is to look at brief descriptions as a label; these tell you something of an event, experience or feeling in the client's inner world, but they are still labels because they do not go any further or deeper. Like the synopsis or "blurb" of a book gives you an idea of what the book is about, it does not tell you everything you need to experience to understand it deeply – to do that would require thorough, attentive, absorbed reading and feeling the words expressed by the book.

A *descriptive label* may just be stated without any follow-up. There is a lot missing in the description; that is why it's like a label too.

> "I had an argument last night with my partner, I told him he didn't care and was just using me.. But it didn't work and he just said I need to keep space from him now. I think it is over and I've got to accept it, that's that."

This is a label of an experience that does not go further. For example, what was the argument about? What didn't work? Why is it over? What's your feeling? Therapists are trying to connect with the client's inner world. The labelling occurs here because there is no broader and deeper elaboration that tries to understand circumstances of what happened and their feelings.

That is not to say that a mental health diagnosis and labelling is bad or wrong when it comes to defining the emotional state or experience you're in. It is more of a concern when it hides you, your true feelings, emotions, thoughts, and experiences. You are more than a label.

Reasons for using labels

How do you use labels? It may be something to explore further in therapy?

- Because it is easier
- As a starting point and to share initial information
- The labels are what people told you. Do you believe others labels of you?
- The labels block the desire to understand further. Labels can be detrimental if it blocks self-understanding.
- It keeps you safe from difficult feelings. Are labels a way of feelings safe from exploring more difficult feelings?
- You prefer the label
- Your ashamed of part of you, so the label is a relief

- A label makes you feel it's not you; rather, it's something outside your control

Spot the labels

Notice the labels in these quotes:

"I'm just too **needy** for my own good. My husband gets annoyed with me when I get needy. I'm worried he will leave me. I'm just going to stop it now."

"I've spent too long in therapy; I'm a **failure.**"

"I'm just **angry** all the time; every time someone tries to dominate me, I try and destroy them."

"I read online about **avoidant personality disorders**. I definitely think that's me."

"I keep pushing people away because I am too **needy.**"

Examples of labels:

➤ Shy/quiet
➤ Needy
➤ Jealous
➤ Angry
➤ Introverted
➤ Bossy
➤ Good, bad or fine
➤ Not normal
➤ Nag
➤ High-maintenance
➤ Crazy
➤ Right or wrong
➤ Attention seeker
➤ An official diagnosis
➤ An unofficial self diagnosis
➤ I'm fine

Self-Reflection

- What labels would you use on yourself, in life, in therapy or to label your emotional world?
- What labels do you like or don't like?
  - Do you notice any "that's that" type of statements? For example, "I'm ADHD, that's all there is to it."

- Do you understand where the label came from?
- Are your labels useful? Why?
- Do you want to explore more of who you are under the labels? Why?

But I had a good childhood

When you reflect upon your childhood, especially your caregivers and family, it may appear to you that any problems you have now are in no way related. This can be especially true if you did indeed have a good childhood. However, there are a number of perspectives you may wish to consider when deciding whether to bring your childhood into focus within therapy.

Regardless of the way you grew up, the environment, your family, or lack of family, would've had an influence on you, whether it's your beliefs, values or how you experience relationships. I am sure we can all think of something, such as a good teacher who encouraged you to pursue your career or being anxious speaking in front of the school. So, therapy can give you the opportunity to understand how your childhood impacted you and whether it's relevant to your problems. This awareness has the potential to open doors inside you that can guide and deepen your therapy.

Here are a couple of examples when talking about having a *good childhood* was found useful:

> *Charlie was only 4 years old. He was regularly dropped off to his grandma's house every Tuesday and really enjoyed his time. However, on one occasion, his grandmother was not available, so his father took him to stay for the day at Mike's house. Charlie got on pretty well with Mike and had no issues with staying with him, although it was an unfamiliar environment. As Charlie's dad left him, he said, "Now, you be good boy and have fun but now I have to go." In that moment, Charlie froze and was confused and assumed his dad meant that he may never come back. He was quiet and withdrawn for a while but enjoyed the rest of the day. The fear he experienced was not due to any poor parenting, but now as an adult, he felt those same fearful feelings when he was separated from his partner for long periods of time.*

> *Shirley was an only child and brought up by loving, caring and supportive parents. She could not really wish for more in her childhood and looked back at her childhood as the "best time of her life." She really loved her parents and felt really close to them. However, what she struggled with in adulthood was her confidence and fears of making decisions in her life. She was able to link these problems with her childhood, particularly as her parents would make most decisions for her and tell her what she needed to do. But now she constantly needed their approval to make decisions whether in relationships or when buying some trainers. She said her parents had somewhat "wrapped her up in cotton wool" contributing to her feeling of being unable to face decisions or take personal responsibility for them.*

Another common theme in therapy is where you feel conflicted about whether you should talk about your caregivers. The conflict may be because there is a part of you that wishes to talk about your childhood as you have an intuition or even foresight that it's something relevant, but another part of you has an overwhelming feeling of guilt, anxiety or even fear about talking about your caregivers in a "negative" way. It just feels judgemental, critical and disloyal. After all, it's not their fault and you're responsible for your problems, aren't you? You don't want to play the "victim" by blaming others for your issues. You have an instinctive protectiveness for them given the importance of the relationship and how you've been supported by them you all your life. Here is an example of this type of conflict where a client is right on the edge of exploring their feelings about caregivers:

> "I really don't want to talk about my feelings; it's difficult and I don't want to blame them. I do think my past is related to the way I try to control my emotions and my health anxiety, but I'm worried what happen if I do. I'm scared my relationship will change if I go there."

One way of gently working with your conflicts and anxious feelings is to simply talk about them in therapy and see where it leads you. Exploring feelings about feelings, or meta-feelings, may naturally lead you to the answer of "what to do" and help you to decide whether you want or are ready to explore your childhood further. Sometimes, just by talking about your worries, and their reasons, such as fearing the consequences of disclosure, can lead to more exploration in other areas, and create more safety and a stronger relationship with your therapist.

Exploring your childhood can be about understanding how your caregivers impacted you in life, rather than blaming them, absolving your responsibility, or painting them in a bad light. Looking at your childhood is more about understanding the circumstances of your childhood and whether that can be useful to your healing process. Of course you may blame them, but therapy is about what you feel regardless.

Possible reasons for not wanting to talk about childhood

Remember, these reasons should be seen as valid reasons rather than wrong; it is about whether you wish to challenge them or not.

- You had a good childhood
- Painful experiences
- Unknown consequences of disclosure
- Cannot see how it's relevant to your situation now
- You've got so much other stuff to explore, it's simply not a priority
- You don't wish to be disloyal, critical or blame them

- You wish to take responsibility for your life now
- You wish to keep the image of who your caregivers are in tact
- Feelings of shame
- Wanting to distance yourself from the younger you and the past

Self-Reflection

After you have read this section, reflect on how you feel about your childhood.

1. How would you describe your childhood?
2. What are your best memories?
3. What are your worst memories?
4. Who did you feel closest to?
5. Who hurt you the most?
6. How has it shaped who you are today?
7. Do you believe your childhood is related to your current problems?
8. Are you ready to talk about your childhood more? Why?
9. Do you have any conflicts about talking about caregivers or childhood? What are they?

Summary

- Childhood experiences do influence how we develop into adulthood
- Childhood experiences, even good ones, may be relevant to self-awareness and your problems
- It's not uncommon to find it difficult to talk about childhood. For example, because of guilt or feelings that you're blaming caregivers
- Your conflicting feelings about whether to talk about childhood may in itself be useful
- Talking about childhood is about understanding how your childhood affected you and how it relates to your problems or goals

As always, you decide what feels right for you.

But I'm feeling worse now!

Therapy is not always a straight line, nor is it without difficulty. You may feel worse before feeling better. A narrative of someone who feels worse:

> "I wasn't expecting this. I feel worse than I did at the start. This can't be good! Every time I come here, I'm more and more in touch with the pain of my wife cheating on me! It just stirs things up more."

Well, it's an understandable sentiment that getting in touch with pain is difficult. It is a bit like exposing an open wound to the air or putting you hand near the fire you'll want to be cautious. However, it could be also be a significant sign that therapy is working and on your way to feeling better longer-term.

There are a number of reasons why you may feel worse, but essentially, you're getting in direct contact with your feelings and thoughts, which may be difficult to face and include bad memories, grief and other emotions that were previously hidden from your immediate attention (or suppressed, as therapists refer to it).

> "My dad died 12 months ago and we didn't really have a relationship. He would never really make the effort. I always had to make the effort for him to come around. I'm okay because he wasn't there for me at the start and was never there so it's not like having a real dad. There is nothing I can do about it; I just have to accept it."

Here, a client is starting to touch upon something early on that could be, unbeknown to him, a set of complex painful feelings underneath that are causing his downward spiral into depression. Once revealed, the painful emotions can come to the surface, such as feeling rejection and guilt for losing the father he never really had.

In some cases, the pain could be totally hidden until associated memories come up which you did not even know existed. In the excerpt below, the client has realised a painful memory he had "forgotten," and getting in touch with the feelings of being abused made him feel worse and even more ashamed at first but he had made the first step.

> "I had a good childhood. But I remember always being the one who listened; no one appeared to listen to me about my feelings. I just became a listening robot to get attention and fit in. One day, I was coming home from school, and a bunch of kids attacked me. I remember going home in shock and for some reason, I don't know why, I never told anyone. I was so ashamed. It's only after talking about it that this memory came to me."

Once the therapeutic process brings these hidden or untouched feelings out to the fore to be worked on, you can feel worse because you're now feeling parts of the original pain and the feelings surrounding them, which brings an opportunity for healing.

"Feeling worse" in therapy can appear to be self-defeating or hopeless, when in fact, it could be the opposite. The therapeutic journey should not be seen as a straight line but more as a road with many contours, turns, and twists. You could be well on your way to feeling better and you just don't know it yet. So, if you get into this situation, you should not just ask, am I feeling better, but also is it working? I also recommend not leaving the therapist without exploring the "worse feeling" first. Sticking with the process, working through the difficult feelings could be the path of recovery you just might need.

Warning. We have to caveat this section a bit. If you're not ready to go deeper into your feeling, then you are not ready. It has to be what you want to do. Also, just because you're feeling worse or if more pain is being experienced, this does not imply that it's healthy either. Talk to your therapist and/or physician if you have concerns and you are feeling worse.

Self-Reflection

- What are your past experiences of feeling worse with regard to your physical or emotional wellbeing? What did you learn from it? Do you see a pattern of how you deal with difficulties in life and in your mental wellbeing?
- If you have felt worse after a session or for a while during therapy, can you pinpoint possible explanations as to why that is?
  - In general, therapy can be very exhausting and draining. Working on feelings you are facing anew or having to delve into them can be straining. On the other hand, it can be very lifting. What do you normally experience?

Calm the inner critic

You may already be familiar with the sandwich approach to giving feedback. You begin with what went well, what you may wish to work on more and what you did well again. Coming from anyone in the true spirit of learning and with the purpose of teaching and helping, critique is one of mankind's greatest achievements and it is needed for any form of development. How is it possible to make progress in our learning if it does not contain a critique? Here, the critique is termed feedback, and it is an important part of making judgements necessary to improve the self, others, relationships, work or any learning. Criticism offered in the true spirit of learning is a gift.

However, when it comes to criticising ourselves, we can be the harshest of all critics.

Consider the following examples:

"I should have done better at school."

"Why was I so scared? Why didn't I just defend my friend from being attacked?"

"Arghh, I *hate myself* for being so fat. I just can't seem to stop eating!"

"I don't know what to do here. I've been doing therapy for so long, I just feel like a *failure*."

"I'm so *boring;* everyone seems to have such interesting things to say. I *can't stand* myself."

"I am *disgusting. I hate* what I see in the mirror. I hate when my partner even touches me."

In these examples, criticism takes on a different form; rather than being supportive to improve, it is very harsh and punishing. The problem with these types of criticisms is they are shaming, demotivating, anxiety provoking and can be downright scary. The effect of being on the receiving end of these messages could be extremely damaging to how you feel about yourself. The longer-term impact of harsh criticism could include avoiding any situations that trigger these thoughts, and instead of dealing with the problem, you keep busy, procrastinate or even turn to unhealthy addictions. So for example, someone who criticises themselves as boring may avoid social situations and turn to constantly working long hours to avoid feeling.

These criticisms may also impact how we view ourselves overall, that somehow we are defective, weak or bad. When we feel shame we withdraw and disconnect from people as well as ourselves, by finding unhelpful comfort in things like food or drugs, we may mistakenly believe that this will take away the shame and it does but for a short while.

In therapy, you can see this as applying a "hammer to your head." Ultimately what you need to do is find a way of working on ourselves by calming these criticisms and thereby your take care of yourself. So, if you can become aware of an unhealthy critical voice within, you can explore it further during therapy. Notice your self-criticisms and process them "down and out." Having an objective learning mind rather than harsh critical one ultimately is going to give you space to learn and learning involves making mistakes to improve too.

Possible Reasons for the harsh critic

- Introjected messages from experiences of caregivers and people around us. That is, you have taken on board others' views of you and swallowed it as your truth.
- Perfectionism, idealism or very demanding expectations.
- Highly focused on comparison with others.
- Being bullied.
- Linked to how you judge and feel about yourself.

Possible ways to calm the critic:

Usually, the more ingrained and aggressive the criticism, the more therapeutic work is required. Here are some starting points:

- Just be aware and notice it. Say, "Ah, I noticed it."
- Be vulnerable and journal the reasons why, or talk to someone safe about why you feel critical about something.
- Next time you get something wrong, see if you can be more relaxed about not getting it right.
- Use the feedback approach on yourself – what did you do good, what could you improve and what did you do well again?
- Label the inner critic metaphorically, with humour or visually. For example, it could be a big plastic hammer hitting your head or even an obnoxious parody of a colleague criticising you.

Self-Reflection

1. What self-criticisms do you tell yourself? You could also ask someone what they think you do that is detrimentally self-critical.
2. What would you say if someone said those things to a loved partner, friend or child? What do you think the effect of that criticism would be longer-term?
3. What do you feel when you hear those criticisms?

4. What issues does the criticism cause? Does it cause an avoidance of feelings and situations? What behaviours does it influence? For example, not wanting to do things you want.
5. What do you really need to take good care of yourself? Or, what is it that you really need to hear? Express this to your inner critic with feedback.
6. Talk to your critic or write it down as a dialogue as if it were a different person and see what conversation you could have with that part. See if you can gently give that part feedback. You certainly don't want to give the critical part harsh treatment (two wrongs don't make a right!).

Themes in relation to the process

In this section, some patterns which occur between you and the process of therapy, and their possible meaning in your journey, are described. In this sense, it's your "process" about the process of doing therapy. As with all patterns, not all will be applicable to you, but if any resonate, then that is a good opportunity for further self-reflection and potential work with the therapist.

I know

Socrates, the Greek philosopher, was astonished when the oracle of Delphi said, "There is no one wiser than Socrates!" He did not believe that of himself, and asked, how could that be? Given the reliability of the source, he spent time investigating various experts on all matters to determine how that could be. He finally came to a conclusion and said, "Ah, I get it: they think they know something, but I know I know absolutely nothing."

That's part of how therapy can be effective: be tentative about what you know about yourself, what will be the solution and what will happen next. Be fluid and open to the idea you don't know everything yet and any conclusions are tentative as you go through your journey. For example, do you know what is causing the symptoms? do you know what you understand about yourself and your needs, and your childhood?

Why is this important? Well, it is a bit like excavating an archaeological site for treasures and thinking there are no more rooms left to explore after two or three, when there may be dozens more; you don't know, but you reserve that judgement. Your awareness and understanding of yourself and how that influences your issues is usually of paramount importance when healing. Blocking further investigation can pre-emptively block access to more inner doors. Simply put, any understanding you have may have not be the whole picture.

A classic way of describing this need for tentative knowledge we have was laid out by Sigmund Freud. He describes what we know about ourselves as an iceberg: the tip of the iceberg is what we know about, yet there is a whole lot more going on underneath!

A narrative that may indicate a block to further discoveries may sound something like this:

> "[beginning therapy] I've been through therapy before over many years. So I know it's about my anger towards my parents. I don't think repeating that with you is going to make a difference. I've also done the 'punch the bag' and 'get your anger out' bit. Can you give me some techniques to make this anxiety drop?"

Other types of voices that may indicate this type of thinking include "there is nothing that can be done now,", "I don't see how this can help,", "I know that already," or "I had a good childhood." While these feelings are real and are to be respected; having an open mind to other possibilities and new experiences can open up new possibilities, particularly if the problems still remain.

Here is a pattern of narrative of what happens when you discover something new about yourself in therapy:

> "I never knew my work-performance anxiety was also to do with how I felt that my mum took sides with my stepfather rather than with me. I thought this was really all about my boss at work. I don't know how, but exploring that stuff seemed to help with my anxiety at work. I poured my heart out to my mum, and hearing her say sorry helped."
>
> *Note: confronting people about harm they caused you is always something I recommend reflecting on in therapy first.*

During therapy, be open and curious about yourself, people and the world around you. Learn about yourself just like you would go about any type of learning. For example, if as you learn to juggle balls, you accept that it's a process, you'll learn by experience and making mistakes, and in your own time, you will improve. You can only know what you know about how to juggle at a point in time even with assistance. The learning process may involve looking at your posture in the mirror, how the palms of your hands are placed or where your eyes should be focused. You only know what you know at a point in time; there is plenty more to learn, and that applies to yourself too.

Have no conclusions, don't assume where things will lead to and what can or will help the most. Letting go of fixed conclusions leaves the door open for new ideas, possibilities and ultimately growth and healing. You don't assume you know the answers until of course you're in a better place or at the end of therapy. It is common for life-long travellers to never say they have seen all parts of the world, and that can apply to yourself too. Socrates believed he knew nothing, and that is the true spirit of living and learning.

Self-Reflection

- How do you generally approach learning, e.g., a hobby, learning to use a device or even some DIY project?
- Do you learn analytically by following instructions or by feel and through experience?

- Do you notice what you feel during the process of learning? Feelings including being absorbed, frustration, impatience, or wanting the learning process to end or continue further.
- How do you feel usually when someone else knows more about a subject than you? How does it feel in competitive situations? School? And at home?
- Do you feel you are open to learning and letting the therapist help you?

When there is a physical injury, our body tells us very quickly when something is wrong. If we injure our leg, we are soon aware of our condition because of pain or a limitation, such as not being able to move the leg freely. We usually realise because of these symptoms and their impact on us that we need to seek help. A doctor may suggest we go on some medication, do some exercises, and go through a rehabilitation programme of physiotherapy and rest to take off the full weight of the body on the leg. We may have to take a bit of time off work, forgo the exercise we once enjoyed and reduce our social activity. If we do not heed the advice of doctors and give ourselves time to heal, we could end up in a cycle of recovery that is far longer, and our leg may get worse, causing a more permanent impact or just prolonging the recovery. Bottom line: if we don't give time or priority to the injury, we don't give ourselves the best chance to heal.

In comparison with mental health, it is common to ignore psychological symptoms because of their lack of externally visible signs. With psychological symptoms, such as anxiety or prolonged low moods, we can still be highly functioning and have no apparent physical limitations, so we may choose to ignore them and carry on business as usual. Even when we know something is wrong, we may end up putting it off and even feel ashamed of the stigma of seeking mental health support. We may make some moves to help ourselves, like get more sleep, but we don't fully perform the necessary steps to give us the best chance of recovery. For example, we may continue working long hours and continue to expose ourselves to mentally stressful situations, causing our anxiety to spiral. A voice may be saying something is wrong but because we appear to be functioning "as-if" these problems were non-existent, the symptoms become easier to ignore. The necessary care is simply not present. After a while, our mental health issues can start interfering not just "inside" of our mind but they can also spill over into the physical and impact external situations, such as anxiety at work, anxiety attacks and not being able to enjoy life anymore. Just like walking on an injured leg, the more we "push through" emotional injuries, the more the issues can grow and the emotional injury gets bigger and more severe, increasing the time we need to recover fully. It could even result in what is popularly referred to as a "nervous breakdown" where the level of depression, anxiety or dissociation is to such an extent that you are not able to function without resolution.

Mental health requires metaphorically the same type of attitude to healing as a physical injury. This may include finding time to heal, changing lifestyle, and seeking support, advice and therapy. Therefore, the commitment to the act of a therapeutic process is analogous to not simply pushing through and standing on an injured leg but giving yourself the "space" mentally to work on yourself. By working on recovery through therapy, you are accepting the fact that there is an emotional injury, just as you would for a physical injury. Through accepting the need to make changes to recover, we are doing the equivalent of taking the weight off our emotional injury, which provides us a clear space to heal emotionally.

If you feel this is you, perhaps it's time to explore that further because sometimes, people are good at valuing others more, or they are less inclined to treat themselves as well.

Self-Reflection

1. Do you suffer from any psychological problem, e.g., low moods, anxiety, stress, fears or sadness?
2. How are you generally with caring about yourself? Attending to yourself and your needs?
3. Do you give yourself time and priority when it comes to your wellbeing? If not, why?
    a. As an experiment, think about someone you have responsibility for or care deeply about. It could be a child or an elderly parent. Now, imagine they are struggling with the same problems you are experiencing. What advice and/or care would you provide them? Would your approach to care change? Would the priorities change? Would you invest time and money on them?
4. If you believe you need to spend more time on yourself, how can you achieve that? For example, you could change priorities or give yourself more time and space in your spare time.

Fred came to counselling because of the relationship difficulties he was having with his wife. He had a turbulent history with his stepson, and he often clashed with his wife over him. It had gotten to a stage where he was feeling disconnected with his wife and things were not being shared freely between them. It felt like he was in a triangle, and she would keep the relationship with her son away from him. Fred shared their history, the pains and how his stepson had disrespected him many times. He understood what he was feeling, and at the end, he decided to reach out to his stepson to try and fix it. But as a few sessions proceeded, he could not understand why he was not feeling any better and neither was she. They continued to be short with one another, distant and missing each other's needs. What was going on? What was missing?

It was only when he got in touch with his true feelings –feelings of being second-best and anger that his wife would allow her son to get away with things, even though she knew her son could be very "difficult." He realised why his fix of reaching out to his stepson and talking to his wife was a start and not a fix. So although reconciliation with his stepson was welcomed by his wife, it hid the anger, resentment and pain that was buried deep within him. His anger of being left out, her anger at him, and their 18-year history of turbulence remained, so no matter his reconciliation with her son, it could not fix his relationship with her.

Fred and his wife took up the suggestion of couples counselling and engaged in a process over a number of months to heal their real underlying feelings of resentment, disappointment and hurt. Fred and his wife realised that fixing things was only a start, and that a natural inclination towards a quick-fix was not possible because of missed or dormant feelings underneath. They learnt that through experience, the answer lay not in the apparent fix, but in the process of healing, which includes reciprocal understanding of feelings, what happened and why. Only then did the underlying feelings begin to subside and move on. The fix was not the answer; the process was the answer.

In another example, the process can be missed because of assumptions about what would make healing work:

> Jim came to therapy looking for answers. He would often analyse his feelings, thoughts and childhood. He wanted answers in the hope that by having the answer, he would be able to relieve himself of symptoms of feeling low. He was quick to be anxious and frustrated in session that he could not find it. Later, he discovered there were many reasons for this but one factor was his assumption that he had to find the golden answer. But in fact, by processing his feelings in the here and now, and by simply being with his feelings, somehow over time, he began to feel better. He had

assumed nothing would happen unless he found something, an analytical answer, when in fact, his commitment to the process, including time and effort, allowed him to heal. He had assumed that since nothing was being found out in therapy, nothing was happening in his recovery. What was happening underneath was that he let go of thinking there was a single golden egg to be found in the basket of recovery.

If you are not getting anywhere with trying to fix a problem, consider whether that fix bypasses the process. The process is a continuous journey, full of ideas, new perceptions and thinking, feeling, and understanding as well as emotions. The journey of healing when dealing within ingrained feelings usually requires a process rather than a fix.

Self-Reflection

1. When something goes wrong, what do you normally try to do in life? How do you handle it? Think about the answer for emotionally distressing situations, e.g., stress, grief as well as practical matters, such as finances or a complaint.
2. How do you demonstrate your way of caring when someone is going through a difficult time, such as stress, difficult life events, and bereavement? (Ideas: avoid, fix it by direct suggestions, listening, empathy, understanding, hugs)
3. Ask yourself and someone else what they need when things out of their control go wrong or when they make a mistake?

Supporting Ways: All of this book is based on this premise

Whatever problems you bring to therapy, no matter what path you take, roads you cross or decisions you make, you'll always find that to the largest degree, you'll invariably come back to you. The examination and change of the self is the heart of change. There are three reasons why this is a common factor in the therapeutic success.

First, the obvious fact is that because you want change, only you can change. It is your mind, it is your life and you will only change if something makes sense for you to do so. Regardless of the many talents of a good therapist, they cannot reprogram your mind for you nor would that be ethically right to do so. By spending time in your own mind, sometimes called internal frame of reference, therapy enables you to untangle, restructure and change you. You do it, you really do.

Second, everything in your life is in "relationship" to you. If you're hoping external things like money, career or relationships will alleviate or fix your problems, invariably, they won't, not in themselves. This is particularly true when there are deeper entrenched problems. Because you can't always control external situations, it's the way you relate to external factors in life that usually lead to deeper change, as well as increased resilience to suffering. You changing has primacy rather than relying on others or your external situation necessarily changing.

One way to look to change yourself in your relationships is to continually relate you're suffering back to you, the "I." For example, "my friend went behind my back and bad mouthed me to others" can be related back to the "I" by adding, "this made me [I] feel hurt and humiliated." By sticking with and relating to the "I," there is possibility of your relationship with events and suffering changing over time. By sticking with the "I", you have more chance of experiencing inner change.

Third, sometimes deeper contact with the core hurt inside you is required, and only you can do it with the aid of a good enough therapist. The sad tragedy of a lot of serious psychological problems is that not only do problems in many cases originate outside your control, but you're also left with the hard work of healing sometimes deep inner wounds over many years. In many cases, you will be faced with lines of defence inside you, and it's only with the aid of a good enough therapist that you can "pass defence" and encounter the core hurt within.

Keyword: Defence mechanisms (or as I prefer Protective layers) can be seen as ways of coping, of deflecting from anxious or difficult feelings that are embedded in the mind and body. For example, extreme anger may through work be seen as a defence against feeling the pain of being wrong, inferior or less powerful. " Defence is usually a mechanism, particularly in insight oriented analytic psychotherapy definition, of protecting and surviving in the world. In many cases defences can remain because of life experiences even if they no longer serve you best in the here and now.

Themes in relation to the therapist

In this section, some patterns which occur between you and the therapist, and their possible meaning are described. In this sense, it's your "process" about the relationship you have with the therapist or others in the case of couples, group or family therapy. As with all patterns, not all will be applicable to you, but if any resonate, then that is a good opportunity for further self-reflection and potential work with the therapist.

As you are

Therapists work with you as you are. Just bring you and they will accept whatever you bring in as the starting point to therapy. Being nervous arriving for therapy is a normal response; after all, it is something new, and it may be exciting heralding a new chapter in life.

However, attending therapy can be worrying and anxiety-provoking for many. Your feelings may relate to fear of the unknown, what you will learn, being emotionally triggered and being judged by the therapist. You may also have "performance anxiety" of therapy and feel that you need to do therapy right and are worried you'll not be able to express yourself and say what you need to say. Underlying that may be a feeling of "am I good enough for the therapist or to do what is needed to heal?"

Although you may feel that way, the safe environment of therapy with a "good enough" therapist isn't anything like your fears and anxieties you have about therapy. The therapist is there to accept you, not judge you, to empathise and understand your world. Therapists are not there to say that you are wrong or defective, to shame or criticise you. They are there to work with you. In fact, therapy is about enabling you to be "as you are" regardless. They will welcome you and invite you to be as you are, regardless of your nerves, anxieties and worries. The therapist accepts whatever it is you think, feel, say or don't say, your symptoms, even if those feelings are directed towards them.

They will work with whatever you present to them. So, being as you are is welcome. You can express whatever it is if you can. For example, if you express that you feel the therapist may judge you, they will work with that. If you feel anxious, they will work with that; if you don't want to talk, they will work with that; if you feel you don't want to share, that is okay too. Of course, you may wish to share all those anxieties, worries and feelings, and it can be beneficial, but you are autonomous and free to choose.

This does not mean that therapist won't challenge you or doesn't care, but they do so in a way that will help you with your problems and goals. Therapists don't have a preconception of how you should be and from that point, anything is possible. Just bring yourself, as you are and however you want to present yourself in therapy.

Here is a narrative of someone who was being himself, regardless of not being able to show all of himself to the therapist. It is not wrong; it is right.

> For a number of sessions, Dave had taken charge in therapy and worked with efficiency through his issues, finding solutions and answers. However, it was only when he let go of the mask of "being in control and knowing the answer" that the therapist got to know and understand him more. Deep down, he felt a need to hide that part of him that felt "depressed" and "not understood." He was presenting part of himself, rather than the whole. He began showing who he was rather than what he ought or thought he should be in the room.

Of course in therapy, you may not know who you are. You are likely to discover that as a natural consequence of therapy, and so who you are in therapy is also likely to change as the process unfolds.

Self-Reflection

1. Do you feel you can be you? Reflect on differences between work, family, social, therapy or other activities.
    a. Carrying multiple personas (or masks) is a normal way for us to be. We may present ourselves very differently depending on the situation.
2. What are the different types of mask you wear in different settings?
3. Ideally what type of persona would you like to carry most of the time?
4. If you feel you can't be you a lot of the time, reflect on reasons why.
5. What persona(s) do you carry in therapy or in different settings? Here are a few ideas:
    a. The Good Client
    b. The Appeaser or Pleaser
    c. Joker
    d. Hero/Anti Hero
    e. Rational/Logical or Emotive
    f. Professional
    g. Controlled
    h. Romantic
    i. Independent/Self Sufficient

Gareth had met the woman of his dreams, she was smart, successful and so caring. Gareth held her tightly in his mind, first thing in the morning, at work and at night. People noticed how distracted he was, but he didn't care because he was in love. As long as she was with him, he would never need again. He lived to see her and counted the days and hours till their next meet. The only problem, it was his therapist and he knew he needed to leave her but could not. He was dreading her next two week break.

The foundation of therapy is built upon the relationship you have with your therapist, which on the whole is empathic, accepting and caring. The building of this foundation takes place over time as you start to feel, to varying degrees, safer, stronger, deeper, and more connected. This is really healthy and shows the work you're both putting in. It is also quiet natural that feelings arise within you, where you do feel a sense of care or even love towards the therapist. If you chose them proactively, it's likely there must have been something that "attracted you" to them. These feelings can be mutual and respectful with boundaries, and they have the power to fuel your healing process.

You may also encounter stronger emotional, romantic and sexual feelings towards your therapist. These feelings may also be familiar to you, resembling love towards a partner, father, mother, friend, brother or sister. You may feel you want to be with the therapist more and more in the room or even outside of therapy, and ending the session and being without them may be painful. If you recognise these feelings in you, I would say congratulations; they are acceptable, you are not wrong, and these feelings are not something to be ashamed of, in fact, quite the opposite as they have the healing potential within them that may be the most important part of your therapy. These feelings may be healing due to the relevance they have to your problems, your ability to love, care, and see beauty, and provide a windows into what's missing. I can't stress enough the normalisation and acceptability of these feelings; this happens a fair amount in therapy. In this section, I hope to help you understand these feelings, what you can do with them and how they can be used to accelerate your healing process.

Keywords: Strong feelings that are of a romantic and sexual nature are sometimes called erotic transference.

It must be said at the outset that the relationship between therapist and client can never be more than that. Not only is it unethical for the therapist to engage in anything other than the important therapeutic relationship, it would interfere and be detrimental to helping you in your goals and could result in hurting you more. A therapist is always your therapist only, and that way applies for life (although there may be some exceptions depending on your country or region). However, the good news is that therapists are generally aware of the possibility of this type of attraction and know how to accept and sensitively handle the subject to use it as fuel in aide of your healing.

> *Warning*: Before making the decision to disclose feelings to your therapist, please reflect on whether your therapist makes you feel safe and secure, keeps boundaries and behaves consistently with you. For example, a therapist who switches between caring, distant, critical or punishing is NOT the therapist to do deep work with on client-therapist attraction, or indeed any therapy. See Way 19: Watch out for signs of inefficient, poor or harmful therapy.

There are a number of reasons why disclosure of your feelings, rather than keeping them "below the covers," may be important. Reasons to disclose may be because therapy is stagnating or frozen, your feelings are interfering with the process, and you already feel pain and preoccupations associated with your feelings. There is also a danger that without resolution, therapy will eventually end and you could end up in a worse position than you started, even to the extent of having to spend more time in therapy recovering from this experience.

Regardless of these reasons, you can use therapy to gain a deeper understanding of what these feelings are about, what they mean to you and importantly whether they're related to your problems. You can start by just being curious, accepting and being reflective about them. So, in this context, working through your feelings towards your therapist, either on your own or with the therapist could be a very important part of the work you do. I really recommend you take some steps to work on these feelings; this does not necessarily mean you disclose but it does mean you work on it and make decisions appropriately for your wellbeing. You have four main options: stick with it, disclose, get outside help or move on. The other option of course is to work on these feelings by yourself, reading this section and reflecting and journaling your process using the questions at the end of the section.

Stick with it
If you've just begun therapy and feel the immediate attraction as a distraction, it may subside and you can buckle down without it interfering at all. In this case, your "distraction attraction" will eventually fade into the background, and you can continue without feeling your goals will be impeded. Equally, you may feel the attraction and it does not dissipate, but you may feel you are able to hold the attraction like a separate compartment in a box and thus interfere very little with your therapy. You're able to contain it.

If the feelings are really strong, you may feel not ready, unsure, embarrassed or ashamed of disclosing, which may be a sign that you're just not comfortable yet and the relationship is not strong enough. Part of therapy is about recognizing and respecting your feelings. The decision to stick with it is totally acceptable. You can see how it goes, how your feelings evolve and decide later on whether you want to do anything with those feelings and their relevance to your process.

Disclose to the therapist

If you have built a trusting relationship with your therapist, consider talking about your feelings, especially when they feel intense, reoccurring and distracting. However, I know that disclosure can often be anxiety provoking, but therapists in general are aware of the possibility of client attraction and know how to sensitively handle it to support you in your goals. Although the therapist cannot enter into anything other than a therapeutic relationship, there are a number of reasons in practice why disclosure can be a useful part of the process, lest not because you're already vested in the process; you may have built a good relationship, made progress, and spent time, money and effort in being where you are in therapy.

Here is a non-exhaustive list of potential reasons for disclosure:

- If your process is not moving on or if it is stagnating and you feel the attraction is hurting you or stopping you from making progress.
- It can reveal your missing needs and thus guide you towards a better understanding of yourself. For example, if you have not experienced a warm and safe relationship, the attraction can be identified and explored further.
- Help with patterns of attraction in relationships. You may see similarities of strong feelings with other people or even other therapists, such as unrequited longing or painful rejection that open new paths to explore.
- Uncover how childhood relationships, particularly with caregivers, impacted you in general as well as in adulthood relationships.
- Overcoming your fear, shame and embarrassment of disclosure. Disclosure could alleviate those feelings and help you move forward. Just by disclosure and non-judgmental acceptance by the therapist, you can build confidence in yourself, determine a way forward and relieve the tension. The process can model how shame can be overcome through your courage to be vulnerable.

Because of the dynamic between attraction and rejection, many people find it difficult to make the decision to disclose. These are understandable concerns as you feel the stakes are high when disclosure could lead to loss, rejection, extreme pain and shame. This could in itself be damaging to the extent of having to go into therapy again to overcome the loss. Unfortunately, there are not guarantees whether your therapist will take your disclosure seriously, work with it in depth, or refer you on. I believe most therapists would work on your feelings, but there is no research to back this up. However, in my experience, the following factors, in addition to having already establishing a good relationship, may provide some clues to the therapist's ability to work with your feelings:

- They work for themselves privately. If the therapist works as part of an organization or agency, they may be under outside influence because of internal supervision or policy.
- The therapist has at least five or ten years of experience. It's very unlikely in that time the therapist has not encountered this type of issue directly or raised their own awareness of the possibilities and how best to work with these types of feelings.
- The therapist works psychodynamically/psychoanalytically (insight oriented therapies). These therapists are very likely to be more aware of the possibility and how to work with your feelings. In fact, the term erotic transference comes originally from psychodynamic theory.

Another way of de-risking your concerns is to ask them a few lead-in questions:

> *"I was reading this book that talks about transference and how past experiences with people can follow you. What do you think about it? Is it real?"*

> *You could even ask, "Do you think it applies to me?"*

> *Another way in is to use feelings you have towards a third party. For example, "I think sometimes that happens to me. I get strong feelings when I like someone a lot and then I get so upset and just think about them so much, and when they leave, it really hurts."*

In short, disclosure is an opportunity, maybe the perfect opportunity, because of its intrinsically safe and accepting environment, to gain better understanding of yourself and to take charge of your process.

Consult with an external therapist

If you are unsure of your feelings and need some help to determine what you wish to do, talking to another therapist may be useful. You should see that as therapy coaching rather than your main therapy. Another therapist can provide an opinion, help you understand yourself and help you determine risks to disclosure. A session or two with another therapist maybe useful for coaching you on your process. Another source of external help could be through the country specific regulator or voluntary organizational bodies who may have a helpline for consumers of therapy. See Way 21: Get help from outside therapy if needed.

Move on

At any point, you can move on. You may not feel comfortable disclosing, or you may feel that by sticking with it, you're not getting what you need in therapy. Alternatively, if you have already disclosed, you may feel the therapist has not accepted your feelings, did not help you explore it further or even ignored it. It may have driven a wedge in the relationship. In any case, where possible, consider whether you can talk about how you feel with them; another option could be to call for a review of your therapy with the therapist to see where that leads (See Way 20: Don't walk away from therapy without talking to the therapist).

Ultimately, you are free to decide to move on. This shows that you are in touch with your feelings and taking responsibility for your decisions; you are not failing but becoming empowered. If you decide to move on, you can learn about what you need if you move to another therapist. You may learn that you would prefer someone of a different gender. Also remember, you have the option to talk through these feelings at the outset with your new therapist.

Regardless of what you decide to do, don't feel you have to disclose; you are free to choose.

Possible reasons for attraction

- You just are!
- The feelings awaken your dormant child feelings of needing caregivers who were present, attentive, empathic, caring and attuned to your needs.
- They provide a strong emotional crutch, and you feel life would be empty without it.
- The therapist represents a relationship you never had, such as mentor, teacher, family member, or friend.
- You've never really experienced being accepted and cared about.
- Early exposure to sexuality.
- They show your unmet needs as an adult.

Possible reasons to disclose

- The feelings relate to the problems you want to overcome.
- Therapy appears to be stagnating.
- You may already be in emotional pain over your feelings. For example, ending sessions may be difficult and you're preoccupied with the therapist.
- When therapy eventually ends, it may hurt or damage your more.

Possible reasons not to disclose

- You're not ready, or you feel uncomfortable, embarrassed or ashamed.
- You fear you will lose them. They won't accept your feelings or they will "fire you."

- The relationship is not well developed and you feel the therapist will block your feelings rather than work with you in an accepting and non-judgmental manner.

Self-Reflection

When reflecting on your relationship with the therapist, remember it is one-sided; they are offering undivided caring attention, so there is a natural gap in your understanding of who they are. We all make judgements, and it is possible to imagine personal qualities of the therapist by "filling in the gaps" and imagining how they would be in a relationship. It can in some ways be easier to love someone who spends all their time together completely attending to your feelings without asking anything in return, rather than being in a relationship that is based on balancing two people's needs. Here are some questions for reflection:

What's going on?

1. What are your feelings towards your therapist?
2. What qualities about the therapist appeal to you?
3. How much do you miss or want to be near your therapist when you are or are not with them?
4. Are the feelings intense, persistent, painful, and distracting?
5. How would you label your feelings? For example, one or a combination of emotional, romantic, sexual.
6. Do your feelings resemble particular types of relationships? For example, brotherly, lover, partner, fatherly, sisterly, friendly, teacher or motherly?
7. Are you acting out on your feelings? For example, persistently tracing them on social media, being the "good" client, going out of your way to spot where they are or what they are doing?
8. When did your feelings start to appear? And what was happening? For example, immediately or when you felt more comfortable and shared more?

Understand yourself

9. Does the therapist have any weaknesses or flaws?
10. Have similar feelings occurred with other people or other therapists? Is there an underlying pattern that repeats itself?
11. Did you have caregivers who cared and were empathic and tuned into your needs?
12. Is this the first time you've experienced someone who is totally accepting and is attentive, listening and caring about what you say and about your feelings?
13. Do you struggle with intimacy, or idealizing relationships? Do you control the intimacy where you can keep them at arm's length?
14. Do you find it difficult to love someone with flaws when all is revealed about them? Do you love the idea of the "perfect" partner?

15. How do you prefer relationships to be: mostly focused on them, on you or equal? How does this relate to decisions, intimacy, power, money, love, giving and receiving?
16. Do you want to change anything about your relationships in life? What's missing? Do any of your therapeutic goals relate to relationships, your needs in relationships and what maybe missing?
17. What do you think are the reasons why strong feelings have been evoked?
18. How much do you know about your therapist?
19. What do you imagine they are like outside the room?
20. Is there an element of the unobtainable in your interest? Is the "pining" element of interest to you?
21. Are you fearful or anxious about losing the feelings you have towards your therapist? Why?
22. If you were together outside the room, what would the relationship be like? Imagine it fully. Where would you see it going? What would be happening? Go into lots of detail and write it down. Go into all matters: domestic, intimacy, children, financial, friends, and family. How would the relationship be in 1 month, 3 months, 1 year, and 5 or 10 years' time

What to do

23. Do you feel you are staying with the therapist more because of these feelings rather than your own growth? Or are you conflicted and don't know?
24. Do you feel your feelings for the therapist could interfere and hinder your healing process?
25. Do you want to understand yourself better through the attraction you are feeling?
26. Are you invested in the process? Has it been useful so far? Given your investment of time, effort and money, would it be worth exploring this with your therapist?
27. Do you feel you have a good relationship with the therapist, and have they been accepting, non-judgmental and caring so far? Do you think your therapist would be able to accept your feelings and work with them?
28. Are you fearful of the disclosure? Why?
29. Are you worried the therapist will end your relationship if you disclose? Why?

Summary

- Feelings of attraction and attachment toward the therapist is a known occurrence in therapy.
- Therapists are never allowed to enter into a relationship with you other than a therapeutic one.

- Developing feelings of intense attraction and attachment towards the therapist has healing potential and may be related to your problems.
- These feelings are never wrong or something you need to feel ashamed of.
- These feelings may arise because of your own personal history, particularly your childhood and relationship with caregivers.
- These feelings may block your healing process but if handled well, they may also accelerate it considerably.
- Consider the quality of the relationship before disclosure. Ask whether they accept your feelings, don't judge you, and have consistent boundaries.
- Disclosure has the potential to heal your missing needs.
- Other benefits of disclosure can include alleviation of shame, working to understand your inner child, practicing talking about missing needs, and strengthening your relationship with the therapist.
- If you feel you're in danger of harm because of these feelings, please look after yourself by taking steps that will keep you safe.

Idealised

There are two particular patterns that frequently occur when clients think about the therapist. The first is the therapist needs to *be* the ideal; the second is the therapist *is* the ideal!

In the first sense of needing the therapist to live up to an ideal, remember the therapist does not have to be perfect or indeed tick all your boxes; they just need to be "good enough." I use the term "good enough" throughout this book but what does "good enough" really mean? The phrase "good enough mother" was termed by a British psychoanalyst, D.W. Winnicott. He coined the term to express the idea that while a mother starts by sacrificing her needs to fulfill her child's, such as sleep, later in development, the mother allows for small frustrations, for example, a delay in responding as the child starts to cry. She is not "perfect" but she is "good enough" in that the child only feels a slight amount of frustration, which gives the child space to learn about her place in the world and to develop. I refer to the term "good enough therapist" throughout this book to allow for that development. The therapist may not always be attuned to your needs in the room. A good therapist is never able to be "perfect" at all times or know what is going on or what you need, but they can be "good enough," which is not only realistic but it may even be an important part of your healing.

In the second sense, the therapist *is* the ideal. You may hang on everything the therapists says; they represent the perfect therapist or the perfect imagined caregiver, partner or friend. Whatever they do and say is golden; they are golden. While that can be a great sign that you have a good relationship with the therapist and they are competent, it is also an opportunity to understand what is going on as these feelings may mean more than what appears to be apparent. However, what does it mean in reality? Does it in reality mean you see others as more important, more competent and better that you? Does it mean you want to please or be a good client? Or is it that they fill a need, such as a good role model or someone who cares and provides love?

If you have become aware of this pattern in other relationships, write it down and identify if anything comes up you can explore with the therapist. It may be useful to relate these feelings to your self-worth, which is how you judge yourself. While there are external things, like work satisfaction, that can build your self-worth, the type of self-worth people often have difficulty with is self-judgement, which is not tied entirely with external achievements, such as personal success, wealth or being appreciation. Self-worth is a deeper sense of judgement and feelings about yourself, such as feeling damaged, unworthy of love, abandoned, or self-loathing. These themes can remain static, having been "created" in our history of childhood, culture, family relationships, school and society. For example, feeling secure with your parents and being able to explore and make mistakes is going to be positive for your self-worth, but being persistently scolded, abused, and bullied and having a lack of feelings of belonging in the world is not a recipe for good self-worth.

Here is an example of a client idealising the therapist:

> Karim came to therapy and had a good relationship with the therapist. He would often compliment the therapist, "You must be so good with being assertive with people," "You have so many qualifications,", "You always seem to calm me down." However, he was putting the therapist on a podium, and wanted to follow the therapist's lead, looking for the therapist's judgements, even by trying to read his body language. When the therapist shared his feelings about it, the client said "Well, I want to know what you think and what you need me to say." The therapist replied, "I appreciate that you have faith in me and in the process, but I'm sitting here thinking, it would be nice to hear about you, what you feel and what you want to talk about." In this case, Karim was so focused on the therapist, he had not yet developed the trust in himself to know the answers from inside himself.

Whether you see the therapist as an ideal, less than ideal, or want them to be the ideal and these feelings interfere with therapy, you will likely want to explore it further.

Self-Reflection

1. Were your caregiver's ideal? Why?
2. Do you tend to attach or value others' opinions and knowledge more than your own? Under what circumstances?
3. When you idealise, have you ever been disappointed, feeling they did not meet the ideal standard?
4. If applicable, what is the impact of you not feeling self-worth? Do you feel the therapist has good self-worth? Is this something to explore in therapy?

Chapter 6 – Understanding the therapeutic process

It is recommended you read Chapter 5 – Oliver's journey before reading this chapter. See Appendix E for references to therapeutic change models.

If you're going on a significant journey, it is important to know what to expect, even if it is only to expect the unexpected, and to know how to deal with hardships on the way. In this chapter I describe how the process of therapy tends to unfold and what happens as change occurs.

The questions addressed in this chapter are:

- What is the therapeutic process? What sort of attitude should you have towards it?
- What actually changes "under the covers" as you move through the process?
- Are there particular stages that people go through?

What do we mean by the therapeutic process?

The therapeutic process is the mind, heart and body activity you go through over time to overcome your problems. Healing and growth occur during the process as you work on yourself and your mental world, both inside and outside therapy. The consequences of this activity can lead to changes in the way you feel about your situation, and it is that change that fuels your recovery over time.

Processes of change occur in many systems, like converting milk to cheese, sand to glass or a seed to flower. However, as part of that system of change, there may be multiple steps in the process before arriving at the final product. For example, to produce glass, sand has to be prepared for the correct granularity, and then heated to the right temperature. However, the process does not stop there because it needs further ingredients and activity before it becomes glass.

The process of therapy also involves various ingredients, with multiple steps and activities. However, unlike mechanical processes, the human change process cannot be a cookie-cutter approach. You cannot apply one structured process to everyone and expect it to lead to the desired change. Further, as I describe in this book, change can happen across a number of dimensions in parallel, e.g., less confusion, more action, sometimes seemingly in parallel.

So, how is it possible to convey such a fluid process that will be practical and meaningful? After all, everyone is unique, with their own sets of problems and needs. While it is not possible for me to answer definitively the process you will follow, it is possible to identify the general stages by which people tend to move towards psychological wellbeing and growth. By viewing from the bigger picture of experience and theory, I describe the common stages of healing, as well as the common events that trigger movement towards your desired outcome.

As change occurs, a common set of inner changes may be observable as you move towards wellbeing. Examples of mental change processes may include converting fogginess to clarity, inauthentic self to a more authentic one, anger to understanding, and fear to safety. However, in order for that change to occur, a bridge is needed, i.e. the process. For example, fogginess to clarity is likely to include making available all the facts about a situation and understanding what caused them.

What changes exactly?

One way to understand the process of therapy is to look below the covers of common changes that take place during the therapeutic process as people move towards psychological wellbeing and growth. So in the example of Oliver, what types of psychological and physical changes led him from feeling low and confused to energised and hopeful?

In this section, I'll highlight the areas where change commonly occurs, acting as a catalyst for moving the process forward. These dimensions of change can be seen as a continuum from one end to the other, for example, from rigidity to fluidity. As clients move towards overcoming their problems, certain dimensions will be moving, often unnoticed, alongside their process.

It does not mean that everything listed here must change for you to get what you need from therapy. Therefore, you should not make these dimensions into therapeutic goals unless it's something you really want to aim for. How you change and what you change inside is something only you can determine.

Awareness

From being unaware and confused you become fully aware of yourself, your reality and why your difficulties make sense. You're aware of your truth. Awareness has primacy in therapy, as all the other dimensions of therapeutic change may involve significant moments of awareness which can lead to insight and thus change.

An example of awareness leading to insight was when Oliver realised he was pretending to be someone he was not. He was being tough and sarcastic like his friend, but this was something he had outgrown. He had made the link between a past way of being and here-and-now reality.

Safety

From feeling unsafe and untrusting you move to feeling safe. This applies to therapy, the therapist, the process of therapy and ultimately to all other relationships.

In Oliver's case, he went from feeling he would not be in therapy for long and not knowing his feelings, to feeling safe enough to express them to the therapist. Safety increased as he felt more comfortable in the relationship.

Disclosure

From feeling fearful of disclosing deeper feelings, even to yourself, you feel that you can be open to talk about all sorts of feelings that occur within your inner world, such as memories, shame, fantasies, darker feelings or anything you may have previously felt ashamed to say.

In Oliver's case, his feelings about aggressive behaviours in the family may have been locked away from entering his own consciousness, or he felt ashamed to reveal them to his therapist. Either way, he went from not expressing the truth about his childhood to disclosing more. It is possible that only when he became more himself and more trusting of the relationship with the therapist could he talk about his parents' aggressive behaviours.

Feelings

From feeling numb, disconnected, suppressing or minimising feelings to become in full contact with your true feelings.

Oliver expressed a feeling of numbness, or he was not heard or understood. However, as he listened to his inner voice and confusion, he found that he did have feelings to express, including real anger and sadness. He had made contact with his buried truth.

Bodily feelings

From feeling heavy, tense and worn down you feel light, joyful and alive. Sometimes, symptoms may be physical, such as anxiety or panic. Quite often when clients begin to feel better the body feels lighter too.

Oliver came into therapy feeling low and anxious, but towards the end of his process, he expressed feelings of calmness, vitality and excitement.

Thoughts

From thoughts that are overly critical of both the self and of others (including obsessions), thoughts become rational, balanced, assertive and protective of the self.

Oliver's thinking process changed, particularly once he understood his feelings more. For example, he went from "I can't confront anyone" to "although it's difficult, I need to sometimes confront people [parents]."

Self-Worth (Self-Judgement)

From feeling unworthy or inferior, to you feeling worthwhile.

Oliver's self-worth improved from being concerned about "rocking the boat" and suffering in silence, to feeling good enough in himself to seek his own needs as he began to value his authentic self. He became more important to himself. For example, he wanted better relationships and directed his life based on his current needs.

Acceptance

From rejecting yourself, your feelings or parts of you, you fully accept yourself, your feelings and your truth. This does not mean you don't want to change things further but feel accepting of it in the moment.

In Oliver's case, his acceptance came once he understood that he was "right to have his feelings". Once the confusion began to dissipate, he was able to validate himself, knowing it was okay to be himself. He owned his feelings, sat with them in therapy and worked on them, rather than rejecting them.

Moving forward

From being caught up and unable to let go of difficult events and experiences, you go to being able to let go and move forward dynamically, all the while still recognising past significance. Being "caught up" can feel like being trapped in a net and unable to find a way out.

In Oliver's case, he came into therapy having been unable to be himself for a long time, and his life was on hold. However, as he confronted and expressed his feelings more, he was able to let go, to the extent that he could focus his attention on his life rather than solely worrying about his parents' future.

Holism

From having many conflicting, confusing, fragmented or disowned parts you feel resolved, complete and whole.

Oliver's problem could be seen as fragments of anger, confusion and a desire for something better in life. Once these parts had been worked on he gained a sense of wholeness, where all parts of him were working together without conflict. The good, bad and ugly were not separate to him but became a single unifying truth in his life.

Separation and Boundaries

You are totally enmeshed in other people's worlds, where you lose yourself and you lose who you are. At the other end of the continuum, you see yourself both as an individual and in relationships with others. You have your own individual needs, thoughts and feelings. You know where you start and others begin.

Oliver started therapy lost in his situation. He was not able to be himself because he was "lost" in his parents' relationship or in a version of himself that he would portray as being socially acceptable. This caused him to disconnect his feelings and to stay focused outside of himself, moulding himself more on the external world, rather than his own. During therapy, Oliver worked towards gaining separation from himself and others. He eventually asserted his boundaries: "he was not going to sit back" and continue in this way while his parents continued to behave badly. His solution was to confront them, express himself and stay in the relationship with them without being lost within it. He was no longer solely caught up in their world, but allied to his own.

Identity

From having no identity or misplaced identity you have a genuine connection with an identity. Identity relates to a sense of being and belonging in the world as part of something other than being individual. This may be a culture, spirituality, history, heritage, aesthetic, family, ancestry or personal passions, interests and hobbies.

It is not totally clear whether Oliver felt a sense of a belonging in the family or with friends at the beginning. If he did, it would likely have been on a false self in order to fit in and survive. He identified strongly with the Samurai, which he was passionate about; however, could that symbolically also be expressed as a numbing of feelings or having a "stiff upper lip" as the Samurai story was focused in on self-sacrifice, respect and ritual? Either way he tried to repair the bonds that were broken in his friendship and family which may be the beginning of having a sense of identity and belonging.

Relationships

From having painful feelings or no feelings when experiencing relationships you have healthy and joyful relationships. This is not only about relationships with others but also with yourself and the therapist.

Oliver took charge in his friendship group by taking chances to tell them about himself. He told his parents how he felt and even got his father to go on a Samurai weekend with him. He took steps to improve and repair relationships as far as he could control.

It is well recognised that improvements in relationships tend to contribute to improvements in psychological wellbeing.

Fluidity

From holding rigid beliefs and judgements about yourself, others and the world, you become fluid, holding many differing perspectives, and being open to your views being challenged. You move away from black-and-white thinking to exploring many parallel possibilities or solutions. Visually, the stone becomes water.

In Oliver's case, he was always willing to explore possibilities, even if he initially hesitated or did not expect therapy to be the "answer." This openness led him to discover what lay under his confusion, numbness and low mood. He felt he was able to separate and accept his parents, even though they could not meet his own needs fully while moving forward in his life. He was able to accept the shades of grey in his life.

Confidence or Grounding

From feeling small, powerless and submissive you feel confident and grounded with a sense of inner agency. You have an inner strength or belief in yourself that you can engage more confidently in the world. You are happy with yourself, and happy in your own skin.

Oliver clearly had a sense of powerlessness in his childhood, and his survival solution had been about making himself smaller. He was not in a position to emotionally protect himself and did not know that it would be okay for him to be himself. Oliver gained confidence that his feelings "were not wrong" and that it was okay to assert himself, thereby strengthening his own belief in himself.

Action oriented

From being a passive bystander in life you become fully active in making changes outside the therapy room.

Oliver took a number of external actions alongside therapy, including writing a letter to his parents, sharing more feelings, and setting up a day out with his father. He took action as a result of his process to improve things for himself. He realised he could not wait for others to fix things; only he could do it.

Purpose

From feeling no purpose in life you feel life is full of purpose and meaning, which can be seen as "what makes life worthwhile". For some, it is about a social or political cause, for others, it can be spirituality and relationships. Meanings may change over time for all of us, and can come into focus at various times and stages in life.

Although this was not explicitly mentioned in the case of Oliver, he did have a passion for the Samurai, which would have given him some direction in taking an active life. However, if we had asked the question, "What is the purpose of your life, Oliver?" it may not have been clear. However, towards the end, he became a "glue" of sorts in the family, taking a parental role to some extent, which may have been a catalyst for his parents seeking couples therapy. Whether he knew it or not, his life did have meaning beyond his personal next steps in life. It would be for Oliver to determine his meaning or "calling".

Responsibility

From taking little responsibility of shaping your life to taking full responsibility of your life, its meaning and direction.

The moment Oliver came into the room, he had taken responsibility for himself. He knew something was wrong even if he did not know what it was. However, this responsibility also translated to the outside world. He asserted his life force and worked out what was wrong. He took responsibility as far as he could to make his life better. Only he could take responsibility for what he wanted in life.

Stages of the therapeutic process

This section presents a framework for understanding where you are in your therapeutic process and the stages you may go through to overcome your problems. Each stage is compared and contrasted with Oliver's journey (Chapter 4).

Each stage has an overarching process theme consisting of various feelings, thoughts and attitudes expressed or unconsciously held. For example, someone who is in the "hesitation" stage will not yet believe therapy can help, or they may guard their feelings involuntarily. However, as the client's inner world evolves they will come to recognise those beliefs and feel safe enough to explore them, moving towards a stage where they are more open with their feelings, even if they feel they "should not" have them.

As you read through the stages, reflect on anything significant that comes up for you and notice whether some of the ideas and inner beliefs resonate. Understanding the process may give you an insight into what you can identify within yourself that you want to work on.

Remember this is a framework to stimulate reflection, rather than an absolute path which you will or must follow to achieve your growth or healing aims. It's a blueprint rather than a map. Only you can define your map.

Key points about the stages:

- The stages are generic and indicative rather than specific to any individual.
- Not all aspects described at any stage will be relevant to you.
- Stages you go through are non-linear. You don't have to pass one stage to get to the next.
- The stages may repeat routinely. You may be at separate stages for each theme you are working on. For example, childhood bullying may be on one track and work stress issues on another.
- Expect plenty of overlap between stages.
- The stages you go through will may be iterative depending on the depth, complexity and scope of change you are looking for. There is a big difference between redecorating a room and rebuilding a house.
- If you're working in short-term therapy, you can still experience all these stages, even in a short period of time.
- Only you can determine what is relevant to your process.

The rest of this section delves into each of the stages.

Stigma (Stage 1)

In the first stage of the process, there is a complete wall against showing feelings and thus therapy is simply sought regardless of any psychological issue. A number of internal beliefs will be at play blocking access to therapy, from feeling "It's not something I do", "I don't believe in therapy" and "There is nothing wrong with me" to feelings of shame or fear of the consequences of therapy.

In very rare cases, such clients may enter therapy but only because of outside pressure or due to a level of mental distress. In such cases, the hope of many clients is that therapy is a procedure to obtain a fix rather than a process. For example, people may enter therapy due to a concerned parent or as a mandatory step during a couple's separation. People at this stage are likely to divert attention away from themselves and their feelings and thoughts may be seen in black and white terms e.g. good or bad, right or wrong. While there is always hope, it is very unlikely that a client will move forward in the therapy process unless there is a "light bulb" moment that removes some of these barriers.

In Oliver's case, he felt he wanted help but was not hopeful of therapy, stating he would likely get some anti-depressants after attending a session. However, he did mention that his mother did not want him to attend therapy because "he was okay, and it's not something we do". It is assumed Oliver had an alternative view point to his family system. He showed courage to defend his position to stay in therapy against his mother's wishes, which eventually led to his parents seeking couples therapy. You could say through his struggle, he broke the cycle of stigma about therapy within his family. Because he acted from his own will he did not enter therapy at this stage of the process.

Self-Reflection
Here are some of the characteristics of this stage. Did you encounter any of these?

- Cut off from feelings
- Rigid and way based thinking when making judgements
- Fearful of judgement and consequences
- Feelings of shame
- Holding on to inner and outer exterior image of the self (a social mask)
- Therapy is not an option

In this stage, you're totally against entering therapy and cut off from your feelings with regard to your problems. Which of these voices/beliefs apply to you? If any apply, ask whether they are they holding you back. Reflect on these beliefs and how you arrived at them.

- **"That's just not what we do."**
    - We don't go outside of the family for help
    - People will judge you and you'll regret it
    - We have never done that before so were certainly not going to start now
    - What doesn't kill you makes you stronger
    - I never talked; it never did me harm
    - There is nothing wrong with us

- These sort of things happen to other people not us
- People who enter mental health support are dangerous people
- If you're feeling suicidal or anything else it's your fault no one else's
- People who have mental health issues aren't normal, but were normal
- Talking about Feelings shows weakness
- I don't need therapy
- I'm better than this
- Suck it up and sort yourself out
- It's so shameful to disclose the things you've done
- Be a strong boy/man or woman
- There is nothing wrong with me
- Therapy is a waste of time and money
- Other people have it worse than me, I'll just be wasting the therapists time
- Therapists pretend to care and are just in it for the money

- **"It's so shameful to disclose the things I've done."**
  - What will people say or think
  - That'll be on my record
  - If I talk I will no longer be able to work / drive
  - Sharing personal issues outside of the family is shameful

- **"I fear the consequences."**
  - I'll be judged, criticised or told I'm wrong
  - People won't treat me the same if they know
  - Work will discriminate against me if they find out
  - I won't be able to get work
  - It'll be a waste of time
  - The therapist will say I'm to blame and wrong
  - I don't want to know what's wrong
  - I'm afraid what I will find out about myself
  - Things will never be the same once I know what I've got (a label)
  - I've well to hide parts of me from myself, the therapist may see it
  - It'll be scary and painful if I explore my feelings
  - The therapist will see the guilt, shame and wrongness in me
  - You'll get a brain lobotomy, you won't be the same anymore
  - It's not safe you'll get hurt/worse or abused
  - You'll remember things that aren't real
  - I'll lose friends
  - People will pity, avoid or not trust me anymore
  - People will gossip – school, work, friends and my community
  - I'll be rejected by my group
  - People will be scared to be around me

Hesitation (Stage 2)

In the hesitating stage of the process the client enters therapy reluctantly, maybe as a last resort. They may want the therapy but are—consciously or unconsciously—closed off from the therapy process and the therapist, as well as their own feelings. It seems like they are there in the therapy room but stay away from exploring deeper thoughts about themselves, and certainly no feelings are expressed in the room. Where thoughts are expressed, they can feel like being expressed about someone else, as being remote from themselves or as a generalisation. They may also see therapy as similar to going to a doctor, where they tell the therapist what is wrong and the therapist gives them tools that will "cure" their ailment.

Their own ideas about life may be seen in black and white terms and so could be closed off to the idea of the possibility of seeing things differently. While they may be outwardly confident and in control, they may be unconsciously fearful about therapy, the therapist and the expectations upon them. Clients at this stage may be inwardly conflicted between staying or fleeing therapy, so while there is no guarantee a client at this stage will want to continue, they may, with the right therapist, decide to stay in therapy to see where it leads.

Overall, Oliver was not at this stage of the process when he began therapy. Even though he was unaware of the deeper feelings of his childhood, and was perhaps even guarding them, he was, nonetheless, in touch with his feelings and expressed them to the therapist, as much as he could understand of them, for example, exploring his sadness and confusion. In addition, he did not state that he wanted the therapist to fix him, even though that may have been his wish. He was able to speak what he knew as best he could and was open to possibilities.

Self-Reflection

Here are some of the characteristics of this stage. Did you encounter any of these?

- The reluctant or tentative client
- See therapy not too dissimilar to going to a doctor
- Will talk about the issue in a general way
- Guards feelings
- Confusion about what to say, think or how things work
- Therapy can be a threat to self-image, values or beliefs

Which of these inner voices/beliefs apply to you?

Feelings inside you:

- I don't have the time or energy for this
- What do I do
- Tell me what to say or do

- I'm scared to tell
- I feel numb or empty
- I feel powerless and hopeless
- I've got to be strong and not show feelings
- Why me?
- I'm useless. I'm not good at anything else how am I going to be good at this.
- No one understands me
- I feel weak
- This is bizarre
- I don't trust myself to know what to say
- Get me out of here as fast as possible I've got other important things to do

Feelings towards the therapist

- Why doesn't the therapist talk more
- Why is the therapist so quiet and just stares
- She seem so cold or strict
- I'm small and they are so big
- They are OK but I'm not OK
- Fix me
- This is not going to work
- You don't matter
- You don't care
- You won't understand
- I feel weak
- This isn't going to work
- I've got to be careful what I say
- I've got to be a good client

Minimisation (Stage 3)

At this stage of the process, the client's initial reluctance to engage in therapy begins to diminish. They begin to feel safer when talking and have developed a level of comfort—but not necessarily trust—with therapy, and in the presence of the therapist.

During this part of the process, the client minimises their feelings by talking about day-to-day things that have happened, as well as symptoms, and the issue. When beginning to talk about feelings they are minimised or avoided outside of awareness, for example, they compare themselves to others, or believe they "should not" be indulging in feelings. These voices may be echoes of past ways of coping with difficult feelings—by suppressing them.

They may still see things in black-and-white terms, either "I" or the "other" is to blame. They feel guilty for talking about those who may have hurt their feelings or contributed to their problems.

Minimisation may also be about what they feel about themselves, such as the lack of ability, capability and power potential they have in life. So going to feelings will feel unsafe, because they don't want to show the person behind the "social mask". They may see the therapist as someone who is more important, more knowing or more powerful than them.

Regardless of how minimisation of themselves is present in therapy, at this stage the client is actively working to get to their subjective truth, even if they feel confused, blocked or unaware of their complete life narrative.

Overall I would say Oliver started therapy at this stage of the process. He worked with the therapist with whatever he knew at the time. However, there were many ways his feelings were diminished or minimised. The most obvious sign of minimisation of the self was him putting on a mask to "be likeable" because "no one likes a moaner." This belief was prevalent in his life, but minimised his own feelings for the sake of getting by. This type of self-minimisation had been going on for years; it was a solution to a problem of feeling that "people were not interested". However, this was also causing his sadness and confusion. He was not being true to himself and recognising his own feelings, beliefs and needs.

Self-Reflection
Here are some of the characteristics of this stage. Did you encounter any of these?

- No one else is to blame but me
- Sense of personal responsibility for others
- Talks about issues, everyday matters rather than feelings
- Any feelings touched upon are blocked or rationalised quickly
- Feels unsafe or cut off from feelings to talk about deeper matters
- Confusion about what is going on within
- Scared to tell or don't know what to tell

Which of these inner voices/beliefs apply to you?

- Disloyalty
    - o I feel guilty for talking about myself because I'll be criticising others
    - o It's not my parents fault; I owe them everything, after all (not that it must be the parents fault)
    - o It's no anyone's fault
- It's my fault, no one else's
- I'm not normal

- I'm wasting the therapist's time
- There are other people who need more help than me
- I can't feel anything
- I just need to talk about the "symptoms"
- I feel bad for being here
- It's not safe to talk about the real me
  - I'll be hurt
  - Don't trust
  - I'll be judged
- It's me. I'm the problem, not others
- I'm confused
- Everyone else is to blame
- I shouldn't be feeling this way

Revelation (Stage 4)

At this stage, clients will be openly reflecting and overcoming barriers to their subjects of discussion in therapy, such as what happened, and how they feel about themselves and their situation. They begin to join the dots in their understanding of themselves and to gain insights into their way of being, and why that contributes to their difficulties. Things that previously may have felt too difficult to disclose are brought into the room, including feelings of shame and how they feel truly and deeply about themselves.

While they express feelings, they still they have not realised in a true, felt sense the enormity of their loss in life and the impact of it in the here and now. They still see themselves as being unacceptable, even if there is no logical reason for it in the present.

The client takes more responsibility for their own process, sets their own agenda and starts to see therapy and the therapist as being valuable. Confusion begins to subside and their reflections become open, fluid and free. The client goes wherever their mind takes them in the therapy room and begins associating past with present, and in doing so becomes more aware of why they feel the way they do, even if they still encounter conflicts and see themselves as fragmented parts rather than a whole. This part of the process can typically be the longest period in therapy.

Oliver began to actively explore and seek answers at this stage of the process. He became more trusting and open with the therapist. He explored his life, friendship groups, family life and in particular, his childhood and aggressive behaviours in the home and their impact on him. He connected the dots between who he is now and who he was in the past, for example, that anger is still scary now because of feeling unsafe in the past, or he became a listener because that was his way of pleasing his parents (a solution to ensure they would not separate or become aggressive). He even recalled memories he had forgotten including when he would "wet himself" while witnessing his parents being physically and verbally aggressive. These insights enabled him to feel less confused about why he felt so low, and he began to experience his own truth. However, he was still experiencing conflicts during this stage of the process, for example, you "should like your mum" or "how can I call my dad a coward?"

Self-Reflection

Here are some of the characteristics of this stage. Did you encounter any of these?

- I should or wish I was x
- I am not really acceptable as I am
- I see myself as parts not as a whole (e.g. I avoid certain parts or feel ashamed of them)
- Feelings begin to simmer
- Small Insights or "A-ha" moments
- Start to talk in first person "I feel x"
- Understand how and why
- I feel lighter and less confused

During this stage, you will also begin to hear a more hopeful inner voice that is becoming more self-aware. Do any of these apply to you?

- Not everything is my fault
- A-ha! I'm starting to get it
- There is a reason I'm feeling this way
- That is not me, this is me
- I feel x
- I can do a, b or c rather than stick with d
- I'm less confused
- Sometimes people let me down

Contact (Stage 5)

Here, the client begins to reach a deeper and broader understanding of their issues and begins to express deeper feelings. They become more aware of themselves, whether it's about relationships, their beliefs, needs or feelings. During this process they will contact more of their raw feelings which may even be felt viscerally, or they may be bodily felt rather than simply narrated. They feel the truth of things in their life in a very real way with any suppressed feelings coming to light. Feelings such as anger, frustration, sadness, and emptiness can be felt in the voice as a "live" happening in the room.

In Oliver's case he showed visceral feelings in the room as he encountered his own painful feelings towards his caregivers; going from a feeling of numbness to a more lived-in anger and sadness. For example, when he talked about the fact that things went from chaos and aggression to calm as if it didn't happen, he raised his voice as he demonstrated his felt anger, rather than expressing it in a monotone way. His came to be in sync with the feelings he had held below the surface. They were not just intellectually real, they were real in a felt sense. His head, heart and mind had connected as one.

Self-Reflection

Here are some of the characteristics of this stage. Did you encounter any of these?

- This really happened to me
- I'm really angry/sad/teary!
- This really hurts bad
- I get why x
- I can really feel my anger, rage, sadness
- I feel worn down
- I feel as if I could explode
- You show your "teeth"

You may encounter some of these changes:

- You feel the feelings not just talk about them
- You understand why you're feeling the way you do
- You react to feelings e.g. emotive and angering
- You realise your loss e.g. opportunities, time.
- Felt heartbreak
- Beginning self-care
- Feeling mentally lighter
- More accepting
- Awareness grows
- Feelings and behaviour change outside of the room
- Hope and trust build
- Self-love

Rebuilding (Stage 6)

The client starts to rebuild their life around what they have learnt during the process. They make life changes over time, sometimes small and sometimes big.

They gain a level of acceptance of themselves and what has happened, and generally feel much lighter in their body as well as in their mind. Their judgements, feelings and thoughts about themselves and others are seen in multiple perspectives, rather than binary. They feel they are able to let go of aspects that were holding them back, although feelings can remain raw. They are in a more self-aware state, and this change of attitude can be seen by others.

Their self-structure (identity, beliefs and mental attitudes) begins to change once they accept themselves, their situation and the reasons for experiencing their problems. However, they don't necessarily know who they are or what it means for them going forward, and they are still undecided on what version of themselves they want to be. They feel more hopeful and optimistic about their life.

For Oliver, after exploring and experiencing his feelings in relation to his past and to himself, decided that he needed to move forward in life. He rebuilt his own sense of self by asserting his feelings both in the therapy room and outside of it. He challenged his parent's arguments by writing a letter to them and began to share his beliefs and likes, such as the Samurai with others.

He no longer held his true self back from being in the world, rather he accepted that it was okay for him to be who he was. He rebuilt his self-structure, not by dismissing the past because that was a part of him, but by asserting his needs now.

Self-Reflection
Here are some of the characteristics of this stage. Did you encounter any of these?

- I believe I am really acceptable as I am
- I'm ok
- Phew... I feel lighter
- I know what I need to do
- Excitement, joy and energy
- Acceptance of difficult parts such as anger
- Who am I now?
- I care about myself and have compassion towards myself

Freedom (Stage 7)

At this stage, inner and outer changes are bedded down and are consistently applied. Clients see themselves as not needing to have a fixed way of being, and can accept themselves for who they are. They accept the whole of themselves, including shades of grey, and their darker sides. They have found a new sense of care, energy and passion in life. The individual trusts their own feelings and life is filled with meaning and purpose.

They continually develop themselves further, have no set structure of who they must be, and are free to choose the direction of both their inner world and life. They are "centre stage" in terms of taking responsibility for their direction. There are no fixed limits to the way they shape their inner life, regardless of external constraints.

They become their own therapists, free to evolve in any way they choose to do.

Towards the end of his process, Oliver realised he was a separate individual but also part of the family. He could define himself as he wished to, even stating that he wanted to act his age and have carefree fun, rather than worry about his family. He had the freedom to decide who he would be now, and he took the responsibility to change his situation. His was freer. Where would his travels and his new sense of freedom take him? No one knew but him. What is known is that life changes, challenges abound but a therapist's door, time willing, is always open.

Self-Reflection:
Which of these feelings / beliefs apply to you?

- Permanent change. A significant shift in your personality.
- You trust yourself
- Life feels full of meaning
- Joy and trust in yourself
- Inner freedom to evolve and choose
- Love unbounded
- Belonging to group(s)
- Deeper connection between self, others, society, world and universe

Chapter 7 – Client topics, questions and concerns

In this chapter, I have collected – based on my experience of coaching clients in therapy – a response to nearly seventy of the most common questions, dilemmas, and concerns that consumers of therapy have. This chapter aims to empower your journey in therapy by helping you feel more confident about the work you are doing and, in particular, the issues and obstacles that inevitably arise from it.

At different stages, you will be faced with decisions and inner obstacles, and in my experience, many of those are to do with the nature of the process, your relationship with the therapist, and your concerns about it. Here is a random sample of questions answered here:

- Why are boundaries important?

- Is it okay for a therapist to use touch?

- How do I know if I am doing therapy right?

- How do I know my therapist is working safely with me?

- Are my memories true? What are false memories?

- I am in love with the therapist. What shall I do?

- Does therapy blame parents?

- Will I still recognise myself at the end of therapy?

- I feel the counsellor isn't on my side?

- Do therapists prefer working with "Good clients?"

- I just found out my counsellor is seeing someone I don't like. Shall I tell the therapist?

This chapter is split into six areas:

- In relation to the therapist. Questions related to the therapist.

- In relation to the therapy process. Questions relating to the process of therapy.

- In relation to yourself. Questions related to your concerns about using therapy.

- In relation to safety. Questions about the safety of therapy.

- Extra-therapeutic matters. Questions that are external to therapy, but which may impact it, such as stigma.

- Specific questions and answers. Other questions that are very specific.

I hope this chapter will act as a guide to your journey. It won't always tell you all the answers or what to do, but it will tell you a method of how to get there, wherever that may be. Remember not to take all these answer as necessarily being absolute answers, rather indicative because context will be important. If you need further helping talk to your therapist or use Way 21: Seek further support.

In relation to the therapist

In this section, I provide answers and reflections on questions that relate to your therapist, including the relationship, boundaries, or feelings about the therapist.

How do I find the right therapist for me?

The most concise answer is to work with a trusted therapist, one who meets country standards and has experience working with your problems, whom you feel safe with and who believes the approach you are undertaking with them has the potential to help you achieve your goals.

In Way 2, Find the right therapist and approach, I go into detail of the process, considerations, questions, and reflections to assess the therapist's suitability for your needs.

What are some signs of a good or bad therapist?

Overall, you should choose someone you feel safe with, who makes you feel accepted and not judged, and who you can foresee being able to create a relationship in which you could disclose whatever you feel you'll need to.

I describe this in detail in Way 19.

Common questions about therapist selection

This section looks to answer particular questions related to therapist selection.

Is it important the therapist come from a similar background to me? Or that the therapist has overcome similar problems?

Do you prefer a therapist who has a similar background to you? Perhaps the same cultural or national identity? Or you may prefer someone to have the same stance on spirituality, religious or non-religious? Or even that they have experienced the same problems as you such as abuse, addiction, or trauma? There are two views on identification with the therapist.

On one side, a therapist who you identify with may be able to understand your concerns quicker and relate to your life and difficulties. You may perceive they will naturally be on "your side," not judge, and understand why things have been difficult for you. Having someone who has been through recovery of addiction or child abuse can be beneficial because they have the experience of the process, its struggles, pitfalls, and moments of insight.

However, on the other side, there is a school of thought that having a therapist who does not directly identify with you means they won't have preconceived ideas because they recognise you for you, with unique experiences that are separate to themselves. So in that sense, having someone who does not have the same beliefs or background is thought to be beneficial because they do not hold any fixed view of your world, the outcome, or the solution.

Remember that the therapist is there to accept you as you are and not judge you. They will be beside you trying to tune into your and their feelings, rather than making assumptions about your unique experiences. This does not mean the therapist cannot separate themselves from your experience; it is just a theoretical perspective, as it depends on the therapist. So I would, unless it is important to you, not dismiss therapists solely on the basis of them having a different background because their competence and the relationship are the foundation of therapy. However, if it is important to you, your beliefs and in feeling safe, I would say go with that.

Does it matter what gender the therapist is? Aren't women more caring?
I know that it's fairly common for clients to have a gender preference and usually that is based on who they feel or imagine being more comfortable with. This comfort could be to do with the material to be disclosed or fear that the therapist will judge them.

Gender preference could be to do with societal or negative past experiences which become generalised, such as women being more caring and nurturing than men. Some schools of therapy also believe preferences could be related to past experiences with caregivers and are more subconsciously held, e.g., because of a difficult relationship with their father. Whatever the reason, you should choose the gender based on who you would feel comfortable with.

However, if you are working on issues you have with a particular gender and you are working through that in therapy, e.g., lack of trust in men, it could be worth considering working with that gender, as it can be used to check out your assumptions and provide new perspectives that ultimately provide a healing experience. However, do what you feel is right for you, including the feeling that it may be beneficial to work with the opposite gender you normally work with.

Does the age of the therapist matter? Surely if they are too young they won't have life experience?
There is a misconception I feel that age, or greyness, is an important factor in deciding on a therapist because they must know more, be more experienced in years, have more wisdom, knowledge, etc. There may be truth to that but in my experience, this is not necessarily true. Consider that regardless of age, someone could have stagnated in their own learning, lack passion, or not had the life experience you would perhaps imagine someone of that age has.

A younger person could in fact have more life experience, be more passionate about therapy, have an openness, or be "wise beyond years." Yes, you need life experience, but being younger should not put you off. Life experience is certainly an important factor, as it in itself can indicate outlook, knowledge, and wisdom. Also, remember that a younger person being closer in age to your age may be an advantage in terms of similar experience. Age is not necessarily the key, I feel.

Why do some therapists charge so much and others very little? Is it better to work with the most expensive therapist?

Sometimes it is easy to be impressed by a beautiful setting, office building, and letters after a therapist's name, their qualifications and expertise. One therapist may charge £150 an hour and another £35; surely we will be better off with a therapist who charges more? In my experience not really. I would not look at these things as being the most important, going back to "who they are" and their competence, rather than "what they are" as being more important. Unlike products where you can usually recognise its quality, its function, and therefore its value, in therapy that is not always the case. I have been to therapists who charged £35 and ones who charged £90 and the one who charged less I made more progress with; it's not the important factor. Good enough therapists may charge £150 or very little.

Is it okay to work with trainee therapists?

The short answer is "yes," you can work with trainees as long as they are working within limits and those limits accord with what you need to achieve your goals. Trainees can have pretty much all the qualities of a good enough therapist; after all, it's the person, so it's not in itself an issue. However, my recommendation is that when you are severely distressed or with issues that require specialist training and skills, e.g., with PTSD, you need to feel assured the therapist has the requisite training and experience, so in those cases I would not recommend using a trainee. Also, if you are working with a trainee, ask that they are supervised and that they have been given the clear to work with your type of issues. As with any other therapist, only work with them if you're comfortable. It's your therapy and your choice.

What are therapeutic boundaries? Why are they necessary?

When I talk to clients who are in or have been through therapy, they can be curious or confused by its peculiarities. For example, why the therapist does not say more, disclose more, and be open about themselves, or tell you more of what they are thinking about or what you're working on.

Confusion of this nature is understandable; we have all sorts of relationships, and a relationship where it's one-sided is rare. In this section. I will help you understand why therapists keep, sometimes very tightly, to boundaries when working with you.

Boundaries in therapy are there to clarify roles, the goals of therapy, the relationship, and what can and cannot be provided as part of the service.

Here, the key reasons for boundaries during the process of therapy:

- Boundaries can make you feel safe. You know what you're getting and what you are not getting.
- Therapy is about helping you develop your own sense of self and independent thinking and direction. Therapists are there to help you find your own way, not their way.
- Therapy is about working with your needs. How will the therapist talking about themselves benefit you?
- Boundaries are an important part of what makes therapy work. Boundaries allow you to have an impartial place to talk where the therapist has no agenda other than working in your best interests.
- To assure your vulnerabilities are not exploited. Boundaries protect you from being consciously or unconsciously being taken advantage of by the therapist. For example, if you have difficulty setting your own boundaries, then you know your boundaries will not be violated.

Boundaries are also crucial for the therapist too because it's important they too retain a sense of self. After all, they have a life outside of therapy and are likely to see other clients too. So, for example, they don't end up feeling burnt out, and a burnt-out therapist would not be useful to you.

Often people think about boundaries being fixed by the therapist, but many types of boundaries can be negotiated or demanded by you. Examples of boundaries that maybe negotiated include time, and approach. While an example of boundaries can be demanded is not to use touch or to be able to reject a particular technique.

Dual Relationships - Why therapy and friendship don't mix
Combining a therapeutic relationship with friendship, business, or even a romantic relationship is fraught with issues. Therapy is about the client's needs, and any other type of relationship is usually reciprocal, where both parties gain something from the relationship – whether it is help, support, advice, sympathy, empathy, or intimacy. However, in the client-therapist setting, the focus is very much on the client and the client's needs. Having any other type of relationship in tandem can distract and interfere in the therapeutic process and cause harm.

A vital part of how therapy is known to work is through the nature of the therapeutic relationship, which is fundamentally different to friendship. Therapy works at a different level to friendship because the connection between the therapist and client is based on empathy and unconditional acceptance. The therapist will tune in and focus in on these elements because of their expertise and training; they will want to fully understand how and why things are the way they are for their clients. On the other hand, if this relationship was mixed with friendship, these elements of the process could be detrimental or harmful to the process. For example, during a relationship breakup, friends may have more of a judgement about what you should do. They may tell you not to worry because you'll find someone else or you need to get over it by now. They may have their own agenda; for example, in order to keep you in their social circle, they inadvertently give you advice that is not in your best interests. Therapists work in your interests and help you arrive at your own answers, not their answers for you.

Another reason a friendship would not help is that clients may not want to talk about certain things to a friend or they may need to talk about the friend themselves. Not all clients are in a position to be able to trust a friend, so a stranger that offers an impartial confidential space can be exactly what is needed. Similarly, other types of dual relationships, including partner, business, and financial relationships, have the ability to interfere with therapeutic goals in different ways

The therapeutic relationship should be seen as another type of relationship on its own merit. There is no need to treat it as a friendship, partner, mother, father, brother, sister, romantic or business partner, it's its own type of relationship (although if you do experience them in that way it could be useful to explore). This does not mean the therapist is not "friendly" or caring or that you cannot feel a deep connection with the therapist, but it's geared towards your goals.

Boundaries as a model in life

An additional benefit of boundaries is that they also act as a model for having boundaries in all sorts of relationships. Clients may have had their boundaries violated, and this may even be the norm for them; for example, in an abusive relationship. So the therapeutic boundaries act as a learning tool that can in itself heal and enable clients to establish their own safe boundaries outside of therapy.

For clients, the structure inherent in a boundaried relationship can make clients feel in control and empowered, as they know what to expect and feel they are safe in the process. This can then translate to asserting boundaries to feel safe in life.

And why don't they share personal stuff much?

In addition to the aforementioned reasons for boundaries, therapists don't usually disclose much personal information because it could inadvertently interfere with your process. For example, if a therapist tells you they are not having a great day, it could stop you wanting to share difficulties that will burden them. Similarly, if a therapist shares something you don't like or don't respect, such as a political view, it won't give you a clear canvas to work on. This does not mean therapists won't share, but they do so if they believe it is in your interests. For example, depending on the therapist, they may consciously share they overcame an addiction similar to yours as a way of demonstrating experience, and to strengthen the relationship.

Having said that, some therapists may consciously choose to share more personal details, including their history, beliefs, and political views openly in public forums and in their profile. In this case, it will be up to you if you feel it's something you can work with or not.

Is it okay for the therapist to use touch?

Some therapists do use touch, only for specific interventions such as in hypnosis, or body psychotherapy, but in all cases, you would have to give consent for touch to be used (of course, touch will be of a practical nature rather than used in a sensual way). If you feel uncomfortable with touch, you have the right to say "no." You can ask them whether there is an alternative approach that does not involve touch.

How come some therapists hug and others do not?

In general, my experience is that therapists do not hug. However, not all therapists work in this way, and some may hug by exception, perhaps once therapy has completed or as even as a general greeting. Of course, if you feel uncomfortable with the hug, you have the right to say "no."

There are a few opposing views about hugs; first, because it is relational, and that can be a good thing in therapy as long as it is appropriate and consensual. The other view is that hugs can create confused feelings in clients; for example, what the hugs mean, what it means when you either receive or don't receive them, or it may create feelings within you which interfere with your process, perhaps to an extent of feeding a dependency on them.

For handshakes the same applies, although you'll find that is more of a possibility. However, there are many therapists who don't engage in any contact whatsoever.

Of course, we can't way out the possibility it could also be fostering inappropriate intimacy, so be wary of any touch that feels inappropriate (Way 19).

Since you're asking the question, can you reflect on how you feel about it? Whether it feels good or bad? What happens if you don't receive a hug?

Why can't I have an outside relationship with the therapist?

Ethical standards determine that having a dual relationship has the potential to harm you and the work you are doing. In addition, the therapist is in a position of power where they know more about you and not vice versa. Here are some reflective questions to consider:

- What if the outside relationship went wrong? How would it interfere with your therapy?
- What agenda would they have for you? Therapy vs. outside relationship?
- What if you need therapy after therapy ends?
- How could all the information they know about you be used against you?

The therapist is your therapist for life and never anything else, even after therapy finishes.

Do therapists prefer working with "good clients"? Because I think my counsellor finds me difficult to work with and doesn't like me.
No, good enough therapists work with you as you are, not because you are a good client. They want to help you achieve the goals you came in for. Ask yourself, what makes you believe that they find you difficult? Is there a possibility it is not true? Do you recognise that with other types of relationships?

If you feel the therapist doesn't like you, then reflect on these feelings, check out any signs of unprofessional practice (Way 19), and then, if you feel safe, tell the therapist. Good enough therapists know that clients may have negative feelings towards them even if there is nothing obvious or unprofessional that generates it.

Why does my therapists keep quiet a lot? She just nods and looks at me when we first start a session.
Your therapist may be keeping quiet a lot because they are trusting the process, which gives you space for your mind to show you the way. The reason why therapy works is because of you; you heal yourself, provided the right conditions are offered by the therapist. However, this doesn't suit everyone and if that is the case then you can raise the issue with the therapist.

Questions for you to reflect upon: What is the impact of the quietness? Do you feel the therapist is distant or present with you? Do you feel judged? Anxious? If you can and you feel safe to do so, you should talk to the therapist about these feelings.

I am attracted to my therapist, is it okay?
The foundation of therapy is built upon the relationship you have with your therapist, which on the whole is empathic, accepting, and caring. The building of this foundation takes place over time as you start to feel, to varying degrees, safer, stronger, deeper, and more connected. This is really healthy and shows the work you're both putting in. It is also quiet natural that feelings arise within you, where you do feel a sense of care or even love towards the therapist. You could say there must have been something that "attracted you" to the therapist in the first place if you were the one who chose them. These feelings can be mutual and respectful with boundaries, and they have the power to fuel your healing process.

You may also encounter stronger emotional, romantic, and sexual feelings towards your therapist. These feelings may also be familiar to you, resembling love towards a partner, father, mother, friend, brother, or sister. You may feel you want to be with the therapist more and more in the room or even outside of therapy, and ending the session and being without them may be painful. If you recognise these feelings in you, I would say congratulations; they are acceptable, you are not wrong, and these feelings are not something to be ashamed of, in fact, quite the opposite as they have the healing potential within them that may be the most important part of your therapy. These feelings can be healing due to the relevance they have to your problems as your ability to love, care, and see beauty through the therapist provides an awakening of an inner door that needs attention, care and understanding. I can't stress enough the normalisation and acceptability of these feelings; this happens a fair amount in therapy. In this section, I hope to help you understand these feelings, what you can do with them and how they can be used to accelerate your healing process.

Keywords: Strong feelings that are of a romantic and sexual nature are sometimes called erotic transference.

It must be said at the outset that the relationship between therapist and client can never be more than that. Not only is it unethical for the therapist to engage in anything other than the important therapeutic relationship, it would interfere and be detrimental to helping you in your goals and could result in hurting you more. A therapist is always your therapist only, and that way applies for life, although I know some professional bodies allow relationships after a certain number of years since therapy ended. However, the good news is that therapists are generally aware of the possibility of this type of attraction and know how to accept and sensitively handle the subject to use it as fuel in aide of your healing.

> *Warning: Before making the decision to disclose feelings to your therapist, please reflect on whether your therapist makes you feel safe and secure, keeps boundaries, and behaves consistently with you. For example, a therapist who switches between caring, distant, critical, or punishing is NOT the therapist to do deep work with on client-therapist attraction, or indeed any therapy. See way 19.*

There are a number of reasons why disclosure of your feelings, rather than keeping them "below the covers," may be important. Reasons to disclose may be because therapy is stagnating or frozen, your feelings are interfering with the healing, and you already feel pain and preoccupations associated with your feelings. There is a danger that without resolution, therapy will eventually end and you could end up in a worse position than you started, even to the extent of having to spend more time in therapy recovering from this experience. Regardless of these reasons, you can use therapy to gain a deeper understanding of what these feelings are about, what they mean to you and importantly whether they're related to your problems. You can start by just being curious, accepting, and reflective about them. So, in this context, working through your feelings towards your therapist, either on your own or with the therapist could be a very important part of the work you do. I really recommend you take some steps to work on these feelings; this does not necessarily mean you disclose but it does mean you work on it and make decisions appropriately for your wellbeing. You have four main options: stick with it, disclose, get outside help, or move on.

See Chapter 5: Process themes in therapy: Love in the room for detailed guidance.

I bumped into my therapist outside therapy and they ignored me
Therapists don't usually acknowledge people outside of therapy because they want to protect your privacy as well as keep boundaries in the relationship. Not all clients want to inform people about going to therapy, therefore want to keep it private, so the therapist will not usually acknowledge you in public in case you feel uncomfortable or others you are with ask questions about the nature of your relationship. You felt ignored; that is a feeling to be respected, and I would recommend exploring it with your therapist.

My therapist ignored my request to connect on Social Media. I feel rejected by them.
Therapists won't connect with you on social media in the same way they won't have dual relationships. However, since you felt rejected I recommend you reflect on or write down your feelings and use it as an opportunity – if you feel safe and ready – to explore with the therapist.

In relation to the therapy process

In this section, I provide answers and reflections on questions that relate to your therapeutic journey.

How do I know if I am doing therapy right?

There are two ways to answer that question. First, there is no right or wrong way to do therapy. As long as you're committed and participating in therapy, that is a significant part of doing therapy "right."

However, if you feel blocked or you don't feel better after a period of time, then it could be time to look at what attitudes, skills, and tools you can apply in therapy. The first tool to use is the therapist as a sounding board for your concerns and reflect on your feelings about doing therapy right. For example, reflect on what is behind the question. Is it curiosity, anxiety, or is it because you feel you're stuck?

If I had to make a short list of good signs you're on the right path, it would be:

- You are committed to the process, including attending regularly and participating actively.
- You feel comfortable with the therapist and are able to say what you feel you need to.
- You are describing your feelings, giving concrete examples of difficulties and memories, as well as their impact on you.
- You are reflecting on yourself in order to increase self-understanding of how and why you feel the way you do.
- If appropriate, actively trying to bring in new perspectives.
- You tell the therapist about your "process," i.e., about any feelings below the material you talk about, including about therapy and the therapist.

I am feeling worse because of therapy. Is that normal?

Yes, it can be. Therapy is not always a straight line, nor is it without difficulty. You may feel worse before feeling better. A narrative of someone who feels worse:

> *"I wasn't expecting this. I feel worse than I did at the start. This can't be good! Every time I come here, I'm more and more in touch with the pain of my wife cheating on me! It just stirs things up more."*

There are a number of reasons why you may feel worse, but, essentially, you're getting in direct contact with your feelings, memories, and thoughts, which may be difficult to face. In the following example, feelings of grief about an absent dad could be lying under the surface:

> *"My dad died 12 months ago and we didn't really have a relationship. He would never really make the effort. I always had to make the effort to ask*

him to come around. I'm okay because he wasn't there for me at the start and isn't there now, so it's not like having a real dad. There is nothing I can do about it; I just have to accept it."

In some cases, the pain could be totally hidden until associated memories come up that you did not even know existed. In the excerpt below, the client has realised a painful memory he had "forgotten," and getting in touch with the feelings of being abused made him feel worse because he felt more ashamed, even though he had taken a brave first step.

"I had a good childhood. But I remember always being the one who listened; no one appeared to listen to me about my feelings. I just became a listening robot to get attention and fit in. One day, I was coming home from school, and a bunch of kids attacked me. I remember going home in shock and for some reason, I don't know why, I never told anyone. I was so ashamed. It's only after talking about it here that this memory came to me."

Once the therapeutic process brings these hidden or untouched feelings into the foreground to be worked on, you can feel worse because you're feeling parts of the original pain. However, it could be the beginning of working on feeling better through a healing process.

"Feeling worse" in therapy can appear to be self-defeating or hopeless when in fact it could be the opposite. The therapeutic journey should not be seen as a straight line but more as a road with many contours, turns, and twists. You could be well on your way to feeling better and you just don't know it yet. So, if you get into this situation, you should not just ask if you are feeling better, but also you should ask if it's working. I also recommend not leaving the therapist without exploring the "worse feeling" first. Sticking with the process, working through the difficult feelings could be the path of recovery you might just need.

Warning. *We have to caveat this section a bit. If you're not ready to go deeper into your feeling, then you are not ready. It has to be what you want to do. Also, just because you're feeling worse or if more pain is being experienced, this does not imply that it's healthy either. Talk to your therapist and/or physician if you have concerns.*

I want more sessions per week so I can get better faster; isn't that better for me?
Maybe or maybe not. If you feel you need more therapy because you think it will make you recover faster, that is something to talk to your therapist about. The therapist may agree or have other views. Of course, the therapist may not be able to accommodate your needs because of their schedule.

Therapy, in general, is fairly intensive, with lots of thoughts, feelings, and new understandings coming up. It can be tempting to work harder, but in working harder you may reach full capacity where its no longer useful to push through. That's similar with mental activity or work where it feels you've reached your limit and anything more just isn't productive.

Further, in therapy, the time between sessions for reflection is regarded by many as being an intrinsic part of the therapeutic process rather than "dead" time. Therefore, there is a general tendency for regular, paced sessions rather than intense, long sessions.

That does not mean more sessions, longer sessions, or even fewer sessions won't be helpful or better. For example, you may feel that you are in an emotional crisis and need more time to work through your feelings, or you find you only start getting into feelings after 40 minutes into the session. Speak to the therapist to see what they think and see if it is appropriate.

I recommend identifying why you think you need more sessions. For example, maybe you want to recover quicker, or you want the care and closeness of the therapist. Whatever your reasons, take it to therapy and explore with your therapist.

I am worried about ending therapy. What can I do?

Thinking about endings can stir up many different types of feelings, including loss, anxiety, or painful feelings. Anxiety may be about being able to cope without therapy or even the relationship with the therapist. Endings can bring about feelings of confusion, uncertainty, joy, happiness, and even anger.

Whatever your feelings about endings, it is a topic you can bring up in therapy, as these feelings may influence whether or not you want to end with the therapist and, equally, it could be related to your problem. In short, use therapy to talk about how you feel about endings and reflect on previous endings - good, bad, or indifferent. Talk about the feelings, the loss, and about ending with the therapist. Also, you don't need to leave it to the end; if endings are a concern, talk about it during therapy and at different stages.

I cover this topic in Way 14: Use your feelings about endings.

I feel stuck. What shall I do?

Ultimately, on a path towards growth and healing, stagnation may be one of the many things that you encounter during the process. Stagnation is a feeling to be confronted along the journey, just like other feelings, such as guilt or anger. However, left out of the room and out of your awareness, it can become the elephant in the room, unspoken but doing a lot to block your progress. How can you work on

346

something if it is not brought into awareness? It's part of the problem and thus part of the process, not an aside from it.

I cover this topic in Way 15: Don't let things stay stuck without taking action.

Will I be cured or will I be brainwashed?
Were you sick in the first place? Not in terms of how you feel now because you could be in a dark and painful place. But to be sick and be cured implies that you've caught something, perhaps some nasty germs or a virus. Therapists, in general, believe things that have happened in life play a large part in contributing to your problems, i.e., its not just nature that has struck you down with a mental health illness. Therapy is about working with you as you are, regardless of personality, diagnosis, neurodiverse or neurotypical. Those things may inform practice but they don't define it.

I do really hope no therapist tries to brainwash you, dominate, and direct you to think or feel a certain way (that would be unethical). Brainwashing implies a therapist taking away your rights to freely think and choose for yourself. However, good therapy is the opposite of that because you change your mind because you have decided to do so rather than the therapist entrancing (brainwashing) you into their way of thinking.

Doesn't therapy blame everything on parents?
No, therapists and therapy do not aim to blame your parents. However, your caregivers will have had a major influence on you, and that is why some modalities are focused in on developmental theories associated with your relationship with primary caregivers. In reality, your pain, learning, and suffering have to start from somewhere, and that can include caregivers too. Some therapists may suggest how parents influenced you and help you explore your feelings, but they are not there to pass blame (unless, of course, you do) but to help you recognise your truth. You are free to choose how you see it.

However, that does not mean you have to talk about your parents if you don't want to, and you should not feel as if you must. You decide.

Will I still recognise myself at the end of the process?
During a process, you may change, but you are in control. You may change a little or drastically based on what it is you were after. So, sometimes, it can be that you see yourself very differently at the end because you decide to choose a different path.

However, to not recognise yourself would mean that you would no longer see the past as being part of you. In general, therapy is geared towards integration, or including, rather than giving up parts of yourself, your history, or identity. Of course, you may want that, but that is your choice.

So although you may change quite drastically, therapy is not by design aimed at helping you become unrecognisable to yourself; rather, integration means all of you coming together as a whole, and that includes any historical parts of you. You choose who you would like to be, not the therapist.

I am worried about what I will discover and how it will change my relationship.
If you are feeling concerned about what you will find out in therapy, say a previous event you're not ready to face, or even a possible diagnosis (although diagnosis is rarely the remit of therapy), you can talk to your therapist about your concerns. For example, you can tell them that you don't want a diagnosis or you don't want to talk about childhood issues but only your "here and now" problems.

If you are choosing to go to therapy, especially longer-term therapy, there could be changes to you as a result. There is no guarantee that you will not do so, even if you benefit from therapy. Therefore, it is definitely possible that you may see relationships in a different light.

However, you are in control. You can decide what you choose to reflect upon and you choose your goals. The therapist will not force you to change or make you talk about things you don't want to talk about. You can reflect upon what aspect of changing concerns you: relationships, lifestyle, the past, your existing view of who you are, etc. That decision can only be yours to determine if therapy is worth it. Remember, just because you decide this is not the time to work on something does not mean you can't return to it at a later date.

How long might therapy last?
Therapy can last anywhere between one session, even to 3, 5 years or more. In general, the more complex, ingrained or characterological change required the more time it takes. It also depends on extent of the change needed, sometimes you just want to change the furniture in the house but other times you want to go for a major overhaul.

In relation to yourself

In this section, I provide answers and reflections on questions that relate to yourself being in therapy, especially your role, worries, or concerns.

I am really nervous about therapy. What can I do?

Concerns about the encounter with a therapist can range from feeling worried about being alone with the therapist, being judged or made to feel you are wrong, to feeling that the setting of therapy is just too intimate. Being nervous about therapy is very normal, especially if it's your first time and you have not been used to talking about yourself before.

If you feel you can, I recommend talking about these feelings with your therapist. They can lead to important new areas of exploration, insight and collaboration to see what can be done to help you settle your worries so you can get the most out of the sessions.

If you are feeling that you will be judged or made to feel wrong, remember that therapy is not about telling you you're bad in some way or forcing you to do or talk about things you don't want to or telling you that you need to do better in therapy. Therapy is an open invitation for you to be yourself as you are, not as you may believe the therapist expects you to be. Therapy is about providing an accepting, empathic and safe environment for you to work on what you want or need to work on. If you feel nervous about sharing something that you are embarrassed about, those feelings are accepted too and it is quite normal; you can go at your own pace, when and if you're ready. You may *feel* the therapist will judge you or say you are wrong, but therapy is quite the opposite.

You may also be nervous about being alone with the therapist or engaging in therapy because of the problems you would like to work on, for example, because of a past traumatic incident, anxiety or phobia. That is perfectly understandable as it could trigger heightened emotional or physical responses that make it difficult for you. Some of these triggers could be because of the gender of the therapist, fear of leaving home, social anxiety, relational problems, or even particular keywords associated with a phobia. If this is the case, you can inform the therapist prior so they can adapt their approach with you, but if you feel it is not an option, you could also consider other access methods, such as online audio, phone or even instant messaging. Eventually, you may feel ready to meet the therapist face to face if appropriate.

If your worry is that you will be asked to talk about things you're not ready to talk about, or even that you know deep down you need to at some point, for example, a past abuse, then that is respected. Perhaps you are not quite ready for that, in which case you can even tell the therapist. Therapy is a process. If you're not ready, you can talk about other important or related aspects such as your family history, stresses and feelings that are present in the "here and now" rather than particular events. The therapist should respect your feelings and not push you to talk about things you're not ready for. If you feel nervous about sharing something you are embarrassed about, those feelings are accepted too and it is quite normal; you can go at your own pace, when and if you're ready. You can also consider talking about feelings such as shame or judgement, or of not wanting to disclose with the therapist and only explore the elements or feelings you are ready to explore.

If you feel you will be blocked, clam up or won't be able to speak in therapy, you may wish to reflect on what you feel is the reason you are anxious about that in particular. Remember, the therapist is the one who is professionally trained and if good enough, they will be able to work with you as you are, as they have likely encountered and worked with a very broad range of client experiences, including complete silence and little expression at all. They may introduce other methods of expression, such as emotion cards, to help you and to give you time and space with empathy and acceptance to allow you to open up gradually in your own time.

You should also consider whether your anxiety about the encounter could actually be related to what you are trying to work on. For example, you may feel the therapist may judge you because that is how you experienced your own childhood.

I am concerned about showing vulnerability. What can I do?

Is your worry about talking about your personal life and in particular showing deeper emotional feelings including anger, sadness or even tears? If so, reflecting on why this is the case in therapy may be useful. For example, is it because you were not brought up in an environment where feelings were expressed? When you tried to express feelings, were you made to feel they were wrong or did no work? Or, is it simply something you're not used to doing? If you had experiences in the past when your feelings were not handled well, understood, validated, accepted and cared about, it can cause you to feel you don't want to share; after all, why would you want to share when feelings are not valued by people around you or when you're made to feel ashamed, rejected or not right? You may have come from an environment of "stiff upper lip" or "boys don't cry," so now, opening up feelings can be a scary thing to do. The downside of this approach is that it can block being able to form deeper connection with people. If you're not ready to trust, it can expose you to hurt, especially if your vulnerabilities are rejected.

As a thought experiment, conjure up the last situation when someone opened up, either to you or you saw the situation in a film or read it in a book. What did it feel like to you? My guess is you would have felt more empathy and you would have felt closer to understanding them. By being vulnerable, if and when you are ready, a better connection with yourself, the therapist and importantly with your own healing in therapy will be created. If it is difficult, try opening up in smaller units first and then move towards what you feel would be more difficult. For example, talk about feeling angry with your partner and then graduate to why it makes you feel hurt inside. This does not mean being unguarded with feelings, but with a good therapist you could begin to see vulnerability as a strength that makes you feel better connected, rather than a weakness.

I'm really worried I won't be able to perform in therapy. What shall I do?
After concerns about therapist competence and getting a therapist that is the right relational fit, the most frequent concern is the worry about "doing therapy right." If you're reading this, then I presume you will have picked up some of the ways in which you can help yourself.

I believe above all, being you, as you are, is a big part of "doing things right." Therapy is an open invitation for you to be yourself as you are, not as you may believe the therapist expects you to be. By just being you and sharing with your therapist your true feelings, worries about "doing therapy" right, about the therapy process or about the therapist, is "doing therapy right" because it encapsulates a number of therapeutic qualities in one swift move. It involves talking about your worries, expressing feelings, allowing the relationship to deepen through understanding, letting the therapist know something about you, asking for help, as well as opening up the possibility of new insights that may directly link to the problem you are trying to resolve.

Therapy may also make you feel that you have to perform well, like a "good client" or you must know the answers. You may feel internal pressure to perform, or to meet the therapist's expectations as well as ultimately to achieve a good outcome. Part of this may have to do with being vulnerable, having difficulty asking for help, feeling less power or feeling you need to be competent and good at therapy. You can reflect on what the need is about in therapy to see if it leads to new insights and whether it links with what you are in therapy for. If you have become aware of these feelings, that's a great step and opportunity. Of course, therapy relies on your commitment to want to work on yourself, but therapy does not intrinsically require a particular standard or ideal for you to be present. It's about working with you as you are.

I'm worried the therapist just won't understand me. What shall I do?
If you have a concern about the therapist not being able to understand you, remember that the therapist will by nature of therapy be concentrating on understanding your world, which is what they are there for. They will try their best to understand what you are saying, to get into your world and to get to know you and why you feel that way. This understanding is intrinsic to therapy. However, if your worry about being understood comes more from your own life experiences of not

being understood, heard, dismissed and invalidated, you can reflect whether that concern is born out of your life experiences.

Of course, it may be that you do feel the therapist does not understand, and you feel the therapist does not get you or is not attuned to what you're saying. These feelings may be occasional blips or you may feel it is a continuous problem. The stage and maturity of the relationship will also be a factor as attuned understanding may not be present yet. For example, you feel they don't understand the impact of the session on your wellbeing, they are holding something back or even they are distant. Not only is it possible for this misunderstanding to derail your therapy, it may also be an opportunity for you to discover something related to your problems, particularly as it is thought that any relational difficulties outside of the therapy room can "show up" in the room too.

One way to overcome this is to write down what specifically makes you feel the therapist does not understand and how you feel it is impacting you. Be open to having a conversation with the therapist, listening and taking in what they might say as they may say something that helps with your feelings and whatever it is you are working on. Although it may feel uncomfortable to talk about your feelings, the discomfort may open new doors in your process. After talking to them, reflect on how the conversation felt to you. Did you feel energised and hopeful? Did it feel neutral or did it make you feel worse? If it does not improve, then moving on could be an option if you feel you're not getting your needs met and therapy is stagnating.

What if my feelings are wrong?
If you think that your feelings are wrong, that is something to work through in therapy. It's tempting, especially when you observe strong feelings, to rationalise them or "fix" them away, but if you feel something, you feel it! Ignoring those feelings would be equivalent to ignoring a child's feeling and saying, "Don't be silly, just grow up!" That is not to say that rationality is not important; it may be a critical part of this solution, but give yourself time first, understanding, nurturing, self-care, and compassion to understand all parts of you too. Respecting your feelings is part of caring for your wounds.

Of course, feelings may be echoes of the past, so using your feelings wisely is something to consider in your process. Just because you feel something now does not mean you will feel the same about later in the process.

Caution: If you have feelings that you feel like you need to act upon that are harmful to you or others, please talk to your therapist or call emergency services as appropriate. Having feelings that need to be processed and worked out does not mean free reign to act in harmful ways.

How come I don't always feel anything in therapy?

If you're not feeling anything in therapy, that is how you are. You have noticed it and are curious, and now you can work to understand it. Does the lack of feeling relate to your problems? Is it because of the therapist? Or is it a general feeling in life? What caused you to feel less in the first place? When do you feel something?

Non-feeling can be treated like a feeling in therapy. By exploring its root or associated factors, you may find things like a lack of meaning, belonging, apathy, or boredom behind it. One of the reasons people can feel numb, or empty because it is a reaction to life's suffering. This is really a complicated question to answer completely without knowing your context; it requires you to work with the therapist to figure it out. It may even be why you wanted to undertake therapy in the first place.

In relation to safety

In this section, I provide answers and reflections on questions that relate to feeling safe in therapy, both in terms of therapy and the relationship.

How do I know I am safe in therapy?

Safety in therapy means a number of things, including:

- The therapist is competent and experienced in working with the types of problems you are experiencing.
- Your personal view of feeling safe. For example, some clients are okay being alone in a building, while others are not. Some feel safe being challenged by the therapist; others do not. These safety aspects relate to your personal level of comfort of being in therapy.
- You feel the information you disclose won't be used against you or shared without your consent – It is confidential.
- You feel you won't be emotionally hurt. You feel free to talk about what you want, and you don't feel judged. A therapist, for example, does not blame you or get frustrated. A common area of therapist complaint is where you feel stuck in therapy, and the therapist takes their own frustrations out on you.

See Way 19: Watch out for signs of inefficient, poor, or harmful therapy

I am concerned I will have triggers in therapy. What can I do?

As long as you have a good enough therapist, safety will be an intrinsic part of what you need to feel to enable the work you are doing.

However, you may have existing problems that, once triggered, cause difficult emotional or physical reactions, such as a phobia, anxiety, or a previous trauma. If you feel you will get triggered emotionally or physically, for example, flashbacks, a phobic reaction, panic, emotional state, fainting, and anxiety, you should let the therapist know beforehand. You can also enquire with the therapist how they intend to keep you safe as possible while working on these problems. The therapist should be able to explain how they might mitigate some of the risks through their approach with you.

For example, if you have emotions that trigger when you talk about a trauma, the therapist should be able to offer techniques as a way of mitigating the difficulties, such that you don't feel as if you are completely reliving the trauma in the room. Ask the therapist how they intend to keep you safe if you feel you may have these preexisting triggers.

What is processing and how do I do it safely?

Processing feelings means to become aware of them, understand them, to gain perspective(s) of them, or even experience them bodily so they can be healed. A metaphor of healing is taking the plaster off a wound, caring for it, letting it air, bandaging it up, and allowing it time to heal.

When you are actively working on yourself, your feelings, reflecting, bringing in new perspectives, joining the dots, and gaining insight into your difficulties, you are said to be "processing."

Sometimes when you are experiencing feelings, thoughts, images, and memories, and paying attention to them, it can cause you to react by experiencing strong feelings, alongside physical symptoms, such as anxiety. That does not mean having those feelings is a bad sign, and you could feel worse before getting better, but your therapist is there to help you, and it is their responsibility to keep you safe.

In general, you should be allowed to go at your own pace, not feel compelled to talk about anything you don't want and be given tools that can help you stay "grounded" or present. However, if at all you feel things are going too far in therapy and you are not feeling safe or good about what you are experiencing during the process, you can ask to halt the process. If you're worried about this occurring in therapy, talk to your therapist first. Tell them your concerns and see what can help you feel safe.

Note: Some approaches to processing (for example, EMDR) allow you to process your thoughts and feelings using a more structured approach led by the therapist.

I've heard of false memories. What does it have to do with therapy?

Have you ever doubted your memory? Perhaps whether you forgot to lock a door or turn off the cooker, and then you go back and check. Research and our own experiences validate that memories are not always reliable. Further, your memories can change based on others influencing you; therefore, therapists are mindful not to suggest something that has the possibility of leading you to create or change the memories you have.

In therapy, you may be working on memories of huge significance to you; for example, witnessing a crime, an incident of childhood abuse, or a new memory that was previously suppressed. For example, if a client described a past experience at his old home, he might describe the house, doors, the furniture, who was there, and what was being said. If the therapist added "now, go upstairs and enter the bedroom," that suggestion has the potential to lead the client to infer what it means, perhaps that he was abused. The difficulty that could come into question is whether that memory was effectively implanted or actually true.

Therefore, you may find even the most directive therapist stays out of your process whenever you explore events related to your past so as not to suggest something specific, but rather to let you find your own truth.

This is not something you should be overly concerned about. It is for the therapist to work appropriately, but if you are concerned or are being asked to identify a perpetrator or be a witness in a trial, you must raise it with the therapist and your legal team prior to beginning therapy.

What is the therapist's code of ethics? What is it for?

Therapists are in a powerful position; not only do they have more knowledge about the healing process, but they also meet people who could be very vulnerable. Therapists, therefore, are in a very responsible position to ensure you come to no harm and work in your best interests. The principles of integrity are enshrined in the ethical standards of therapy, which all good therapists must adhere to. By adhering to a code of ethics and complaints procedure, you can gain a level of trust that the therapist is working in your interests and keeping you safe from harm.

The core principles of ethical practice are:

- Autonomy – Therapists must respect your rights to be free to choose.
- Non-maleficence – Therapists commit to avoiding any harm to you.
- Beneficence – Therapists commit to doing what is best for you.
- Justice – Therapists provide a fair and impartial service to all their clients.

I am a victim/perpetrator/witness in a trial. Is it okay to do therapy?

If you have been asked to identify a perpetrator or provide evidence at a trial, then you usually must inform and seek permission from your legal team and the court prior to attending therapy. A lot of this is to ensure that any information you give is not tainted by outside influence (See False memories above) and therefore jeopardises evidence for the case. In addition, your therapist needs to be informed so they adapt their approach and know what records to keep according to country guidelines. Generally, therapy that is non-directive is preferred, such as a person-centred approach (Humanistic school).

Variation: Country/region variations apply. Seek reputable advice and guidance.

How do I make a complaint?

While most therapists are there to do the best they can for you, like any profession there are therapists who do not behave ethically and can cause harm either consciously or unconsciously to you because of their own issues. If you believe a therapist has not worked ethically with you, then you have the right to make a complaint or seek assistance. Each country has its own approach to regulation of therapy; some countries regulate it by law, such as the USA and Italy, while other countries, like the UK and France, do not have state regulations. To fill the gap where there is not central government regulation, the concept of voluntary Membership Bodies exists, whereby therapists may volunteer to join an independent organization that assures the consumers of therapy that they adhere to what is thought to be an acceptable standard of practice, including qualification, experience, and ethics. Regardless of the situation, if you wish to take further advice or make a complaint against a therapist, you should contact the regulator or membership body the therapist belongs to. In the case of a complaint, they will inform you of their process of investigation. The penalties applied to therapists range from further personal development, suspension, or even being struck off the register as being unfit to practice. Of course, if it is a criminal matter, such as fraud, sexual abuse, or physical abuse, you may decide to take that through the criminal justice process.

Here is a list of the types of published complaints where therapists have worked unethically:

- Use you to offload their own problems and disclose personal information about themselves that is irrelevant to your goals. This could be a sign of the therapist not keeping within boundaries, having their own needs met, or wanting to befriend you. They are trying to get you to be their support. Remember, some therapists do disclose but there is usually a reason, for example, to model vulnerability or to help you connect with them on a human level.
- Forming or asking for a dual relationship such a friendship, business arrangement, romantic or intimate relationship.
- Asking for favours that have nothing to do with therapy, such as business services you offer, or financial support.
- Critical or punishing. Therapists are there to make you feel safe. If you're being criticized, judged, or scolded for not doing something, you are likely to be entering or in an abusive relationship. The therapist may act inconsistently, such as one day they maybe caring, withdrawing another time, then becoming inattentive or outwardly critical another day. This sets up a cycle of abuse. This should not be confused with therapists calling out inappropriate behaviour or being more challenging, which is done in a non-critical adult voice to help with your process of healing.
- Therapist always thinking they are right and do not appear to consider the client's feelings or opinions. They have rigid opinions of what is right, wrong, or what you should do, rather than being open and fluid about the situation, allowing you your own judgements and answers to healing to evolve. Therapy is about you finding the answers, not the other way around.
- Try to pressurise you into undergoing particular approaches or techniques or make you feel guilty for your issues or even not wanting therapy with them.

What are the signs of therapist abuse?

The signs of therapist abuse are largely very similar to that of any other abuse. The therapist gains your trust, makes you feel special, and entraps you in a relationship that is abusive.

I cover this topic in Way 19: Watch out for signs of inefficient, poor, or harmful therapy.

Extra-therapeutic matters

In this section, I provide answers and reflections on questions that relate to matters that are external to the therapy process, but which may impact it.

Therapy costs too much. I am not sure I can afford it. What do you suggest?

The question of time, effort, and money needing to be spent on therapy to recover and heal is a concern for over 70% (Appendix A) of people attending therapy. After all, you may be just surviving financially or have a packed life where you don't have the time to add therapy to the list of things you need to do. In this case, clearly you can't do therapy. However, I feel it is worth looking closer at the underlying reasons for not entering therapy. The question to ask: is it really about money and time, or are there other factors at play too?

Why would it not be clear whether it's about the money or not? One theory is that money has at least two value factors embedded within it. Money means survival, buying power, and opportunities, but it can also represent a relational attachment to money. Because the relationship with money is intrinsic in our lives from childhood, the loss of money or the keeping of money has an underlying "feel" or "thought" process attached to it. The belief may be of "I must not lose money," "I have to save," or even "I will feel down when I spend money," or "I have lost when I lose money." This relationship is built very early in life and is reinforced continuously on a daily basis. It is not surprising that our judgements about money and value can be clouded. Having awareness of this, I believe, can be a useful insight in helping us live the lives we want.

To see if it is really a money issue, do the following:

- Write down all your expenses and put a value against each (say, 1-10).
- Ask: What value do you give yourself in healing and growth as a priority against those? Consider the potential future benefits as well as "managing or coping," e.g., better relationships, better mood, or more at peace.
- Ask: Are the things you prioritise above yourself related to basic survival, you only, the whole family, or to others?
- Ask: What specifically would you need to go without to do therapy? Can the priorities below your own priority be forgone, cut out, downsized, or put on hold?

You may find going without is easier than having others going without. For example, you may feel guilty that your kids can't go to dance class, go on holiday, or it may be that you just want to sustain an accustomed social lifestyle. Really reflect on what it is that you worry about in terms of the financial or time investment.

A natural sticking point in people's minds is how the benefits of something might be measured when you don't know if it is going to be of benefit, or you don't know exactly how "big" that benefit would be. After all, how can you value something when you have not experienced its value? I would recommend considering the risk and impact to you if you don't get help. For example, the risk to your wellbeing, quality of life, work, relationships, lost wages, sleep, and time. Even if you do put more value on others, you can see that in fact by devaluing you, it could still have consequences on you as well as others regardless. Ultimately, going to therapy can be seen as a sign of valuing yourself, self-care, compassion, and the courage to be open and vulnerable regardless.

In most cases, you will come to one or more of these conclusions: you really can't afford therapy, you value yourself less than others, or you could actually afford it if you cut down in some areas such as your social life, or there are other factors of concern, such as encounter concerns.

If you conclude you could afford therapy perhaps at a stretch, you can consider other factors discussed in this book that are reasons for your reluctance, such as stigma of attending therapy, or performance anxiety. An oft-overlooked factor is that the reluctance to attend could actually be related to what you are actually trying to overcome such as apathy, hopelessness, anxiety, or being judged. Knowing what blocks you from attending therapy should be seen as a good sign of progress and an intrinsic part of the healing process.

I have a small budget. What are my options?

One of the most significant challenges society has is providing access to therapy to those who need it. Therapy has to be paid for somehow, regardless of whether it is free or paid for by the consumer. Unlike the medical model, service costs for therapy have no guaranteed time limit for when you may get better. As a solution to reduce costs, a number of approaches are available to provide cost-effective therapeutic options that are generally short-term-based, for example, solution-focused therapy and CBT are generally applied for the purposes of overcoming specific problems generally over 1 to 12 sessions.

However, although short-term models of therapy have been hugely beneficial, it does leave a gap because depending on complexity, severity, and how ingrained the problems are, there are people who would really benefit from a longer-term approach. The rub is that as per my survey, 70% of people are very concerned about the financial implications of therapy on their lives. So, the natural question asked is whether there is a lower cost option that can provide the benefits of a longer-term model. Here, I present some ideas for you to consider.

Caution: Please don't take the following ideas as an alternative or equivalent for long-term therapy. They are just ideas that have come about from discussions with others who have had to work on a budget. Seek advice from your physician/doctor and therapist first prior to taking on an alternative route.

- Find a therapist as per the guidance provided in the book that you feel is a right fit for you. You can ask them about the possibility of a "sliding scale" fee based on your affordability.
- Use your own reflections and/or a few short-term sessions to identify your problems you are experiencing in detail. You can ask the therapist also what they think you may need to work on. Write down the top 10 underlying difficulties you would want to address. Don't just write addiction or depression; make the difficulties underlying these problems explicit. Examples include jealousy, performance anxiety, anger, finding meaning, boredom, hopelessness.
- Do more reading and education about the problems you have identified through reputable self-help books or online resources. As there are so many to choose from, ask your therapist for any recommendations. Generally, go for books or resources produced by experienced and qualified therapists.
- Use a focused block of sessions to understand how current problems relate to the past. Focus on childhood, family, and your upbringing. Try and write a journal or story of your life and how it has affected you. You can return, rewrite, and update the narrative of your life as you discover more.
- Read the story and share with any person you trust. They need to be someone who can hear, understand, and can keep your personal information private.
- Use several blocks of short-term therapy to work on specific related focused issues you have identified above. For example, relational difficulties and anger.
- Supplement short-term therapy with support groups. Many support groups are usually low cost or voluntary and contribution based. You may be able to find support groups that align to your particular issues, e.g., social anxiety, addictions, survivors of abuse. Although these are not therapy groups, they can be used to give and gain feedback, improve communication skills, and help you communicate your thoughts and feelings, as well as improve relationships.
- If there are particular traumas that have bodily reactions when triggered, plan to work on these longer and consider using trauma-focused therapies, such as EMDR.
- Use group therapy. Group therapy is typically lower cost than individual therapy and it gives you a chance to explore things such as difficulties in forming relationships, patterns of painful relational experiences, or addictions.
- Once you have worked through all your underlying issues, have a block of sessions to bring together and consolidate what you have learnt into a unified whole that is you.

- Remember, you don't have to work with the same therapist or approach for each block of sessions you use. For example, you could use psychodynamic for talking about childhood impact and existential therapy for looking at purpose in life. In general, I would recommend retaining one therapist who has had the continuous understanding of your therapy process, even if you used several others at different stages.

I feel ashamed that I am going to therapy and everyone is saying there is nothing wrong with me. What shall I do?

Do you feel very reluctant to enter therapy because of an inner voice that says, "What if someone finds out?", "This is not something we do!", "It's shameful to talk to a stranger about feelings." Or "Only crazy people go to therapy."

It is understandable that you may feel this way because historically, mental illness and mental health and therapy have been treated as something that is shameful, inferior, and a sign of weakness or craziness. If the collective society or family buys into that narrative, then it is self-fulfilling because it can be used as a rationalisation to stop people getting the help they need. Imagine saying to someone, "Don't go to the doctors because your leg is painful." At the extreme, mental health, just like physical health, can kill if left untreated.

Although I am writing from a non-political perspective, a lot of that stigma can be traced back to controlling, hiding shame, secrets and ultimately power. There will be many reasons historically for this stigma to perpetuate, including the fear of outsiders using information against a family or group. This sentiment is perfectly understandable from a survival perspective since "good" and "bad" is determined by a set of ways, and if people found out, those secrets could be used against them. The darker side is that secrets can also give rise to insulating negative behaviours, including abuse. In short, there is a historical background and real-life consequences to receiving emotional help, so much so that the term "mental health" can feel scary, which perpetuates the stigma of seeking help through therapy.

However, now many societies, families and people are moving away from the sentiment of "there is something wrong with you" to "there is something right with you," and therapy can be applauded as an act of self-respect and compassion for individuals and the larger collective human race. That does not mean it is all safe sailing because there is still unfortunately a wide variation of opinions, and stigma does still exist.

Nonetheless, feeling worried about your family, work, or friends knowing you are in therapy is still a common position to take. There may be some reasons for that. You may feel people may use it against you, you will be going against the family ways, or you will be asked questions about it that you don't want to answer. The thing to think about would be the benefits vs the rewards. Also, ask the question, if someone you cared about was going through what you are going through, what would you recommend to them?

So, how do you mitigate this risk of someone finding out information about your therapy? First, remember the therapist won't force you to talk about anything you don't want to talk about. They won't judge you, but they accept you as you are. Remember that therapists abide by a code of ethics which includes a confidential agreement; they are not allowed to talk about your matters with anyone, including family, unless it is of a serious concern (see section on Disclosure). Even if a therapist talks about you to a supervisor, they won't reveal any identifying information, e.g., your name.

Second, if you are worried about people finding out you're in therapy, talk to your therapist and assess the risk. Of course, there is always a risk of bumping into someone and some places may have more risk attached to that because of the amount of people moving through the environment or some counselling agencies having waiting areas. You can check this out with the therapist or agency prior to attending therapy for the first time. One strategy people sometimes use is it to locate a therapist outside of the area they live or work in.

If you have any misgivings about therapy, you could reflect on whether the benefits may outweigh your reservations. Reflect on what you would lose or gain by talking to a therapist. Of course, it is up to you if you feel ready to enter therapy; you are free to choose.

International Variation: There is a wide range of views about the stigma of therapy, which will vary across people, families, communities and countries.

My therapist has not diagnosed me. Isn't it better to have a diagnosis?
There are over a hundred possible mental health diagnoses that are contained in the Diagnostic and Statistical Manual (DSM V). Examples of diagnosis may include depression, general anxiety, autism, bipolar disorder, or post-traumatic stress disorder. Generally speaking, counsellors and psychotherapists don't diagnose and certainly don't provide medication unless qualified to do so. Some therapists may "screen" you for possible diagnosis, which can be seen as a way of determining the likelihood of a formal diagnosis. You will typically need to seek out a clinical psychologist, physician, and psychiatrist if you wish to seek a formal mental health diagnosis.

In many cases, having a diagnosis can be a personal decision. The therapist should also be able to help you explore the possibilities and feelings around diagnosis, to help you clarify your own position with wanting a diagnosis. Therapists usually act impartially about whether you would be better off with having a mental health diagnosis. They are generally not against labels or diagnosis, and it can certainly be helpful for them to know, but it's just that therapists don't want to see you only as a label with a set of symptoms to fix, but as a human being.

The subject of getting a diagnosis is usually a personal choice. Some find it useful—at least they have an idea of why things have been the way they are—for example, having Bipolar can cause moods to switch between extreme highs and lows. People can obtain a great degree of comfort with the feeling that they are finally understood and there are reasons for the issues they have experienced. Having these reasons can then enable someone to accept themselves more and work with who they are. In addition, for some, the diagnosis can help with the right treatment options, which could also inform medical and therapeutic options. Also diagnosis may, in some countries, mean the ability to demand rights, such as justification for time off work or insurance claims.

On the other hand, people can be reluctant to obtain a diagnosis for fear of being mistreated, being labelled, excluded, or they feel it may be detrimental to their future, e.g., in their career. All these things are definitely worth considering. You could also seek guidance for civil rights and the law to determine the possible impact of the diagnosis on you.

One concern about diagnosis is that, if left unchecked, it can end up becoming a *self-fulfilling prophecy*. For example, if you believe no one will like you because of your diagnosis, you may become reluctant to engage with people because of it.

Keyword: Self-fulfilling prophecy is any held belief that causes, either directly or indirectly, that belief to become true.

From a therapeutic perspective, it is not to say that diagnosis is bad or wrong when it comes to defining the emotional state you're experiencing. It is more of a concern when it hides you, your true feelings, emotions, thoughts, and experiences. Diagnosis can inform therapy, but it doesn't define it.

Is it okay to be on medication as well as therapy?

Yes, in most cases. The main concern therapists have about any medication is that it has the potential to suppress or numb emotions, and given that therapy, at least for some, is about experiencing feelings, it is not ideal. That does not mean all medications suppress feelings in the same way or that you won't be helped with medication alongside therapy.

On the other side, medication can, in fact, help therapy because it enables you to engage better. For example, if you are highly distressed, or feel too low, then you may not be able to focus in and actively participate and make the best use of therapy.

The choice to medicate or not is between you and your physician, and it may be unavoidable due to the type of problem being experienced. The therapist is not going to recommend medication (unless qualified to do so), although they may ask whether you are on medication or have sought that option. Although they won't recommend, they will help you to reflect on your decision whether to medicate or not. Knowing you are on medication may also inform them of how best to work with you.

If you are concerned about the effects of medication on therapy, talk to your therapist.

I am concerned about someone who is doing therapy. What can I do to help?
If you are a friend, caregiver, parent, or partner of someone who is suffering psychological problems, it is only natural that you are concerned about their suffering and want to help them.

It is understandable that you may want to know how things are going for someone you care about in therapy. Some people may wish to talk and some prefer to keep information about sessions to themselves. I would advise you to be guided by the person attending therapy and to respect their stance on the matter.

However, this does not in most cases mean total disengagement; just show sensitivity to what they are going through and make sure they know they can talk to you if they wish. Being transparent and telling them your reasons for not asking them, i.e., because you are respecting their privacy and space, can let them know you're there for them if needed. This can be very important, given that clients can sometimes get the message that people close to them don't care; they could perceive lack of interest as lack of care, which can be especially true for young people. For example, a parent can sometimes be scared of talking to their child because they believe it will cause them distress or to spiral into self-harm.

If you can you should try and find out if there are any triggers in the environment or in relationships that cause them to feel worse. Here are some examples (not to be used as representative):

- If you say they will be back to work in no time it could trigger them to feel worse because they are letting people down if they don't get better soon.
- If you get frustrated at them for "not trying to get better", it could trigger them to feel not good-enough.
- If you feel down around them or because of the stress they are causing it can trigger suicidal thoughts.

You may also be worried about the content of what is being talked about in therapy, including about you or your family. The therapist is not there to judge you or your family but to help them overcome their problems. It is important to give approval to the person receiving therapy so they can talk about what they need to. You should bear in mind that good therapists will follow a strict code of ethics, including clauses about confidentiality. Confidentiality naturally extends to all relationships outside of the therapist-client relationship, so therapists are unlikely to give you information about how things are going in the therapy process. The only rare exceptions to this would be if there was a serious risk of harm to the client, especially children.

Someone I care about needs help, but they won't go to therapy. What can I do?

I often get asked by concerned others what they can do for someone who does not want to get help with psychological problems. If they are an adult (18+ in the UK), you cannot do anything unless they are a vulnerable adult or posing an immediate danger to themselves or others. Ultimately, you cannot force anyone into therapy or any psychological treatment; it has to be their decision. The best you can do is be patient, listen, offer empathy, provide information, and provide possible ways they can get support. Try not to make assumptions and stay as calm as possible. If you believe someone may act on suicidal feelings or is at risk of serious harm to self or others, then you should call their doctor and / or emergency services.

Can I arrange an appointment on behalf of someone else?

If you contact a therapist on behalf of someone else, the therapist may or may not be able to arrange an appointment on their behalf. If the referral is for an adult, some therapists will insist the adult make the appointment themselves, while for children, it is more acceptable for guardians or parents to refer them into therapy. Either way, the therapist will want to know that the person being referred actually wants to attend therapy for themselves. The reason is twofold: the first, its unlikely therapy would be helpful for someone who really does not want to enter therapy; secondly, therapy is intended to be safe, and that safety begins from the start with a relationship where information comes from the client, not from outside sources. Therapists in general will not want to know your feelings about an adult client and the issues and problems they have, but rather they want to be informed by the client themselves. However, with children, it is more common to take a few more details.

Note: Although clients may arrive to therapy "reluctantly" at the beginning, it does not mean that once they begin, they won't change their minds about therapy and its benefits. There is always hope.

Specific questions answered

In this section, I cover a small selection of questions and answers to very specific and less common questions I have been asked over the years.

My partner thought if I came to therapy I'd be fixed, but I'm starting to realise that it's my partner who has many issues and when I try and express them we get into arguments. Is this normal?

In therapy, you may gain insight and shift perspectives that lead to you feeling you want to improve yourself, your relationship, and get your needs met, both individually and also within your relationship.

When you change, it is not unusual for it to impact your relationship(s) because they are not used to your new way of being. When change occurs, usually it can be a positive step for you and your relationship; however, it can impact your relationship because your partner will have to adjust to your change. For example, if you are asserting yourself more and realise what is missing in your relationship, it could be difficult for them to receive your needs and change with you.

When you are communicating with your partner, you could try, unless you are already doing so, empathic interpersonal skills (Chapter 3: Tool #10). With these skills you can learn to both state your feelings/needs as well as empathising your partner's feelings and differences. For example, using "I feel" statements rather than "you are x." e.g., the dialogue "you never listen" can be converted to "I feel ignored by you." By learning to use these skills, it may take down your partner's walls. Another suggestion is to give it time and space rather than trying to fix it; you can both work on whatever is missing in the relationship over time to see where it leads.

Of course, you may be more ready for a more open conversation with your partner, but they may not. Relationship (couples) counselling is an option if you're struggling in the relationship. Whatever is going on, it is something to talk to your therapist about.

I bumped into another client and I don't want to go back

Reflect on why you feel you don't want to go back. For example, is it about feeling you are sharing the therapist? They are giving someone else attention? Or you felt vulnerable being spotted by someone? Or perhaps you knew the other client? You can write down your feelings about it and use it as an opportunity, if you feel safe and ready, to explore your process with the therapist.

My therapist doesn't always answer my emails and it upsets me.

Given it has upset you, then those feelings are to be respected. You can write down your feelings about it and use it as an opportunity, if you feel safe and ready, to explore your process with the therapist.

When you work with a therapist, they usually set out the service they provide, including the format of therapy and how it is accessed. Was there anything in your agreement about emails being allowed and being responded to? Was there something about responding in a certain time frame?

Some therapists may allow you to share feelings via email, but this is usually by formal agreement. Usually contact is about logistics, such as timings or access to resources, rather than anything more.

Of course, if you have an agreement to respond at a certain time, or they said they would acknowledge your reflective feelings, then I would suggest talking to your therapist about it.

My therapist says that they will send me resources to help me, but always seems to forget. Is that because I'm not that important to them? Because that's exactly how it feels.

The fact that the therapist always forgets what they have said that they would do is not great; a therapist should be reliable and model consistency in the relationship. However, therapists are human too, and they can get things wrong (See Way 19), so you should tell them how you feel about it.

Reflect on feeling unimportant. Questions you could ask include: Other than this, do you think the relationship is good and you are getting something from therapy? Do you feel safe to tell your therapist how you feel? Do you think this is getting in the way of creating a safe space for you? Are the feelings familiar, perhaps of being let down? You can write down your feelings about it and use it as an opportunity, if you feel safe and ready, to explore your process with the therapist.

My counsellor told me a little about his past heartbreak and started to cry. I felt like I needed to help him and didn't want to talk anymore.

That does not sound appropriate, particularly as you say you felt you needed to attend to your therapist. Therapists are there to attend to your needs, your goals, and difficulty, not the other way around. However, you may wish to consider further perspectives before making a judgement on their professionalism, and whether they are the right therapist for you.

First, therapists may disclose personal information appropriately, but it must be to serve your needs and not the other way around where you feel you need to look after them. For example, a therapist may disclose something that was intended to help you, but unwittingly caused them to focus in on their pain (sometimes called countertransference). So you should reflect on whether the therapist's disclosure was intended to help you, i.e., their intentions were good.

Secondly, therapists in general don't see getting a little misty-eyed a problem because it shows their human side and may even be helpful to the relationship. So therapists can feel emotional during sessions, some even shed tears, so tears don't always mean poor practice. But the way you ask the question seems to indicate something beyond being misty-eyed and still in control.

Third, therapists can make mistakes and get overwhelmed. If this is a one-off occurrence, they may have gotten it wrong and I hope they allowed space to openly talk about it after. Therapists have supervisors who they should be getting help from, not you, to help them do the best work for you.

If you feel safe, you should talk about your feelings with them, including how you felt a need to help them and how it interrupted your process. However, if the therapist is disclosing personal information that is unrelated to your goals and/or this happens often, then I would suggest you question whether they are the right therapist for you and seek support, because it does not sound like professional practice (See Way 19).

My counsellor fell asleep in our session. Am I boring?

Your therapist needs to be present and give you complete focus during the session. They must not be falling asleep regardless of whether you feel you are boring. If the therapist has made a one-off mistake and it has not derailed your therapy, you can overlook it if you wish to, particularly if you are getting something from the therapy. If they were aware of it, I hope they apologised. But if they were unaware of falling asleep, then the only thing you can do is to make them aware of it and that it has brought up feelings in you.

If you feel that it is your fault because you are boring, you can explore this further with the therapist. For example, you can ask yourself: is that how you feel about yourself? Do you find life boring? And what have been your experiences of boredom? Maybe you feel this way because you really are feeling bored?

My counsellor kind of gives me the creeps. Like she enjoys that I'm sad and feeling like rubbish.

Reflect on the following: Is there a particular thing she does that makes you feel that way? Or is it a general feeling? For example, is the therapist asking you questions that feel voyeuristic or intrusive? Does she smile or say something that is inappropriate based on what you are saying? If that is the case, then you need to determine whether she is the right therapist for you (See Way 19).

Sometimes clients can view therapists negatively without logical reason or unprofessional practice, and if that is the case it's important material for you to work on. A good therapist knows that this can happen for no particular reason. If you can and you feel safe to do so, you should talk to the therapist first to check out your feelings.

My therapist charges me for cancellations but I don't get compensated if they cancel. That's not fair.

If you feel it is unfair and you feel safe, then I recommend talking to your therapist about your feelings, especially if it could interfere with you continuing therapy and trusting the therapist.

I also recommend you check the terms of the contract you have with them. You may find some therapists compensate you, especially if it's very short notice or you have been detrimentally impacted. If it's not offered in the contract, therapists should still listen to your perspective and may even compensate you for it.

I feel like my counsellor isn't on my side.

Reflect on the following: Do you feel judged by the therapist? Is there something they say or do that makes you feel that way? Or is it a more general feeling? Then check out the following perspectives.

Although therapists are there to accept you and not judge you, it does not mean they will agree with everything you say or not use their feelings to give you alternative perspectives. If it was a particular matter that made you feel this way, you can reflect on why they may have done so.

Sometimes clients can view therapists negatively without logical reason or unprofessional practice, and if that is the case, it's important material for you to work on. A good therapist knows that this can happen for no particular reason. So if there is no particular reason or unprofessional practice, just be curious about your feelings.

If you can and you feel safe to do so, you should talk to the therapist first to check out your feelings, particularly about feeling they aren't on your side. Regardless of the reasons, being able to work on these feelings sounds important, as you will need to feel safe to get the most from your therapy.

Of course, if you feel the therapist is being unprofessional, see Way 19 to help you assess the therapist.

My counsellor is always running late and finishing early.

Unless there is a particular agreement to do that, then I would say this is unacceptable, particularly as you say it sounds like it is happening often. The therapist needs to be providing reliable and consistent boundaries so you can feel safe. Sometimes, clients may want to finish early, but it should not be instigated by the therapist unless they can justify doing so would be best for your interests. If you can and you feel safe to do so, you should talk to the therapist first. Depending on the response, and whether you feel you're getting anything out of therapy will determine whether you wish to continue with them or not.

Paying my counsellor makes me uncomfortable. It keeps me from being cared about. Money can, sometimes, get in the way of clients feeling the therapist could care about them, and thus can be an obstacle to recognising the relationship between you and the therapist. You may feel the therapist is paid to care, pretends to care, or because they have other clients, you wonder how they could care about you. The truth is, the therapist is usually paid and will most likely have many clients. Ultimately, therapists are human and will have expenses and bills to pay for, like others.

One way of looking at this issue is based on your own experiences. Are there people you have cared for in work or where your services were paid for? Also, is it possible to care for many people simultaneously? Like friends, family, or clients? Can you "fake" care? An oft-quoted phrase in the counselling world is, "You pay me for my time, but my care is free," because you can't force someone to care by paying them; humans simply don't work that way.

If you feel the therapist cares, maybe it is because they do and they have a lot of passion and heart in working with you, so feel free to allow yourself to feel the care. If it feels important, talk to them and see what comes up. You can use this as a springboard in your healing process, as the relationship is core to how therapy works.

My counsellor said it's her job is to listen and analyse. That made me feel like its only a job for her.
In therapy, analysis, particularly if you have chosen analytical psychotherapy like psychodynamic therapy, can be an intrinsic part of their approach to help you.

However, if you are asking this question, I suspect it is more to do with how the "analysis" makes you feel uncared for. I would advise you write down reflective feelings on the experience. For example, is it because you feel you are not heard, empathised with, or understood or that your feelings are minimised because of the analysis? You can, if you feel safe, share those reflections with your therapist.

You should consider your needs against what the therapist can provide. Maybe analysis is not what you need right now, and you can discuss this with the therapist to see what comes out of the exploration. If you decide this approach is not working for you and won't meet your needs, then an option would be to consider a more relational therapist (assuming you don't experience your current therapist as overtly relational).

I've been with my counsellor for 5 months and I still feel like rubbish.
Reflect on chapter 5: I feel worse now and Way 15: Don't let things stay stuck without taking action.

I would recommend talking to your therapist about your feelings. If you still have difficulty, then it may be worth seeking outside help (Way 21).

I just found out my counsellor is seeing someone I don't like. They are a close family friend. Do I tell my counsellor or leave it?

I would advise you reflect on your worries or concerns about it. Is it that the family friend may be talking about you in their session? Or is it because you feel the therapist will share information? Or you'll bump into them?

Remember that therapists are not allowed to share information about you with others. If you are worried, explore it with the therapist and/or obtain more information from them about confidentiality and disclosure. It's important for your work to feel safe from outside interference, so working on that is recommended.

Can I ask whether my therapist is on medication?

You can, and you may or may not get an answer. When you ask questions that can be deemed personal, therapists are usually cautious about sharing.

It may be more useful to understand what is behind your question and what your concerns are. Perhaps it is because you feel the therapist is not performing well, or giving you what you need. Or it may be that you have had negative experiences of people on medication, or you have read something which indicates you should not see a therapist on medication. Another reason could be that you're on medication and you would feel more hopeful if a therapist had been able to safely withdraw from medication.

So one way of approaching your questions is to talk about underlying concerns about medication rather than ask the direct question. Of course, a good therapist will be able to handle and work with your questions, however personal, rather than stonewall them. In any case, you can bring that up with the therapist if it's important to you.

My therapist told me to come back when I stop drinking. But I told him I that I could not do that completely. He told me to return in two months after I had tried. It doesn't make sense.

There may be a reason why the therapist told you that, and I hope they explained their rationale for their instruction. They should also help you reflect on your feelings about not feeling able to completely stop and work collaboratively to help you achieve your goal(s).

Reflect on the following: Did they listen and accept your feelings? Or did you feel dismissed? Do they appear to be working in your interests? Therapists work in different ways; some will take your lead and others will have their own ideas of what would help you. Certainly, you should not feel so criticised, judged, or blamed for your viewpoint that it would be too difficult to give up alcohol completely. If you are unsure about their reasons for therapy being paused, you could try secure messaging your therapist to ask for clarification.

My therapist cried in therapy. Is that right?

Maybe or maybe not. The main thing to ask is how did you feel about your therapist crying? And do you feel it interfered with your therapy? Also, how long and how often does it occur? Therapy is about the therapist attending to your needs and therefore if the therapist crying took you away from that by interrupting your process, e.g., you felt sorry for them, it irritated you, or made you feel you did something wrong.

However, therapists are human and sometimes therapists may shed a tear or get misty-eyed, so it can happen; it does not necessarily mean they are a poor therapist overall.

Everyone is different, and some may not mind the therapist showing visible emotion, as they feel the therapist is connecting with them. However, if it moves the focus of therapy away from you, if you feel it's something that blocks or interferes with your process, I recommend talking to your therapist. If it is happening a lot, then I would consider the therapist's competence (See Way 19).

Appendix A – Survey of consumer concerns

The chart below shows the % of respondents in sample of 113 what their concerns were when they first began therapy. By far the most dominant concerns are the therapist being right for the consumer including being competent and non-judgemental, the financial commitment, and personal performance.

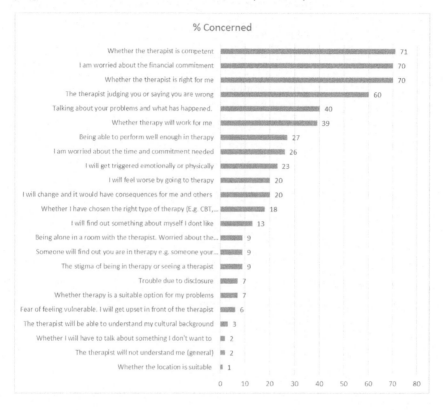

% Concerned

Concern	%
Whether the therapist is competent	71
I am worried about the financial commitment	70
Whether the therapist is right for me	70
The therapist judging you or saying you are wrong	60
Talking about your problems and what has happened.	40
Whether therapy will work for me	39
Being able to perform well enough in therapy	27
I am worried about the time and commitment needed	26
I will get triggered emotionally or physically	23
I will feel worse by going to therapy	20
I will change and it would have consequences for me and others	20
Whether I have chosen the right type of therapy (E.g. CBT,...	18
I will find out something about myself I dont like	13
Being alone in a room with the therapist. Worried about the...	9
Someone will find out you are in therapy e.g. someone your...	9
The stigma of being in therapy or seeing a therapist	9
Trouble due to disclosure	7
Whether therapy is a suitable option for my problems	7
Fear of feeling vulnerable. I will get upset in front of the therapist	6
The therapist will be able to understand my cultural background	3
Whether I will have to talk about something I don't want to	2
The therapist will not understand me (general)	2
Whether the location is suitable	1

Appendix B - Mental health support numbers

If you have seriously harmed yourself – for example, by taking a drug overdose – call your local emergency services or go straight to Accident and Emergency. Or ask someone else to make the call or take you there.

In this section you'll find the international mental health organisations, UK specific mental health support services, reputable UK based counselling and psychotherapy voluntary membership bodies and find a therapist directories.

International mental health organisations

- International Suicide hotline numbers: www.suicide.org, www.befrienders.org
- Worldwide support numbers: togetherweare-strong.tumblr.com/helpline
- Alcoholics Anonymous: http://www.aa.org/
- Narcotics Anonymous: https://www.na.org/
- For people concerned about someone with an Alcohol problem: https://al-anon.org/
- Overeaters anonymous: https://oa.org/worldwide-oa/

UK Based mental health organisations

Childline: 0800 1111
Samaritans: 08457 909090
Abuse Not: 0808 8005015
Brook Young People's Information Service: 0800 0185023
Eating Disorder Support: 01494 793223
Anxiety UK: 0844 477 5774
Depression Alliance: 0845 123 23 20
Rape Crisis Centre: 01708 765200
Rape/sexual assault: 0808 8000 123 (female) or 0808 8000122 (male)
Miscarriage Association: 01924 200799
LLGS Helpline (LGBT): 0300 330 0630
Sexuality support: 01708 765200
Bereavment: 0800 9177 416
Runaway/homeless: 0808 800 70 70
CareConfidential Pregnancy/post abortion: 0800 028 2228
Women's Aid National
Domestic Violence Helpline 0345 023 468
National AIDS Helpline: 0800 567 123

Mental Health Foundation
020 7803 1101
Improving the lives of those with mental health problems or learning difficulties.

Together
020 7780 7300
Supports people through mental health services.

The Centre for Mental Health
020 7827 8300
Working to improve the quality of life for people with mental health problems.

Depression Alliance
0845 123 2320
Provides information and support to those who are affected by depression via publications, supporter services and a network of self-help groups.

PANDAS Foundation
0843 28 98 401 (every day from 9am-8pm)
PANDAS Foundation vision is to support every individual with pre (antenatal), postnatal depression or postnatal psychosis in England, Wales and Scotland. We campaign to raise awareness and remove the stigma. We provide our PANDAS Help Line, Support Groups offer online advice to all and much more.

General advice and support

Young Minds
020 7336 8445
Provides information and advice for anyone with concerns about the mental health of a child or young person.

Childline
0800 1111
Free, national helpline for children and young people in trouble or danger.

Nightline
Listening, support and information service run by students for students.
Other places you could go for support

Age Concern
0800 009966
Infoline on issues relating to older people.

Lesbian and Gay Switchboard
020 7837 7324
Provides information, support and referral services.

Refugee Council
020 7346 6700
The UK's largest organisation working with refugees and asylum seekers.

Relate
0300 100 1234
Offers advice, relationship counselling, sex therapy, workshops, mediation, consultations and support.

Education Support Partnership
08000 562 561
A 24/7 telephone support line which gives teachers access to professional coaches and counsellors 365 days a year. The network also campaigns for change within schools and education policy in order to improve the wellbeing, mental and physical health of teachers.

Anxiety UK
08444 775 774
Works to relieve and support those living with anxiety disorders by providing information, support and understanding via an extensive range of services, including 1:1 therapy.

Generally recognised UK Voluntary Membership bodies

Please note your therapist may belong to another membership body not listed here as there are many others that are equally recognised.

British Association for Counselling and Psychotherapy (BACP)

Address: BACP House, 15, St John's Business Park, Lutterworth LE17 4HB
Telephone: 01455 883300
Email: bacp@bacp.co.uk

UK Council for Psychotherapy (UKCP)

Address: America House, 2 America Square, London EC3N 2LU
Telephone: 020 7014 9955
Email: info@ukcp.org.uk

British Psychoanalytic Council (BPC)
Address: British Psychoanalytic Council, Suite 7, 19-23 Wedmore Street, London N19 4RU
Telephone 020 7561 9240
Email: mail@bpc.org.uk

British Association for Behavioural and Cognitive Psychotherapies (BABCP)
Address: Imperial House, Hornby Street, Bury, Lancashire BL9 5BN
Tel: 0161 705 4304
Email: babcp@babcp.com

Reputable UK directories for finding a therapist

BACP: 01455 883300
Through the British Association for Counselling & Psychotherapy (BACP) you can find out more about counselling services in your area.

Counselling Directory: Counselling-directory.org.uk

UKCP: Psychotherapy.org.uk

Psychologytoday: Psychologytoday.com

Appendix C – Further support

Are you in therapy or are you about to embark on a therapeutic journey? Do you need help? Are you feeling stuck, emotionally overwhelmed, or confused by the healing and growth process of therapy? Do you want to know what direction your healing process should take? Do you need help in figuring out what you need to do to make the process as effective, efficient, and safe as possible? Then these services could be for you.

To support your therapeutic process, I offer the following:

- A secure "Ask the therapist" messaging service
- Online secure coaching (instant messaging, audio, or via web conference)
- YouTube channel "Dear Therapist" for each of the ways
- Consumer events (online/offline)

You can find details of each service at empoweringyourtherapy.com.

*These services are for anyone around the world where there are no legal constraints in providing support. It is not for **previous or existing clients for ethical reasons.***

Ask a therapist

If you want to ask me a specific question, you can contact me on the "Ask a therapist" page at empoweringyourtherapy.com.

You can ask questions and they will be answered by a therapist. We will provide some thoughts, reflections, and guidance. The guidance will not be telling you exactly what to do.

Please note that due to legal jurisdiction I may not be able to answer questions if you are based in a particular country.

Online therapy coaching

I also hold confidential online coaching session for clients who need external support for their therapy process. Coaching is based on the principle of working on things that help or hinder you. I do not tell you what to do, but I help to inform your decisions.

The ethics of this services are the same as for psychotherapy and counselling. In particular please note:

- It is confidential unless there is serious harm to yourself or others
- We will provide a safe place for you to share thoughts and feelings from different perspectives and help you to find your own answers
- We will ask questions to help you focus on what's going on but we remain impartial to any decision you make about the direction of your therapy

- We share concerns if something about your process is or maybe harmful to you.

During this process I ask you to fill in a 50 point questionnaire to elicit your feelings and how you are in the room in order to provide some suggested activity to help you with whatever you are struggling with in therapy.

Consumer events

I also hold regular events online and in person for consumers of therapy services. Regular event dates can be found on empoweringyourthearpy.com. Here are the general event details:

This is a psychoeducation event for general public/clients, who are stuck, confused or have overwhelming feelings and emotions that have been created by the therapeutic encounter and process (counselling and/or psychotherapy of any form including individual, couples, group and family therapy).

The types of issues that clients can encounter that could impact their lives include:

- Unsure of direction therapy should take.
- Unsure how to make therapy work for you.
- Don't know whether to stay or leave the therapist.
- How to make therapy efficient, effective and safe.
- Not sure if the therapist is right for you.
- Not sure if you are using the right type of psychotherapy (counselling, CBT, EMDR, DBT etc..) or what options I have.
- Confused feelings towards the therapist.
- Stuck and not making progress.
- Feeling that no therapist is able to help.
- Continuous cycle of starting/ending therapy.
- Finding it hard or ashamed to say things to the therapist you would like to.
- Feeling a loss/attachment towards the therapist even after ending therapy.
- Feeling abandoned by the therapist.
- Feeling angry/frustrated at the therapist.
- Feeling your being blamed by the therapist.
- Feeling the therapist is not being open and/or withholding information.
- Constant thinking about the therapist.
- Emotional and/or therapist abuse, e.g., anger directed towards client.
- Difficult endings in therapy.
- Love and/or sexual attraction.
- Finding it hard to end therapy.
- Detangling feelings between that of a friend and therapist.
- Boundary/ethical issues.

Please note I do not provide a complaints service or a mediation service between the client and therapist or between the client and a professional body.

Contact the author

For questions relating to this book email: ma@paththerapy.co.uk

Appendix D – Inventory of client concerns

Clients can begin therapy with questions, concerns, and worries, not only about overcoming their problems or growth but also about therapy, the process, their performance, life impacts, and of course the therapist. Given the range of concerns addressed in this book and described in the questionnaire below, I believe working with these concerns actively has the potential to reduce dropouts, activate client empowerment, align expectations, identify constraints, correct misinformation, identify process interference, tune in your approach, build the relationship, and of course, enable the client's process.

How you wish to work with these questions and concerns will depend on your own approach. There are three approaches, ask direct questions, use an assessment questionnaire or a more client centred approach that naturally falls into talking about concerns.

See my event at onlinevents.co.uk for further discussion on how these concerns can help clients and be integrated into the initial session.

The big questions

Based on the sixty or so concerns that have come up in my research, the following specific questions condense these concerns down into five high-level categories. The following questions do more than simply asking a client "do you have any questions or concerns about therapy?"

- Do you have any questions or concerns about the **suitability** of therapy, the approach or even the therapist to help you achieve your goals?
- Do you have any questions or concerns about yourself, your role and whether you have any worries about being able to "do" therapy? [**personal performance or ability**]
- Do you have any questions or concerns about **safety**, being here with me, saying what you need to say or even about confidentiality?
- Do you have any questions or concerns about therapy **impacting your life**, such as the time commitment or consequences of change?
- Do you have any questions or concerns about how this can help, what will happen or what to **expect** in therapy?

Indirect questions

Questions that can lead to talking more in depth about client concerns include:

- Have you had therapy before? This can lead into discussions about any of the main areas of concerns – Life Impacts, Expectations, Suitability, Personal Ability and Safety.

- Do you have a rough idea of how therapy works? This can lead to discussion about differences between talking in general vs. therapeutic talk, the client role and any concerns
- What expectations do you have about therapy or myself? Or what will work? This can often lead to discussions on expectations, answer concerns and enable work to be tailored to client needs
- What's your journey been like in find a therapist?

Inventory of client concerns (M-CC)

Apart from achieving your goals in therapy. What are you concerns you most about undertaking therapy? Please remember you are in control, you are not required to answer anything here you are not ready to - just leave any questions blank if that is the case.

Type	Description	Significant Concern	Some Concern
	About you in relation to therapy		
Suitability	Whether therapy is suitable for my problems		
Expectations	What therapy is and what it is not		
Suitability	Whether I will choose the right type of therapy		
Expectations	What I can expect during therapy		
Suitability	Whether I will choose the right therapist		
Expectations	How and why therapy works		
Suitability	How can this help when it's just talking/venting		
Suitability	It will be just like the last therapy e.g. CBT, no direction		
Expectations	What is expected of me in therapy		
Expectations	What will happen in therapy		
	About you in relation to the process		
Personal Ability	Don't believe I can change		
Personal Ability	Won't feel motivated enough for therapy		
Personal Ability	Unsure whether you are ready to commit or face things		

Type	Description	Significant Concern	Some Concern
Personal Ability	Being able to perform to use the sessions to get the most from them		
Personal Ability	I will get triggered emotionally or physically by the experience of therapy (e.g. flashback, phobia, anxiety)		
Personal Ability	I will have to say or answer questions I don't want to		
Personal Ability	Being able to say what I need to say about the problem and what has happens		
Personal Ability	I am fearful of being vulnerable in front of the therapist e.g. being upset in therapy		
Personal Ability	I will feel embarrassed about talking about things that have happened or have experienced in the past		
Personal Ability	I will freeze up and not be able to talk and I'll get blocked		
Personal Ability	Concerned about silences in therapy		
Safety	Confidentiality of sessions (including to spouse, parents)		
	About you in relation to the therapist		
Suitability	The therapist is competent		
Suitability	The therapist has experience with types of problems I am experiencing		
Suitability	Whether the therapist is the right relational fit for me		
Safety	Therapist will judge, blame me or say I am wrong		
Safety	Being alone in the room with the therapist		
Suitability	They will not understand my race/ethnic background		
Suitability	They will not understand my religious/spiritual beliefs		
Suitability	Whether they can help if they have not been through similar problems or experiences		

Type	Description	Significant Concern	Some Concern
Suitability	They will not understand my sexual orientation		
Suitability	They will not understand my lifestyle or behaviours		
Suitability	They won't be able to understand my gender		
Suitability	Therapist won't be able to understand me because of my education, social, or financial status		
Suitability	Whether they will understand me because of age differences (generational)		
Suitability	The therapist is able to meet needs for diagnosis, reports and letters		
	Life Impact to me		
Life Impact	The cost of therapy		
Life Impact	The duration of therapy		
Life Impact	The effort and commitment required of me		
Life Impact	I will feel worse by going to therapy		
Life Impact	I will change and it will have consequences to myself and others		
Life Impact	I will find something out about myself or others that I don't like		
Life Impact	Someone will find out I am going to therapy		
Life Impact	People will not like that I am in therapy and use it against me e.g. Stigma		
Life Impact	I will or someone will get into trouble if I disclose information to the therapist		
Life Impact	I'll be diagnosed		
	Other		
Safety	What information will be kept and how it will be used (Record Keeping)		

Type	Description	Significant Concern	Some Concern
Safety	The impact on an imminent trail (Pre-trial therapy)		
Suitability	Suitability of the location e.g. including for accessibility needs		
Personal Ability	Attending frequency of sessions needed		
Personal Ability	Ability to attend sessions e.g. due to transport, having to care for someone or caring for children.		
Personal Ability	I'll be reliant on medication as a solution		

Appendix E – Further reading

Case studies
This is a list of example therapeutic demonstrations based on a particular school of therapy

- Humanistic (Person Centred): Gloria & Carl Rogers: https://www.youtube.com/watch?v=24d-FEptYj8
- Cognitive Behavioural school: Gloria & Albert Ellis: https://www.youtube.com/watch?v=odnoF8V3g6g
- Solution focused school: https://uk.sagepub.com/sites/default/files/upm-binaries/41673_Case_Study_add_on.pdf
- Integrative school: https://youtu.be/PETvBmNlGtg
- Expressive therapies (Psychodrama): https://youtu.be/OdvErKtIVUE

Therapeutic change models
If you have an interest, here are some different models of therapeutic processes that have been created to describe the process of therapy.

Modality: Non-specific personal change models
Transtheoretical Model or Stages of Change
Health Belief Model (Medical)
Theory of Planned Behaviour
Theory of Reasoned Action

Modality: Gestalt
The Paradoxical Theory of Change' by Arnold Beisser.

Modality: Focusing theory (Eugine Gendlin)
Theory of personality change.
See:http://www.focusing.org/personality_change.html

Modality: Jungian Analysis
Individuation process.
See:https://www.carl-jung.net/individuation_steps.html

Modality: Person Centred
7 Stages of process (carl rogers)

Codes of Ethics
UKCP Code of Ethics 2019: See psychotherapy.org.uk

Appendix F – References

These references are for therapy students and therapists. All references relate to client perspectives of therapy.

1. Howe, D., 1993. On being a client: Understanding the process of counselling and psychotherapy. Sage.

2. Dinnage, R., 1988. One to One: the experience of psychotherapy. Viking.

3. France, A., 1988. Consuming psychotherapy. Free Association Books.

4. Tallman, K. and Bohart, A.C., 1999. The client as a common factor: Clients as self-healers.

5. Bohart, A.C. and Tallman, K., 1999. How clients make therapy work: The process of active self-healing. American Psychological Association.

6. Bohart, A.C., 2000. The client is the most important common factor: Clients' self-healing capacities and psychotherapy. Journal of Psychotherapy Integration, 10(2), pp.127-149.

7. Dr Phoebe Lambert (2007) Client perspectives on counselling: Before, during and after, Counselling and Psychotherapy Research, 7:2, 106-113, DOI: 10.1080/14733140701345919

8. Barry A. Farber, Matt Blanchard, and Melanie Love (2019) Secrets and Lies in Psychotherapy.

9. Cozolino, L., 2017. The neuroscience of psychotherapy: Healing the social brain. WW Norton & Company.

10. Bates, Y., 2005. Shouldn't I be feeling better by now? Palgrave Macmillan.

11. Ahmad, M., 2020. Client Perspectives of Being in Therapy. PT Publishing (Independently published).

12. Lambert, M.J., 2017. Maximizing psychotherapy outcome beyond evidence-based medicine. Psychotherapy and psychosomatics, 86(2), pp.80-89.

13. Richards, C., 2011. Alliance ruptures: Etiology and resolution. Counselling Psychology Review.

Appendix G – Worksheet exercises

Johari window

Ways applicability: Way 10: Peel back the layers

Johari window is a 2x2 grid which can help you to understand what you know about yourself, what you've shared with the therapist, and what you've not shared. In therapy things that you are not aware of can sometimes be termed blind spots. These blind spots may be in your therapist's awareness or at the edge of your own awareness that come out during the process.

Now imagine you whole life experiences, memories, personality, beliefs, feelings and behaviours as parts (well small circles in the diagram). Now put each circle with a label in one of the windows below. Example parts are joker, neglected, wise, pure, or sad.

Now take the next step and draw in any parts of you find difficult to talk with your therapist about, including how you feel about yourself.

Johari Window

The Arena (Known to self and therapist)	The blind spot (Known by therapist not by self)
The facade (Known by self not by therapist)	Unknown (not known by therapist or self)

Patterns and rationality
Ways applicability: 7, 9 & 11

This catch-yourself exercise helps to understand patterns in your thoughts, feelings and behaviours. Try catching yourself in situations where you are reacting negatively. For example, a performance, meetings, being criticised or meeting new people

For each situation:

- What were you thinking?
- What emotions were you feeling?
- As a result how did you behave in that situation?
- What body sensations did you feel?

Here is an example of a negative situation where you felt treated unfairly:

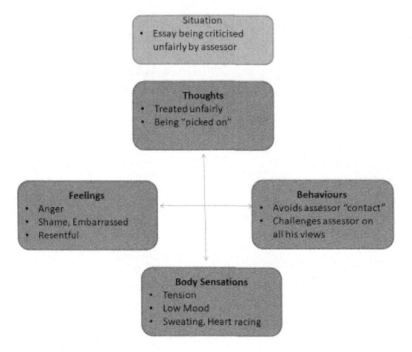

Here is the same situation where your feelings are tempered with new kinds of thoughts:

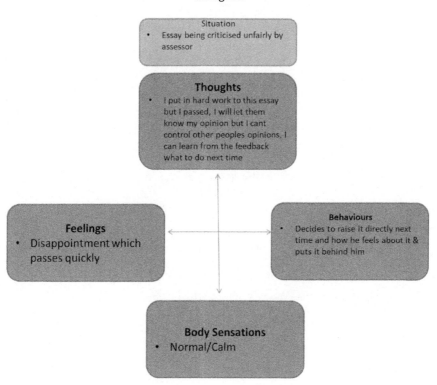

Appendix H – Full table of contents

About the author

Mamood Ahmad is a clinical psychotherapist (UKCP Registered), workplace speaker on mental health and therapy, and author who originated and developed learning-oriented therapy, a form of therapy coaching. It focuses on empowering clients to affect their own change within safe and ethical healing relationships, including counselling and psychotherapy.

Prompted by his own experiences of not knowing what to do in therapy, he provides specialised *therapy coaching* to consumers of therapy who feel stuck, emotionally overwhelmed or confused by therapy. His research interest is client perspectives of therapy and how they inform practice.

He has nearly 10 years of therapeutic experience working in private practice with adults, young people, and couples. He is based in the village of Binfield, Berkshire, UK. He is passionate about family, wing chun (A Chinese martial art), and philosophy. **Empoweringyourtherapy.com**.

Learning oriented coaching focuses on the client's learning process to affect their desired change against their goals, rather than any specific theory of psychological disturbance.

Printed in Great Britain
by Amazon

87539390R00235